AF887646

THE LACAN TRADITION

LINES OF DEVELOPMENT

Evolution of Theory and Practice over the Decades

Series Editors: Norka T. Malberg and Joan Raphael-Leff

Other titles in the series:

The Anna Freud Tradition: Lines of Development—Evolution of Theory and Practice over the Decades
edited by Norka T. Malberg and Joan Raphael-Leff

Fairbairn and the Object Relations Tradition
edited by Graham S. Clarke and David E. Scharff

The Winnicott Tradition: Lines of Development—Evolution of Theory and Practice over the Decades
edited by Margaret Boyle Spelman and Frances Thomson-Salo

The W. R. Bion Tradition: Lines of Development—Evolution of Theory and Practice over the Decades
edited by Howard B. Levine and Giuseppe Civitarese

THE LACAN TRADITION

Lines of Development—Evolution of Theory and Practice over the Decades

Edited By

Lionel Bailly, David Lichtenstein, and Sharmini Bailly

Routledge
Taylor & Francis Group
LONDON AND NEW YORK

First published 2018
by Routledge
2 Park Square, Milton Park, Abingdon, Oxon OX14 4RN

and by Routledge
711 Third Avenue, New York, NY 10017

Routledge is an imprint of the Taylor & Francis Group, an informa business

British Library Cataloguing-in-Publication Data
A catalogue record for this book is available from the British Library

Library of Congress Cataloging-in-Publication Data
A catalog record has been requested for this book

ISBN: 978-1-78049-151-6 (pbk)

Typeset in Palatino LT Std
by Medlar Publishing Solutions Pvt Ltd, India

CONTENTS

PART II: SOME CENTRAL CONCEPTS

PART III: SOME CLINICAL REFLECTIONS

PART IV: BEYOND THE CLINIC

ABOUT THE EDITORS AND CONTRIBUTORS

Lionel Bailly is a Psychoanalyst and a Child and Adolescent Psychiatrist. He is a Practicing Analyst of the Association Lacanienne Internationale and an Academic Associate of the British Psychoanalytical Society. He is Honorary Senior Lecturer at University College London Psychoanalysis Unit where he is particularly involved in the doctoral school. He trained in medicine and psychiatry at the Salpêtrière Hospital in Paris. After a long collaboration with Jean Bergès he became head of Sainte-Anne's Biopsychopathology Unit, which he led until moving to London in 2000. He is the author of two books, one on Psychotrauma in Children (in French) and *Lacan* in the Beginner's Guide Series (One World Press) in English.

Sharmini Bailly is a psychoanalytic psychotherapist and member of the British Psychotherapy Foundation in London. A former news and arts journalist, she currently works in the National Health Service and in private practice. She edited *Lacan* in the Beginner's Guide series published by One World Press.

Gabriel Balbo is a psychoanalyst in private practice in Paris. He has published extensively in the field of theoretical psychoanalysis, child psychoanalysis, and psychoanalytic psychodrama. In collaboration with Jean Bergès, Gabriel Balbo also wrote four books in which they put forward innovative ideas in child psychoanalysis. In 2005 he founded the psychoanalytic association La Libre Association Freudienne (LAF).

Jean Bergès (1928–2004) was a psychiatrist and a psychoanalyst. Having qualified in medicine, Jean Bergès became Chef de Clinique in Prof Jean Delay's unit at Sainte-Anne Hospital in Paris. Before undertaking a specialisation in child psychiatry, he worked with Professor Alexandre Minkowski being involved in research into the development of premature babies. This led him to develop new models of children's relationships with space, time, and motricity. After a long collaboration with Professor Julian de Ajuriaguerra, in 1960 Jean Bergès became head of Sainte-Anne's Biopsychopathology Unit, which he led until retiring in 1995. An analysand of Jacques Lacan, Jean Bergès was one of the founding members of the current Association Lacanienne Internationale (ALI), together with Charles Melman, Claude Dorgeuille, and Marcel Czermak. He was actively involved in training within this organisation, in particular within the Paris School for Child Psychoanalysis (EPEP). Having held for over fifteen years a monthly seminar first at Sainte Anne then at the ALI and having published extensively, Jean Bergès wrote four books in collaboration with Gabriel Balbo about child psychoanalysis.

Néstor A. Braunstein is a former professor of Psychoanalysis at the Universities of Córdoba (Argentina) and UNAM (México), and a pioneer of Lacanian Psychoanalysis in Mexico. He is the author of *Memory and dread or the memory of childhood.* (2010), *La jouissance: un concept lacanien* (1994 [2006]) and *Traducir el psicoanálisis Traduire la psychanalyse*, which was published in Paris in November 2016. He lives and teaches in Barcelona (Spain).

Bernard Burgoyne is a psychoanalyst practising in London. He was educated at Clare College Cambridge, the London School of Economics, and the University of Paris. He is a Member of the World Association of Psychoanalysis and a Founder Member of the Centre for Freudian Analysis and Research, London. He has published widely on the relation between mathematical structure and the structure of the mind, and has given more than four hundred presentations on these themes at many universities and clinical training organisations across the world. He recently gave presentations on the mathematical structure of boundaries in psychic structure at the Tate Modern in London; he is currently working on the relation between the mathematical theory of space, and the tension of desire in the human soul.

Sara Flanders is a Training and Supervising Psychoanalyst of the British Psychoanalytic Society and has worked since 1989 at the Brent Adolescent Centre. She is the editor of *The Dream Discourse Today*, and with Dana Birksted Breen and Alain Gibeault, edited *Reading French Psychoanalysis*. Both books were published by the New Library of Psychoanalysis. She has published a number of articles pertaining to dreams and to adolescence. Having received a PhD in English prior to training as a psychoanalyst she retains an interest in the reciprocal illumination of psychoanalysis and literature.

Cormac Gallagher is a Psychoanalyst. Following a traditional Jesuit training in philosophy, theology, and spirituality, he started to train in psychoanalysis in Paris in 1970. He attended Jacques Lacan's seminars and case presentations and obtained a doctorate with Jean Laplanche. He returned to Ireland in 1974 and while working as a clinical psychologist in St Vincent's University Hospital, founded The School of Psychotherapy and set up undergraduate and postgraduate programmes in Freudian and Lacanian psychoanalysis. Cormac Gallagher started to translate Lacan's texts into English and made the translations of most seminars available to the public, first through books and more recently through the website "Jacques Lacan in Ireland" that he created. He was involved in the foundation of the psychoanalytic journal *The Letter* in 1994 and founded The Irish School for Lacanian Psychoanalysis (ISLP) in 2007.

Maurice Khoury is a Psychoanalyst, co-founder, and President of the Lebanese Association for the Development of Psychoanalysis (ALDEP), full member of the Paris Psychoanalytical Society (SPP) and the International Psychoanalytical Association (IPA), and works in private practice in Beirut, Lebanon.

David Lichtenstein is a psychoanalyst in New York, Editor of *DIVISION/Review: a quarterly psychoanalytic forum*, faculty at NYU Postdoctoral Program in Psychoanalysis and Psychotherapy, and the CUNY Graduate Center. He is on the editorial board of the Journal of the American Psychoanalytic Association and was co-founder of the Apres-Coup Psychoanalytic Association. He is the author of numerous articles and book chapters.

Charles Melman is a Psychoanalyst and a Psychiatrist. A trainee and analysand of Jacques Lacan, he was Director of Teaching in Lacan's École Freudienne de Paris and also in charge of its journal, *Scilicet*. After founding the Association Freudienne Internationale with Jean Bergès, Marcel Czermak, and Jean Dorgeuille in 1982, he started the journal, *Le Discours Psychanalytique*. Together with Claude Dumézil, Gérard Pommier, and Moustafa Safouan, he created the European Foundation for Psychoanalysis, and in 1994 *Le Journal Français de Psychiatrie* with Marcel Czermak. In 2001, following his suggestion, the Association Freudienne Internationale was renamed Association Lacanienne Internationale. Since 1982 he has explored and built upon Lacan's work in his seminars. Having published many books, in particular on hysteria, obsessional neurosis, and psychosis, Charles Melman has engaged in the elaboration of what he describes as a New Psychic Economy.

Dany Nobus is Professor of Psychoanalytic Psychology and Pro-Vice-Chancellor for External Affairs at Brunel University, London, where he also directs the MA in Psychoanalysis and Contemporary Society. He is the Chair of the Freud Museum London, and the author of numerous books and papers on the history, theory and practice of psychoanalysis.

Jean-Michel Rabaté has been Professor of English and Comparative Literature at the University of Pennsylvania since 1992. He is a curator of Slought Foundation, an editor of the *Journal of Modern Literature* and a Fellow of the American Academy of Arts and Sciences, and has authored or edited more than thirty-five books on modernism, psychoanalysis, and philosophy. Recent books include *The Pathos of Distance: Affects of the Moderns* (Bloomsbury, 2016), *Think, Pig! Beckett at the limit of the human* (Fordham, 2016), and *Les Guerres de Jacques Derrida* (U. de Montréal, 2016).

Colette Soler, Professor of Philosophy and PhD in Psychology who trained with Jacques Lacan. She founded the Forums du Champ Lacanien and their school. She is a practicing analyst in Paris and teaches in Paris and in many Forums du Champ Lacanien around the world. Having extensively published books and papers in French, she has published in English: *What Lacan Said About Women* (Other Press, 2006), *The Unconscious Reinvented* (Karnac, 2014), and *Lacanian Affects* (Routledge, 2015).

Alain Vanier is a psychoanalyst and a psychiatrist. He is professor at Paris Diderot-Paris 7 where he directs the Centre for Research, Psychoanalysis, Medicine and Society (CRPMS). He also teaches at the École Nationale Supérieure des Beaux-Arts de Paris (ENSBA). He is an analyst member of Espace Analytique (AFPRF). Having extensively published books and papers in French, he has also published in English, *Lacan—The Lacanian Clinical Field* (2000) through Other press, New York.

"Lines of Development": evolution of tradition, theory, and practice over the decades

Norka T. Malberg & Joan Raphael-Leff

In a 1974 interview given to the Italian magazine *Panorama*, Jaques Lacan was asked about the crisis in psychoanalysis. He replied: *Psychoanalysis has not come close to finding its own limits, yet. There is still so much to discover in practice and in consciousness.... How can it be said that Freud has been left behind, when we still not yet entirely understood him? ...* (Verso Books Blog, 2014)

In this volume, the sixth installment of the Lines of Development Book Series, the editors, Lionel Bailly, David Lichtenstein and Sharmini Bailly bring to life the very sentiment expressed by Lacan in that 1974 interview. They amass an erudite group of contributors who in truly Lacanian fashion filled the pages of this book with their frankness, lucidity and precision and yes, at times, eschew what Lacan called in the same interview: "the comforting psychoanalysis established by some of Freud's students". Given the complexity of this tradition, and respecting the structure originally established in our first book in this series, the co-editors offer a helpful overview and insightful commentary prior to every section. This provides a thread throughout the book which serves as a guiding light to those of us just beginning to explore the depth of Lacan's thinking.

The aim of the 'Lines of Development' Series is to offer an in-depth exploration of the theoretical contribution of specific thinkers and pioneers in psychoanalysis. A second goal is to trace and acknowledge the expansion of their concepts and technique, and applications of these beyond the original intention. Furthermore, each volume invites the student, the teacher and the practitioner to broaden and diversify their knowledge of the language and practice of psychoanalysis. This book meets the mark and exceeds it by drawing a true developmental line of Lacanian thinking, its roots and its evolution. This is apparent in the superbly orchestrated historical journey exemplified by Bernard Burgoyne to Lionel Bailey's clinically useful elaboration of Lacan's ideas on the Oedipus Complex, and specifically clarification of Lacan's paternal metaphor and other concepts. Similarly, explorations of the Lacanian view of human emotions such as love and hate in the poetic writing by Colette Sofer to the application of Lacanian theory to today's complex reality, its impact on the human psyche and the role of mental health in the collective as explored by Charles Melman.

In sum, '*The Lacan Tradition*' invites us all to move away from what Lacan called 'a few banal psychoanalytic formulas'. It challenges us to imagine, to reflect and most of all, to dare beyond that which is easily seen.

PREFACE

Lionel Bailly

One could introduce Lacan, paraphrasing the great Victor Hugo, by saying that the century was one year old when he was born. That made him very much a "*début de siècle*" creature, someone living at a time when the new was made. Sciences, arts, social rules were changing at a dizzying pace in the first part of the twentieth century and Lacan wanted to be part of it. His personality was characterised by an infallible desire to understand, associated with an inability to accept as true what he felt had not been demonstrated as such.

He would use these traits in the pursuit of a career in Medicine. This is particularly important for several reasons. The first one is that being a doctor in the France of the nineteen-twenties meant belonging to an elite, being member of a very privileged club where you really had power. This position of power meant that trainees were expected to "treat" patients not because they were themselves trained and ready but because it was the privilege of their function. Long before even having finished his doctoral dissertation or his analysis, Lacan was in charge of treating extremely complex cases. Having been pushed in at the deep end by the system, he could have been cautious and unadventurous, he could have shied away from it all and blamed degeneracy, a frequent 'answer' to psychological problems at the time. Instead, he embraced the challenge and searched in all available sciences for what could help him in his work as a clinician. This is a crucial point: Lacan's theoretical elaborations were aimed at achieving clinical success. At a time when no psychotropic drugs were available and when most psychological models were rather weak, Lacan turned to psychoanalysis—in itself a daring move in a very anti-German society, in which the work of Freud was largely unknown. Beside psychoanalysis, Lacan harvested ideas from other sciences. However, while strongly influenced by philosophy Lacan's work was not philosophical; although he initially drew heavily from the work of Henri Wallon, his model is not psychological. It remained psychoanalytical and aimed at clinical practice as illustrated by the very title of his first important paper, "The Mirror Stage", described by Lacan: "as formative of the function of the I *as revealed in psychoanalytic experience*" (my emphasis). A second aspect of his work was influenced by his training: having worked in psychiatric hospitals with deluded, hallucinating, psychotic patients, Lacan's experience was somewhat different from that of many lay analysts more used to the neurotic anxiety of their analysands. Lacan felt it was important to be able to theorise psychosis within a psychoanalytic framework and it is from his work on psychosis that he developed central concepts such as the paternal metaphor, which could then be applied apply universally.

From the very beginning of his work Lacan's manner of thinking seems to have been similar to that of mathematicians—his ideas rested initially on intuitions that he would then try to demonstrate to be true. The method he used for demonstrations involved critical logical analyses of psychoanalytical arguments and was in fact a variation of the methodology of scholasticism. Like a modern Abelard, Lacan engaged in his seminar in dialectical reasoning, trying to extend knowledge and to resolve contradictions. This does not always make for easy reading. His seminars were not made to be read but to be heard, and heard from the mouth of the author, a particular situation that allows the auditor to understand more than they would on their own. Also, as with mathematical intuitions, Lacan's theoretical hypotheses were quite difficult to put into words and he attempted to present them in a visuo-spatial way, a topologic way, in many different schemas and diagrams.

The complexity of Lacan's model and the format of his seminars meant that his pupils and his followers engaged in the necessary work of elucidation, which over the years seems to have unfortunately become for some analysts an end in itself. These appear reluctant to use Lacan's theory as Lacan used Freud's, and they go on commenting on the previous comments of others in a curiously Talmudic way. When the oral scholarship established in Lacan's seminar (though some had made private notes) could no longer be maintained, what had been fluid knowledge still under discussion came to be written, and these writings then became the object of discussions, structured as an exegetical commentary, stifling the possibility of innovation. Worse, some authors seem to have moved from exegesis to eisegesis, in the sense of "importing" or "drawing in" his or her own purely subjective interpretations into the text, unsupported by the text itself.

Thirty-four years after Lacan's death, many of his concepts have spread into mainstream psychoanalysis and the number of Lacanian psychoanalysts worldwide is broadly similar to that of IPA members. In addition, the Lacanian model is extensively used in many parts of academia, from literature, cinema, critical theory, gender studies, to politics and philosophy. Despite this blatant and enduring success, the wounds resulting from the split from the IPA have not healed with several deleterious consequences. On one side there are analysts who continue to refuse to consider Lacanian theory, or use it without quoting their references. On the other, some Lacanians don't read the work of other major analysts and ignore the ongoing debates of the rest of the analytical world. There is also a curious tendency in some Lacanian analysts to identify with the master in such a way that they seem to seek rejection, as if being excluded from an institution was a necessary initiation and a guarantee of quality. At a time when worldwide, worryingly simplistic models of the psyche have become the received view and when money from the pharmaceutical industry rules a large part of psychiatric academia, it would seem reasonable that the practitioners of the unconscious start at last to genuinely exchange and work with each other, sharing their experience of a very difficult profession. This book, hopefully, will contribute to this exchange.

Lionel Bailly,
London, September 2016

INTRODUCTION

Lionel Bailly, Sharmini Bailly, and David Lichtenstein

This book finds its place in a series about "psychoanalytic leaders whose ideas have generated a tradition of thinking and working in particular ways". From the beginning of his career, Lacan seemed set on contributing ideas to the field with a conviction that has been considered either prophetic or somewhat grandiose. In the thesis he presented for qualification as a medical doctor in September 1932, Lacan suggested that the findings of the founder of German psychiatry Emile Kraepelin "confirm mine"—a statement that reveals his ambition to be the leader in a new tradition. Eighty-four years later, one can admit that his wish has been realised: there is indeed a Lacanian psychoanalytic tradition and concepts such as the Name-of-the-Father and the Real, Symbolic, and Imaginary have constituted a breakthrough in the understanding of psychosis, the field that Lacan explored in his thesis.

Throughout the first decade and a half of his career, Lacan was highly influential within the psychoanalytic establishment. In 1953, he was president of the Société Psychanalytique de Paris, the French branch of the IPA. When a conflict around the issue of the analytic training led to a split in the SPP, Lacan followed Daniel Lagache, who led the separation, into a new organisation. A later split occurred when Lacan was banned from training analysts by the IPA, who gave as a reason his use of variable length analytical sessions. This "excommunication" however seemed to result in the strengthening of his influence within his own analytic following.

The story of Lacan's history and role in the development of French psychoanalysis has been told well by Elizabeth Roudinesco (1990, 1999, 2014) in several books. We revisit this in Part I of the current volume in the two essays by Flanders and Gallagher. Histories could also be written about Lacan's influence on psychoanalysis and intellectual history in other countries aside from France. The variety of these stories would reflect the multiplicity of Lacan's appeal, the range of his concepts, and the specific cultural and historical dynamics of the respective national communities. Thus, in Argentina and other parts of Latin America where there are currently large and vibrant communities of psychoanalysts influenced by Lacan's work, distinct political, cultural, and intellectual factors there contributed to establishing and nourishing that interest. The histories of Lacan's reception in the Anglo-American, Irish, and Australian contexts are similarly rich and reflect particular cultural dynamics as much as diverse aspects of Lacan's thinking.

The Lacanian tradition goes beyond psychoanalysis. Its relationships with authority within the psychoanalytic world and with other critical intellectual currents gives it an appeal beyond that of just another psychoanalytic school. Lacan's critique challenges ideas about the dialectic of knowledge and power itself and thus has a reflexive function on the very processes of teaching and the transmission of knowledge in psychoanalysis. Like Freud's "Copernican revolution" that displaced the self-conscious human subject, Lacan radically interrogated the subject of knowledge in the psychoanalytic encounter. The Cartesian subject that links being and thinking (*cogito ergo sum*; I think therefore I am) is forever altered by the psychoanalytic discovery of unconscious thinking that leads to a modification of the Cartesian assertion such that it might better be phrased as "I am where I think not" (Lacan, 1966).

The ethical and political ramifications in the fields of culture and history of Lacan's radically altered self-conscious subject have in turn affected the very reception of his model. There are parallels between the psychoanalytic enquiry into questions of ethics, culture, and politics and Lacan's enquiry into the ethics, culture, and politics of psychoanalysis as reflected in his professional history, the "excommunication" from the IPA and his establishment of an independent school, but also in essential elements of his conceptualisation of psychoanalysis. For example, the slippage of the signifier (the over-determination of all representation) as a reflection of the subject's division by unconscious knowledge, the Real as impossible (as a boundary of knowledge), and the imaginary fictive character of subjective wholeness and self-certainty are all basic ideas in Lacan's view of psychoanalysis and are all ideas that likewise contribute to the appeal of his thought in the context of cultural critique.

Lacan repeatedly asserted that his intent was to teach psychoanalysts but his students always included others, non-psychoanalysts who heard the ethical, epistemological, and political ramifications of his thought. The context of his seminars and the resonance of this wider audience altered the significance of the ideas for the psychoanalysts who were present as well.

There is a striking and somewhat tragic parallel, however, between Lacan's influence and that of Freud. Both expressed a commitment to intellectual scepticism, to ongoing critique, in the Kantian sense, and to the continual reassessment of ideas and formulations, yet each generated a community of orthodox followers, followers who insisted instead on a rather set and unchanging theory. This is a problem encountered in many intellectual communities; however, it is particularly poignant for psychoanalysts since at the heart of the psychoanalytic process as understood by both Freud and Lacan, is an encounter with the unconscious construction of authority relations and, in principle, the working through of idealisation in this regard. Yet the problem of idealisation of Lacan and his teaching can be seen in every community influenced by his work. In considering the influence of Lacan especially in light of this view of his work as an ongoing critique, it is therefore necessary to also take into account the particular ways that the dogma in his teaching has also been used to obscure its truths.

Lacan's reception in the United States

In his talks and seminars in the 1950s and 1960s Lacan used as a foil for the elaboration of his ideas what was then the dominant approach to psychoanalysis in the United States, the approach associated with Hartmann's (1939) notion of *Ego Psychology*. At the time, the field of psychoanalysis was more powerful in the United States than anywhere else in the world and thus in spite of its Germanic origins, Ego Psychology could be seen as an American phenomenon.

Lacan used the emphasis on so-called autonomous ego functions as a springboard for his critique of the field and for the development of his new conceptions of the divided subject; a conception that Lacan asserted was more consistent with Freud's intent than the later ("American") emphasis on a healthy integrated ego. And while Lacan was also a close reader and frequent critic of other approaches of the times, such as the British school of object relations theory and the work of Melanie Klein, his critique of the then dominant American school of émigré analysts, including Lacan's own analyst and founder of the first French psychoanalytic society, Rudolph Loewenstein, was a central foundation point for his teaching. To be an American student of psychoanalysis at the time was therefore to be addressed by Lacan's project in a particular and challenging way. Indeed, the American psychoanalyst was interpellated by Lacan in a debate on the fundamental principles of the field.

Ego Psychology, while still extant and influential, no longer has anything like the hegemonic authority it once had. It may therefore be difficult to recall how bold and revolutionary Lacan's critique seemed when it first appeared in the US in the late 1960s. Given the social and political upheavals at the time, the idea of revolutionary critique resonated on a cultural level as well. Radical political ideas regarding power, class, race, and gender were linked to a growing literature on the radical potential of psychoanalytic thought that had begun with the work of writers such as Marcuse (1955), Brown (1959), and Jacoby (1975). The ground was thus over-determined for receiving Lacan's radical critique of established psychoanalytic authority and his attack on the current affirmation of the conflict-free zone of the ego, and "the problem of adaptation" (Hartmann, 1939). In the context of the times, it was possible to portray this concern with adaptation and freedom from conflict as a distinctly American style of psychoanalysis associated with the post war conformist consumer society that developed first and foremost in the US.

The Ego Psychology that Lacan was critiquing in the 1950s and 1960s had, by that time, assumed the authority of orthodox Freudian dogma in the United States. Freudian psychoanalysis in the US *was* Ego Psychology. There was hardly any other approach that yet called itself Freudian.

However, there were other schools of psychoanalytic theory and practice in the American scene at the time. Indeed, by the late in 1960s and early in 1970s psychoanalysis was becoming a pluralistic field in the United States in ways that threatened the hegemony of Ego Psychology quite independently of Lacan's critique. Heinz Kohut's *Analysis of the Self* (1971) was a significant break with Ego Psychology but also a portent of a broad re-examination of the psychoanalytic theory of the subject that would expand in both scope and influence in the years following, to what has since come to be known as the "relational turn" in American psychoanalysis.

Thus, the challenge to contemporary orthodoxy was being mounted from a different direction in the United States and indeed, the shift in American psychoanalytic practice away from

Ego Psychology since 1970 is owed far more to the impact of relational and self-psychology theories, as well as the various indigenous inter-subjective theorists, than it does to Lacan's influence. This is one reason why the initial reception of Lacan's work in the US occurred mostly in the non-clinical, wider intellectual, and academic community. The clinicians already had their alternatives, and didn't immediately see the relevance of Lacan's work.

There was however a major difference between the interpersonal theories, self-psychology, and various so-called humanistic therapies evident on the American scene in the late 1960s and 1970s, and Lacan's work. Unlike Lacan, they based their approach on a departure from and indeed even a rejection of Freud: to distance oneself from the dominant authority of Ego Psychology was to distance oneself from Freud as well. To some extent this remains true among the current adherents to these alternative frameworks: they begin from a rejection of Freud, that is entirely counter to the position taken by Lacan.

However, especially in the early years of Lacan's reception in the US, to affirm a Freudian commitment one would necessarily be loyal to Ego Psychology as its most fully realised representative. Janet Malcolm's *The Impossible Profession* (1981) is an important and still relevant examination of this particular position in the intellectual and cultural history of American psychoanalysis. Lacan's work gets merely a brief and dismissive mention in that book. However, in truth Lacan differed from all of the clinical reforms taking place at the time and that were the subject of the debates she wrote about. Lacan instead reaffirmed a commitment to Freudian thought and a rigorous reading of Freud's texts.

Lacan declared that it was those very analysts who called themselves Freudian, the émigré analysts of the American orthodoxy, that were instead betraying the truths of Freud's discoveries. He called for a more attentive and respectful reading of Freud especially of his earliest work—a "Return to Freud" that was a direct challenge to the so-called Freudians. Putting in doubt the current orthodoxy in the name of a new critical and rigorous reading of the sources had a tremendous appeal to those of us in the United States at the time, who found the reigning authorities too rigid and unimaginative yet were not interested in rejecting the Freudian foundations in the drives, the unconscious, and the interpretive role of the analyst. Lacan represented a new dialectical challenge regarding the rigorous reading of Freud that preserved an appreciation of the Freudian project in the context later developments in philosophy, linguistics, and anthropology.

Was there indeed more to be found in Freud than had been recognised either by the orthodoxy or by those who were post-Freudian? Did the route to reinvigorating psychoanalytic theory and practice pass back through Freud, Lacan's famous return, rather than by turning away? This is Lacan's wager and the current volume is an occasion to evaluate its success.

Lacan's wager is to reread and reconfigure the basic elements of Freudian thought in a way that is both true to their intention and yet allows them to be worked with in a more expansive and effective way. Does his appropriation of the Saussurean signifier for instance successfully preserve the meaning of Freud's unconscious *Repraesentanz* while yet allowing us to work with it in a more effective and rigorous linguistic framework? Does Lacan's invention of the object *a* effectively preserve Freud's idea of the vicissitudes of the drive while yet knitting that theory into a consideration of the subject/other dynamic, a critical inter-subjectivity, that was later to become the focus of relational schools? Does his proposed structure of the Imaginary, Symbolic, and Real effectively enhance Freud's efforts to map a structure of the psyche? The evaluation of Lacan's project should take place on his own terms: a return to Freud and respect for the core of Freud's work in order to find new and more effective ways of conceptualising and working with it.

Perhaps because the clinicians were engaged in other battles, the initial interest in Lacan among North Americans was found in the Academy and especially in the humanities and human sciences there, rather than among clinical psychoanalysts. The first translations of Lacan's work that appeared in Yale French Studies (1966, 1972) were part of a more general intellectual interest in Structuralism and the potential that the structuralist perspective offered for invigorating psychoanalytic thought as a critical discourse rather than as a clinical profession. The academic interest in Lacan was part of a general interest in "French Theory", a designation for post-war philosophy and cultural theory ranging from existential phenomenology through structuralist and post-structuralist theory. Lacan was encountered as part of this field and as part of the interest in psychoanalysis as a discourse within cultural theory, as a sort of anthropology rather than a clinical practice.

Anthony Wilden, a British expatriate who was studying with Rene Girard, the French historian and social philosopher at Johns Hopkins University in Baltimore, provided the first important introduction to the work of Lacan. *The Language of the Self* (1968), appeared in the US only two years after Lacan's first major publication, *Ecrits* (1966) was published in France. In 1971, American Imago published a review of the Wilden text by Octave Mannoni, a psychoanalyst who was then working with Lacan. It was one of the first essays to appear in an American psychoanalytic journal addressing Lacan's work and his place in the history of psychoanalytic thought. Mannoni's reflections on Wilden's book not only set a context for the book's significance in the Anglo-American world, but also its significance for what was then still a developing appreciation in France of the relationship between Lacan's thought and other contemporaneous intellectual currents.

At the same time, Wilden's text introduces English and American theoreticians (Bateson, Laing, and others) to France by putting their ideas in parallel or in opposition to Lacan. In a more generalised fashion, we see from his later work that Wilden is working to identify and synthesise the new orientation of scientific thought under the influence of linguistics, information theory, and systems theory. His interest in Lacan results no doubt from this general orientation of his researches. Naturally, similar efforts are being made in other countries—in Italy, for example. But they are far less advanced—and above all less embracing and less ambitious. At the present time, Wilden's work remains unique in the world, including France (Mannoni, 1971, p. 96).

In fact, it was only in the mid 1960s and especially after 1966, with the original publication of *Ecrits*, that Lacan's work began to be widely known in France outside psychoanalytic circles. The introduction of Lacan's texts within the Anglo-American world was thus not long delayed in relation to the wider dispersion of that work in France. One fundamental difference of course was that in France there had been a group of analysts who had worked with Lacan both as his analysands and as his students or colleagues since the 1950s. As his work became known this group was supplemented by philosophers and others who took an interest in psychoanalysis largely through Lacan's teaching (Roudinesco, 1990).

The Lacanian school in the broadest sense of the term that thus came into existence was unlike any other in the psychoanalytic world in that it was entirely the outgrowth of one person's elaboration of psychoanalytic theory and practice and stood apart from any already established psychoanalytic institute or society. This differed from developments in London or Chicago, for instance, where important figures like Melanie Klein, Donald Winnicott or Heinz Kohut emerged within the psychoanalytic institution and then developed a following. For some, the Lacanian organisation around the work of one person was a reason to question it, but in any case it was a unique phenomenon in psychoanalytic history and should to be taken into account in understanding the particular character of its influence. For those of us who became interested in the texts of Lacan as they began to appear in increasing volume from the 1970s on, there was always also the question of the phenomenon of the Lacanian school, its rebellious history, internal conflicts, schisms, its ultimate dissolution near the end of Lacan's life, and the subsequent proliferation in France of a remarkable multiplicity of Lacanian groups after his death in 1981.

As an American analyst, interested in the phenomenon and the teaching of Lacan, one never encountered Lacan alone but always also the Lacanians. Indeed, to be a Lacanian was not only to be interested in Lacan's approach to the theory and practice of the field but also to be interested in the unique sort of organisation and transmission that accompanied Lacan's career and therefore might accompany the transmission of psychoanalysis in general. Questioning the formation of psychoanalysts and the study and transmission of psychoanalytic practice was a central element in Lacan's work, not an incidental by-product. Cormac Gallagher's essay in the current volume takes up this matter more fully.

To follow an interest in Lacan therefore meant to form a group in order to study the texts but also in order to experience the unique approach to transmission that this "de-institutionalised" psychoanalysis offered. In many ways, this is still the case. Young psychoanalysts in New York who are interested in Lacan today attend various formal courses and or workshops, but just as often form semi- or fully independent working groups to study together and to present work to one another. They do so not simply to supplement formal teaching, but because there is something in the Lacanian approach itself that invites this act. These then are the characteristics of the Lacanian reception in the US. A critique of both the American orthodoxy of Ego Psychology and the post-Freudian relational, interpersonal, and inter-subjective reforms in the name of a radical and dialectical theory of the subject that is nevertheless an affirmation of the Freudian foundation of psychoanalysis, a call to link psychoanalysis with Post-Structuralist theory, and finally, an invitation to rethink the transmission of psychoanalysis, i.e., to form new groups for both the study of psychoanalytic texts and the supervision of psychoanalytic work.

Lacan and the current psychoanalytic field

The ambition of rethinking psychoanalysis has led to an efflorescence of work and reflections worldwide; however, it has also had the effect of keeping Lacanian and non-Lacanian thinking separate. It is as if since the split of the SFP, two groups of practitioners working on the same subject have decided splendidly to ignore each other and refuse to benefit from the others' advances. The French singer and poet Georges Brassens at the time of the SFP split mocked nationalists in a song where a Frenchman chose to die rather than to be saved by a treatment invented by a German: a metaphor unfortunately very meaningful in the field of psychoanalysis.

In opposition to this sectarian attitude, one of the ambitions of the editors of this book is to help integrate Lacan's ideas with the main body of what is thought of as psychoanalysis by the other schools. Some of these ideas have already been absorbed into this "mainstream" without being recognised as being Lacanian in origin (see Flanders, S., Chapter Two), because the French tradition within the IPA is so heavily influenced by Lacan. Terms such as the Symbolic, the Paternal Function, Desire, and notions of representation (or figuration, as the French say) have their origins in his emphases upon these matters, but the current IPA discourse around them has diverged from his own views, which are sometimes misrepresented but more often ignored.

Psychoanalysis is still in its infancy as a clinical discipline and our understanding of the human psyche very far from complete. It is the view of the editors that no particular school of psychoanalytic thought has a perfect model of the workings of the human mind, not to mention its interface with the body. It is also our view that Jacques Lacan's contributions to our understanding and more specifically to the building blocks with which we can build concepts about the human mind and its functioning are too important to remain ignored by the "mainstream". Doing so retards the evolution of psychoanalytic understanding in a way that a "split off" part of the personality retards creativity until the subject (or ego, for non-Lacanians) can reclaim it.

Many papers published in the *IJP* begin with a thorough "review of the literature", which seems necessary in order for the author to justify the particular definition of the terms she or he uses in the discussion; it sometimes feels like nobody is quite sure that what they mean by a word fits with what others mean by it; and the basis for employing a term seems to be that if enough people have used it in a certain way, then that must be right. This may be the way in which language evolves naturally, but when applied in the context of a natural science, it can lead to collective thinking going down the wrong path for generations. We follow Hobbes (1909) in feeling that "when men register their thoughts wrong, by the inconstancy of the signification of their words; by which they register for their conceptions, that which they never conceived [...] deceive themselves". Understandings built upon vaguely understood terms are fundamentally shaky and lead to what Ferenczi called a confusion of tongues, and in Lacanian terms, imaginary-to-imaginary dialogues.

Lacan certainly felt that a confusion of tongues was arising in the 1950s, when James Strachey was still in the process of translating Freud's complete works and thereby laying down definitions of the terms that have come into standard usage, and he very much wanted to contribute to the defining of the field. It is a pity that the successors of Freud in the IPA, who may have been talented clinicians, were not receptive of his exceptional talent for theoretical abstraction. Lacan was too ambitious merely to accept Strachey's translations and add to the discussions taking place in London and New York; he challenged the developing "establishment" view of the Freudian fundamentals of how to think about the psyche. This is precisely what makes it so difficult to integrate Lacan's theory into the mainstream: he did not come up with ideas with immediately obvious clinical resonance, so that readers can easily say, "that is just like my patient so-and-so", he went back to the basics and sought a re-examination of terms: what do we mean by ego, or by id? How does the Oedipus Complex work? What is psychosis and what is meant by psychotic? What do we mean by "unconscious"? What did Freud mean by *Darstellbarkeit*? By *Vorstellungrepräsentant*? And in his examination of the fundamentals, he coined new terms and ideas of his own.

The problem for us now is that his split with the IPA was so thorough and took place so long ago that the understandings he brought to many basic terms and the usage they have acquired in Lacanian psychoanalysis have diverged so widely from the way in which the same words are conceptualised and used in the "mainstream" that they have become *"faux amis"*—false friends: they exist side by side in different languages, meaning different things. There is a work of translation to be done—a work of enormous importance and difficulty and beyond the scope of this introduction; indeed, it would constitute a book in itself. However, it would be negligent of us not to at least provide some indications and clues for non-Lacanians as to the different meanings psychoanalytic terms have in the Lacanian Tradition.

The Ego and the Ich

Freudians, both classical and contemporary, Kleinians, British Independents, American ego psychologists, and others in the IPA tradition of psychoanalysis take the Ego to be the agency of reason that mediates between the savagery of the id, the demands of reality and those of the superego. Freudians also focus upon the ego as the agency of repression and pathological defences, which would bring them closer to the Lacanian position. However, Lacan never accepted the translation of Freud's *"das Ich"* into "ego", and himself preferred to speak of the Subject as the experiencing and active self. Lacan never bought into the idea of a fundamentally "good" agency that mediates between id impulses and superego demands, fantasy and reality, or whose function is that of adaptation to external reality, and moreover he disliked the implicit moral judgment bound up in such a definition. Lacan retained the Subjective *"Ich"* and saw the neologism of "ego" as a fiction constructed by the Subject: it is what the Subject says to itself about itself, after the radical splitting that occurs when the baby, upon encountering its own image, recognises itself as an object embedded in the Other. In this sense, the Lacanian ego is a narcissistic construct, which is however more than just "one's view of oneself" as it is also the active agent involved in a more or less permanent act of self-construction and maintenance. The extent to which the constructions of the ego coincide with the Subject's true relation with the Other is a measure of its authenticity. Some Lacanians have widened the concept of ego to see it as almost synonymous with the Lacanian *sinthome*—the "cotter pin" that stops the Subject from unravelling into madness (see Braunstein, N., Chapter Eight).

Lacan's detestation of the ego psychologists was one of the many unfortunate antipathies that have sprung up in the psychoanalytic movement. His ultimately unsuccessful analysis with Loewenstein, one of the movement's founders, might play a part in this. But Lacan's characterisation of Ego Psychology as an attempt to "educate" patients better to adapt to reality and to "strengthen" ego defences is an over-simplification. The ego psychologists, particularly those concerned with childhood development like Mahler and Jacobson, recognised ego defences as the keystone of pathological personality traits and this could have been an area of potential common ground with Lacanians. We wish to emphasise not the differences but the common ground between contemporary Freudians and Lacanians: both take cognisance of the objective world, fantasy and the area between the two in which psychic functioning belongs. However, it was in characterising the objective world that Lacan took a step forward in the invention of a new term.

*The Other (*Le Grand Autre*)*

There is something in the vagueness of this term coupled with the importance suggested by the capitalisation that seems to inspire mystical speculations about it. What has been obscured by this is the important recognition contained in this term that the objective world that most profoundly affects the Subject is the *human, cultural* world, created, defined and represented by speech and language. It is this deeply rooted relationship between the objective social world and language that caused Lacan to define the Other as "a locus in which speech is constituted" (Lacan, 1993); and it is by means of language that the Other infiltrates and shapes the psyche.

One continuous criticism of Lacan by the psychoanalytic mainstream is that he reduced everything to a matter of language. However, the Other is not only the social-cultural world, but also the physical human world—the world of "*la jouissance Autre*" in which the baby resides until its submission to the paternal metaphor. Lacan used a capitalised Other to denote the social cultural world, and lower-case "other", sometimes emphasised as "*les petits autres*"—small others—to denote other people, who might at times be seen as representatives of the Other but who by and large are individuals just like the patient—the subject to themselves and object to others. Relations between others are predominantly within the Imaginary realm, where the relationship between the subject and the Other is predominantly (though by no means exclusively) within the Symbolic.

Objects and others

The use of "object" is a confusing *faux-ami* for the uninitiated. This is not the place for a lengthy discussion of British object relations or recapitulation of its Freudian origins but in brief, in its classical Freudian character, an object is the vehicle by which the drive attains its aim. Object relating begins with the relationship between the baby and the breast—the infant's first relationship with a non-me object. Up to this point, most psychoanalytic schools can agree—but divergences begin hereafter. Freudian and the British object relations schools (Kleinian and Independent) hold that at this point, the baby makes no distinction between self and non-self; Kleinians also make a direct equivalence between the breast and the mother or even the maternal environment, which are seen as an extension of the breast. Internal objects in the adult individual are seen by non-Lacanian analysts as psychic representations of objects that have been experienced by the subject; more bluntly (and admittedly simplistically), internal representations of people with whom the patient has had a relationship. These are often projected onto real people in the external world and form the basis of transference phenomena.

Lacan instead recognised that from extremely early in life, the human infant is able to distinguish between the breast and the mother and to accord to the mother her own subjectivity, a viewpoint taken up more recently in infancy research. The primary relationship for Lacan is tripartite: an intersubjective relationship between baby and mother over an object, the breast.

Contemporary Freudians see the individual's personality and identity emerging out of an initial "merger" with the maternal object by means of a series of phases of separation and individuation. In the Lacanian view, there is no merger with the first object, which is the breast, but there is instead a non-differentiation between the mother, who is in reality merely an "other", and the Other. To the baby, the mother is the whole human and social universe and Lacanians have come to represent this by writing "mOther". However, it is because of the baby's recognition of the subjectivity of the mother that it is able to posit as a question in its mind, before it can even speak, the proto-question—what does she want?—that leads to the phallic hypothesis and paternal metaphor (see Bailly, L., Chapter Four).

In general, Lacanians are not very concerned with object relations *per se*, but have focused instead on the aspect of objects that causes desire. When we talk about *the* object, in general we mean object *a*, the cause of desire. Object *a* may take many guises; its origin and evolution is complex, shaped out of the incapacity of language fully to represent what is lacking, and is built around the idea of the Other's desire. Because desire and subjectivity are products of language, the object *a* is closely linked with master signifiers which give direction to all other signifiers, rather like a magnet with iron filings; this gives object *a* a central place in the constitution of the Subject.

Lacanians think less in terms of object relations than intersubjective relations, between the Subject and others (*petits autres*) or between signifiers. These relations have been conceptualised in great detail in the famous *Four Discourses* (Lacan, Four Discourses), and in his later work on sexuation and his focus on the linkage (articulation) of signifiers S1—S2 (Lacan, 1972–1973). This can be seen as an attempt to reduce to the barest atoms the ways in which Subjects might relate, by the linkage of the signifiers that define them and by which they define themselves and others.

The phallus

The Lacanian phallus is not derived in the same way as Kleinian or Contemporary Freudian objects and does not represent the same thing. While we can all agree that the word is used "symbolically", this is as far as the common ground goes. The differences between the Lacanian phallus and the term as employed in Anglo-American analysis stems from radically different ideas of representation developed by the different schools. The way Lacanians conceptualise psychic representation has little overlap with the Kleinian view of symbols and their formation: Lacan's ideas on representation and signification are the gold thread that runs through his work while the ideas of symbol formation that dominate the British object relations schools are so different that a full discussion and debate upon the issue is warranted, and indeed was begun by Lacan himself (Lacan, 1958, 1959). Interestingly, it was around the notion of the phallus and castration that Lacan seemed to realise that a better definition of ideas of representation and symbolism needed to be developed, and he recognised his debt both to Klein and to Jones in refining his idea of the phallus (ibid).

We wish to underline here that to think of the Lacanian phallus in terms of a Kleinian "symbol" is to misunderstand and indeed to misrepresent it badly. He says himself that it is "not a fantasy, if we are to view fantasy as an imaginary effect. Nor is it as such an object (part-, internal, good, bad, etc.) inasmuch as 'object' tends to gauge the reality involved in a relationship. Still less is it the organ—penis or clitoris—that it symbolises" (Lacan, 1958). It is derived *not* from any "*a priori* knowledge" of bodily parts, as hypothesised by Kleinians (Birksted-Breen, 1996) who believe in "innate" pre-conceptions or proto-symbols in the mind of the neo-nate. It does not pass through stages from "concrete representation" through to "predominantly verbal" thought (Money-Kyrle, 1968). It *has* something in common with the views of Ernest Jones on symbolism (Jones, 1916), whom Lacan felt "loses his way" but whose ideas he credited sufficiently to debate and elaborate (Lacan, 1959). And most definitely, the Lacanian phallus does not take its shape in the mind by introjection, via the experience of a particular interaction with someone or something. Thinking about the phallus in this way gives rise to all kinds of misconceptions and pointless arguments, e.g., about phallic monism.

The Lacanian phallus is the product of logical abstraction and the effect of language—of the ability of the infant to wonder and to form hypotheses. Lacanians would also say that it arises out of unconscious knowledge, except that here again it is important to state that this is not the same kind of unconscious or "*a priori*" knowledge coded in proto-symbols or pre-conceptions as conceptualised by Kleinians and other object relations theorists (Bion, 1962; Money-Kyrle, 1968), but knowledge that arises from the unstoppable tendency of signifiers to form links within a language—the unconscious knowledge contained in language itself. The Lacanian phallus begins as the missing signifier that answers the questions that arise in the infant's mind in response to the repeated losses of the mother: what takes her away from me? What does she want? It implies a hypothesised object that lacks any fixed signifier, because neither mother nor infant can actually answer the question: what does she/what do I want? But for the infant Subject, it is the thing that rivals "me" and is supposed ultimately to fulfil mOther's desire (at this stage the mother can still be written in this way, as representing the child's whole human universe); and who can imagine a more compelling object of fantasy than this?

We see Lacan's insistence that the phallus is neither fantasy nor object as his attempt to stop it becoming conceptualised as an "imaginary effect" in the subject's mind (e.g., an unconscious proto-symbol) and to avoid object relations theories being built upon it. He posits instead the phallus as the unknown signifier that could answer the questions in the child's mind about mOther's desire: "the privileged signifier of this mark in which the role of Logos is wedded to the advent of desire" (Lacan, 1958). To use Lacan's bridge-dummy metaphor, the subject will relate *according to* it but not *with* it.

The Lacanian phallus is therefore a representational element in the subject's mind around which fantasy will be built, "the signifier that is destined to designate meaning effects as a whole" (ibid). In the Oedipal constellation, the child will build its fantasies and object relations by trying to embody it (identifying with it), or trying to master and possess it, or in opposition to it—the choice of positions adopted *vis-à-vis* the Phallus is quite individual (see Bailly, L., Chapter Four). While following the lure of the Phallus in its investigations of the Other, the child is simultaneously being introduced into language and is thereby forming its own unique system of representations of the world. Because the phallus takes up the place of the absent signifier of mOther's desire, and because the infinitely linking and substituting nature of language allows the phallus to give way to the object *a*, cause of desire, one's own desire comes to be shaped through language and over time by the desire of the Other.

Drive

There is a surprising myth around that Lacan "moved away" from the concept of the drive or even discarded it. We are not sure how it arose but it seems important here to correct it. What could be said is that Lacan's conception of drive came to differ from those developing within the IPA. Within that organisation, drive is now one of the most eclectic of notions and is used to mean almost anything from affect to creative and destructive urges, in the form of life and death instincts. If the Lacanian view on drives has not undergone such a transformation or elaboration, it is because Lacan was himself for once rather clear on the subject. It has not changed much in conceptualisation for Lacanians since he gave it prominence as one of the four fundamental concepts of psychoanalysis.

Lacan's explication of the drive in that seminar, although he refers in the main to "Instincts and their Vicissitudes", returns us to the Freud of the "Project"—the Freud whose scientific training in the Helmholtzian tradition strove for "the integration of physiology with the fundamental concepts of modern physics, especially those connected with energy" (Lacan, 1981). Lacan is clear that drive is "a potential energy, for [...] the characteristic of the drive is to be a [...] constant force" (ibid). He goes further: "In the drive, there is no question of kinetic energy; it is not a question of something that will be regulated with movement" (ibid). In other words, drive does not "evolve" and has of its own accord no particular direction; and it most certainly cannot be assigned any moral qualities. All these qualities are carried by other factors but derive their power from investment with drive.

In terms of its observability, drive again is analogous with an electrical potential: it can only be seen in its effects, which could lead Lacan to say, "if, for lack of representation, it is not there, what is this *trieb*? We may have to consider it as being only *Trieb* to come." And just as an electrical potential causes a current to flow, the current itself cannot be seen but is theorised as being packaged in moving electrons, which again are invisible. For Lacan, the "current" would be the signifying chain of fantasy and its "electrons" the signifiers within it.

And what is the place of the object for the drive? Lacan, quoting Freud, states: "it [the object] is a matter of total indifference"—but refuses to go as far himself. In looking at the relationship between the object and the drive, he concludes that "the drive turns around the object", meaning that the signifying chain invested by drive is one that revolves around, is given direction by and is in some ways tricked by the object. In another unusually clear statement linking drive with objects, he writes: "the activity in the subject I call 'drive' consists in dealing with these objects in such a way as to recover from them, to restore to himself, his earliest loss" (Lacan, 1964). But because of the incapacity of signifiers to capture the lost object *a* and the consequent emergence of desire, Lacan focused his later efforts on analysing desire, not to the exclusion of drive, but with the implicit understanding that desire is the consequence of drive that best reveals the object relationship within which drive is bound up.

This very short glossary of terms highlights the differences in conception that have grown up between the Lacanian and other psychoanalytic traditions. We hope that our explanation does not have the effect of making the reader feel that the differences are too vast for common understandings to grow up, but of stimulating the reader to think further about the basic concepts of psychoanalysis and how they can be clarified, sharpened, and rendered more useful. The Lacanian tradition, with all its complexity, difficulty and at times self-indulgence, is nonetheless possessed of a wealth of ideas that have been found to be helpful in fields as far ranging as literary criticism, anthropology, art, and politics, and we feel that non-Lacanian psychoanalytic clinicians should no longer deprive themselves of the chance to benefit similarly from an understanding of the paternal metaphor, a psychic model based on Symbolic, Imaginary, and Real, the signifying operation in the constitution of the subject and other Lacanian formulations that it would take too long to list here. One of the aims of the editors of this book is fairly, albeit not comprehensively, to show where the Lacanian tradition has arrived at this point, and to hope to steer its future course slightly further in a direction in which cross-fertilisation with the IPA will become not only possible but also generative of greater clarity and creativity in psychoanalytic thinking. Another aim is to bring together in one volume papers from authors belonging to different affiliations *within* the Lacanian tradition, for there has been a divergence of views on some matters and a divergence of emphasis or focus on others—divergences that have all too often carried the full adversarial charge and embattlement of Lacan's original split with the IPA. We hope that showcasing work from different parts of the Lacanian spectrum will reveal to Lacanians that their common ground is fertile enough to bear their diversity and that their common heritage worth celebrating, critiquing, enjoying and drawing inspiration from together.

References

Bion, W. R. (1962). The Psycho-Analytic Study of Thinking. *Int J Psychoanal, 43*: 306–310.

Birksted-Breen, D. (1996). Phallus, Penis and Mental Space. *Int J Psychoanal, 77*: 649–657.

Brown, N. O. (1959). *Life Against Death: The Psychoanalytical Meaning of History*. Middletown: Wesleyan University Press.

Hartmann, H. (1939). Ego Psychology and the Problem of Adaptation. New York: International Universities Press, pp. 1–121.

Hobbes, T. (1651). Oxford at the Clarendon Press, 1909 edition, Leviathan; chapter 4, Of Speech.

Jacoby, R. (1975). *Social Amnesia: A Critique of Contemporary Psychology*. Boston: Beacon Press.

Jones, E. (1916.) The Theory of Symbolism. In: *Papers on Psycho-Analysis*. Boston: Beacon Press.

Kohut, H. (1971). *The Analysis of the Self: A Systematic Approach to the Psychoanalytic Treatment of Narcissistic Personality Disorders*. New York: International Universities Press.

Lacan, J. (1955–1956). *Seminar 3—The Psychoses*. R. Grigg (Trans.). New York: W. W. Norton & Company, 1993.

Lacan, J. (1958). The Signification of the Phallus. In: *Ecrits* (2006) B. Fink (Trans.). New York: W. W. Norton and Co, Inc.

Lacan, J. (1959). In Memory of Ernest Jones: On His Theory of Symbolism. In: *Ecrits* (2006), B. Fink (trans.). New York: W. W. Norton and Co, Inc.

Lacan, J. (1964). Position of the Unconscious. Remarks made at the 1960 Bonneval Colloquium. Rewritten in 1964 in *Ecrits* (2006), B. Fink (Trans.). New York: W. W. Norton and Co, Inc.

Lacan, J. (1966). *Ecrits*. Paris: Éditions du Seuil.

Lacan, J. (1972–1973). *Seminar 20—Encore*. C. Gallagher (Trans.). Unpublished.

Lacan, J. (1981). *The Four Fundamental Concepts of Psychoanalysis The Seminar of Jacques Lacan (1964), Book 11*. J.-A. Miller (Ed.), A. Sheridan (Trans.). New York and London: W. W. Norton and Co, Inc.

Malcolm, J. (1981). *Psychoanalysis: The Impossible Profession*. New York: Alfred A. Knopf.
Mannoni, O. (1971). About Jacques Lacan: Anthony Wilden: *The Language of the Self*. Baltimore, Johns Hopkins Press.
Marcuse, H. (1955). *Eros and Civilization: A Philosophical Inquiry into Freud*. Ann-Arbor: University of Michigan.
Money-Kyrle, R. E. (1968). Cognitive Development. *Int J Psychoanal, 49*: 691–698.
Roudinesco, E. (1990). *Jacques Lacan & Co.: a history of psychoanalysis in France, 1925–1985*, Chicago, Chicago University Press.
Roudinesco, E. (1999). *Jacques Lacan*. New York: Columbia University Press.
Roudinesco, E. (2014). *Lacan. In Spite of Everything*. London: Verso Books.
Segal, H. (1957). Notes on Symbol Formation. *Int J Psychoanal, 38*: 391–397.
Yale French Studies [1966]. Structuralism. #36–37. New Haven: Yale University.
Yale French Studies [1972]. French Freud: Structural Studies in Psychoanalysis. #48. New Haven: Yale University.

PART I

SOME HISTORICAL REFLECTIONS

CHAPTER ONE

Editors' introduction

S. Bailly

It is rare to be presented with a paper of such ambition and scope and even rarer to find that it succeeds in more than its aim. Burgoyne takes us through Lacan's entire programme of work, presenting the deceptively simple thesis that it was ultimately a search to define psychic space, and incidentally revealing not only its intellectual riches but also the clinical applicability of ideas that may occasionally appear to be intellectual whimsy.

Burgoyne's reflections upon the ideas of identification that Lacan took from Koyré's work on Meyerson are particularly useful, at a time when the passing of this term into common parlance has made it lose some of its original scientific meaning. Here, we are reminded that "identification" as used by Meyerson in the philosophy of science denotes a tendency towards unity (oneness) and assimilation that is Janus-like in being both reductive and excluding on the one hand and creative of coherence on the other. In psychology, identification is then a transformation in which there is a tension between the strengthening and extending of psychic structure by the assimilation of new material and the destructive riddance of elements of that cannot be made to fit the formula of fantasy. As a tension between creation and conservation, it is of the same kind that Freud noticed existing between his sexual and self-preservative drives, so that one can always expect there to be a tipping point in psychic functioning between consolidation and sterile enjoyment. It is then possible to see how while psychoanalytic dialectic strives against identification in the sense of "reduction to identity or sameness", it is nonetheless the mechanisms of identification—digestion and insertion into the signifying chain—that are also its tools and could by consequence produce a change in psychic space and structure. It is also possible to see from this why self-analysis cannot work.

The distinction made by Lacan between discourse and dialectic is another clarification with immediate clinical resonance, and Burgoyne's presentation of Lacan's use of Riguet's mathematical tenets in the formulation of ideas such as sexual non-rapport is enlightening. Burgoyne uses new material helpfully to explicate Lacan's view of the constitution of the body within the field of signifiers, which should give new life to an area of Lacanian theory that remains relatively undeveloped.

This paper seeks to establish firmly a link between what Burgoyne calls Lacan's General Topology—the ideas we tend to think of as "earlier Lacan"—with the Borromean Knot theory that so greatly dominated the last eight years of his life that it has caused many to feel that the "late Lacan" constitutes an entirely different theory to the earlier work. Burgoyne's analysis reintegrates Lacan's BK theory securely *within* the General Topology. We feel he has here produced a key work that will open up Lacanian studies further, although it is ultimately also a little sad to see in it how at the end of his life, Lacan's own thinking and that of those around him suffered from the tendency to impose an identificatory structure upon all and "reduce to a one" what perhaps should always be left open to a dialectic, rather than a discourse, with other analysts and with posterity.

CHAPTER ONE

The changing forms of a research programme

Bernard Burgoyne

Introduction

There are many interpretations of the differing phases and periods which can be found in the development of psychoanalysis constructed by Lacan over a period of fifty years. These interpretations usually propose answers to a number of questions. What are the problems addressed in each of these periods? Do the solutions proposed in one period replace those found before? What are the divisions between the various periods, and why did they come into being? Do the formulations put forward in later periods—and particularly in his last period, that of the introduction of a topology of knots—allow for a reconstruction of all, or of many, of Lacan's previous results? The thesis that I maintain here is quite straightforward: it is that there exists throughout the body of Lacan's writing a programme that is constitutive of the direction of his work. This programme remains central throughout all the developments that he introduced over these five decades; and it is this programme that explains the choice of problems addressed in the successive phases of Lacan's thought. Both clinical and theoretical problems are included within this programme: it intended from the beginning to relate conceptual and clinical theses. The programme could be called Lacan's General Topology programme, since there is one fundamental problem that is placed at the centre of this programme: it is the problem of the nature of psychic space.

This General Topology programme itself contains seven distinct programmes: each of them being a development of previous periods of his work. Before giving the fuller detail of these—which I will call programmes [R1] to [R7]—I will first of all give an outline sketch of their structure. Some explanation of their content, and of the relations between them will follow.

The first research programme [R1] addresses the structure of psychic space—paths, boundaries, limits, interiors, the relations between outside and inside, neighbourhoods, disconnection.

[R2] concerns itself with the effectiveness of dialectic in the analytical situation, and also in wider situations.

[R3] focuses on desire, the dialectic of its recognition, and its interpretation.

[R4] bears on the relation of jouissance and desire.

[R5] investigates a field that can be called the embodiment of relationships.

[R6] contains a (clinical and mathematical) renewal of the original form of his General Topology programme, placing it at the centre of research, and finding new axes of development.

[R7] addresses the particular topological structure of the Borromean Knot.

The timing of these periods may give rise to some discussion: I shall try to refer any transition to a particular year, and sometimes to a particular month of that year. A number of themes can be found from the start of these programmes—desire, dialectic, identification, and the structure of the mind. In each of the epochs of Lacan's work, I will present selected elements of his writings that I take as exemplifying the main characteristics of his work throughout that period.

R1

By 1931, after five years of psychiatric publications, Lacan's work had begun to maintain an explicit focus on psychic structure, and more particularly on signifying structure and its relation to dialectic. His paper "Structure des Psychoses Paranoïaques" (Lacan, 1931) was given in July of that year in Paris: in it he presented paranoia as moving towards a halting of judgement, one brought about by an "unboundedness—a virulence—of the logical function". This excess brings with it "the appearance of rigour" accompanied however by an absolute "lack of variation". The structure of paranoia, he claimed, will incline all judgements towards a system, and it is this system that will impede the "dialectical faculty".

"Under the influence of some triggering cause, often hidden, sometimes represented by a toxic episode [...] [or] an emotional trauma, there comes into being a sort of precipitation of significant elements, impregnating at the start a throng of incidents which the subject stumbles upon by chance, and whose bearings for the subject become suddenly transformed." This delirium occurs only in certain sectors of the mind, and not in a network. It produces a broken logic, and—*pari passu*—it is organised around desire. In describing the structure of the mind in these terms, some mathematical notions have already been introduced, amongst them network and bound; Lacan continues this when he claims that the sector affected by the paranoia is the sector of interpretations that are "within the angle opened up by the precipitating event".

This paper then begins to construct some concepts that allow for a formulation of the activity of dialectic in the structure of the mind. It investigates the nature of this dialectic and the forms it can take: from the functioning of logic within the "awakening" of the first notions of reasoning, to the debilities introduced into this function by the system of the paranoia. The propositions of this logic contain some preliminary proto-mathematics which have bearings on what will later become the space of signifiers: it is within such a space that there can be "a sort of precipitation" of a number of signifying elements which become significant in the life of the individual. But this space is not yet formed by means of explicit mathematical notions.

Lacan continued to work on these notions: some two years later he returned to an explicit consideration of these themes. He was one of the participants at the eighty-fourth Congress of the Swiss Psychiatric Society, in October 1933—together with, amongst others, Jung, Menard Boss, and Théodore Flournoy from Switzerland; and Henri Claude, Raymond de Saussure, Jean Lhermitte, and Henri Ey from France. Lacan wrote a "*compte rendu*" of the session held on hallucination at this Congress, and his report was published in the journal *Encéphale* in November 1933. Lacan started his account by commenting in particular on the problem of the relation between sensation, perception, and representation: this is one of the problems that had led Freud to formulate his initial theory of psychic space in 1895 (Freud, 1950a [1895]). In addition, Lacan raised questions of the relation between imagination and sensation in the construction of a hallucination, and, in relation to the presentation by Henri Ey, the problem of the relation between the organism and the structure of psychic space. Lacan then moved on to present problems that would inform his own researches over the oncoming years: he agreed with Flournoy as he described the view "commonly held in psychoanalysis" that psychogenesis is constituted "by the realisation of a desire". Lacan noted that Lhermitte added to this "dynamism of desire" additional functions of "the hallucinatory state", and Lacan presented both of these concepts—particularly in relation to the presentation by Morel—in relation to the problem of interior language. Additional problems of the speech apparatus were raised by Morel—again continuing the initial problems of psychic space raised by Freud in his early work (Freud, 1891b). Lacan, in his comments on these themes, can be seen to sketch out the beginnings of a theory of differential representation within the space of signifiers: he referred to the paper presented by Montet: "*rien ne possède de signification sinon par rapport à autre chose*"—"nothing possesses any power of signification except in relation to something else".

There are explicit—though rough and ready—references to mathematics in his commentary: "*les discriminations* [...] *de nos théories ne sont que le reflet de cette relativité entre un nombre infini de singularités*"—"the discriminations made by our theories are only the reflection of this relativity between an infinite number of singularities". Lacan chose to place the emphasis here on questions of truth in relation to a science of the mind: "*il semble que le problème qu'on agite ici* [...] *c'est le problème de la vérité*"—"it seems that the problem that one is working with here [...] is the problem of truth". There are found together then in these themes questions of the Imaginary, of the structure of signification, and—in relation to the development of the child—of the "evolutionary phases of the constitution of the real". It would take some twenty years for these themes to take the form of the theory of the Symbolic, the Imaginary, and the Real: but the beginnings of it are here, in relation to a theory of the structure of psychoses, and the structure of psychic space.

By 1936 Lacan was regularly working with questions of the existence of paths and chains connecting elements of psychic structure (Lacan, 1936): I have described this in some detail elsewhere (Burgoyne, 2003). In describing the function of the analytical rules of free association, he constructs them as laws of non-omission and non-systematisation. The formulation he gives to this I have described as follows: "What is apparent in his description of this structure is its proto-mathematics. He calls the implementing of the law of non-systematisation 'respecting succession'—preserving, that is, the relations of order. He describes the 'chaining' or connectivity between the elements of the material presented to the analyst, and the relation of the fragments of this material to the structure of which they are a part. The initial chaining of the narrative is different from the one that the analytical work is trying to construct. These are all notions that call on the terms of mathematics, and the question of formalisation in these texts is already present" (Burgoyne, 2003).

[R1] contains an investigation of paths and structure: the framework of the mind is here being investigated in terms of the topology that constitutes psychic space. The question then arises: by what means is access to the material of this framework hindered? Lacan's answer is that this is the main function of the ego.

Lacan's text on the "mirror phase" contains this hypothesis, which most radically differentiates his work from the programmes more generally accepted in the Anglo-Saxon world: that the ego—far from being an instrument that constructs any kind of realistic adaptation to the world—is an instrument of systematic misunderstanding and misrecognition ["*méconnaissance*"], undermining by its very functioning any means of access to the history of the analysand. Such a theme exists in Freud's work: it is the notion of "false connection" ("*Falsches Verknüpfung*") that Freud takes to characterise the way that the ego constructs reality by means of a web of fictions[1] (Breuer & Freud, 1895d). Initially Freud had found the clinical origins of this problem in the relation between negative hallucination and false connection. One could put things then in the following way: "Effectively, the false connection articulated by Freud is Lacan's *méconnaissance*" (Burgoyne, 2015).

Elisabeth Roudinesco has been able to reconstruct much of the original content of Lacan's paper of 1936.[2] Roudinesco has also brought to the attention of historians the content of an unpublished article that Lacan had written in April 1936—for Alexandre Kojève. In this second essay three main themes appear—"the ego as a source of illusion and error"; "the I set out as the subject of desire"; and "desire as the function of revelation of the truth of being" (Roudinesco, 2001). These themes clearly raise many problems for a formulation of the aims of psychoanalytic technique. The relation that they propose between the ego and "the subject of desire" entails that access to what is real in the psychic life of the analysand has—of necessity—to use techniques that do not rely on any functioning of the ego. Lacan's aim then is to determine the properties of human subjectivity that allow for the side-stepping of this functioning of the ego.

In their construction of recommendations regarding the technique and aim of analysis, both Freud and Lacan seek to move from away reality to the Real that underlies it—to a real that the fabrications of reality conceal. Access to what Lacan will later call the Real is gained by means of pathways through the structure of the psychic apparatus—through, that is, the spaces of the mind. The ego is not an ally of the analyst in seeking to open such pathways: rather the ego of the analyst, the ego of the analysand—as well as the ego of any theorist of psychoanalysis—hinder and resist the gaining of access to the Real. So here in [R1] the theme of *méconnaissance* raises questions of epistemology and questions of technique, as well as questions of the relation of psychoanalysis and science.

Very early in this period, Lacan makes a number of explicit references to the literature of the philosophy of science. His Doctoral Thesis—which contains his famous Aimée case—had been submitted in the Autumn of 1932. Towards the end of it he referred to "the most recent epistemological research", by which he meant "the epistemological studies that are fundamental for all philosophy of knowledge, those of Meyerson"[3] (Mayerson, [1907] 1926). Lacan takes from Meyerson the notion that "progress" in the analysis of the mind—what he in this thesis calls "dialectical progress"—takes place in the context of *"la fonction identificatrice de l'esprit"*, the context of the forms of identification operative within psychic space. At this early date, the problems raised by these notions already gave Lacan a number of questions about the nature of science—about the nature of a science of the mind, and in particular about the question of a science of psychoanalysis.

In his thesis, Lacan presented the aim of psychoanalytic technique as a gaining of access—one operated by a dialectical intervention—to the strata that underlie "the personality of the subject". At this time Lacan refers to ego functioning as "the personality of the subject", and he takes it to be the locus of resistances formed out of "misrepresentations and systematic negations". The subject is a repository of historical truth, but unconscious structure is located in regions of psychic space that are in no way immediately available for inspection.

Six years later, Lacan was still pursuing questions of the relationship between space and analytical technique. In a presentation to a session of the French IPA Society—the Société Psychanalytique de Paris—on the 25th October 1938, he raised the question of the relation between structure and recommendations for technique[4] (Lacan, [1938] 1939).

In this paper, Lacan presents two cases that he has chosen; he notes that although they seem to be close (*"apparemment très voisine"*), they are such that psychoanalytic investigation reveals them to have structures that are different in the extreme. In the first case Lacan takes it that a simple elucidation of Oedipal episodes is sufficient to resolve the symptomology. The second case however was one that required a reconstruction of "extremely archaic" phantasies, using dream material, and raising the question of the origins of the elements found within these phantasies. In this second structure there are themes of dismemberment, combined "within the structure" with a "state of passive beatitude". Lacan calls this structure "Saturnine"—with regard to the figure of eating one's own children—and in terms of the drama presented here being the reverse of an "Arcadian dream".

How can one progress in obtaining access to such an underlying structure? Lacan claims that this can only be done by means of "different perspectives" and multiple narrative or interpretative takings up of questions that arise in the course of the "psychoanalytic monologue". This "monologue" actually has two protagonists, and the relation between them—the analytical relation—is given its outline and its boundaries by means of a dialectic. The ensuing dialogue then progresses with the force of a logic. Lacan claims that he can isolate in this way the structure of the first case—that of an obsessional neurosis: the aim there, he says, is a remaking of the personality and "a systematic reform of the deepest attitudes towards reality". Both in this more straightforward, and in the more difficult case, what is involved is an actual "recreation by the subject of his ego and of his world". The two cases together show how great is the separation that exists between the more immediate evidence of clinical facts and the primordial world of images: but this archaic world needs a different approach in each case. However, in both these cases, Lacan takes it that articulation of the structure of psychic space will lead to "the primitive drive in its pure state".

There is also an aim here to determine the characteristics of a neurotic structure—specifically that of obsessional neurosis—and to differentiate this structure from that of a psychosis. Lacan claims that he takes "great care" in each case to outline the "psychological evolution of the subject"—while still differentiating the two structures involved. In working with these cases, his aim was to develop a vocabulary that, while being adequate for each structure, at the same time stayed as close as possible to the phenomena. This entailed, according to Lacan, not restricting clinical concepts to supposing only mechanisms already recognised in the domain of pathology: the analysis of clinical phenomena needs to be organised around a method that maintains a distinction between the content of symptoms and the structure that generates them. Such a method is required, he claimed, in order to "reveal the structure" of a case.

At the culmination of this first programme, fifteen years after its start, Alexandre Koyré wrote a commentary on Meyerson's posthumous volume of essays (Koyré, 1946). The themes that he discussed there are all pertinent to this question of the structure that underlies the phenomena present in a world of experience. Koyré describes Meyerson as "a great thinker … [producing] magisterial work", whose aim had been to produce a general theory of scientific thinking, a theory of how reason functions within the sciences. From sensible perception to scientific theory, there is—in Meyerson's account of things—no leap. Perception is already penetrated with reason, since the perception of problems is itself already dependent on a history of prior problems. Theories presuppose prior theories, and—in every case—perceptions of facts are already laden with theory.[5]

Koyré presents some of Meyerson's central themes. Reason always has a tendency towards repeating the same, in such a way that "everywhere and always it opposes itself to, and seeks to impose itself on … the Other" (*"toujours elle s'impose, et cherche à s'imposer* […] *à l'Autre"*). Reason thus seeks to reduce the Real to "the one" (*"expliquer le réel en le réduisant à l'un"*) to reduce appearances to what is "always the same". Dialectic, says Koyré, operates against such identification, and allows access to the Real that underlies any apprehension of the world. Lacan—at the end of this first version of his programme—is ready to transpose these themes into a clinical context: this context is also that of the problem-situation of the relation of psychoanalysis to science. Science operates, according to Meyerson, according to a principle of identification: although it is clear that this involves a "projection by the mind onto the real", nevertheless, scientific explanations "put this process to work without scruple" (Meyerson, 1936). Of the thousands of traits that make up the particularity of an event (*"des milles traits que nous pouvions observer"*) only a small number are taken up by the process of identification: the rest are "eliminated, ignored, treated as if they did not exist[6]" (Meyerson, 1921). The psychology of the mind, and the structure of scientific explanation are put into close relationship in this account: each identification is "a rent in identity"; at each reduction there is left behind a "scrap or residue" (Meyerson, [1907] 1926); the traits by which identification replaces the actual perceptions can be reduced—as Lacan later does, in his account of Freud's theory of identification—to a single trait.[7]

Over these years, other psychiatrists were also drawing on Meyerson's work to explain the nature of their science.[8] However, only Lacan took up the central theme of identification in Meyerson's account of the sciences, and took it as a bridge linking the structure of the sciences to the field of psychoanalysis. These ideas of the nature of science in relation to psychiatry and psychoanalysis were widely worked on and formulated in the mid-to-late 1920s,[9] and they form a backcloth to the themes developed by Lacan during the first decade and a half of his psychoanalytical work.

This then is [R1], and it was focussed on topology from the beginning. Such a primary focus on the structure of psychic space will stay with Lacan throughout all the fifty years of the further development of his programme. Initially this topology remained implicit in his work—later it was to become explicit. In [R1] Lacan constructed an initial investigation of general properties of psychic space: the research orientation generated by this can be taken to be Lacan's operative research programme between November 1931 and the Autumn of 1946.

R2

In September 1946 Lacan participated in a critical debate with his friend and colleague Henri Ey; their interaction was part of a series of seminars at Bonneval that had started in 1943 and was to continue to include the famous Colloquium on the unconscious in 1960[10] (Ey, [1960] 1966). The project to set up a debate between Ey and Lacan—and thirty of their colleagues—on the nature of psychic causality, and had been devised as early as December 1943 (Ey, [1943] 1950). There had been an initial intention to hold this Colloquium in the autumn of 1944, but war conditions had delayed this by a further two years. The theme in his interaction with Ey was the causality of the mind: it is clear that any investigation of psychic causality presupposes a concept of psychic space.

Lacan had visited England in September 1945; there he had met and discussed psychoanalysis and its research themes with—amongst others—John Rickman and Wilfred Bion. Rickman had earlier that year presented a paper on topology to the British Psychoanalytical Society—in February 1945. In this presentation he had used the mathematical notions of region, path, limit, and connection in order to explore the nature of boundaries in psychic space. Lacan wrote a paper describing these discussions at the same time as he was preparing his presentation at Bonneval: both these papers were published in *L'Evolution Psychiatrique* (Lacan, 1947). So apart from the two papers that Lacan published in 1945—each of them bearing on the existence of algebraic structure, and particularly permutations, within psychic space—the further development of Lacan's topological researches can be seen to represent a coming into alignment with work being done in England during and immediately after the War.

In his own investigation of psychic space, Lacan had taken one of the terms proposed by Rickman—limit—and used it to orientate the position he gave to psychoanalysis in relation to psychiatry: Clérambault's work, he claimed, contained as a central element "a search for the limits of signification" (Bonnafé, Ey, Pollin, Lacan, & Rouart, 1950). In relation to work with psychoses as well as in relation to work with neuroses, Lacan stressed the topological structures introduced into the mind by the function of language: he proposed that a word presupposes a point with several paths through it. In his presentation Lacan praised Guiraud, whom he claimed knew how to detect in the resonances of a word the nature of a delusion—and by means of it to establish the structure of what Lacan called "a semantic system which has formed the child"[11] (ibid). And this theme allowed Lacan to formulate an aim couched in terms of the topology of psychic space—to make "a structural analysis of space and time constituted by the Imaginary, together with the connections between them". His hope was that "the authentic dialectic" employed in the seminar series at Bonneval would guarantee the progress of this programme: "I myself take up the support provided by this dialectic [...]." So, in this paper Lacan focussed his work around three central terms: language, space, and dialectic.

As he responded to Ey's final allocution, Lacan reflected that the discussions had displayed the virtue described by Heraclitus—that of opposing tensions (Bonnafé, et al, 1950). He had ended his own paper with the expression of a certain regret: he could have started his account, he says, by referring to the exchange between Parmenides and Socrates.[12] He took Socrates to have initiated a programme of research that had "the passion to unveil [...] truth": the instrument that had been devised within this Socratic research programme was dialectic.[13] It remains to be seen to what extent this dialectic is necessary for psychoanalysis.

Lacan surprised his audience as he drew together these themes in his most striking presentation during this period: his intervention—on the 1st November 1951—at the XIVth meeting of the Conference of French-Speaking Psychoanalysts in Paris (Lacan, 1952). In this presentation, he gave an account of Freud's technique in the Dora case, an account which presented Freud's technique as being entirely organised around a Socratic dialectic. The aim of such a dialectic is to weaken the attachment that someone has to certain theories of the world—by drawing their attention to the absurdity of the consequences that follow from them:[14] in the cases of psychoanalysis, the particular theories involved are theories of sexual love. In his intervention Lacan described in some detail the dialectical structure of Freud's technique in the work with Dora: a positioning that Freud was able to maintain up until the last moments of his interpretation of Dora's second dream.[15]

Freud's attention had been drawn to the theme of dialectic very early in his work: in 1879 he had translated a lengthy paper by John Stuart Mill (Mill, 1866, Freud trans. 1880a). It contained a detailed commentary on what Mill and his colleague George Grote saw as a Socratic revolution, and it gave Freud an extensive insight into the nature of Socratic dialectic.[16] Grote investigated the changes brought about by dialectic—the shift from a previous vision of the world, the resistances against such a shift, and the circuitous pathways that needed to be taken to achieve such a shift. He also described the way in which earlier fixities of opinion had been inherited from previous generations: these inherited fixities, Grote claimed, were "imbibed by the [child] almost unconsciously".[17] It was in this work that Freud found a range of themes that allowed him later to formulate the protocol for the analytical situation (Burgoyne, 1995, 2001, 2007).

In the years prior to this intervention in 1951, Lacan had frequently formulated Socratic dialectic as an agency of change within the spaces of the mind:

1. Socratic dialectic searches for the truth; it is the tradition that "conditioned the appearance of all our sciences".[18]
2. In psychoanalysis, as in the sciences, what brings about the organisation of truth is not a body of facts, "but rather a dialectic".
3. (There are) questions that "only psychoanalysts" can answer, since "only they have a dialectical experience of the subject".
4. Verbal dialectic has frequently met an impasse.
5. Resistance stemming from the ego is opposed to the deployment of any dialectic—"here we see the ego, in its essential resistance to the elusive process of Becoming—to the variations of Desire".
6. The dialectic encounters resistance: it is hindered and obstructed by the ego's reluctance to allow the opening of pathways that may lead to pain. Where Freud pictured this resistance in terms of contours on a hillside, Lacan is content to describe its effect on the dialectic as that of a "backcloth of inertia".

In an address to the World Congress of Psychiatry in 1950, Lacan posed a question: "why resort to 'fallacious objectifications'", when a more reliable method has been available for many years? And as for the method that he is referring to, it is "a familiar dialectic, operated on the level of the particular interests of the subject"; a dialectic which acts "by virtue of the signifiers included within language"; a dialectic that operates on relations of sexual love (Lacan, [1950b] 2001).

He continued: "In fact, it is this dialectic which operates in the treatment, and that one discovers there since it has been at work in each human being since their coming into the world up to the point of penetrating into the entire nature of a person through the formative crises where the subject identifies themselves." In the same year he had elsewhere outlined "the radical structures that language transmits in the unconscious" (Lacan, 1950a). So, at this point of his programme he is reformulating the problem of space in terms of structure and language, identification and dialectic.

The dialectic—as Lacan formulates it—is a means of dealing with the unreliability of the ego; it represents his way of dealing with Freud's problem of false connection[19] (Breuer & Freud, 1895d). This problem is: how to gain access to the strata that underlie the fictive opinions put into place and maintained by the ego? Freud proposes the same solution as Lacan: the access is given by dialectical or logical threads. Ordinary discourse obscures and hides what is real, whereas dialectic is the instrument—the only instrument—that regains any regular access to the Real. The ego, while it maintains its version of reality, is an unreliable guide to what is real; resistances hinder—or cut off—access to what is real, to what the ego finds most painful in the structure of the soul.

In 1952 Lacan started a seminar on the Wolf-man: it was organised around a number of themes. The system of the unconscious, he claimed, "has its own inertia"; as he continued the seminar he maintained his topological terms—the patients hold on to something "up to the last limit"; resistance, he claimed, is overcome by a dialectic; but the dialectic of the analytical situation is affected and changed by proximity to the primal scene. This seminar is organised in effect around a study of the "the mode of dialectical relation" between the child and the function of the father (Lacan, 1952–1953). The notion that Lacan works with here—closeness to the primal scene—incorporates spatial notions within the dialectic of the analytical work. As this seminar progressed, Lacan made some additional discriminations. In the movement from rivalry with the father to an elective affinity with the father he distinguished an imaginary father, a symbolic father, and a real father: this triple provides the matrix that a few months later will generate his registers of the Symbolic, the Imaginary, and the Real. The themes at play then in this early seminar are those of dialectic and the structure of space.

This period had started in the Autumn of 1946, and it ends on the Wolf-man, early in the Spring of 1953.

R3

In July 1953, Lacan gave an introduction to his new registers of the Symbolic, the Imaginary, and the Real.[20] The registers stemmed from the scientific development, he said, of his two previous years of seminars:[21] the triple formed by these registers has the structure of a Freudian topic that brings with it the ability to display the topological structure of the mind[22] (Lacan, [1953] 2005). Lacan tested these registers in terms of their ability to give an account of all of Freud's major cases:[23] the structure of these registers will lead him to introduce a series of mathematical relations explicitly into the analysis of the mind.

At the end of this 1953 presentation, Didier Anzieu asked Lacan whether his registers were to be understood as models of the psychic apparatus, of the kind that Freud had used. Lacan, in his reply, claimed that he—like Freud—was formulating hypotheses which worked on the highest level of assumption about the mind, and that the structure of language, rather than being a component of a model—or a tool-to-hand in everyday life—worked on this formative level, and that the formalisations undertaken by Freud and by himself were to be taken as primary hypotheses regarding the structure of the mind.

The fuller presentation of this programme took place two and a half months later, in Rome. At this Congress—held in late September—Lacan presented the place of the Symbolic within the trinity of the Symbolic, the Imaginary, and the Real (Lacan, [1953] 2006; Lacan, [1953] 2001). Lacan there claimed that the Symbolic register was central within this set of relations—it allowed for the establishment of the structure, for the functioning and the limits of psychoanalysis. In his commentary on the discussions at this Congress, he stressed the presence of dialectic in analytical work. He described his programme as concerned with "dialectical concepts: speech, subject, language", and he went on to claim that it would be a true recognition of his work, were someone to suggest giving it the motto: "let no-one enter here unless they are a dialectician" (Lacan, [1953] 2001). This weaving together of dialectic and structure was immediately followed up by what was to be the beginning of a twenty-six-year long series of public seminars.

Lacan's first seminar in this series was devoted to Freud's papers on technique. He started the seminar with a declaration of intent: "We are going to follow the techniques of an art of dialogue"; [...] "we have to know what links, what resistances we will encounter"; [...] "the point to which analysis leads, the end point of the dialectic [...] is *You are this*"; [...] "[the aim of analysis] is to render the subject capable of bearing the analytic dialogue" (Lacan, [1953–1954] 1975). And in this seminar, by "dialogue" Lacan means—as always—"Socratic dialectic".

Here then in 1953, twenty-two years after the start of his first programme, space was still analysed by Lacan in terms of dialectic: "Psychoanalysis is a dialectic, what Montaigne [...] calls an *art of conferring*. The art of conferring of Socrates [...] is to teach [the analysand] to give his own speech its true meaning"[24] (Lacan, [1954–1955] 1988). This central point was developed by Lacan in a variety of ways: in a dialectic, he said, "the point is to link the subject to his contradictions, to make him sign, and to pledge his speech"[25] (ibid).

Lacan had intended these comments to bear initially on questions involving the classical psychoanalytical technique of working with neurosis. His dialectical theme can also be extended however to the different clinical context of work with psychosis—"it is precisely because there has always been a radical misrecognition of the dialectical dimension in the phenomenology of pathological experience that the clinical has gone astray"[26] (Lacan, [1955–1956] 1993). So, across the field of psychoanalysis, Lacan's three registers announce a necessary presence—of the structure of dialectic.

The problem of structure in psychoanalysis introduces a fundamental question: what is the relation between the structure of the unconscious, and mathematical structure? Lacan had always been tempted to take it that there was a close relationship between the two.[27] Actually, he went somewhat further than this: he held the taking up of such mathematical relationships to be a first step that was necessary in order for psychoanalysis to become a science. In addition to his early interest in the work of Emile Meyerson, Lacan had kept in close contact with workers in the history of the mathematical sciences—Alexandre Koyré and Alexandre Kojève, for instance—and had always maintained a close friendship with an important French mathematician—Georges-Théodule Guilbaud.[28] So, his considerations of dialectic had always taken place against a backcloth of the structure of mathematics. Soon after the beginning of Lacan's third programme, this network of themes[29] was to be extended by an engagement with yet another mathematician.

Lacan met Jacques Riguet in May 1954: Riguet was a leading French mathematician—his researches at this time were in relations of partial order, and more particularly, in the relations between algebra and geometry. The two men had been introduced at an interdisciplinary conference organised in Paris by Claude Lévi-Strauss: Lacan was there together with linguists, physicists, and mathematicians. After the meeting, both Lévi-Strauss and Lacan wanted Riguet to work with them: Riguet fell for the charms of working within psychoanalysis. So, from the Autumn of 1954 Riguet would regularly visit Lacan at his country house in Guitrancourt, and the two would work together on the structures of the unconscious. They talked of cybernetic loops, of networks and of pathways; later, says Riguet "I taught him several notions of topology, of the theory of surfaces, graphs on surfaces, and so on. When I explained to him the notion of a projective plane, and [its figuration as] a cross-cap, he found it bedazzling" (Riguet, 2011). Riguet left Paris for Zurich in 1958, but during these four years, he participated in Lacan's seminar, and made many contributions to the formalisations that Lacan was introducing at that time into psychoanalysis.[30]

Riguet was at home with the functioning of dialectic within mathematics: he worked with the notion of proof being a means of "destroying certain illusions" (Riguet, 1989). Moreover, he saw that this functioning extended well beyond the domain of concepts and their consequences: he played on the notion of a "certain sadness" when reaching the end of a proof, going as far as to propose "a kind of parallelism between the resolution of a problem and the accomplishment of a sexual act".[31] Riguet wanted to work with the "most general" structures, so he was at home also with the structures of the human soul.[32] In this respect, he was well aware that his own family "romance" revolved around a question of separation from the mother—and that any question of separation leads directly into questions of the nature of a general topological space. Something extremely deep is lost in such separations, and Riguet knew that this kind of loss was located within the history of the formalisations that he proffered to Lacan. He took it that the steps towards successful sublimation lead away from a fixation to the mother, and that the mathematical parallels to these steps can be seen to produce purely algebraic results extracted from what had previously been only a misapprehension of underlying themes. All of this he says, comes from "a dissatisfaction which goes back very far".[33]

In his reflections on his work with Lacan (Riguet, 1989), Riguet produced a series of what could be called desiderata on questions of method. There is a fundamental parallelism built into them—so they apply to work in mathematics, as well as to psychoanalytic technique.

1. There is a pathway—rather a series of pathways—leading away from the "imprisonment" of attachment to the mother [fixation].
2. Detour[34] are recommended for (dialectical) technique: never move straightforwardly towards an obstacle.
3. A pathway in the advancement of mathematical work represents a movement towards better (and more general) problems, driven by a certain dissatisfaction.
4. The structure of mathematics and the structure of psychic spaces are in a relation that can be called a parallelism: that is, to any part of the one structure, there is a corresponding part of the other which exactly recapitulates its problems. The work done on either side of this parallelism is internal to that domain; whether the domain is mathematics or the field of trajectories through conflicts in sexual love. Riguet stresses that mathematics in this sense is not directed by something outside of it: he talks of disengaging the mathematical material from the envelope of "philosophico-logical gangue" that surrounds it. He claims that the dialectic within each field obtains an access that cuts through the worthless material that "surrounds, or is closely mixed with" a wanted mineral.
5. At each step in this process something is lost.
6. What is lost is never quite forgotten; and in the construction of such pathways, a separation and a relative freedom are gained.

During the course of *Seminars V and VI* Lacan used Riguet's graphs to formalise circuits of desire. Over this period, their collaborative work had led Lacan to construct a range of mathemes organised around the structures that Riguet had provided. Riguet is mentioned, or intervenes, nine or ten times during the course of *Seminar II*: the first of these occasions was when he was called on by Lacan to intervene in a discussion of the dialectic in Plato's *Meno*.[35] Koyré had given a presentation—just over a week previously—on this theme of dialectic and the constitution of knowledge. In his seminar, Lacan continued with Koyré's themes: the mathematical dialectic and the analytic dialectic have this in common—they bring about a shift "from the plane of an intuitive bond to a plane of symbolic bond". In the case of the analytic dialectic, this shift allows access to the "founding speech" which has brought into being the space of desire in the human subject[36] (Lacan, [1954–1955] 1988).

[R3] is effectively in two parts—*Seminars I to III* study the spaces of desire; the next three seminars move from the dialectic of desire to the relations between jouissance and desire.[37] In *Seminars I—VI*, Lacan formulates clinical and conceptual problems in both formal and informal ways; Jacques-Alain Miller has said of these years—from the beginning of [R3] onwards—that the strata that make up their themes "pass insensibly from one to the other [...] [developing] as if by topological transformation".[38] The second phase of [R3]—particularly from the start of 1957—contained a burst of creativity unparalleled even for Lacan: in the two and a half years leading up to the Summer of 1959, he completed eight major papers—whilst continuing with other presentations and giving over seventy crucial sessions of his seminar. The collaborative work with Riguet continued for nearly the whole of this period, to creative effect.

This third programme then spanned six years: from July 1953 to July 1959.

R4

The four seminars of the fourth period start with an investigation of the relation between the analyst and the analysand: this in turn raises many questions about human nature, just as the Socratic questioning of Plato's dialogues had raised many questions about human nature and its structurings.[39] The determination of the analytic relation by what Lacan then calls the law of desire is at the forefront of the first of these seminars: such a moral law is intrinsically different from the law determined by the ideal systems and the superego. By using the new registers that he had established over the six years of [R3], Lacan found that he was able to differentiate between these laws, and to devise solutions to this and a range of other problems in psychoanalysis that had until then shown themselves resistant to formulation. After this initial investigation of what Lacan calls the ethics of psychoanalysis, the work of the three following seminars moved on to a study of the RSI-structures operative in three foundational clinical realities—transference, identification, and anxiety.

Central to this formulation of the analytical relation is the question of what traditionally has been called the good of the patient. Since the determination of what is good is usually subservient to some moral law, this is also a question of some complexity, as well as of considerable delicacy. Freud himself had always refused proposals to have the direction of analytical work determined by any notions drawn from moral philosophy. In a discussion with the American psychiatrist and psychoanalyst James Putnam, he had insisted on the direction that governs psychoanalytical work being determined by "the method of the sciences"[40] (Freud, 1933a). So, Lacan seeks to investigate how analysis determines the good through its own scientific apparatus. His answer is as follows: there are regions within psychic space that are insistently avoided—they are regions that open the possibility of revisiting some fundamental loss. These regions are approached, in other words, at some cost, and the price of such access raises questions about the nature of the good—"there is no other good than that which can serve to pay the price of the access to desire"[41] (Lacan, [1959–1960] 1992).

The relations between the Symbolic, the constitution of the body, and jouissance are complex: an affected body takes shape within the field of signifiers. Jouissance emerges with characteristics of "inaccessibility, obscurity, and opacity" at key points within the body of signifiers[42] (ibid). It brings the drive into attempts made by the subject to reconstruct their own history: it therefore functions as a body of inertia and resistance to the analytical dialectic. In its functioning, it introduces an alternative: insistence or desire. The ethics of psychoanalysis is the ethics of finding pathways through spaces that give access to desire.

The working of the analytical dialectic finds pathways that lead to the traces of childhood loves, to the zone of broken love relations of childhood. In the four seminars of this period, Lacan looked for a mathematical structuring that would account for the facilitation and hindering of these pathways through psychic space—pathways that lead to representations of the lost love relations of childhood. The broken knowledge introduced by the analytical dialectic is evocative of these relations of broken love: in the transference relation that this engenders there is a putting into words of imaginary versions of love—a symbolisation that reshapes the Imaginary. It also introduces a new approach to limits, a changing of limits, and a restructuring of the world of the analysand.

Towards the end of [R3], Lacan had constructed an entire paper around the theme of the direction of analytical work[43] (Lacan, [1958] 2006a). In it he had introduced the idea of interpretation within the transference: any interpretation within the transference is a particular case of the working of the analytical dialectic. It is not the same therefore as an interpretation of the transference—it is actually its opposite.[44] Lacan's recommendation for technique proposes a movement away from the Imaginary of the present into the field of the Symbolic that historically underlies it—whereas interpretation of the transference in the here-and-now of the session is organised around an imaginarised version of the symbolic determinants of childhood loves.

The love-transference invokes an introjection of an aspect of the analyst's person or environment: a form of identification that draws the analyst into the circle of the analysand's loves.[45] Early loves deploy on the terrain of the setting up of the ego-ideal—an ideal identification that allows a movement from oedipal love to a form of renunciation of its aims. The analysis of love exhibits new limits in the field of desire, limits which in their turn call for an analysis of the mechanisms of identification, and of the constitution of ideals.

Seminars VII and VIII investigate the functioning of the analytical dialectic. It acts as the major instrument for the investigation of love: in this investigation limits are encountered, frontiers are found between what one is and what one is not, between what one has, and what one lacks. Lacan calls this the entering of an inner limit zone in relation to desire[46] (Lacan, [1959–1960] 1992). The zone is that of the pursuit of desire, and the space involved in this region Lacan calls the topology of tragedy, the topology of desire. Entering this space allows for the analysis of desire—but it also leads to a recognition of fundamental loss: "in an even more fundamental way than through its connection with the Oedipus Complex, tragedy is at the root of our experience".

Lacan takes this theme back to its origins in Greek tragedy: "as the key word, the pivotal word *catharsis* testifies"[47] (ibid). Catharsis here means the purification of the signifying apparatus: it can be represented as (I; S) → S. This process is what Lacan had earlier described in terms of a "reshaping of the Imaginary". In the process of this reshaping, the analysand gains coordinates that lead towards losses in love: Lacan brings to bear several tragic figures—Oedipus, Antigone, Lear—as he investigates the structure of these spaces of tragedy. Lacan actually takes this tragic theme further—but this will not detain us here.

Seminar VIII is in two parts—the first is organised around a questioning of love, via the *Symposium* of Plato; the second part investigates fundamental loss in relation to the love of the mother—and this via the *Coûfontaine* trilogy by Paul Claudel. The twin themes of this investigation are the dialectics of love and the constitution of desire in relation to the function of the Father. This seminar on transference develops its themes almost entirely without mathemes: it forms a sort of literary preparation for the subsequent seminar on identification—a seminar which contains a mathematics of the human soul.

The first explicit taking up of topology as an organising principle of Lacan's seminar occurs in *Seminar IX*—in the session of 7th March 1962. From the 1930s Lacan's central problem had been the nature of psychic space, and from the 1950s his formalisations had been buttressed by the introduction of algebraic, combinatorial, and geometrical apparatus. Now however his problem-situation had developed: into an investigation of the changes undergone by the subject in the processes of identification. In order to analyse this Lacan introduced the topology of a number of surfaces.[48] He continued with Claudel, Euripides, and Sophocles, as he proposed the mapping of the domain of signifiers into a variety of number fields.[49] But in the main, in this seminar, he investigated the construction of psychic surfaces from the sticking together of the points of more elementary or archaic surfaces—that is, by means of identification.

Lacan then moved from a seminar organised around topology to the consideration of anxiety. The last phrase of *Seminar IX*—at the end of the session of 27th June 1962—is the following: "Next year I will work on anxiety for you, following strictly the point of view that I have been developing today". So how is this transition possible? Topology studies boundaries, and anxiety can be seen as the recognition of a sudden change in the perception of a boundary. Either a previously unseen boundary is suddenly perceived, or an anticipated encounter suddenly displays itself to have a boundary in an unexpected place. Anxiety particularly arises when the boundary concerned is one that indicates the presence—or the lack—of desire.

Transference, identification, love, phantasy, anxiety, and desire: all show that they need topology to investigate their structure, and their content. Anxiety takes a central place in Lacan's theory of psychic structure: anxiety contains a signal about limits, and in this respect it is an index of truth. As Lacan develops his theories of psychic space, he finds that he is committed to providing an extensive account of the structure of affects and their transformations.[50] With anxiety, love, hate, ignorance, fear, and pity at their core, the passions of a human being demand both dialectic and topology for their analysis.

But by the time of his *Broken Seminar*,[51] it seems that Lacan began to be tempted to take up a series of propositions that left behind dialectic—the apparatus of question and answer—that up to this point he had taken to constitute the structure of psychic space. Starting at around this time, Lacan began to formulate the notion that there are fixed limits within which the dialectic works; and that beyond this there exist more encompassing structures that come into play "before any question is put"[52] (Lacan, [1963] 2005). During the single session of his *Broken Seminar* Lacan assessed the claims of dialectic. Progress in the history of mathematics, he claimed, had demonstrated the falsity of the Hegelian dialectic. But it is not a Hegelian dialectic which is being put into question here: rather an Eleatic instrument for the discovery of truth.

Lacan traced the history of psychoanalysis back to the position that it had been given within the history of science—he thus saw the inception of psychoanalysis in the first birth of Greek mathematics. So his problem at this time was how to incorporate jouissance—and what he then called the *a*-object—into the body of a science, and the assumptions that he made about the nature of mathematics led him to propose this pathway of the curtailment of dialectic within the framework of this science of the mind.[53] Lacan seemed torn. On the one hand—in *Seminar X*—he comments "this path reanimates the whole dialectic of desire"[54] (Lacan, [1962–1963] 2004); on the other hand he simultaneously felt that he was forced to take this *a*-object to be a (non-dialectisable) residue of the relation of the subject to the field of A[55] (ibid).

It is as if these two pathways in Lacan open up at this moment. However, anyone who takes up the mathematical structuring of a space is committed to a methodology that is dialectical. Pathways through psychic space are made through dialectic: connectedness and disconnection are determined by proof and dialectic. Any object, and perhaps particularly an *a*-object is concerned with the determination of limits, connectedness, borders, interior, and exterior. In this way topology can be seen to work through the functioning of the everyday mathematical dialectic of proof and refutation.

The relation of jouissance to desire had become a central theme of Lacan's work by the start of [R4]. The more that jouissance took up this place, the more that discourse—with its reliance on limits established by settled and socially approved meanings[56]—made inroads into the domain previously reserved for the working of the dialectic. Within this new framework, Lacan continued to talk in terms of dialectic: the responses of the analyst, he says "suspend the subject's certainties". But the tension between this fundamental dialectic, and the more fixed forms of discourse, will continue in Lacan's work; it will lead him eventually to seek an apodictic form of topology in his last programme: [R7].[57]

There is then a tension introduced into the theme of the analytical dialectic in relation to the content of these four seminars: ethics, transference, identification, and anxiety. Over the entire period of Lacan's work, there are scores of references to the relation between dialectic and transference, and he will come back to this question of the subject-supposed-to-know—the question of suppositions and limitations of knowledge—in six sessions at the start of [R5].[58] Moreover, Lacan is still speaking of the "dialectic of the subject", for instance, in January 1967—in the last year of [R5]. At this period of Lacan's work, many questions are raised as to the relation between philosophical themes and the topics of dialectic and space.[59]

Traversal of psychic space had been at the heart of this programme: [R4] had covered the period of these four seminars together with Lacan's interrupted seminar—from the Autumn of 1959 to the end of 1963.

R5

This programme spanned four years. An overview of it can be obtained from a glance at three presentations that Lacan gave in the final months of the programme—on 22nd October, 10th November and 29th November 1967.

A Congress on Child Psychosis was organised by Maud Mannoni, and other child-analysts within the Ecole freudienne de Paris, in the autumn of 1967 (Mannoni, 1972). Lacan gave the closing address on 22nd October: in it he raised the problem of moving towards a conceptualisation of the body, and in doing this he referred his audience back twenty-one years, to his debate with Henri Ey at Bonneval at the start of [R2]—in September 1946.

The construction of the body is clearly a complex issue, as it involves the field of relations between the body and the mind. From a very early age, signifying structure affects the mind of the child; moreover, the incorporation of signifying material has an effect on the formation of the body. That the body is affected by signifying structure can be put more strongly: the constitution of the body—*in utero*, and in the years immediately after birth—is dependent on signifying structures. Before a child is born, its first perceptions of the voice of the mother—and thereafter its choice of what to take in of other voices and sounds—initiates the construction of a body of relations[60] that both direct and affect the body of the child. From the moment of the mirror phase—the structuring which engenders primary narcissism—there exists the symbolic body, the imaginary body, and the real body, none of which can be investigated without taking into account their relation to the others. Many bodily functions—including the construction of the brain and the nervous system of the child—suppose for their operation that they are embedded in this larger field of relations.

Signifying structures fragment the body—more precisely, they cut the body's experience of excitation into regions and cantons. There is a further effect: in the constitution of the body a part of the body is lost. Lacan's *a*-object finds a place in these voided regions of the body, particularly within rims, and within regions of the perception of loss.[61] The embodiment of relations takes place in this way, involving what Meyerson had called "a rent in identity". The body of the Symbolic maintains its priority in determining all forms of embodiment,[62] so it is the structure of the Symbolic that determines how a body of relations is given shape within the topology of psychic space. It is this space—a space that is already in place in the life of a very young child—that Lacan now proposed to investigate.

Lacan had asked Winnicott to contribute to the congress: Winnicott's paper was on autism, and drew on his own theory of psychic space. He put forward his concept of "the lost memory of an unthinkable anxiety"—this "primitive anxiety" being experienced before the child has separated an external world from the spaces of its internal experience. So, both Winnicott and Lacan were proposing to investigate the same space—and the functioning of the object within it.

In the second of these three accounts—on the 10th November—Lacan gave an overview of his programme, and where it had got to by the end of [R5] (Lacan, 1967). He reminded his audience of psychiatrists that "it is now seventeen years since I started to speak of language"—to psychiatrists, at the First World Congress of Psychiatry in 1950. To this new audience, he effectively enumerated the steps in the development of his work in psychoanalysis: he formulated them as follows—

(1) The unconscious is structured like a language.
(2) This raises many questions as to the nature of psychic space—questions that only exist in the dimension of language: the nature of translations, for example.[63]
(3) There is firstly the question: "what is a language?" And to this question Lacan adds a correlate: "what does language bring about?"
(4) Lacan gives an answer to this further question: it makes the subject.
(5) And Lacan proposes a parallel question: "what is produced by language?" He also responds to this question—his answer is: the texture of desire.
(6) Lacan claims that it follows that a science of the subject is a science of desire.
(7) He claims also that "the first steps" towards such a science are taken by means of formalisation—*à la* Spinoza, and those mathematicians who followed him.
(8) A language is made of signifiers, not signs with fixed reference; its domain is made up of networks or pathways of signifiers, subjective trajectories which go around a void in the space of representation.
(9) The networks of language determine order relations—mathematical structures that can be analysed by means which "come within the province of combinatorics".
(10) Where many Anglo-Saxon analysts had tended to centre their work on access to the unconscious gained by some functioning of the ego, Lacan focuses on the analysis of the subject: the signifying batteries are prerequisites to this subjectivity.

(11) What Lacan calls the A [*le grand Autre*] is precisely the body of structuring that is necessary to the primacy of the signifying chain.
(12) The functioning of truth arises from the moment when there is a signifier. It arises therefore from a field which escapes the captivations found within the register of the Imaginary.
(13) The experience of analysis is nothing other than this realising of the function of the subject.[64]
(14) The signifying operations contain elective falterings—weaknesses that derive from the subject's being affected by the field of sexual love.[65]
(15) That this subjective weakness is experienced not totally within the interior of a signifying medium is what Lacan calls [Symbolic] castration.
(16) Such elective faltering is organised around the place of the loss of an organ of sexual love. The Freud-Abraham theories of partial love derive from such "cut-outs" within the functioning of the body-image: Lacan will organise them around the functioning of "cessible" parts of the body—void; voice; look; breast; shit.
(17) The formalisation of the signifying chain—the field of the Symbolic, together with the body functioning derived from it—explains all effects within psychic space: "reaction, defence, resistance, affect, transference [...] and what you will".
(18) The sexual act fails on account of these frailties of the signifier.
(19) The subject is determined by the signifying material that preceded him: that is, by the desire of A; by the desire of the Mother; by the no of the Father; by ideal-functions; and by the phantasies inherited from previous generations.
(20) Lacan finally stressed the extent of the consequences that follow from his distinction between desire and demand.

The above is what Lacan offered to this audience of psychiatrists, as an account of what his work had consisted of "over the last seventeen years". He added to this list one further theme: it is a complex theme but it can be summarised as follows—

The lacking bodily-organ takes the form of what Lacan—"in my algebra" he puts it—called the object *a*. The existence of this object introduces the division of the subject; as other objects come to replace the lost organ, they are so placed that it is not noticed that the organ is lacking.[66] The divided subject maintains a certain relation to this *a*-object, a relationship that is the basis of the construction of phantasy. The play of demand in relation to the *a*–object constitutes the functioning of the subject in relation to desire.

The *a*-object and its lures make up the circuits of jouissance: these circuits of jouissance give Lacan the elements of his later theory of discourse. Whenever the body of socio-cultural relations efface boundaries, these circuits will introduce modern forms of segregation. This last piece of prescience—from the last months of [R5]—has been sadly but extensively corroborated in the almost fifty years that have followed. When socio-cultural boundaries are effaced, internal boundaries come into place, and move into the socio-cultural space, so as to stand in for them: Lacan states that there is a problem of "how to bring about separation" when these boundaries have been lost (Lacan, 1967–1968; also in Mannoni, 1972). Unless some discrimination—and some dialectic—is available, this separation will be done by the ideal and superego system: mercilessly.

In so far as there is some structuring within the public sphere that is inherited from the domain of love, it follows that a change in these established relations in the socio-cultural sphere will render certain states of affairs impossible in the domain of love. The space inhabited by jouissance is characterised by isolation: in this space lost boundaries are replaced by new determinations of what jouissance is deemed to exist on the right side of the law. These determinations produce new segregations: outsider—scapegoat—ignoble—vermin. In a time when the Nazi death camps were only a few decades past, Lacan gave early warning of the continuation of segregationist pathways that lead towards genocide and civil war.[67]

Finally, in November of that year, Lacan proposed a parallelism—between the content of his work in the four years from January 1964, and the first eight of his seminars: "a certain correspondence could be made between each of these years, and two [of the years or seminars starting in 1953]"; in this way, says Lacan, his seminar "up to its seventh and eighth year" corresponds to the content of [R5][68] (Lacan, 1967–1968). I have reconstructed this parallelism as follows:

1964: *Seminars XI & XII: Fundamental Concepts & Crucial Problems*
//
Seminars I and II: Relations between theory and practice in Freud's papers on technique + problems relating to the ego in psychoanalytic theory and technique;
1965: *Seminars XII and XIII: Crucial problems & the Object of Psychoanalysis*
//
Seminars III and IV: The structure of psychosis + object relations;
1966: Seminars XIII & XIV: The Object of Psychoanalysis & the Logic of Phantasy
//
Seminars V and VI: Formations of the Unconscious and Desire and its Interpretation.
1967: Seminars XIV & XV: The Logic of Phantasy & The Psychoanalytic Act
//
Seminars VII and VIII: The Ethics of Psychoanalysis and Transference.[69]

This series of parallels had been occasioned a retrospective look at the question of knowledge in relation to Socratic dialectic; it involved Lacan in again surveying the question of the approach to truth, and its bearing on the handling of the transference. It was a survey that would be followed [in R6] by the introduction of a new formulation of his topology programme, this time making explicit use of General Topology.

[R5] was a programme that covered four years: from January 1964 to December 1967.

R6

Lacan introduced explicit topology immediately after his eighth seminar. The existence of a parallelism between his seminars—as he described it in late November 1967—indicates that this might also happen at the start of 1968.

In November 1967 Lacan had started *Seminar XV* with a reference to a mathematician—and one of the greatest. Gauss, he said, knew that the consequences of his work had transformative effects on the question of mathematical truth: he therefore kept some aspects of it unpublished—for around three decades.[70] Right from the start of [R6] Lacan began to reformulate questions of the nature of psychic space, looking for general mathematical structures with which he could articulate problems that he had been working on since the 1930s.

In January 1968, Lacan summarised some of the content that he had been occupied with in his seminar of the previous year. The terms that he chose to refer to are mathematical notions, and he formulated three of them as follows—operation transference, operation truth, and operation alienation. They can be described more fully as the movement of transference towards the object, the movement of truth towards the unconscious, and the movement of alienation towards the subject: these three, he says, form "half a Klein group". So, the mathematics that he was working with in this seminar was embedded in this way within a range of particular clinical problems.

In the two sessions of this seminar immediately before Christmas, Lacan had discussed the relation of Winnicott's work on transference and counter-transference to the question of the interpretations and the interventions of the analyst: he also discussed at this point the relation of his *a*-object to Winnicott's transitional object.[71] In these sessions Lacan expressed his indebtedness to Winnicott—"I remember [...] the help the transitional object, as he put it forward, gave me when I was questioning myself about the way to demystify the function of the so-called partial object". He also commented on the relation between these two formulations of the object-function: "The *a*-object commands the subject [...] which functions at first at the level of the transitional object". Both Winnicott and Lacan had investigated questions of human nature, and both had used lines, regions, and boundaries to investigate it (Winnicott, [1936–1954] 1988). Lacan stated that he will comment on his relation to Winnicott at greater length in the New Year—in the coming session of 10th January, but he did not: apart from a passing comment on differentiations between subject and self, he moved on to looking for more general mathematical structures which will help grasp the intricacies involved in the analytical relation.

[R6], like [R3], is in two parts. The first part, covering three years, lasted from January 1968 to December 1970. Its extensive development of the mathematics of the previous years' means that it could be seen as Lacan's post-Winnicott era. The work of these three years had followed on from the close—personal and theoretical—relationship that Lacan had maintained with Winnicott, and it continued to maintain the close inter-relationship that Lacan had ascribed to the handling of the transference and the question of transformations of knowledge within the analytical space. The succeeding part of [R6] was made up of an intense investigation of properties of space. This second part ran from January 1971 to the summer of 1973, and it contained—starting in January 1972—a mathematical analysis of psychic space that can be seen as the peak of Lacan's General Topology programme, a peak that he was to maintain for a further year and a half. This second part of [R6] comprises *Seminars XVIII, XIX, XIXA*,[72] and most of *Seminar XX*.

By the start of [R6], topology and logic had come into close relationship; and a movement from geometries to questions of topology became re-established in Lacan's work.[73] Erik Porge has commented in the following way on Lacan's work in the mid-to-late 1960s: it contains an investigation of the construction of subjectivity, and of the nature of the object by means of the (non-Euclidean) geometry of projective spaces.[74] In this context, Porge cites the psychoanalyst Imre Hermann—"A child up to a certain age perceives, not in a metrical, but in a topological way [...]. The works of painters have convinced me that there exist within us primitive spaces and primitive topological surfaces, but that demands for their becoming metric forbid them from becoming conscious"[75] (Porge, 2015).

So, in January 1968 Lacan commented on Cantor's theory of transfinite numbers in relation to his own theory of the desire of the analyst; in the same session, he took up Frege's logic—as Bion had done—particularly in relation to the functioning of negation and quantification. He was working on Peirce by the start of February—using elements of Peirce's logic that he had previously worked on in *Seminar IX*[76] (Lacan, 1961–1962); and soon after this he was raising questions of projective geometry in relation to one of his *a*-objects: the look.[77] At the start of the second part of [R6], he started *Seminar XVIII* by introducing the theme of the tension of the analytical dialectic, which he immediately related to one of his previous topological objects—the Moebius strip. He then took up the relation between the *a*-object and the Ego-Ideal; the question of the *Innenwelt* and its frontier (the relation between the interior and the exterior of the subject); the handling of the transference; and hysteria in relation to the desire of a woman. As he took up these themes, he was looking for a general topological context within which to formulate them.

Lacan then moved to a focus on general—or set-theoretic—topology at the start of *Seminar XVIII*: interior, frontier, cut; network, thread, lattice—these are the themes that occupy him in January 1971. Towards the end of that seminar he investigated femininity, masculinity, symbolic castration, and symbolic wounds—in texts by Nunberg and Bettelheim: and this in relation to a phallic function buttressed by Brouwer, Carnap, and Russell.[78] There are repeated attempts by Lacan in these three years to find the place of the subject in corresponding topological surfaces and spaces. The formulations he gave to subjective reality over this period experimented with a variety of topological structures, in relation to how the subject becomes positioned by phantasies and ideals, by drives and relations to the object, and by the topology of desire.

In this period—January 1971 to May 1973—Lacan was seeking logical systems that explicitly incorporated a notion of the dialectic that he had been working with for many years[79] (Burgoyne, 2016). At the same time, he maintained his previous focus on the condition of dialectic outside of the analytical situation, but now moving a little from an interest in discourse to its underlying logic. By February, he had taken up the constructivist logic of the German logician Paul Lorenzen. You can see why Lacan would have been interested in Lorenzen: his system of proof provides dialogue-based foundations for logic and mathematics—and therefore for any formalisation of psychoanalysis. What Lorenzen offered Lacan was a structuring of dialectic within formal logic.[80]

Contradiction is what leads dialectic to what is real. "The path along which we see science advancing" Lacan said, is one shored up by much logic: by logic Lacan—here as always—means dialectic, and the shoring up that is at play here "is called contradiction" (Lacan, [1970–1971] 2006). Lacan had taken up modern logic before—in *Seminar IX* for instance he had worked with logicians, even algebraic logicians: Boole, Jevons, Frege, Russell, Peirce, and Schröder. The logical themes that he worked on in this period were negation, and the general nature of logical constants; quantification and its negation; and the law of non-contradiction, with or without the law of excluded middle.[81] But through all of this he maintained his focus on non-contradiction—that is, on operations of dialectic: "Thinking cannot be properly speaking conceived of unless it is articulated, unless it is inscribed in language, unless it is sustained in conditions that are called dialectic"[82] (Lacan, [1968–1969] 2006).

Throughout *Seminar XVIII*—and particularly in session VIII—when Lacan says that there is a parallelism between logic and the human soul, it is a parallelism with mathematics that he is actually asserting[83] (Lacan, [1970–1971] 2006). Earlier—in a conversation with Pierre Soury in March 1968—he had said of problems in the theory of logic: "[they) can appear for us as a kind of resonance of something that constitutes […] the field of analysis"[84] (Lacan, 1967–1968). This is the thesis that he is now starting to develop, and it is what I call Lacan's thesis of restricted parallelism: it claims that there are problems in the domain of logic that are exact analogues of conflicts in the human soul. In *Seminar XVIII*, he puts the thesis as follows: "Logic carries the mark of the sexual impasse—by following it in its movement, in its progress, that is, in the field where it appears to have least to do with what is at stake in what is articulated as regards our experience, namely analytic experience, you will discover in it the same impasses, the same obstacles, the same gaps"[85] (Lacan, [1970–1971] 2006). How then had he come to make this claim, to put forward this methodology that would come to underlie the structure of his programme of General Topology?

It will help to look first at how Lacan generalises the thesis. In *Seminar XIXA* he addressed an extensive range of clinical themes: resistance; the pleasure principle and the reality principle; beyond-the-reality-principle—the repetition compulsion; primary process; the body; sexual impotence; the symptom; the Real; psychosis; hysteria; failures of sexual love; *Nachträglichkeit*; and identification in relation to the Father-function. In parallel to this, he worked on the mathematics with which to deal with these themes: number theory, algebra, function theory, topology, the relation of mathematics to logic—including the "topological structuring" of language—and what Lacan calls "the irruption of mathematics into logic". So, this "in parallel" is more than a heuristic tool—in this seminar Lacan formulated it as a thesis about the relation between mathematical and psychoanalytic structure: by now then he had formulated two such theses on parallelism, one in a weak and one in a strong form.

The thesis of restricted parallelism is the weaker form: it proposes an identity of structure between the domain of logic and that of the spaces of sexual love. In order to do this, Lacan first allows logic to take up its place within mathematics: he then, by means of back-and-forth arguments, shows how one domain is homologous[86] to the other. Lacan developed this methodology of restricted parallelism from the Spring of 1968 to the Winter of 1971.

In the second part of [R6], Lacan started an intensive investigation of certain aspects of mathematics: in this period there are references to almost one hundred mathematicians, plus many references to the relations between mathematics and logic—and all of this in relation to psychoanalytic technique. In terms of the mathematics, he drew on some set theory, some general topology, and the theory of order relations. The topology that Lacan uses is sometimes general—or set-theoretical—topology, and sometimes algebraic—or combinatorial—topology. Although these two have been developed almost as separate fields in contemporary mathematics, they are rarely sharply differentiated by Lacan.[87] Topology *tout court* starts to take a central focus from the seminar of 6th January 1972[88] (Lacan, [1971–1972] 2011a); this is the moment where what I have previously called the "peak" of the General Topology programme starts, and this peak is coterminous with his generalisation of the weaker parallelism thesis.

Lacan, that is, moved on to working on the general parallelism thesis from January 1972 to the Summer of 1973.[89]

Seminar XX is a famous seminar: by an act of metonymy, it is known as "Lacan on Love". It is here that Lacan moves to the development of his general parallelism thesis: in its first session—on 21st November 1972, he says that he has—in an earlier text—"demonstrated the strict equivalence between topology and structure". By structure he means psychic structure, and in the earlier text that he is referring to he had claimed "Topology is not 'meant for guiding us' in the structure: it is the structure itself"[90] (Lacan, [1972] 2001).

So, in the greater part of *Seminars XIX, XIXA,* and *XX* there is a claim that can be put as follows: there exists a parallelism between a mathematical domain—the domain of topology[91]—and the structure of psychic space. It is this claim that I call the general parallelism thesis. So, on the one side there is the field of human pathology—the domain of sexual love; and on the other the structure of the mathematical theory of space. Lacan's claim then becomes: to each problem-situation on one side of the parallelism, there can be found a corresponding problem-situation on the other. It has been put as follows—you can resolve problems of sexual love by translating them into mathematics; and the obverse—you can resolve problems in (the foundations of) mathematics by translating them into problems of sexual love. You just have to find the right translations.

The structure of psychic space, it seems, is mathematical by necessity—since mathematics—on rational inspection—turns out to be built of the same stuff as the spaces of the psyche.[92] In developing this part of his programme, Lacan tried to distinguish between topologies on finite and infinite sets, so as to be able to find structures that differentiate between masculine and feminine sexuality. He was led to use the mathematical notion of boundary—or equivalently of open or closed sets: the start of *Seminar XX* then uses this apparatus to address and resolve questions of conflict in sexual relations.[93]

For those who would like some topological detail, a few technical terms of topology may help: but even today, mathematics often hurts people's eyes, so this account will limit itself to very few words. A neighbourhood of a point is made up of points to which it has an elective affinity;[94] a point in general will have many neighbourhoods; such neighbourhoods determine all limits and boundaries (borders; frontiers) in the space. In fact the whole structure of a space follows from points acquiring such neighbourhoods. A point is on the boundary of a set, for instance, if all of its neighbourhoods contain points both of it and of its complement. A set is closed if it contains all of its boundary; an open set is one that contains no part of its boundary; and a set and its complement share a boundary—so if one of these sets is open, then the other is closed. In general, a set in psychic space will lack some part of its boundary. One final notion: a set is compact if every covering of it by open sets has a sub-cover made up of a finite number of sets—so in the case of a compact set, the elements of a covering can be taken one-by-one. An equivalent version of what it means for a set to be compact is this: if any collection of closed sets within the set is such that any finite sub-collection of them has a non-empty intersection, then any sub-collection of them—finite or not—has a non-empty intersection.

Lacan ascribes a (denumerable) infinity to points of the sexual spaces of the woman, and a finiteness to the sexual spaces of the man. In order to relate to a woman, a man would need to enter into an infinite space: there is an embedding involved in this—both the man's space and that of the woman need to be embedded in a—common—space that is infinite. But little is common in the world of impasses in sexual love, and Lacan posits that in such a space, a non-empty intersection of closed sets is experienced by the man as an obstacle—as a gap, or a rent[95] (Lacan, [1971–1972] 2011a, [1972–1973] 1998). Lacan uses the Finite Intersection Property of compactness[96] to conclude that in a compact space, any obstacle encountered by the man would be ineliminable. Lacan then takes this to characterise a sexual encounter: in the compact space of a sexual encounter, *"il n'y a pas de rapport sexuel"*.

Further Elucidation: if the woman would seek to add (an infinite number of) sets to what the man is engaging with—in order to eliminate the obstacles—in a compact space she would fail. In such a space, neither the man nor the woman can eliminate the obstacles. This is even though a woman has greater resources than a man—not being confined within the phallic space that limits a man's position in the world.

The general parallelism thesis draws on the structure of mathematical spaces. It attempts to resolve not only problems of love and desire, but also—more immediately—problems of analytical technique[97] (Burgoyne, 2000). Pierre Soury was Lacan's last mathematical collaborator: the two were looking for mathematical parallels both within Lacan's later knot theory and within parts of the General Topology programme. To this end Soury tried to expand Lacan's half-a-century of work on psychic inertia—or resistance to the forging of pathways in psychic space.[98] So, both Lacan and Soury (working with his guidance) were producing results using this general parallelism methodology—right up to the end of Lacan's active working life. Such a programme is not only intended to extend the research frontiers of psychoanalysis. A methodology such as this draws out consequences for mathematics and its foundations[99]—not only, that is, for the foundations and clinical realities of psychoanalysis.

General Topology is the study of space: one would think that it would necessarily be brought to bear on the study of psychic space. But a considerable number of analysts—particularly in England and in the United States—have seen Winnicott's notion of space as being barely serious, as being no more than a clinically useful metaphor.[100] Lacan, on the contrary, chose to analyse this question of the serial structure of pathways through psychic space: he attempted to take up the question of the nature of psychic space, of its limits and its boundaries, in a very mathematical—that is, in a serious—way. At times Meltzer had attempted this; Bion and Rickman had attempted this; Imre Hermann had attempted this; and Lacan—in a number of ways—continued to advance the frontier of this tradition.

[R6] then covered a period of five and a half years: it started in January 1968, and lasted until May 1973.

R7

While still barely five weeks into the peak of the General Topology programme, Lacan perceived that there may well exist another way through. He was not to act on it however for a further fifteen months—so it is during this period of work on general topology that what was later to become the Borromean knot programme was being developed.

Lacan had first mentioned the interlinking structure of Borromean threads in February 1972—in the fifth session of his *Seminar Ou Pire*[101] (Lacan, [1971–1972] 2011). The daughter of a friend, coming from the seminar of Guilbaud, had showed him the details of Borromean structure in pieces of string: it had left Lacan "wearing the ring" of these threads of string. He thought that the simple topological structure of these threads might to able to formulate and resolve a wide range of clinical problems. But the rings became the central orientation of his new knot-programme only in the last sessions of the seminar of the following year—starting on 15th May 1973. "When I got wind of this knot[102] [...] I immediately had the certainty that here was something that was precious for what I had to explain. I immediately related the rings of string of this knot [...] to what I had recognised from the very start of my teaching [...] I immediately knew that this knot had a relationship that put the Symbolic, the Imaginary, and the Real into a certain position with respect to each other, about which the knot encouraged me to state something". Lacan—in other words—had started to work on what it was that constituted the fruitfulness of his notion of knot[103] while still developing and expanding the topology of his sixth programme.

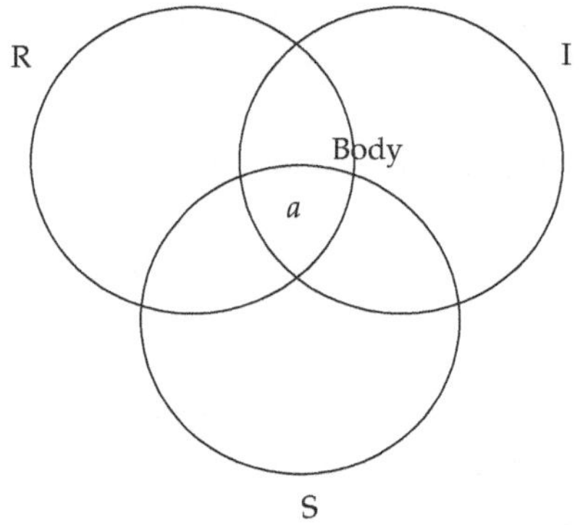

Figure 1. S–R–I–Body–*a*.

A Borromean knot is a number of looped threads linked in such a way that no two are linked together: the typical way that Lacan constructs this is shown in the Figure above. This Borromean knot produces a linking of the body with the Symbolic and the Real: where the Real ring is overlapping the Symbolic, and the Imaginary is overlain by the Symbolic, as it is being underlain by the Real. This basic structure—together with its generalisations—is the field that Lacan opens up with his *noeud-Bo* theory.[104] In this BK programme, Lacan placed an element of the Real at the centre of psychic space: the *a*-object holds the centre, where the Real loop holds together with the Symbolic and the Imaginary. By further adding a fourth loop, and making topological transformations that are structure preserving, one can obtain a number of consequences regarding clinical structure: in this way Lacan, by introducing these particular threads of the BK structure, was making a specialised version of the content of his previous work.

By the time of *Seminar XXII*—the session of 18th March 1975— he could be interpreted as claiming that all his earlier work on RSI could be subsumed under the BK theory of these threaded strings.[105] "I immediately related the rings of string of this knot [...] to what I had recognised from the very start of my teaching" (Lacan, 1974–1975, 1975–1976): many commentators have taken this to mean that the whole of the RSI theory, together with all of its precursory elements—in the earlier forms of Lacan's programme—can be derived from the theory of Borromean knots.

Lacan certainly locates this new form of his programme within the confines of the six previous versions: it had been devised out of these previous forms of his programme. But that it has the strength to recapitulate all the previous forms is far from clear. In *Television*—just a few months before the initiation of [R7]—he speaks of his knot theory as follows: "It is the Real that allows the effective unknotting of [...] a knot of signifiers. Knotting and unknotting are not to be taken here as metaphors, but as those knots whose real construction is brought about by making chains from the signifying material"[106] (Lacan, [1973] 1974). The knots, in other words, are elements that constitute the Real of psychic space. On the other hand, they presuppose certain topological properties, since they are constituted from threads of the Symbolic,[107] and their topology is given to them by the general structure of the space within which they exist.[108]

So where are we now? There are at least two distinct research programmes in Lacan's late work, each of them bearing directly on topology. The earlier—and less known—is what I have called the peak of the General Topology programme, with the general parallelism thesis that it engendered. The better-known dates from the early summer of 1973, where these early forms of "borromeanising" were developed, together with many circumjacent elements of the General Topology programme—many of which were later dropped. As he developed [R7], Lacan came more and more to believe that a particular topology—rather than a general topology programme—will do it.[109] In recent decades, the general topology programme has been comparatively under-developed. Such under-development is a choice, and a choice which is unnecessary; if a choice has to be made from these two formulations of things—the General Topology Programme and the BK programme—it is clear which I take to have priority, which I take to have more resources, and which I take to be more productive.

Many mathematicians advised Lacan over these decades: Guilbaud had been advising Lacan on mathematics even before Lacan's work with Riguet; in the 1970s Soury and Thomé gave Lacan advice on the more restricted topologies of the BK programme; after Lacan's death, Nathalie Charraud continued to develop the mathematical content of his work (Charraud, 1986, 1997). At the end of the century she and Pierre Cartier organised a week-long conversation between psychoanalysts and mathematicians in a Colloquium that was held in the château at Cerisy-la Salle in Normandy (Cartier & Charraud, 2004). Many questions were raised at this meeting concerning the place of general topology in clinical work:[110] many questions were raised at this meeting about the relation of subjectivity to mathematics. Jacques Riguet was at this Cerisy meeting, in September 1999.

The BK programme aimed to give a new form to questions of subjective space—a form which is at the same time more palpable and more specific than the general topology programme. Lacan's claim that this programme is able to replace all the earlier formulations of his work has been taken up by many commentators, but a particular form has been given to it by Jean-Gérard Bursztein—with his construction of a programme that intends at the same time to re-open some of the questions of general topology that are inherent in Lacan's late work (Bursztein, 2012, 2015a, 2015b, & 2015c). Bursztein's aim is to develop a programme which contains a theory of the topological constitution of subjective space—and it is this knot-programme to which he has given the name subjective topology.

In recent lectures (Bursztein, 2015a) Bursztein has worked on the following themes within the BK programme: anxiety, the support of the phantasy; the envelope of the phantasy; mnemic traces of the father; the use of the BK structure for the re-structuring of the subject's relation to the phantasy; the parallelism between the space where speech is deployed and the space of the structure; change of space by compactification;[111] and how the trefoil knot gives a richer representation of the structure of a psychosis than Lacan's earlier formulations and schemas. Bursztein sees the BK programme as a culmination—but at the same time as a programme that is both "highly valuable" and "not finished". Bursztein's own programme takes seriously the location of Lacan's knot-theory within a more general topology. His programme is still under development—as are many other—and differing—articulations of Lacan's theory of knots that are frequently less orientated to general questions of space.

An early appraisal of the strengths and weaknesses of Lacan's knot programme was given by the Belgian psychoanalyst Serge André, who presented an account of this programme to the first meeting of the Ecole de la Cause Freudienne in October 1981.[112] His presentation helps to construct a version of what were taken to be the successes of the BK programme in these early years, and what clinical problems were seen as still remaining for the programme to address. In his talk, André described some of the functions ascribed to the Lacanian registers of the Symbolic, the Imaginary, and the Real. In particular, the Real, he said "sets limits to the power of the Symbolic": now irrespective of any question of power, this formulation allows us to take our first step into topology—the Real is constitutive of limits for the Symbolic, and these limits generate the structure of a space.

As André developed these themes he made two claims: the first being that what I have called [R7] has a close relationship with the preceding forms of Lacan's work; and the second—that the aim of the knot structure introduced by Lacan in [R7] was to renew psychoanalytic practice. I take it that this first claim is undeniable; the second claim has the potential to provide an effective way of testing the effectiveness of [R7] as a programme of clinical research.

In constructing his account, André had made his own periodisation of Lacan's work: we could call the periods that he distinguished [A1]—[A4]. The first of these, which he starts in the mid-1930s, he took to be characterised by a predominance of the Imaginary—the mirror stage functioning indicating that the ego is not a reliable interlocutor in the analytic relation: this theme then already containing a critique of the theories of practice generally held during this first period.[113] André's second period [A2] he then characterised by what he took to be the introduction of the Symbolic as a scheme of differentiation from Imaginary effects; and the third [A3]—starting in 1961—by what he regarded as the aim of the seminar on Identification: to locate the place of the Real within the Symbolic, by means of topology. He claims that throughout these periods—as well as later, with the introduction of the Borromean knot in 1973—there was always present in Lacan's work a persistent attempt to discover relations between the Imaginary, the Symbolic, and the Real.

Let me pause on this claim. André starts with Lacan's article *Beyond the Reality Principle*, of 1936: he formulates Lacan's central problem in this paper as the relation between reality and the Real. Even in this early period, he says, there is a clear notion of "submission to the Real"—to the Real of sexuality, to the Real that underlies symptoms, to the Real of suffering. André in fact takes Lacan in 1936 to formulate the notion of the primacy of the Real over subjective truth; and the ego gives no access to this Real. André calls the programme that was developed by Lacan at this time a form of "negative existentialism"—the Real is not experienced, and by virtue of not being experienced, injects the insistence and repetition of symptoms into the everyday encounters of life. So, André is in fact taking this first programme to be one of investigation of the relations between the Imaginary and the Real.

André's version of the time-scale present in Lacan's work is as follows—(i) from the mid-1930s to 1953: [A1]; (ii) from 1953 to 1961: [A2]; (iii) from 1961 to 1973: [A3]; and then from 1973 onwards: [A4].[114] André proposes that it is during the second period that the Symbolic becomes explicitly intertwined with Lacan's earlier investigations, so that by 1957–1958, according to this account, Lacan is able to formulate—within the matrix of RSI—the key to his investigation of the structure of the Real. This then allows Lacan to move to the following conclusion: within the various forms that shape reality, there is an underlying Real—a Real which is given by the structure of the Oedipus Complex, and by the "function of the Father which is revealed there".

[A3] is a crucial period as regards André's explanation of what Lacan had hoped to achieve by means of the BK programme. By the end of 1963 Lacan had pluralised the notion of no-of-the-Father—in a development very closely tied to his articulation of the *a*-object. The NF outlines the desire of the mother, giving signifying coordinates without which the child would be "left abandoned" in this desire; but in the ensuing world of signifiers[115] there is a real *a*-object, which has been lost between the mother and the child. André raises the question as to whether this functioning of the *a*-object can render unnecessary the additional deployment of the NF function: André's claim is that it is in attempting to answer this question that Lacan was led to introduce his programme of knots.

The manipulation of the knot structure should be able to demonstrate this, claims André. In a Borromean knot, each of the three loops has the same status, and they are intertwined in such a way that—although they link together—if any single loop is cut the other two become freed: *a* takes up its place at the centre. This real centre could then be expected to produce a demonstration of many aspects of psychic functioning. The whole field of psychoanalysis seems to point in a way towards such a cantering says André: "What is a dream, what is a symptom, what is a neurosis, after all, if not a series of attempts to knot together things that are very extraneous to each other?" (André, 1982).

Irrespective of this hypothesis—a hypothesis which André claims had faced many difficulties in being elaborated—one can look for independent clinical and theoretical advances that have been made by the BK programme. Even as it encountered checks to its development, says André, this programme brought out results that led to the construction of new pathways in psychoanalysis: (1) establishing the existence of different knot structures in the cases of neurosis, psychosis, perversion, and phobia; (2) devising a BK structuring for the Father function; (3) the establishment of a series of erroneous-knots that each have a clinical instantiation; and (4) the production of a series of movements, within a number of BK-structures, that allow for the tracing of the direction of analytic work, as it moves from its early moments towards its end.

André takes it that the new programme is sufficiently powerful so as to be able to demonstrate its results—all of the above results he shows to be capable of simple topological proof. But as he points out these results and their limitations, this is exactly what he assumes: the general functioning of limits. "A sign of the extension of the Symbolic beyond the limits which the Real fixes for it" and "(manic states are triggered) where the subject no longer meets the limits [...] the stopping points that the Real imposes on [...] the Symbolic" are just two examples of this. André takes these results to be demonstrable entirely within the BK programme: but the notion of a limit is a part of general topology, and it would need the re-introduction of a programme of general topology to instantiate it.

The points of crossing of the Borromean rings can be seen as moments in the progress of the analytical work. At the start of the work, the Imaginary is dominant over the Real—"at least in relation to these two formations which are [...] the body image [...] and the ego". As the work proceeds, the Symbolic comes to dominate over the Imaginary, particularly as the "ego-Ideal [...] comes to resonate above the mirror-phase functioning"; finally, the Real comes to be dominant over the Symbolic (André, 1982). This progress is represented by a clockwise motion around the *a*-object at the centre of the links.[116] But over and above this, the BK structure produces many further results concerning the end of analysis: the changing of limits in particular. So, while being sceptical as to its fruitfulness, André points out many aspects of its power. "On this point, I'll stop", he said, while giving his excuses for "having formulated so many hypotheses, and having given so few demonstrations".

The BK programme is currently the most extensively developed of Lacan's formulations of his psychoanalytical research programme. Work on its clinical and conceptual content extends to thousands of articles and hundreds of books. The period that starts in 1981 and ends in 2016 extends for over a third of a century: such a period of time is not unusual in the history of science—it took Newton's school a little longer than that to solve the problem of the tides. But the period from Lacan's initial formulation of the BK programme to the present is now approaching half a century, and despite a number of clinical advances that have been made by this programme, relatively little of the progress that had been looked for by André has materialised, at least in any substantial respect. It may now be time then to look for a more extensive field within which to further advance Lacan's clinical programme, and one is immediately to hand: the programme of general topology that formed the central focus of Lacan's work immediately before his giving this last formulation to his programme for psychoanalysis.

The presuppositions of the BK programme would seem to indicate that such an extension into the field of general topology is to be taken as a forced move—further progress in Lacan's account of psychic space would appear to demand a problematising of the assumptions that he made in [R7]. Jacques-Alain Miller has suggested that treating the BK programme as a problem-situation, rather than as an *a priori*, would generate grounds for further clinical advance: "[In the BK programme] there is no Lacanian solution, but rather [...] the variable truths that Lacan encounters in entering this zone. Lacan does not leave us a finished, dogmatic doctrine, but rather a problematic field of investigation where there are places for discussion and elaboration" (Miller, [1996] 2015).

There are many ways of generating topology out of RSI. One of these is to take the relations between the Symbolic and the Real as constructing the limits, and then allowing these limit points to determine the topology;[117] the transformation made by introducing an Imaginary mapping of these relations would then generate the embodied relationships of the everyday world. This way of approaching things stays entirely within the field of general topology. The BK programme however has often been taken to move away from this field, leaving behind more general problems of the structure of psychic space. The particular topological results worked on by Lacan in [R7] can either be embedded in general topology, or rather treated as mere working models, or presentations, of clinical realities. Fruitful lines of advance seem to lie in taking up the topological problems presented by Lacan in the early sessions of his seminar on Love[118] (Lacan, [1972–1973] 1998), and relating them to the formulation of problems that he gave at the start of [R7]—later in this seminar—in May 1973. Lacan concluded one of the last sessions of this seminar—that of the 15th May—with a formulation that would have warmed the heart of an Imre Hermann or a Wilfred Bion: "Only mathematisation can reach the Real, and that is the reason why it is compatible with our discourse, the discourse of psychoanalysis".

Conclusion

Freud formulated theories regarding pathways through psychic space. He centred psychoanalysis around this theme: from his first formulations, in his *Entwurf* of 1895—complemented by what he called associative or logical threads—to his last formulations, over fifty years later in his *Abriss* of 1938 (Freud, [1895] 1950a [German], 1966 [revised English translation], and Freud, [1938] 1940a [German], 1964 [revised English translation]). And he addressed problems of limit, boundary, and interior, as he gave formulations to the pain caused by being caught in the webs of psychic space. Lacan worked on these problems by means of formalisations of Freud's notion of space. In doing so, he moved through a number of different formulations of his research programme: ultimately, he moved from logical thread to signifying chain, and from signifying chain to string linked in a Borromean way.

The Borromean knot theory is a part of the General Topology programme. It uses specialised topological structures, and it is in this sense a particular instantiation of the more general programme. In this form it has taken up, and provided solutions to, a number of urgent and compelling problems of psychoanalysis. It remains to be seen whether this seventh version of Lacan's programme will prove to be the most fruitful, or whether it will, in its turn, itself give way to a more general version, constructed around themes that characterise the nature of topological space.

Notes

1. See the case of Emmy von N.
2. There is further detail of this in Burgoyne (2015). The problem of course is that in the absence of a reconstruction of original version of Lacan's mirror phase paper, one would be left only with the much later version of this paper that was presented by Lacan in Zurich at the Sixteenth Congress of the IPA in 1949.
3. In his thesis, Lacan used the third edition of Meyerson's *Identité et Réalité*.
4. Lacan published his write-up of this session in the *Revue Française de Psychanalyse* under the title: "De l'Impulsion au Complexe".
5. These themes were later stressed by Norwood Russell Hanson, in the 1950s, before the renaissance of scientific methodology brought about by the works of Popper and Kuhn at the end of that decade; see, for instance, Hanson (1958).

6. Meyerson prefers to call this principle of identification a "schema, or process, of identification".
7. Meyerson's theory of the centrality of identification will remain with Lacan throughout all his work: it will take a pre-eminent position in his *Seminar IX—Identification*—in [R4]. An analytical dialectic will be central to Lacan's next programme [R2]: progress in analysis will there be equated with the progress of this dialectic. As Lacan moves into new forms of his research programme, formalisation will take a more central role. In Meyerson's *Essais* one finds reference to a series of mathematicians and logicians—Cantor, Frege, Zermelo, Russell—and discussions of concrete and abstract groups (Meyerson, [1934] 1936). "*Le rattachement au monde du réel est particulièrement apparent dans la théorie des groupes, tant dans celle des groupes abstraites que* [...] *dans celle des groupes de permutations*": these are themes that Lacan will take up in [R3].
8. See, for instance Dide and Juppont (1924). Dide had constructed a programme in psychoanalysis that was a form of the organo-dynamism later developed by Henri Ey—a programme that Lacan engaged with, and criticised extensively. As well as being a prominent psychiatrist, Dide was a hero of the Resistance; one of his colleagues in this resistance work had been Georges Canguilhem. At the age of seventy, Dide was the Head of a Combat Resistance Group in Toulouse where in 1944 he was captured by the Nazis: he was deported to Buchenwald, where he was torn to death by dogs.
9. Lacan, Dide, and Juppont were working on these themes in the mid-to-late 20s. In his Doctoral Thesis (Dide, 1925) Dide attempted to use Saussure's theory of language in order to explain verbal symbolism in states of normality, aphasia, and delirium; in this text, as in his work with Juppont, Dide drew on Meyerson's account of science. The journal *L'Evolution Psychiatrique* had come into existence in 1925. Meyerson had published his *L'Explication dans les Sciences*—in two Volumes—in 1921; his posthumous *Essais* were provided with Introductions by Louis de Broglie and Lucien Lévi-Bruhl in 1936.
10. This (sixth) Colloquium contained detailed psychoanalytic investigations of the relation between the unconscious and language. It was organised around a joust between "juniors" associated with Lacan, and "juniors" associated with Sacha Nacht. The debate—which contained Lacan's response—led to André Green moving to work with Lacan in the 1960s.
11. Part II: "La Causalité Essentielle de la Folie".
12. In the eponymous dialogue by Plato.
13. The programme established by Socrates was actually taken over from Parmenides: for some detail of this see initially Grote, 1865; Mill, 1866; and consequentially Freud, Tr. 1880.
14. From its Parmenides-Socrates inauguration, this method has been propounded as the structuring agency of the sciences.
15. The second, that is, of the two central dreams around which Freud organises his account of the work with Dora. Lacan sees Freud's move towards exhorting Dora at the end of this work as a failure of interpretation stemming from a weakening of his dialectical position. For more detail of this see Burgoyne, 2016.
16. Grote presented what he saw as a Parmenides-Zeno-Socrates programme: he claimed that it constituted a revolution in epistemology, a revolution in the theory of scientific enquiry, and a revolution in the theory of political philosophy. He and Mill attempted to incorporate what they saw as the consequences of this into the programme of their political party at Westminster.

17. Grote: *loc. cit.* The framing effect that Grote describes effectively includes the structure of phantasy.
18. The first three of these references come from Lacan, 1950a; the fourth and sixth from Lacan, 1948; and the fifth is from Lacan, [1951] 1953—a paper that he presented to the British Psycho-Analytical Society in May 1951.
19. The notion of false connection is well described in a lengthy footnote that Freud included in his account of his work with Emmy von N. The note is attached to the session of the 15th May; it is the first footnote, starting with the phrase "the sequence of events".
20. At the first "scientific meeting" of the Société Française de Psychanalyse, held on the 8th July 1953, in the Hôpital Sainte-Anne in Paris.
21. These seminars preceded the start of his public seminar programme; following on from the Intervention on Dora, Lacan's (closed) seminars on the Rat-man and the Wolf-man can be seen as *Seminars 0 and –1*.
22. The three registers then follow on from earlier Freudian topics: unconscious, preconscious, conscious; id, superego, ego; and inhibition, symptom, and anxiety. The topological themes that they disclose as being operative in the mind are pathway, disconnection, interior, boundary, and closure: psychoanalytical correlates of these terms are facilitation, splitting, subjectivity, resistance, and idealisation.
23. Lacan will move on to his account of the Schreber and Little Hans cases in his *Seminars III and IV* (*on Psychosis, and on Object Relations*) in 1956–1957.
24. Session of 7th July 1954. Grote and Mill had claimed as much almost ninety years earlier; Freud had started his extensive contact with this material in 1879.
25. Ibid., 9th June.
26. "The Meaning of Delusion"—November 1955.
27. So had Wilfred Bion, and John Rickman, and Imre Hermannn, and Kurt Lewin. See Bion, [1958–1979] 1994 and Rickman, [1934–1951] 2003. Hermann's work dates from 1923, and Lewin's major text on this is Lewin, 1936.
28. On account of this Lacan would have been familiar with Daval and Guilbaud, 1945. This is a text where Guilbaud points out the virtues of formalisation and generalisation: in particular in relation to what he calls "geometrisation" in the work of Elie Cartan, and in relation to the general topologies constructed by Maurice Fréchet—before the First World War—in his work on function spaces.
29. Bion, over the same period, was to work with a parallel network of themes within the methodology and history of science. This would lead him to take up the work of the Cambridge philosopher of science Richard Braithwaite, the work of the American philosopher and logician Charles Sanders Peirce, and—*inter alia*—the text by Semple and Kneebone on Projective Geometry (Semple & Kneebone, 1952).
30. In particular Lacan's Schema L, the graph structures of *Seminars V and VI*, and the networks, permutations, and transformations of Lacan ([1956] 1966). Notions that thread between Lacan, Riguet, and Lévi-Strauss generate the type of matheme constructed by Lacan in his object relations seminar (Lacan, [1956–1957] 1994); the importance of the notion of permutation as a constituting element of the social bond—both in Lévi-Strauss and in Lacan's work in *Seminar IV*—has been emphasised in Lucchelli, 2014.

31. This particular theme is one that is more likely to have originated with Lacan.
32. He experienced, he says, a *"ravissement"* in being able to resolve problems by moving into a more general space of relations.
33. *"D'une insatisfaction qui remonte très loin"*.
34. Riguet goes as far as to suggest that a history of mathematics could be constructed from an analysis of such pathways and detours: he gives the example of Poncelet constructing projective geometry while a prisoner in jail in Russia.
35. Session 2 of Lacan's *Seminar II*—24th November 1954.
36. This structure of speech "envelops the subject"; it has been put into place by "parents, neighbours, the whole structure of the community".
37. One finds in the last three of these six seminars the themes of the dialectics of frustration, of privation, and of fundamental loss; the dialectic of desire, and its relation to the cut that is operative in phantasy; and what—outside of analysis—functions as the adamantine, that is, non-dialectisable, kernel of the constitution of Ideals.
38. Miller also applies this notion—which looks towards the topological structure underlying the changes of form—to the shifts that can be perceived within the development of a single Lacan seminar: "As *Seminar VI* progresses [...] it transforms continuously. It changes shape without producing a rent, as do topological figures". See Miller, [1981] 2002, and Miller, 2013.
39. Editors' footnote: Burgoyne uses "structurings" to refer both to structural elements and the way in which these underpin the development of further psychic structure.
40. Freud gave an extensive account of his views on this question in the chapter of his *New Introductory Lectures* on "The Question of a Weltanschauung" for the background to the critical interaction between Freud and Putnam, see Burgoyne, 2002.
41. Session of 6th July 1960.
42. Ibid: session of 4th May 1960.
43. In his paper on analytical work with neurosis Lacan proposed an order that establishes a direction for the analytical work. It is made up of three successive steps—(i) a dialectical reconstruction of the frame determining the reality of the relations of love; (ii) the analytical transference; and (iii) interpretation within the transference. Lacan claims that the first step automatically evokes the transference relationship, and that the corresponding direction of analysis is the one that was maintained by Freud.
44. Lacan finds Strachey's paper on mutative interpretation—and how to bring this about—to be very rich. However, Lacan takes this mutative effect to take place in part (iii) of his proposed direction for the treatment. Strachey's account can be found in Strachey, [1933] 1934 and in his contribution to the panel on psychoanalytical technique held at the Marienbad Congress of the IPA in 1936 (Strachey, [1936] 1937).
45. The analyst is then located in a position where the analysand attributes to him or her a "supposition of knowing" the ways through what were previously impasses of love.
46. Session 23 of *Seminar VII*.
47. Ibid: Session 19.
48. In particular, the torus; the Möbius strip; the Klein bottle; the cross-cap; and more explicitly—the projective plane.

49. Particularly the field of complex numbers; at the same time Lacan was starting to investigate the foundations of logic in relation to the constitution of psychic space.
50. The best account of this can be found in Vieira, 1998.
51. The initial form intended for Lacan's *Seminar XI* was broken at the end of its first session, on 20th November 1963. At this moment forced to relocate his seminar, moving it from the Amphitheatre of the Hôpital Sainte-Anne to the Ecole Normale Supérieure, rue d'Ulm, where he started the sessions that replaced the *Broken Seminar* on the 15th January 1964.
52. This formulation is from the *Broken Seminar*—where also you find, in relation to the subject's relation to A ("*le grand Autre*"—usually rendered in English as "the Other"): "in anxiety, the subject is affected by the desire of A", followed almost immediately by "in an immediate, non-dialectisable way".
53. It may be of some importance to note the date: 20th November 1963. This is some twenty months before the International Colloquium held in London where the Lakatos–Szabó programme of Socratic dialectic first saw the light of day. This programme ascribes a dialectical structure to deductive mathematics, to the Greek origins of mathematics, and to the mathematical sciences: it was still being worked on and extended by Popper in the 1990s.
54. Session 27: 15th May 1963.
55. Ibid. The two quotations in question are separated by a few sentences.
56. In this sense, a discourse can be taken to be a standardised form of negotiation of demand and desire; Diderot and Rousseau had worked on a series of problems associated with this in the 1750s and 1760s.
57. Both Charbonneau (1997) and Harder (2013) seem to claim that the dialectic period in Lacan ended around 1960. In Harder's case, he does admit to a movement from "dialectic as a general method" to a series of sub-programmes of "dialectic of": the dialectic of objects of desire in *Seminar XI*, the "dialectic of the Other" in *Seminar XIII*, and the dialectic of the *a*–object in *Seminars XIII and XVI*—all in [R5] or at the very start of [R6]. Of these two accounts therefore, Harder's is more on the right track; but both of them ignore two uncomfortable facts: (i) the greatest part of what takes place in psychoanalytical clinical work remains dialectical, and (ii) there are very good grounds for taking the fabric of mathematics—the material of Lacan's formalisations, and the organisational structure of the sciences—to be structured by dialectics. For these themes see Lakatos, [1961] 1976; Szabó, [1965] 1967 and Szabó, [1969]; 1978; also Szabó, [1993] 2000 and Popper, 1998.
58. And in twenty sessions of the next formulation of his programme: [R6].
59. For the importance of dialectic and demonstration in Lacan, see Miller, 2011. In this text Miller formulates a number of problems concerning philosophical issues that are encountered in psychoanalytic work. Amongst them are questions as to how the topology of psychic space is changed within the analytical dialectic; questions as regards the relation between Real, representation, and truth; and questions as to how Lacan's construction of the drive "draws jouissance into the same dialectic as desire". For a sketch of some of the philosophical backcloth to Lacan's work, see the three parts of Miller, [1989] 1996.
60. In more recent years, Marie-Claire Busnel and Romana Negri—amongst others—have investigated the dependencies of the child on what Busnel calls "pre-natal culture". Busnel's researches have shown that before birth, the child has a preference for voices over other

sounds, for feminine voices over others, and for the mother's voice over other feminine voices. Such research has shown that the child is first able to perceive the mother's voice some eight to nine weeks after conception, and that by the seventeenth or eighteenth week after conception the child is already making complex choices amongst the voices and sounds that surround it—as it is confronted with the problem of finding pathways that lead from one such introject to another. Immediately after birth—at two days—the child shows that it can clearly recognise the affects of joy, anger, and sadness—and that it has a preference for joy. Romana Negri, in Milan, has studied thousands of children in the womb—continuing with follow-up studies that go as far as kindergarten, and using the techniques of child-observation devised by Esther Bick: this work has led her to propose the notion of a foetal "personality". For further details, see Busnel, 2001 and Negri, 2001a and 2001b.

61. These structures of loss are formulations of what has traditionally been called "the form of organisation of the drive". Lacan extends their spectrum—the forms of the *a*-object are void, voice, look, breast, ordure.
62. It is this priority that Lacan will reassess in a later period of his work: the relations of the symbolic body, the imaginary body, and the real body—as they surround the void of the *a*-object—form the kernel of his later programme of Borromean knots.
63. Translations, that is, between different strata of psychic material; between the language of a neurosis and the language of ordinary thinking; or between the language of a dream-thought and the language of a dream.
64. Lacan frequently uses "realise" in the sense of "rendering real" some aspect of the Symbolic structure. This usage simultaneously grasps the more usual sense of coming to a—sometimes surprising, and sometimes shocking—realisation of what had been previously ignored.
65. Lacan may well be calling on a term that Goethe had earlier taken to describe one of the operations of love—"elective affinity"; he may equally well be calling on Freud's notion of the "choice of neurosis".
66. *"pour faire qu'on ne s'aperçoive pas qu'il manque"*.
67. Jean Oury had originally raised these themes at the Congress on Child Psychosis in Paris—in the context of segregationist policies in the institutional treatment of psychosis: see Lacan ibid., and Lacan (1967).
68. In session 3 of his unpublished *Seminar XV*—29th November 1967.
69. Erik Porge has previously commented on the two sides of this homology (see Porge, 2013). Porge gives an—interesting—account of the periods involved in Lacan's work, one that is different from mine in a number of respects. He chose his periodisations in relation to a specific problem, that of the Name-of-the-Father; mine of course follow rather the shifts in Lacan's programme for the analysis of psychic space. I also differ from Porge in the interpretation of the detail of Lacan's proposed parallelism. And of course, these parallels seem to entail that there will be a further development of *Seminars IX and* X—on Identification and Anxiety—that will be located in [R6].
70. Gauss' work had already revolutionised the concept of what constitutes a number; his work on what constitutes a geometry he had kept in reserve.
71. This raises the relation of Winnicott's transitional space to the psychic space that Lacan had been devoting his attention to for over thirty years.

72. In 1971–1972 Lacan gave a seminar at Sainte-Anne, parallel to—and in addition to—his main *Seminar XIX*: I refer to the parallel seminar as *Seminar XIXA*.
73. The relationship between geometry and topology had been there earlier—in his engagement with Daniel Lagache in the late 1950s, concerning the structure of the Ego-Ideal; see Lacan, [1958] 2006b, and Lagache, 1958.
74. There are similar reflections in Bion's work at this time: see Bion, [1958–1979] 1994.
75. The text that Porge refers to here is Hermann, [1947] 1950. In this paper Hermann proposed an exact parallelism between the structure of topological space and the structure of the mind: in fact, from as early as 1929 Hermann had formulated questions of psychic structure—and of psychoanalytical technique—in terms of boundary, interior, and limit. See Hermann, 1929, and for arguments antedating this Hermann, [1924] 1926.
76. In the session of 17th January 1962.
77. In the session of 20th March.
78. Here Lacan moves into questions of the foundations of mathematics, and the methodology of the sciences: questions that have held a place in his work since his initial reading of Meyerson and Koyré.
79. For an account of Freud's taking up of this dialectic theme into analysis, see also Burgoyne, 1995, 2001, and 2007.
80. Lorenzen's structuring was in fact a restructuring—with all that this entails—of the foundations of mathematics, including the foundations of set theory.
81. This latter law can function as the operator of what has been called "double bind".
82. Session of 30th April 1969.
83. Session of 19th May 1971.
84. In session 15th—27th March 1968.
85. Session of 19th May 1971.
86. That is: it "says the same thing".
87. A text that Lacan would have been familiar with is Fréchet and Ky Fan (1946), which stresses algebraic topology. But Fréchet was the great initiator of the study of general spaces, starting in 1906, and continuing into the late 1920s.
88. In the session of *Seminar XIXA* published as "Je Parle Aux Murs", Lacan addresses the question of what it is that resonates in the body—in the structure of the fundamental phantasy. Logic is insufficient to answer this question, he says, and he adds that this has been clear from (at least) the time of Plato. The solution, he claims, is for "mathematics to be brought into play"; and "it is there that the question can be posed as to where to centre this Real that we are led to have recourse to by logical interrogation, and that has its being on the level of mathematics". So mathematics becomes necessary, in order to formulate questions of the relation between the Symbolic, the Imaginary, and the Real.
89. And moved to working on the Borromean knot theory thereafter.
90. *L'Etourdit*—a paper presented by Lacan at the 50th Anniversary Celebrations of the Hôpital Henri Rousselle—in a session given the title *Questions de Méthode*—on 14th July 1972.
91. There is a question as to what constitutes this domain. Lacan would have taken it to mean the structure of topological spaces, as worked on in the second half of the twentieth century. But the structure of his argument would lend itself to a wider interpretation—one formed by

bringing to bear the structure of general spaces, as worked on by Fréchet, Sierpinski, Wilder and others in the first half of that century.

92. This is not news: see Herbart's address to the Royal German Society in Königsberg on 18th April 1822: Herbart, 1822.
93. But not resolve the conflict. Freud had formulated the relations between a man and a woman as follows: the sexual lives of the two seem "out of phase". Lacan reformulates Freud's conclusion by means of mathematics: his version is "there is no sexual rapport".
94. Or rather: by a set of points to which it fails to have an aversion.
95. Session of 1st June 1972 of *Seminar XIXA*, and the session of 21st November 1972 of *Seminar XX*.
96. See above for compactness, and the "Further Elucidation" for the failure of sexual love.
97. I have tried to contribute a little to this general parallelism thesis, using separation properties in topological spaces to formulate the difficulties of the autistic child.
98. The topology contains within it the structure of resistance. As he developed this aspect of Lacan's theory Soury put forward the conjecture that resistance can be characterised by the difficulty of laying a surface flat: see Soury (1981), particularly the session of 4th December 1980. An alternative way of developing this—and one entirely within the General Topology programme—would be to attempt to characterise the difficulty of establishing a pathway between two points.
99. To give just two examples: using properties of psychic space to establish reasons for the development of previously neglected areas of mathematics—such as the structure of spaces more general than topologies; or for reconstructing the history of set theory from Dedekind to Zermelo.
100. And they have seen his diagrams—which are trying to grasp the structure of human nature—as being merely illuminating scribbles. For the wide range of formulations of how seriously one can take structure in psychoanalysis, see the dozen or so papers in Burgoyne (2000) *passim*.
101. Session of 9th February 1972.
102. Lacan may have realised that he was developing what was to be the last of his programmes. "*Le vent du noeud*" is allusive of "*le vent du nord*" with its "*car je croyais ouïr de ces bruits prophétiques*" of the Song of Roland.
103. I will refer to his work on it as the BK programme.
104. This could well be heard as "a *ne-Bo* theory", since in its formulation it is intended to grasp the various forms of negation encountered by psychoanalysis.
105. The seminar is—for this reason alone—appropriately called *R.S.I.*
106. For the structure of chains of signifying material, one needs general topology: Lacan here—for the moment—seems to assume that this can be taken for granted.
107. To put it another way—one involving the body: from fibres within the body of the Symbolic. In terms of assumed topology, Lacan takes the crossing points and the pathways in this network of threads to be determined by the equivocal functioning of language—an assumption which was present at least from the start of the second version of his research programme [R2]. See Lacan ibid, and Lacan, [1946] 1947.
108. That is, it is not only that the BK programme was developed within the General Topology programme, but the development of the BK programme itself presupposes—and needs—the apparatus of general topology.

109. Someone looking for a brief outline of the BK theory can find it in Skriabine, 2011; anyone wishing to see Lacan's own account will find it available in the same issue of *La Cause Freudienne* as Skriabine's article: Lacan, [1974] 2011.
110. The contribution by Eric Porge, for instance, raises the question—already formulated by Lacan—of what it is that follows from topology "being the stuff with which the clinician works": see Porge, [1999] 2004. Porge later develops this theme in a Chapter entitled *L'Espace Topologique* (Porge, 2008), where he makes some assumptions about representation (*Vorstellung*—a term central to Freud's formulation of psychoanalysis) with which I cannot completely concur.
111. That is: transforming a given space into a compact space—a condition that Bursztein takes to be a prerequisite for the deployment of the structure.
112. André had given a preliminary version of this talk at a seminar in Brussels in late September 1981.
113. I have already indicated that in my view Lacan was working with many Symbolic—and even topological—constructs during this first Andréan period, and before it.
114. It is clear that André's [A4] is identical in scope to my [R7].
115. A world which contains the NF [No-of-the-Father] function, and which allows for a signification of jouissance, as well as—ultimately—of what it entails to be a man, or to be a woman.
116. This circular path-structure can be traversed either in the outer regions of the knot's apparatus—in the regions of the body—or in its inner core—the area of loss. In this process, inertias of meaning can block the direction of the analysis—block, that is, the analytical dialectic. At the end of the process, an access to what is Real—in the form of a recognition of impossibility—permits an action to be chosen, where previously there was only a predominance of imaginary flight.
117. As could—equivalently—neighbourhoods, or open sets, or boundaries.
118. Particularly the opening session, of the 21st November 1972.

References

André, S. ([1981] 1982). Clinique et noeud borroméen. In: *Actes de l'Ecole de la Cause freudienne, Vol. 1, Février 1982.*

Bion, W. R. ([1958–1979] 1994). *Cogitations.* London: Karnac.

Bonnafé, L., Ey, H., Pollin, S., Lacan, J., & Rouart, J. (1950). *Le Problème de la Psychogenèse des Névroses et des Psychoses.* Paris: Bibliothèque Neuro-Psychiatrique de Langue Française, Desclée de Brouwer & Cie.

Breuer, J., & Freud, S. ([1895] 1955). *Studies on Hysteria. S. E. II.* London: Hogarth.

Burgoyne, B. (1995). *Freud et la Science.* Thèse de Doctorat de l'Université de Paris VIII. Available online at: www.diffusiontheses.fr.

Burgoyne, B. (2000). Autism and Topology. In: B. Burgoyne (Ed.) (2000). *Drawing the Soul.* London: Rebus.

Burgoyne, B. (2001). Freud's Socrates. In: *The European Journal of Psychotherapy and Counselling, Volume 4, No. 1, 2001.*

Burgoyne, B. (2002). What Causes Structure to Find a Place in Love? In: Glynos and Stavrakakis (2002).

Burgoyne, B. (2003). From the Letter to the Matheme: Lacan's Scientific Methods. In: J.-M. Rabaté (2003). *The Cambridge Companion to Lacan*. Cambridge: Cambridge University Press.

Burgoyne, B. (2007). Socratic History. In: *JCFAR No. 17, 2007*.

Burgoyne, B. (2015). An Introduction to Lacan. In: Klein-Lacan Dialogues II.

Burgoyne, B. (2016). Presentation on Transference. In: Neill, Hook, & Vanheule (2016).

Bursztein, J.-G. (2012). *Sur l'Espace Subjectif*. Paris: Hermann.

Bursztein, J.-G. (2015a). Four Seminars at the Philadelphia Association, Hampstead, 25th January–7th June 2015, unpublished.

Bursztein, J.-G. (2015b). *La Différence Homme/Femme dans la Sexuation*. Paris: Hermann.

Bursztein, J.-G. (2015c). *The Topological Transformation of Freud's Theory*. London: Karnac.

Busnel, M.-C. (2001). Audition Foetale et Réactivité Prénatale à la Voix Maternelle <Adressée>. In: Negri (2001a).

Charbonneau, M.-A. (1997). *Science et Métaphore: Enquête Philosophique sur la Pensée du Premier Lacan (1926–1953)*. Québec: Les Presses de l'Université Laval.

Cartier, P., & Charraud, N. (Eds.) (2004). *Le Réel en Mathématiques: Psychanalyse et Mathématiques*. Paris: Agalma/Le Seuil.

Charraud, N. (1986). Problematique autour de la Topologie. In: *La Lettre Mensuelle de l'Ecole de la Cause Freudienne, No. 46, February 1986*.

Charraud, N. (1997). *Lacan et les Mathématiques*. Paris: Anthropos.

Daval, R., & Guilbaud, G.-T. (1945). *Le Raisonnement Mathématique*. Paris: Presses Universitaires de France.

Dide, M. (1925). *Introduction à l'Etude de la Psychogénèse: Thèse pour le Doctorat ès Lettres Présentée à la Faculté des Lettres de l'Université de Toulouse*. Toulouse: Masson et Cie Editeurs, Libraires de l'Académie de Médecine.

Dide, M., & Juppont, P. (1924). *La Métaphysique Scientifique*. Paris: Alcan.

Ey, H. ([1943] 1950). Les Limites de la Psychiatrie: le Problème de la Psychogenèse. In: Bonnafé et al. (1950).

Ey, H. ([1960] 1966). *L'Inconscient: VIe Colloque de Bonneval, 1960*. Paris: Bibliothèque Neuro-Psychiatrique de Langue Française, Desclée de Brouwer & Cie.

Feldstein, R., Fink, B., & Jaanus, M. (Eds.) (1996): *Reading Seminars I and II: Lacan's Return to Freud*. Albany: State University of New York Press.

Lacan, J. (2006): *Jacques Lacan: Ecrits—The First Complete Edition in English*. B. Fink, (Trans.). New York and London: Norton.

Fréchet, M., & Fan, K. (1946): *Introduction à la Topologie Combinatoire*. Paris: Vuibert.

Freud, S. (Trans.) (1880a). Plato [Freud's translation of Mill (1866)]. In: Mill (1880).

Freud, S. (1891b). On Aphasia. *S. E., I*. London: Imago Publishing Company.

Freud, S. (1950a). Project for a Scientific Psychology (1950 [1895]). *S. E., I*. London: Hogarth.

Freud, S. (1933a). The Question of a Weltanschauung. *New Introductory Lectures On Psycho-Analysis. S. E., XXII* (1932–1936). London: Hogarth.

Freud, S. (1940a [1938]) *An Outline of Psycho-Analysis. S. E., XXIII*. London: Hogarth.

Glynos, J., & Stavrakakis, Y. (Eds.) (2002). *Lacan and Science*. London: Karnac.

Grote, G. (1865): *Plato and the Other Companions of Socrates. Vols. I to III*. London: John Murray.

Hanson, N. R. (1958). *Patterns of Discovery*. Cambridge: Cambridge University Press.

Harder, Y.-J. (2013). Dialectique et Structure: Sartre, Lévi-Strauss, Lacan. In: *Les Temps Modernes, Nos. 674–675, July–October 2013.*

Herbart, J. F. (1822). *Ueber die Möglichkeit und Notwendigkeit, Mathematik auf Psychologie Anzuwenden.* Königsberg: bei den Gebrüder Bornträger.

Hermann, I. ([1923] 1986). La Préférence pour les Marges en tant que Processus Primaire. In: *Les Inedits et les Introuvables de Patio, No. 5.* Paris: Editions de l'Eclat.

Hermann, I. ([1924] 1926). *Gustav Theodor Fechner.* Leipzig and Vienna: Internationale Psychoanalytische Verlag [read originally as a paper to the Hungarian Psychoanalytical Society in 1924].

Hermann, I. (1929). *Das Ich und das Denken.* Leipzig and Vienna: Internationale Psychoanalytische Verlag.

Hermann, I. ([1947] 1950): Rapports Spatiaux de quelques Phénomènes Psychiques. In: *Acta Psychologica, VII, 1950*; translation of Néhány lelki jelenség térvonatkozása. In: *Magyar Psychologiai Szemle, XVI, 1947.*

Koyré, A. (1946). *Etude Critique: Les Essais d'Emile Meyerson.* In: *Journal de Psychologie, Normale et Pathologique, Vol. XXXIX No. 1, Janvier–Mars 1946.*

Lacan, J. (1931). Structure des Psychoses Paranoïaques. In: Semaine des Hôpitaux de Paris, Juillet, 1931.

Lacan, J. (1932). De la Psychose Paranoiäque dans ses Rapports avec la Personalité. Thèse de la Faculté de Paris, Octobre 1932; republished in Lacan (1975).

Lacan, J. (1933). Sur le Problème des Hallucinations. Compte rendu de la LXXXIV Assemblée de la Société Suisse de Psychiatrie. In: *L'Encéphale, Novembre 1933.*

Lacan, J. (1936). Beyond the Reality Principle. In: J. Lacan (2006).

Lacan, J. ([1936] 1949). The Mirror Stage as Formative of the I Function. In J. Lacan (2006).

Lacan, J. ([1938] 1939): De L'Impulsion au Complexe. In: *Revue Française de Psychanalyse, Vol. XI, No. 1, 1939.*

Lacan, J. ([1946] 1947). Propos sur la Causalité Psychique. In: *L'Evolution Psychiatrique, Vol. XII, No. 1, 1947.*

Lacan, J. (1947). La Psychiatrie Anglaise et la Guerre. In: *L'Evolution Psychiatrique, Vol. XII, No. 1, 1947*; translated as British Psychiatry and the War in *Psychoanalytical Notebooks, Issue 4, Spring 2000.*

Lacan, J. (1948). *Aggressiveness in Psychoanalysis.* In: J. Lacan (2006).

Lacan, J. (1950a). A Theoretical Introduction to the Functions of Psychoanalysis in Criminology. In: J. Lacan (2006).

Lacan, J. (1950b). Intervention au Ier Congrès Mondial de Psychiatrie. In: J. Lacan (2001).

Lacan, J. ([1951] 1952). Intervention sur le Transfert. In: *Revue Française de Psychanalyse, Vol. XVI, Nos. 1–2, Janvier–Juin, 1952;* translated as Presentation on Transference in J. Lacan (2006).

Lacan, J. ([1951] 1953). Some Reflections on the Ego. In: *The International Journal of Psychoanalysis, Vol. 34, 1953.*

Lacan, J. (1952–1953): Le Séminaire sur l'Homme aux Loups, unpublished.

Lacan, J. ([1953] 2001). Discours de Rome: Réponses aux Interventions. In: J. Lacan (2001).

Lacan, J. ([1953] 2005). Le Symbolique, L'Imaginaire et le Réel. In: J. Lacan (2005).

Lacan, J. ([1953] 2006). The Function and Field of Speech and Language in Psychoanalysis. In: J. Lacan (2006).

Lacan, J. ([1953–1954] 1988). *The Seminar of Jacques Lacan, Book I, Freud's Papers on Technique.* Cambridge: Cambridge University Press.

Lacan, J. ([1954–1955] 1988). *The Seminar of Jacques Lacan, Book II, The Ego in Freud's Theory and in the Technique of Psychoanalysis*. Cambridge: Cambridge University Press.
Lacan, J. ([1955–1956] 1993). *The Seminar of Jacques Lacan, Book III, The Psychoses*. London: Routledge.
Lacan, J. ([1956] 2006). Seminar on "The Purloined Letter". In: J. Lacan (2006).
Lacan, J. ([1956–1957] 1994). *Le Séminaire de Jacques Lacan, Livre IV, La Relation d'Objet*. Paris: Editions du Seuil.
Lacan, J. ([1957–1958] 1998). *Le Séminaire de Jacques Lacan, Livre V, Les Formations de l'Inconscient*. Paris: Editions du Seuil.
Lacan, J. ([1958] 2006a): The Direction of the Treatment and the Principles of its Power. In: J. Lacan (2006).
Lacan, J. ([1958] 2006b). Remarks on Daniel Lagache's Presentation: Psychoanalysis and the Structure of the Personality. In J. Lacan (2006).
Lacan, J. ([1958–1959] 2013). *Le Séminaire de Jacques Lacan, Livre VI, Le Désir et son Interprétaion*. Paris: Editions de la Martinière.
Lacan, J. ([1959–1960] 1992). *The Seminar of Jacques Lacan, Book VII, The Ethics of Psychoanalysis*. London: Routledge.
Lacan, J. ([1960–1961] 2015). *The Seminar of Jacques Lacan, Book VIII, Transference*. Cambridge: Polity Press.
Lacan, J. (1961–1962). Le Séminaire de Jacques Lacan, Livre IX, L'Identification, unpublished.
Lacan, J. ([1962–1963] 2014). *The Seminar of Jacques Lacan, Book X, Anxiety*. Cambridge: Polity Press.
Lacan, J. ([1963] 2005). [The Broken Seminar]: Introduction aux Noms-du-Père. In: Lacan (2005).
Lacan, J. ([1963–1964] 1977). *The Seminar of Jacques Lacan, Book XI, The Four Fundamental Concepts of Psycho-Analysis*. London: The Hogarth Press and the Institute of Psycho-Analysis.
Lacan, J. (1965–1966). Le Séminaire de Jacques Lacan, Livre XIII, unpublished.
Lacan, J. (2006 [1966]). *Ecrits*. B. Fink (Trans.). Paris: du Seuil.
Lacan, J. (1967). La Psychanalyse et la Formation du Psychiatre (also referred to as: Petit Discours aux Psychiatres), presented to the Cercle Psychiatrique Henri Ey at the Hôpital Sainte-Anne on the 10th November 1967, unpublished.
Lacan, J. ([1967/1968] 1972). Discours de Clôture des Journées sur les Psychoses chez l'Enfant. In: Recherches (1967, 1968); and in Mannoni (1972).
Lacan, J. (1967–1968). Le Séminaire de Jacques Lacan, Livre XV, unpublished.
Lacan, J. ([1968–1969] 2006). *Le Séminaire de Jacques Lacan, Livre XVI*. Paris: Editions du Seuil.
Lacan, J. ([1970–1971] 2006). *Le Séminaire de Jacques Lacan, Livre XVIII*. Paris: Editions du Seuil.
Lacan, J. ([1971–1972] 2011a). *Le Séminaire de Jacques Lacan, Livre XIX*. Paris: Editions du Seuil.
Lacan, J. ([1971–1972] 2011b). *Je Parle aux Murs*. Paris: Editions du Seuil.
Lacan, J. (1972). L'Etourdit. In: *Scilicet No. 4*; reprinted in Lacan (2001).
Lacan, J. ([1972–1973] 1998). *The Seminar of Jacques Lacan, Book XX, Encore—On Feminine Sexuality, the Limits of Love and Knowledge*. New York and London: Norton.
Lacan, J. ([1973] 1974). *Télévision*. Paris: Editions du Seuil.
Lacan, J. ([1974] 2011). La Troisième. In: *La Cause Freudienne: Nouvelle Revue de Psychanalyse, No. 79, Octobre 2011*.
Lacan, J. ([1974–1975] 1975/1976). Dans l'Imaginaire on y Est! In: *Ornicar? No. 5, Hiver 1975/1976*.
Lacan, J. (1975). *De la Psychose Paranoaïque dans ses Rapports avec la Personalité, suivi de Premiers Ecrits sur la Paranoïa*. Paris: Editions du Seuil.
Lacan, J. (1975–1976). Le Séminaire de Jacques Lacan, Livre XXII, R.S.I., unpublished.
Lacan, J. (2001). *Autres Ecrits*. Paris: Editions du Seuil.

Lacan, J. (2005). *Des Noms-du-Père*. J.-A. Miller (Ed.). Paris, Editions du Seuil.
Lagache, D. (1958). *Psychoanalysis and the Structure of the Personality*. Paris: Société Française de Psychanalyse.
Lakatos, I. ([1961] 1976). *Proofs and Refutations*. Cambridge: Cambridge University Press.
Lakatos, I, (Ed.) (1967). *Problems in the Philosophy of Mathematics*. Amsterdam: North-Holland Publishing Company.
Lewin, K. (1936). *Principles of Topological Psychology*. New York: McGraw-Hill.
Lucchelli, J. P. (2014). *Lacan Avec et Sans Lévi-Strauss*. Nantes: Psyché: Editions Cécile Defaut.
Mannoni, M. (Ed.) (1972). *L"Enfance Aliénée*. Paris, 10/18: L'Union Générale d'Editions.
Meyerson, E. ([1907] 1926). *Identité et Réalité*. Paris: Alcan.
Meyerson, E. (1921). *De l'Explication dans les Sciences*. Paris: Payot.
Meyerson, E. ([1933–1934] 1936). La Notion de l'Identique. In: E. Meyerson (1936).
Meyerson, E. ([1934] 1936). Les Mathématiques et le Divers. In: E. Meyerson (1936).
Meyerson, E. (1936). *Essais*. Paris: Vrin.
Mill, J. S. (1866). *Grote's Plato*. In: *The Edinburgh Review, CXXIII, April 1866*.
Mill, J. S. (1880). *J. S. Mill: Gesammelte Werke, Vol. 12*. Gomperz, T. (Ed.). Leipzig: Fues Verlag.
Miller, J.-A. ([1981] 2002). Encyclopédie. In: *Ornicar? No. 24, Autumn 1981*; translated as Jacques Lacan in *Psychoanalytic Notebooks, No. 8, 2002*.
Miller, J.-A. ([1989] 1996). An Introduction to Seminars I and II: Lacan's Orientation Prior to 1953, Parts I to III. In: Feldstein, et al (1996).
Miller, J.-A. ([1996] 2015). The Barcelona Seminar on The Paths of Symptom Formation. In: *Psychoanalytical Notebooks, No. 30, 2015*; a fuller version—in a different translation—can be found in *Psychoanalytical Notebooks, No. 1, 1998*.
Miller, J.-A. (2011). Progrès en Psychanalyse Assez Lents [four sessions of L'Orientation Lacanienne: 19th and 26th January, and 2nd and 9th February 2011]. In: *La Cause Freudienne, No. 78, June 2011*.
Miller, J.-A. (2013). Presentation of Book VI of the Seminar of Jacques Lacan. Available online at: www.latigolacaniano.com.
Negri, R. (Ed.) (2001a). *Que Savent les Foetus?* Toulouse: Editions érès.
Negri, R. (2001b). Quelques Propos sur la <Personalité> du Foetus. In: R. Negri (2001a).
Neill, C., Hook, D., & Vanheule, S. (Eds.) (2016). *Reading the Ecrits—a Guide to Lacan's Works, Volume 1: Between the Imaginary and the Symbolic*. London: Routledge.
Popper, K. R. (1998). *The World of Parmenides: Essays on the Pre-socratic Enlightenment*. London and New York: Routledge.
Porge, E. ([1999] 2004). La Bifidité de l'Un. In: Cartier & Charraud (2004).
Porge, E. (2008). *Des Fondements de la Clinique Psychanalytique*. Toulouse: Editions Erès.
Porge, E. (2013). *Les Noms du Père chez Jacques Lacan*. Toulouse: Editions Erès.
Porge, E. (2015). *Le Ravissement de Lacan: Marguerite Duras à la Lettre*. Toulouse: Editions Erès.
Recherches (1967, 1968). Enfance Aliénée [Parts I and II of the Proceedings of the Conference "Enfance Aliénée" held in Paris on 21st and 22nd October, 1967], September 1967 and December 1968; a selection from these papers was subsequently published in Mannoni (1972).
Rickman, J. ([1934–1951] 2003). *No Ordinary Psychoanalyst: The Exceptional Contributions of John Rickman*. P. King (Ed.). London: Karnac.
Riguet, J. (1989). Interview with Jacques Nimier - Entretien avec le Professeur Riguet. In: Nimier, J. (1989). *Entretiens avec des Mathématiciens*. Lyon: Editions I.R.E.M. Académie de Lyon.
Riguet, J. (2011). Une Analyse Indolore. In: *Le Diable Probablement: Pourquoi Lacan?, No. 9, 2011*.
Roudinesco, E. (2001). *L'Analyse, L'Archive*. Paris: Bibliothèque Nationale de France.

Semple, J. G. & Kneebone, G. T. (1952). *Algebraic Projective Geometry*. Oxford: Clarendon Press.
Skriabine, P. (2011). Lacan Topologue. In: *La Cause Freudienne: Nouvelle Revue de Psychanalyse, No. 79, Octobre 2011*.
Soury, P. (1981). Chaînes, Noeuds, Surfaces: La Topologie de Lacan. J. Lafont (Ed.). Documents et Travaux de la Bibliothèque, Ecole de la Cause Freudienne, Décembre 1981.
Strachey, J. ([1933] 1934). The Nature of the Therapeutic Action of Psychoanalysis. *Int J Psycho-Anal, 15, 1934*.
Strachey, J. ([1936] 1937). Contribution to the Symposium on the Theory of the Therapeutic Results of Psycho-Analysis. *Int J Psycho-Anal, 18*: 136–143.
Szabó, Á. ([1965] 1967). Greek Dialectic and Euclid's Axiomatics. In: Lakatos (1967).
Szabó, Á. ([1969] 1978). *The Beginnings of Greek Mathematics*. Dordrecht and Boston: D. Reidel Publishing Company.
Szabó, Á. ([1993] 2000). *L'Aube des Mathématiques Grecques*. Paris: Librairie Philosophique J. Vrin.
Vieira, M. A. (1998). *L'Ethique de la Passion: L'Affect dans la Théorie Psychanalytique avec Freud et Lacan*. Rennes: Presses Universitaires de Rennes.
Winnicott, D. W. ([1936–1954] 1988). *Human Nature*. London: Free Association Books.

CHAPTER TWO

Editors' introduction

S. Bailly

It is interesting to imagine the state of French psychoanalysis in 1963, when the IPA, having two years previously already suggested that Lacan should receive no new cases as a training analyst, stipulated that his training activities should cease entirely. A generation of analysts, now in their intellectual adolescence, had been taught, supervised and analysed by Lacan. They would have had in their minds *his* take on the ego, narcissism, the subject, representation, language, the Oedipus complex, the maternal signifier and (bearing in mind Lacan was more polyglot than most) *his* take on new theories written abroad. Those of Lacan's analysands and students who chose to stay within the IPA, including Anzieu, Diatkine, Widlöcher, Laplanche, and Pontalis, perhaps made their choice because of new identifications they had made with other influences within the IPA, or perhaps because of a desire to stay within the most powerful organisation in their field, or because of a mixture of the two. The natural process of separating and individuating from a teacher and analyst may entail ambivalence between guilt and triumph, gratitude and hatred; however, the excommunication of Lacan by the IPA might have given this parting of ways a particularly aversive slant and made it less a separation than a repudiation. Because of the lack of contact between these analysts and Lacan afterwards and because of the absence of citations of his teachings in their work, one is pushed to imagine a kind of Cultural Revolution in which the young ones had to deny the father who had taught them the language of psychoanalysis. And yet, these young ones might have discovered, perhaps to their chagrin, that it is not possible to escape entirely the language of the parent, and that even as they came to speak more and more in their new psychoanalytic language, they were found to have "an accent": their understandings were not quite those of the English-speaking world and the new theories they developed were unmistakeably underpinned by the repudiated father.

It may seem curious to readers within the Lacanian tradition that we have commissioned a paper that looks specifically at the work of analysts outside of it, but we feel that Sara Flanders' tracing of developments in French IPA psychoanalysis from the 1960s onwards is in fact a remarkable work of integration: she has shown both what some of these ideas owe directly to Lacan and how they have evolved away from or even in opposition to his thinking, but always in some kind of dialectic with him.

In the years following his excommunication, Lacan seems to have become increasingly isolated from his psychoanalytic peers. Perhaps by choice but more likely out of necessity, he nourished his ideas with material from outside psychoanalysis rather than from within. This would have made it even more difficult for IPA analysts of subsequent generations to relate to his still evolving ideas, and difficult for those who stayed with him to benefit from the evolutions of psychoanalysis outside the Lacanian tradition. And meanwhile, beginning as a rather peripheral group, the new, formerly Lacanian members of the "French school" within the IPA began to enrich the largely Anglo-American theoretical framework with their particular slant on things.

Psychoanalysis has so far resisted defining concepts by theoretical argument, preferring to let its language be shaped by usage and precedence, which may be naturalistic but is also then subject to the irrational forces of identification and allegiance. Flanders' use of psychoanalytic terms illustrates the differences that exist between Lacanians and the IPA in their understanding of many of these and should open up the field for a dialogue that we can hope will create greater clarity and rigour. The phallus she writes of seems to have gained some concreteness and can be displaced "from the Real of the body to the Imaginary". On drive, she reflects both the Lacanian and the IPA views of it, recognising the Lacanian perspective that allows her to write of it as "bound to signifiers", but setting up alongside these non-Lacanian formulations that make drive almost equivalent to affect and that oppose it to representation. There is an interesting distinction to be made between Lacan's drive, upon which we have elaborated in our General Introduction and which remains a constant, "potential energy" and the drive as conceived by Green, who believes in its "movement", and to re-read the exchange between the two in the *Four Fundamental Concepts* in this light (Lacan, 1981).

Flanders' paper also highlights some ideas about Lacan perpetuated within the IPA that Lacanians need to address: that he denied the importance of affect, that his thinking was entirely concerned with linguistics or that he played down the importance of the mother and of the body. We would say that Lacan and Lacanians take affect and the importance of the mother as "givens"—indeed, the givens that constitute the problematic around which psychoanalysis is built. We also hold that Lacan never denied the corporeal, but insisted that the body itself was caught up in the network of signifiers, even before birth (see chapter 1 in this book). He evoked not a disembodied subject, but an embodied signifier. We regret that present theorisers of non-verbal representation and non-represented states have ignored Lacan's formulation of *lalangue*, which bridges the pre-verbal and language, bodily jouissance and the Symbolic, and suggests that it is maternal affect, conscious, pre-conscious and unconscious, that causes the infant to cathect the verbal acoustic image and to become a *parl-être*—a being of speech (Lacan, 1972–1973).

Flanders' paper shows something else the editors consider important: that the IPA of today is *not* that of 1963 and that there is an increasing interest in Lacan within it. If similar interest were shown in the other direction, perhaps we may come closer to speaking a common language, in which different accents can be heard without gross misunderstanding and disagreements can be fruitfully argued, rather than abandoned through the frustration of non-comprehension.

References

Lacan, J. (1981). *The Four Fundamental Concepts of Psychoanalysis—The Seminar of Jacques Lacan (1964), Book 11*. Miller, J.-A. (Ed.), Sheridan, A. (Trans.). New York and London: W. W. Norton and Co, Inc.

Lacan, J. (1972–1973). *Seminar 20—Encore*. C. Gallagher (Trans.). Unpublished.

CHAPTER TWO

French psychoanalysis and Lacan

Sara Flanders

A number of years ago my colleague, Dana Birksted Breen, and I set out to write an introductory chapter on French Psychoanalysis for readers from other traditions, in particular our own, the British Psychoanalytic Society—a complex and heterogenous audience. We aimed to frame the subject as a whole for readers like ourselves, outsiders, who would then be able to dip into a collection of papers, chosen by Alain Gibeault and ourselves, hopefully stimulated by the encounter to explore the subject further. The collection was eventually published as Reading French Psychoanalysis in 2010. I was very happy to share in this task for a number of reasons. As a member of the British society, where the evolution of psychoanalytic thought has been so profoundly influenced by the contributions of Melanie Klein, then the post Kleinian developments of Bion and Winnicott, I often found myself looking to the French for thinking more rigorously grounded in Freud. In France, Freud seemed to remain the fundamental reference, still the source of inspiration for fresh psychoanalytic thinking. It is above all the French who have kept alive the importance of reading and re-reading Freud himself. For me and for many others, the Language of Psychoanalysis by Laplanche and Pontalis, (1967 [1973]) stands as an unsurpassed testament to the value of Freud's work, and is an invaluable aid to reading the texts. Before embarking on the attempt to write an introduction, I was already grateful to Andre Green, who tirelessly theorised both French and English psychoanalysis, integrating the work of Winnicott and Bion with his own richly conceived Freud, forcefully insisting on the centrality of the unconscious and sexuality, challenging the move in Britain away from sexuality and the body. For some of us, these powerful French writers provided invaluable support and illuminating insight, which balanced the developing British focus on object relations and mind.

Although Dana Birksted-Breen had knowledge of French psychoanalytic writing on sexuality and *après coup*, having written about both (1993, 2003), she and I entered the larger field of

French psychoanalysis, with Alain Gibeault as guide from the inside, without a compass or design of our own except our awareness of a sense of difference from British psychoanalysis, a sense that sexuality never disappeared from the French scene, (Birksted-Breen, 1993) and a respect for the Freudian scholarship so evident in these three major authors. It did not take us too long to find our compass. As we studied the history of the development of psychoanalysis in France, we began to fathom how many of the qualities we had come to regard as French, seemed to have grown either out of, or in conflict with the work of Jacques Lacan. Rather than some general cultural difference, which may well exist, we were impressed with something else, something that we identified eventually as a product of the French struggle with the troubling genius of Lacan. We saw a similarity between this influence on French analysis with the impact in British Psychoanalysis of the work of Melanie Klein. And this sense was reaffirmed by the realisation of the patrimony of the great French psychoanalysts: the foundation of our initial reading, Laplanche and Pontalis, were both his analysands; Andre Green had been his student. Moreover we had found, at the Franco-Britannique meeting which takes place once a year, convened by Haydee Faimberg and Anne Marie Sandler, that the style of many French psychoanalysts who are members of the APF or SPP, the two major IPA, non Lacanian French societies, recalled the influence of Lacan's prescription: to offer an enigmatic interpretation, to stay away from the secondary process, to play with the linking of signifiers, and to avoid provoking or invoking compliance with the analyst.

Lire Freud

Lacan was from the beginning, specific in his attack on what he identified as the revisionist ego psychology that had become dominant in the United States after the Second World War, a tradition that in his view completely reversed the radical, destabilising psychological revolution inherent in Freud's assertion of the power of the unconscious. (Roudinesco, 1990; Mijolla, 2004) For Lacan this development in the United States involved a turning away from the early Freud, an embrace of the later structural model, with a particular clinical stress and aim, which was to strengthen the ego in an adaptation to reality. For Lacan, the ego was always the enemy of the psychoanalytic project, aiming at mastery and enslaving the subject to demands often driven by the its "*meconaissance*"—the ego's false knowing—alienating the subject from its truth. In order to free the subject from the ego's grip, according to Lacan, one needed the Freud of the earlier model, the Freud who had "disturbed the universe" with the *Interpretation of Dreams*, certainly destabilised the certainties and pieties of consciousness. Lacan's attack on ego psychology was his preface to the need for a "return to Freud".

Those analysands and students of Lacan who eventually broke away from him, became members of IPA societies and established themselves as the leaders of their societies, always grounded any theoretical move away from Lacan with a reading of the Freud to whom he had insisted they return. It is thanks to Lacan that French psychoanalysis has preserved the grounding of psychoanalytic discourse in interpretation and reinterpretation of Freud. It was in France, several years after the 1963 split within the Société Française de Psychanalyse and the creation of the first Lacanian Society that Laplanche and Pontalis published the as yet unsurpassed *Vocabulaire de la Psychanalyse*, in which they set a new international standard for the study of

Freud's terms and conceptions. Interestingly, to this day, no definitive edition of Freud has been published in France. Rather, the controversy remains alive. In France, different translations have been written, of selected work, coloured by different interpretive emphases, supporting different readings of Freud himself. No standard edition of Freud is in a way a disadvantage, particularly as there have been important papers left out, still unavailable in French. However, as Evelyn Sechaud has written, there has developed in France another approach, or tradition, which has constituted an effort to turn each student of psychoanalysis into a pioneer, a researcher into the mind of Freud himself. Writing in the *International Journal* in 2008, Sechaud tells us that when she grounds her thinking in a reading of Freud, she is "illustrating one of the characteristics of French psychoanalysis"; she calls it "thinking with Freud". This form of learning was influenced by Lacan, who encouraged his students to read Freud in the original German, and so follow as closely as possible the elaboration of Freud's thinking. Sechaud shows her awareness of her Lacanian heritage, affirming that "it is very true that thinking cannot be separated from its language of origin". Reading Freud in this way, ideally in the original German, "enabled us to follow Freud's approach, the birth, the occultation and resurgence of concepts which are often caught up in the unconscious thing itself". The French psychoanalytic students thus learned, to use Jean Laplanche's expression, to "make Freud work" [*faire travailler* Freud] by reading and rereading Freud "in order to identify with the approach that enabled its author to discover hitherto unknown phenomena whose nature is such that they still resist disclosure" (Sechaud, 2008).

It was at a colloquium in 1960 in Bonneville for psychiatrists, psychoanalysts, and philosophers, convened by leading French psychiatrist Henry Ey for the purpose of examining the nature of the unconscious, that Laplanche presented the critique that was to become a cornerstone in the theoretical split from Lacan. (Roudinesco, 1990, pp. 307–318) Laplanche as mentioned before, but as can hardly be overstated for its impact on the development of French psychoanalysis, used as his basis for his argument with Lacan, Freud's 1915 paper on "The Unconscious". In his 1915 paper, Freud states explicitly that the unconscious contains representations, *Vorstellung-Repräsentanzen*, what Strachey translated as "ideational representatives" of the drives. In this paper, Freud also hypothesises "thing presentations"—memory traces of sensory experiences, which have never been conscious, or have become unconscious because they have become repressed. They can only find their way into consciousness if the thing-presentations—memory traces of sensory experiences that develop into images—become linked to word presentations in the preconscious, and so become available to consciousness. Fundamentally, Laplanche is affirming, using Freud, that the unconscious is not linguistic in essence. The beginning of the formation of the unconscious corresponds to the beginning of representational activity, and this activity is linked to the experience of the drives. The drives come first. Representation is a product of the activity of the drives. The movement of the drives lies at the heart of much non-Lacanian French psychoanalysis, always coupled with the relationship to representation of the drives. But as we shall see, there are fundamentally different interpretations of this relationship, which is problematised in French thinking, not taken for granted. What I wish to emphasise here is that by placing the drives and not language at the core of the unconscious, and founding his critique of Lacan on a 1915 paper, when Freud was concentrated on the fate of the drives rather than the functioning of the ego, as in the papers after 1920, Laplanche frees psychoanalysis from the Lacanian emphasis on linguistics prevalent in the sixties and yet rescues classical analysis from the taint of ego psychology, the hegemony of which Lacan had been so successful in undermining (Roudinesco, 1990; Lacan, 1954b). The careful attention to the embedding of the drive in the polysemic words of the analysand, the conviction that the unconscious is speaking through language if the analyst can hear it, has become a *sine qua non* of most French analysis. The significance of the word is saved, even if the unconscious is uncoupled from an identity with language itself.

Laplanche will eventually "make Freud work" for him as he develops a complex and fascinating notion concerning the formation of unconscious phantasy, and he will eventually carry his Lacanian heritage into that field in a convincing and conceptually rich way. Laplanche will make both Lacan and Freud work for him when he links his ideas of the maternal seduction or desire, a Lacanian emphasis, with Freud's theories of primal phantasy, and in so doing discovers his own version of the foundation of unconscious phantasy in the infant's encounter with the "enigmatic message" of the mother. Everywhere in the development of French psychoanalytic theory, Freud will be made to work in original and illuminating ways, for example, by the Botellas, in their exploration of "figurability", a word drawn from the French translation of what is called "representability" in the English translation of *The Interpretation of Dreams*. A chapter often passed through quickly in studying the Strachey translation of *The Interpretation of Dreams*, "figurability" becomes a source of thinking about the nature of representation in images, and forms the basis of an exploration of the psychoanalyst's capacity to "work in the double", to dream for the patient on the couch what the patient cannot dream himself. Again, in the writing of Andre Green, there is always a rich reworking of Freudian texts to deepen a conceptualisation of emotions, sexuality, drive, destructiveness, and a negativity, or death drive eventually conceived as the attack on representation (Green, 1993). Andre Green will do something Freud did not do, which was to gather up his earlier theory and integrate it with his later structural model, the model rejected by Lacan. But Green's integration will be very different from the structural model of the ego psychologists. It will be French, based on the changes in the theory of the drive as it evolved in Freud's writing, linking those changes with the development of relations to the object. In much of this thinking, concerns linked to one or another element in the Lacanian project are challenged and then reworked, the master Lacan pitted against the grand master Freud, the struggle with Lacan keeping Freud alive in a very particular way in the creative life of French psychoanalysis.

On representation

I think the emphasis on representation in non-Lacanian French psychoanalysis is a heritage of Lacan's powerful invocation of linguistics and his scepticism regarding the vagaries of emotional registration. In 1963, Laplanche did not do away with an emphasis on representations in the mind, but re-established Freud's hypothesis of the kind of representation characteristic of the unconscious. Much of the most interesting developments in French non-Lacanian analysis comes back to the theory of representation, an emphasis driven by the formative encounter with Lacan. The great synthesizer of French psychoanalysis, Andre Green, in *Le Discours Vivant*, published in France in 1970, (much later translated into English as *The Fabric of Affect* in the Psychoanalytic Discourse,) aimed to re-insert and reaffirm the consideration of affect in psychoanalytic discourse, the affect of which Lacan was suspicious. Green's analysis included a study of Freud's difficulty with theorising affect, at the same time, affirming that emotional experience of analyst and analysand is central to the practice of psychoanalysis. He draws on theoreticians outside France, notably Winnicott, although later, he will use Bion, to support this reassertion. But as late as 2005, many years after his affirmative action on the part of affect in the psychoanalytic discourse, when he was again looking at what is essential in the psychoanalytic process, he affirmed that the "essential paradigm" of psychoanalysis is "situated without hesitation on the side of representation". "Affect", of which he had been such a compelling advocate, and of which Lacan was so deeply suspicious, he still placed "second". A point of view which explicitly holds in mind a tension between emotional experience and its apparent representation in language has become a strong thread running through much psychoanalytic theorising in France. It is often linked, as it has been by Green, with a respectful and careful reading of Freud's earliest theories about the formations of symptoms in hysteria, where the separation of affect from idea forms the central understanding of the creation of symptom (Green, Gibeault). But the return to early Freud for confirmation of the first principals in relation to symptom, which is the separation of affect or drive from idea in the symptoms of hysteria, supports a concern which Lacan brought to the foreground. In French Freudian theory, the link between affect and representation is not taken for granted, or assumed to be identical, as for example, in Kleinian theory, where unconscious phantasy and emotional life are hypothesised to be congruent. Rather, the gap between representation and drive, between representation and affect, forms a theoretical foundation both for the formation of symptoms, but also for an understanding of the psychoanalytical process. The break with Lacan opened up a field in which the movement of psychoanalytic discourse is toward greater, more meaningful representation, psychoanalysis itself becoming finally in the later conceptualisations of Andre Green, a "work of representation".

Failure to represent therefore becomes a significant element in the understanding of the work of psychoanalysis, not failure to articulate in words, but failure to form the more primitive, visual images which we are familiar with in dreams. Cesar and Sara Botella (1994, 2005) have become theoreticians of the fundamental and terrible anxiety associated with the loss of a capacity to imagine, to visualise, to represent. The field they explore they call "figurability", a neologism in French, *"figurabilite"*, a translation of *Darstellbarkeit*, the word used by Freud in chapter 6 of *The Interpretation of Dreams* (1900a). In describing the characteristics of the dream, he writes, according to the Strachey translation, that the specific form of any dream depends on "representability", referring to the fact that a dream is a visual phenomenon, dependent on what can be expressed in visual terms. One of the fundamental determinants of the dream, the chapter asserts, is the "consideration of representability". This brief section of chapter 6 is often treated as a more obvious, though philosophically and scientifically necessary observation of the qualities of dream, a less important element of chapter 6 than the discussion of the condensation and displacement of the dream work. In the Botellas' refreshed meditation on "figurability" we see illustrated that French ability to "make Freud work", the enduring impact of the Lacanian imperative, *"lire* Freud". And in the focus on the achievement of representation, there is a mining of the field staked out by the 1963 divergence, a consideration of the processes antecedent to the acquisition of language. From the emphasis on this primitive image-making capacity, linked to hallucinatory images and dreaming, the Botellas theorise the capacity in any analytic situation to contact this dream-like expressiveness in the patient, an expressiveness which can enable a deeper reaching into the realm of the unconscious, a realm according to French theory, associated with a regression that is in fact facilitated by the analytic situation, the couch, the invitation to free associate. I should mention here the precursor to the focus on early forms of representation, the classic work of Piera Aulagnier, who looked at early representation, which she called pictogram, the visual precursor of linguistic symbolisms, the early organiser of experience (Aulagnier, 1975).

Another theoretician of the pre-linguistic phase is Julia Kristeva, who, having been very influenced by Lacan, turned her attention to theorising the pre-linguistic experience of the child, arguing a field of "semiotics" the preverbal "sensory substratum" of language, the realm of Freud's "thing presentations". The psychoanalytic process of free association is understood to open up the possibility of a contact with early experience, conceived as a more fluid "relay" system between signs and drives (Kristeva, 2010, p. 425), the metaphor leading to the earlier experience of metamorphoses. Kristeva, like Pontalis, leans on the philosophical work of Merleau-Ponty, theoretician of that which is "in between" or outside signification. In some of her later work, she utilises her study of Melanie Klein to seek within the analytic discourse the "metaphor incarnate" which is essentially the preverbal substratum of language (Kristeva, 2000, pp. 137–157). Her emphasis, as I understand it, is closer to thing presentation and the body than the visual representations which are the focus of the Botellas' thinking. Kristeva keeps an essentially Lacanian emphasis on the primacy of the Oedipal and the fundamental linguistic endeavour of the "talking cure", the psychoanalytic process. But she theorises the preverbal world which informs the trajectory of the Oedipal complex, eventually entering the debate about unconscious phantasy at its most primitive levels, more intrigued than most French thinkers with Melanie Klein's version of pre-verbal experience. Kristeva turns a post Lacanian sensibility to the exploration of primitive mental life, attending to the non-verbal depths Lacan aimed to structure through the Symbolic, organising power of words—a project that built upon another facet of Lacan's interest in language, namely its poetic effects. Most of her compatriots, also turning their attention to non-verbal or preverbal phenomena, look to Winnicott (1971) for illumination of a period still understood to be filtered through the Oedipal phenomena.

At the same time that Laplanche was laying down his foundations for disagreement with Lacan's linguistic reformulation of Freudian theory, returning to a more classically Freudian hypothesis regarding the stuff of the unconscious mind, Pierre Marty was identifying the specific absence of a wide range of mental functioning in the mind of psychosomatic patients. He articulated a failure to "mentalize" in psychosomatically ill patients, who did not dream or imagine or own an emotional experience on which to reflect or to which to associate. The link between mind and body was truncated, disavowed; reality was clung to with almost the same ferocity as the delusion. Instead of hallucinating, such patients develop physical symptoms, they become physically ill. I have no evidence that Marty and the psychosomaticians, David, de M'uzan, and Fain, were involved in the intellectual struggle with Lacan, but their isolation of the theme of the capacity to imagine, fantasise and symbolise bears some connection with the contemporary concern of those such as Laplanche and Pontalis, who were challenging Lacan's powerful focus on language itself. Marty (Marty & M'Uzan, 1963) and the psychosomaticians train their sights on the absence, the very disappearance of the field which Lacan had identified as the true subject of psychoanalysis. *La Pensée Opératoire*, operational thinking, is thinking stripped of the nuance required of free association. The study of this absence took Marty and his group into the area of early object relations, into the failure in the early relations with the primary object, (Marty, 1958), the absence of an internalised, "living other" as foundation for the "mentalization" of emotional and instinctual life. The psychosomaticians learned to work backwards, gradually moving from a discourse in the language of *la pensée opératoire*, to a more richly associative, creative, discourse (Aisenstein, 1993). Marty's studies bravely put movement toward death into the French discourse, what Marty identified as a death instinct, a response to trauma which sparks a movement toward progressive disorganisation or fragmentation, in extreme cases to physical death. Interestingly, Marty never talks of drive, as do most French clinicians; he stays with an idea of death instinct. But he shows a tension between a movement toward death and a movement toward representation, a tension picked up many years later and theorised by Green (see below). What I want to emphasise here is that in 1963, the year of the split between Lacan and some of his most brilliant students, who would go on to form the APF, the second IPA society in France, other French analysts, the psychosomaticians from the APP, were looking at the field of the psychoanalytic process in a new way, shedding a complementary light onto a field that it seems to me that Lacan initially opened up for exploration and elaboration—the achievements and failures of representation in the mind.

The drives

Interestingly, as Diatkine and others have pointed out, it was Lacan who first insisted that the English Standard Edition translation of Freud's "*triebe*" as "instinct" was incorrect, that the translation in French, should be "pulsion", drive in English, which it remains to this day (Diatkine, 1997). Moreover, Lacan early on identified "pulsion" or the drives as one of the four main areas of psychoanalytic concern (the others being the unconscious, repetition, and transference). Lacan's early precision in relation to the language of psychoanalytic theory, his insistence that Freud's conceptualisation of the *triebe* implies a pressure, a push, a drive, not an instinct, has found an established place in French psychoanalytic thinking. Having spent a major part of his 1964 seminar thinking about the drive, Lacan's focus shifted to its linguistic manifestations—the drive bound up in signifiers and orientated by desire—in the consulting room, its relation more to a desire understood in narcissistic terms, as in fulfilling the desire of the other, than as the derivative of drive itself (Diatkine, 1997). In 1960, in his challenge to Lacan, Laplanche reaffirmed the essential relationship between drives and the unconscious, reiterating Freud's hypothesis in theorising the unconscious as constituted by representations in the mind linked to drives and the thing presentations associated with early experience. Freud's 1915 hypothesis regarding the constitution of the unconscious is profoundly linked to the positing of drives, more so in 1915 than in 1900, when the heart of the dream wish is linked to unconscious infantile wishes not quite yet theorised as drives. As Green points out, drive or pulsion, the term originally insisted upon by Lacan, who aimed to "*lire* Freud" rather than his ego psychological interpreters, carries the meaning of a force, a movement, and a direction. Green has harnessed his theory to the movement of the drives of Freud's late synthesis of life drives and death drives (Freud, 1920g, 1923b), the movement either of the life drives towards what he terms "objectalisation" and towards representation, or away from representation and objects, toward death. The movement away from objects and away from representation are contained within Green's over-arching conception of the Negative (1999, 1993). He has made Freud work, utilising the late conceptions of the id, conceiving the death drive posing a constant pressure on the erotic drive toward attachments, toward object life, others, relationships, the complexity and noise of living, the binding of drives in representation. The death drive is unbinding, not so very different from Marty's conception of progressive disorganisation and fragmentation, except that Green's drive is conceived as a Freudian drive (Freud 1905) that exerts constant pressure on the personality—the human personality engaged in perpetual conflict, always susceptible to a destructive internal drive, a negative force in all human life.

The relationship between the formation of the unconscious and the drives has been theorised by Laplanche quite differently from Green. Laplanche's return to Freud has included a different synthesis of his Lacanian heritage, focused more toward the impact of the adult drives on the infant than on the pressure coming internally from the drives of the infant (Laplanche, 1997). Laplanche's understanding of sexuality and the formation of the unconscious eventually turns on the impact of the adult's sexuality on the child, the inevitable precocious intrusion, the transmission coming from the mother to the child. The sexuality of the mother cannot be metabolised, it overloads the psyche, the encounter is with the unconscious desire of the adult, a primal fantasy forms around this encounter, the origins of the unconscious is constituted in this moment, a moment of intrusion. This original seduction is not seen as pathological although it is essentially traumatic, but as constitutive of the psyche. Laplanche's powerful reworking of Freud and Lacan draws on Freud's first seduction theory, in which Freud conceived psychoneurosis as a product of an infantile traumatic seduction, and Lacan's emphasis on the Other, the impact of the Other on the developing human subject. Laplanche eventually links a first seduction by the mOther with the structuring of the psyche, the establishment of the drive, and the primary structuring phantasies with an experience that he identifies not with language, but with a "message". The encounter with the maternal unconscious is an encounter with a maternal enigma, the "enigmatic signifier". Laplanche's fundamental difference with Lacan here is that he sees the enigmatic quality of the signifier to derive from the signifier itself, rather than from its interplay with other signifiers.

Laplanche and Green, two great theoreticians of the drive in modern non-Lacanian psychoanalysis take opposing positions which mark out a field traversed and elaborated by other theorists. Rene Rousillon, argues that it is not necessary to make a choice between Laplanche and Green (Rousillon, 2010). Rather, he finds the fate of the drives to be a product of the interaction between the more biologically founded drives as conceived by Andre Green, based on Freud's final theory of life and death drives, and the traumatic and formative impact of intrusion by the unconscious of the other, the impact of the "enigmatic message" from the sexually mature adult, aligning himself as well with the trajectory postulated by the post-Lacanian Laplanche. Rousillon, following the logic established in the French Freudian tradition, links the development of the drives with the simultaneous development of representation, the specificity of psychoanalytic thought tracing the vector of "the issues of symbolisation and subjective appropriation" which is at the heart of the psychoanalytic process. I think this linking, so characteristic of French psychoanalytical theorising, bears the mark of Lacan's insistence on the importance of language, his embedding of the sexual, the Oedipus, in the linguistic enterprise and correspondingly, in the psychoanalytic project. Here, as in so much of French thinking, the development of sexuality and drive is enfolded in the meditation on the evolution of representational processes. Rousillon continues, the history of the development of drive, is itself "born in/ of difference" though it aims to "reduce difference", pushing toward a sameness, to "produce the identical of the other", a process that is interfered with by the "father's symbolic function, it is the paternal metaphor that makes it possible to transcend the mastery of the pleasure in the same; it is this that blocks the return to origins, to the identical, and opens the way to a pleasure taken in and by difference" (Rousillon, 2010). Here, in this articulation of the role of the father in the evolution of the drive and in the simultaneous development of symbolic capacity is more than a trace of Lacan. He has surfaced unacknowledged in a specifically French consideration linking the relationship between development, sexuality and representation. Rousillon's focus on the sexualisation of experience leans most heavily on Green's emphasis on the "objectalization" of the life drive, the libidinalisation of experience, the "binding" of the death drive in an attachment to objects. But when tracing the development of the drive, Rousillon draws on the Lacanian notion of the paternal metaphor, the oedipal intrusion on the mother and baby union, and he also makes use of Laplanche's Lacanian coloured notion of the "enigma" of the other. In Rousillon's contribution to psychoanalytic understanding of development, the enigma of the other is partially unveiled in the acquisition of adult sexuality in adolescence. The experience of adult orgasm is understood to transform the relationship to the other and to deepen a relationship to the mysterious unconscious, in both self and other. Here, he is finding a place for "jouissance", also beloved of French psychoanalysis, perhaps French culture more generally, and again a concern associated with Lacan.

One last example, and there are many more, of the evolution of the understanding of the drives which holds such a central place in French psychoanalysis, is the idea of a primary masochism, a conception of Benno Rosenberg. (Rosenberg, 1982 [2010]) He looks to the drives to support a notion usually associated with the development of the ego. He links psychic achievements associated with the capacity to delay gratification, the prerequisite to the development of a thinking capacity, to a masochistic contribution to the possibility of waiting. He shows how the investment of primary masochism in the unpleasure which results from the failures of hallucinatory wish fulfilment wish-fulfilment allows time for the recognition of dissatisfaction with the hallucination, and offers the possibility for an investment in the wish to obtain a real satisfaction. Primary masochism thus supports the capacity to wait and look for a real object. "Masochism insures the duration, the internal continuity; it is the bridge which joins the timelessness of the id to the specific temporality of the preconscious-conscious system." What is particularly interesting is this formulation is that it ascribes a capacity, in psychoanalytic theory normally associated with the development of thinking, an ego capacity, to a drive experience. If it is drive related, thinking escapes association with ego capacity alone, and validates the process within the paradigm central to psychoanalysis, as opposed to the psychology of the ego, the field Lacan had so convincingly critiqued (Rosenberg, 1982).

The role of the Other

Jean Laplanche's theorisation of the "enigmatic signifier" displaces the source of infantile drives from the infantile body where they are so firmly anchored by Freud, (1905) and originates their inception in the infantile encounter with the adult unconscious, in an intrusion by an other, the mother. In Laplanche, the mind of the mother, or more correctly, the impact of the mother's mind on the child, is theorised with great attention, and its ramifications in a psychoanalytic situation creatively and precisely interpreted (Laplanche, 1999). Through Laplanche, the Lacanian insistence on what comes from outside, (Diatkine, 1997, p. 44) including the Lacanian notion that the drives are structured by the desire of the mother, finds fresh meaning. For Laplanche, the drives are established in a first seduction, the infant's first encounter with a sexually embodied adult, and it is this encounter which constitutes the source of primary sexual phantasy, and which is the founding condition of the establishment of the unconscious. It is the mother's indigestible too muchness, her enigmatic message, which activates and shapes the drives and establishes the unconscious. Laplanche links Freud's concept of "primal phantasy", the fundamental phantasies which he hypothesised reached back into racial memory, with individual history, resurrecting the seduction theory with it. There is an original seduction which traumatises everyone, and which necessitates the mental work of unconscious phantasy. Laplanche's theory is a heroic reconfiguration of Freudian thought, a powerful creative reworking of conceptualisations generated by Freud over time, from first theories of the traumatic seduction in the lives of hysterics (1895) to the notion of primal phantasy (Freud, 1916–1917, pp. 370–371).

In the concept of the "Telescoping of Generations", Haydee Faimberg (1987) shows how the traumas of previous generations are transmitted and expressed in unconscious narcissistic identifications which take time to disclose in any analysis. Such identifications are made unconsciously, and transmitted unconsciously, eventually revealing themselves in treatment, but only if the analyst is truly listening. One could say that here again the shadow of Lacan's theory of the impact of maternal desire falls on a theorisation of the narcissistic implications of maternal or familial unconscious identifications. The penumbra of meaning contained in these structuring identifications is profound, something the "listening" analyst is alert to, manifesting itself eventually in the patient's material, disclosing the patient's alienation through the unconscious entrapment in familial identifications.

In the work of Lacan, the maternal unconscious is endowed with an otherness with which the baby both identifies and competes, striving to become whatever it is that she prefers to him, the thing that fills her lack, the phallus linked to the maternal desire. Whatever fulfils the mother colours the auto-erotic representations in the mind of the baby. Michel Fain, a colleague of Pierre Marty and others in the psychosomatic school, was concerned like they were with the capacity for representation, and the failures of representation in psychosomatic patients. He locates in the "*censure d'amant*" the function of the mother who, having provided adequate mothering, that is to say, in classical terms, an adequate "protective shield" in the containing or holding function which protects the baby from too much encounter with the chaos of everyday life, puts the baby to sleep, to regain her relationship to her adult lover. The baby is then left to develop autoerotically, to have his own space, to compensate for the withdrawal of maternal protection and maternal soothing to dream, to hallucinate, to represent (Fain, 1971). In Fain's terms, the protection of the mother and the separation from the mother are complementary, and necessary. But when there is insufficient primary care, inadequate provision of a protective shield, then the gaps in the holes of the care are filled by the baby with more chaotic phallic identifications. There is in the premature triangulation, a fundamentally fetishistic therefore avoidant relation to reality. In such a situation, he posits a potential failure to phantasise because the baby cannot bear the absence, and so he predicts in this intolerance of absence a subsequent failure in access to phantasy. Here access to symbolism is associated with the evolution of a capacity for auto-erotism. Perhaps the shadow of Lacan falls more indirectly here than in the synthesis of Laplanche. I think it is nonetheless present in the emphasis on the maternal connection to the father, the production of phantasy understood to be a product of maternal absence, and the acquisition of representation as precursor to the Symbolic, what Lacan would locate as the process leading to the Paternal Metaphor (Bailly, 2009). In this conceptualisation the maternal putting the baby to sleep so that she can return to her adult lover is conceived as a necessary contribution, the absence of the mother, her great and necessary gift to the child and his capacity for autoerotic experience, hence phantasy, the beginning of the structuring of the Oedipus. In Fain's conceptualisation, the necessary precursor to the creative evolution of this capacity is the "protective shield" function of the maternal, not a function emphasised by Laplanche or Lacan, an emphasis that derives from the ego psychologists, some of whom continued to work and theorise in France.

Fain, a member of the SPP, and also a psychosomatician, working with Marty, de M'Uzan, and David, would be deeply involved with the failures of representation, what Marty called the failure to "mentalize", a characteristic of psychosomatic illness. This group linked early object relations to the establishment of creativity of unconscious life. In this conceptualisation, as is so frequently the case in French thinking, the relationship between drive and representation are at the heart of the concern, Fain describing in the maternal putting to sleep the establishment of what in British theory will come to be called a "dream space", (Khan, 1974) or what, much earlier, Lewin (1946) called the "dream screen", a place for the elaboration of phantasy. Fain, unlike Lewin, unlike the British object relations theorists and unlike Bion, emphasises like Lacan the separation from or absence of the mother at a crucial point.

The imagery of Andre Green's famous conceptualisation of the "Dead Mother" (1986), his study of the impact of a maternal depression on the formation of the psyche, has struck a chord with analysts around the world, and offers another illustration of a particular creative synthesis, here of object relations theory informed by sensitivity to the impact of maternal subjectivity, the desire or absence of desire in the mOther. Green's hypothesis is very much coloured by his reading of Winnicott, and Winnicott's understanding of early mother child relations, but the dark and fixating loyalty to the early impact of early experience with a depressed mother, bears some imprint of the emphasis of Lacan, whose baby is enmeshed in maternal signifiers unless helped out by the necessary intrusion of the father.

Narcissism

The impact of the maternal unconscious on the narcissistic identifications of the child, a primary focus of Lacanian psychoanalysis, has penetrated many conceptualisations of the psychoanalytic process in France. Most French psychoanalysts have taken on board the patient's vulnerability to transferring to the analyst this susceptibility to influence. Throughout much of French psychoanalysis, one sees the sensitivity to problems involved in the psychoanalyst's addressing an ego understood to be narcissistically driven, thereby colluding with a patient looking for instructions on how to please the analyst. Lacan's suspicious study of the ego was first articulated in his brilliant paper presented in its earliest form in 1936, at the 14th IPA congress in Marienbad. He was laying down a gauntlet, tackling the ego psychologists, amongst whom would have been his own analyst, Lowenstein, much as later, Laplanche in 1960, challenged his analyst Lacan's insistence on the linguistic essence of the unconscious. Lacan's image of the toddler before the mirror (Lacan, 1949) is unforgettable, a baby narcissus, in love with his own marvellous reflection, in particular, enthralled by the image of coherence and completeness, particularly in the face of the infant's far less organised experience in the world. This intact image constitutes a major element in Lacan's "Imaginary", the illusory "miscognition (*meconaissance*)" of the ego. A concept sacred to most psychoanalysts, Freud's defining assertion of the origins of the ego in the body (1923) is given a disturbing slant here, the experience of the body shown to be, initially, profoundly disorganised and fragmented, only quite suddenly integrated, not on the basis of a continuing dialectic with experience, but by a surprisingly changed perception of a coherent self. The legacy here is of a radically, irretrievably divided self. Lacan portrays an ego continually seeking to identify with its own ideal, an ideal depicted as an image in the mirror, a narcissistic double, a representation of completeness or unity that is not won out of experience. Paradoxically, for Lacan this enthralling alienation is the precursor to a development of subjectivity that is finally structured by language. Language, associated also with the role of the father, the Name-of-the-Father, orienting the developing child through the confusion or tension between the seductive illusion of completeness, and the fragmentariness of emotional and sexual life, contextualises the developing subject in the world of language, history and culture.

This powerful image of the narcissistically challenged child before the mirror, ensnared in what Lacan would call the Imaginary, might be identified with a child that much of non-Lacanian psychoanalysis chose to rescue. In the words of Pontalis, (Pontalis, 2005) it was the work of Winnicott who liberated the *infans* from Lacan's relegation to the realm of the Imaginary. Winnicott was interested in Lacan's baby and the function of the mirror, but he reconfigured the experience, looking to the relationship of mother and baby, and finding there not primarily the seeds of the narcissistic yearnings of Lacan's baby but rather, the mother, out of primary concern for her baby, mirroring the baby and so providing an experience of recognition and love, an embodied sense of psychosomatic unity, the fundamental basis of identity. In the object relations of Winnicott, the development of symbolic capacity and identity emerge out of an interplay with the mother, out of the illusionment and disillusionments of that unity. He calls the field that opens up in the interplay of mother and child the "transitional space" (Winnicott, 1971), and it is in this field, the field of a much theorised capacity to play, that the capacity to symbolise develops. Here, the capacity to symbolise is not linked to language primarily. So, for Pontalis, another of Lacan's students and analysands who formed the APF in 1963, it is the subjectivity of the *infans* that is of interest. "By *infans* I mean one who lacks words, one who even when he finds words is still searching to regain that which escapes language […] our intense emotions like our instinctual urges can hardly be translated into words" (Pontalis, 2005). The intense emotional life of the baby, of emotional experience generally, is rescued by Winnicott, for the field of psychoanalysis, and was grasped by those who had tired of Lacan's linguistic focus.

It seems to me that there are many ways in which the *infans* or the preverbal realm of the child is theorised in French psychoanalysis that is specific to the background of Lacan's formulation, of an infant theorised as occupying a narcissistic place in the maternal mind, then later, the child grasping the illusion of completeness before the mirror. Didier Anzieu, for example, posed an alternative to Lacan's displacement of the centrality of the body ego, and posited the notion of a "*moi-peau*", a skin ego, the basis for a sense of self that derives from experiences in relationship to a containing object, a mother who handles her infant, and endows the infant with an experience of boundaried, embodied coherence. Anzieu, an analysand of Lacan, returns to the Freud of the body-ego (Freud, 1923b) and draws on the Kleinian, Esther Bick (1968), as well as on attachment theorists, to portray a less pessimistic version of the development of a sense of self, an identity in which the relation to the body is central, one which engages with problems rooted in the experience of the *infans*. This state can in his theory be reached in the analytic situation. For Anzieu, there is a reparative capacity in psychoanalysis due to the creative element fostered by the regressive potential of the therapeutic situation; he shows the patient spinning out of her own words a reparative container, her own "ego skin" (Anzieu, 1989).

Lacan's unforgettable child before the mirror has an historical link with what the Botellas have called "working in the double". They describe the analyst allowing himself an empathic immersion in a patient's communication, accompanying the analysand in a regression, and so becoming the patient's "reflection, his complement [...] functioning as his double" in order to begin to provide the possibility of representation for the patient. In the Botellas' thinking, the analyst dreams on behalf of the regressed and terrified patient on the couch, and so brings the possibility of naming the specifics of the patient's fragile and fragmented identity. They describe an analytic frame containing the otherwise frightening depersonalisation of both patient and analyst, and the discovery in the "uncanny" of that moment a psychic truth of the patient's experience. When "working in the double", the analyst works along the lines theorised in modern French psychoanalysis as that of a "primary homosexuality", a crucial libidinal step in the evolution of the self, invoking a benign involvement, again of the drives (Denis, 1982; Kestenberg, 1984). The Botellas note that "It is above all in French psychoanalytic publications that the notion of the double has developed" (Cesar & Sara Botella, 1995). They go on to acknowledge, not only Freud, in the uncanny and in late thoughts on construction in psychoanalysis, but also Christian David, and Andre Green. They do not honour Lacan, who of course, did not dwell on the immersion in the Imaginary, a field which not only the Botellas have creatively reclaimed. But it was Lacan, who, I think, emblazoned the image of the double, and its narcissistic origins in the *stade de mirroir*, in the minds of French psychoanalysts.

The Botellas have other French colleagues who focus on the analyst's willingness to meet the regressive anxieties of the patient, and in so doing, tolerate an element of depersonalisation in the treatment setting. Michael de M'Uzan writes (1994) of the capacity to tolerate a regression to depersonalisation, and how it can yield the production of a "chimera", a product of the intersection of the patient's experience with the analyst. Michel de M'Uzan was an original member of the psychosomatic school, itself immersed in the task of helping patients who do not have a capacity for libidinal elaboration, which Marty called "mentalization". De M'Uzan's work could be regarded as describing another version of the formal regression exploited by the Botellas, a regression that facilitates a reparation in the psychic field of a patient which eventually supports a move toward symbolisation proper, as conceived by Lacan. These analysts are working in the Imaginary, working with the chimera, working in the double, in the primitive world of experience between identity cohesion and the anxiety of fragmentation and boundarylessness, the experience against which the image in "*le stade de mirroir* defends". Finding representations for this experience, working towards its representation in an analysis which is itself, as Andre Green writes, a "work of representation" describes one of the fertile fields of French psychoanalysis, one related to the work of Ferro, in Italy, and Ogden in America.

The Oedipus

In the face of phenomena that is inchoate, non-verbal, or linked to hypothesised unconscious fantasy, Lacan inserts the structuring role of language, introducing a Symbolic order, identified with an Oedipus that is both limiting and infinitely expressive, articulating an ordering law theoretically linked to the father. This is the way he interprets the words of Melanie Klein, in his early paper on "Discourse Analysis" (1954a). Speaking to a very disturbed, autistic seeming child, he approvingly writes that Melanie Klein does not interpret so much as situate him in the Symbolic, saying as she observes him pick up a toy train, "Dick little train, big train daddy train". In so doing, Lacan asserts, she "plastered on the Oedipus myth" and the child begins at that moment to relate, to Melanie Klein, his analyst, and to his nurse, for whom he suddenly calls out for the first time. At that moment he becomes in Lacanian terms, a subject, and he has entered into the human world.

In the Lacanian narrative of child development, the individual is grounded as a subject by his or her submission to the Name-of-the-Father, the signifier presented by the mother to the child in a metaphoric process as a substitute for the Phallus, the imaginary object of her desire. "*Le Nom du Pere*", or "*le non du pere*" separates the baby linguistically and socially from the mother and displaces the Phallus from the Real of the body to the Imaginary and through acceptance of its loss, to the Symbolic. Lacan's trenching the Oedipal complex in the acquisition of language, so directly illustrated in his early seminar paper, insists on the acknowledgment of an Oedipal element in any verbal interpretation in psychoanalytic treatment. The word and the Symbolic, the foundation of the "talking cure", is linked to the father. In France: "It was Lacan's merit to re-establish the paternal function, not only in neurotic cases with an Oedipal fixation, but in general, in all pathology, each form calling for its own particular theorization from which the place of the father could not be erased" (Green, 2005, p. 187). Most French analysts impressively include an Oedipal element in their interpretations, however enigmatic. Julia Kristeva offers an elegantly French version of the Freudian interpretation of transference, "which in the last instance, is Oedipal—is supposed to transform into perception/verbalisation the inexpressible memory-traces of the more or less traumatic 'thing alone' [*la chose seule*]. This means that the formulation will always be a formulation concerning the Oedipus complex, not to be confused with a formulation that can be reduced to the Oedipus complex." She adds an addendum, in her assessment of the Freudian emphasis, that the "concern to focus listening and interpretation on the analysis of the paternal function and its unbearable fragility is forgetting—or underestimating—the mad endurance of the maternal vocation" (Kristeva, 2007). Kristeva, who has long been associated with her own exploration of "semiotics", non-linguistic signification (Kristeva, 1974), alludes here to her developing appreciation of the Kleinian assessment of unconscious phantasy (Kristeva, 2007). There have, in the meantime, been some reciprocal appreciations from the British Kleinians, where since the end of the twentieth century, the father has reasserted his place in the interpretive theories of those analysts most immersed in the Kleinian conceptualisation of early object relations (Britton, 1997). Thus, a French integration of Lacan's theorisation of the relationship of the father to separation and language, using the Father to triangulate the space of the analytic session, has changed the immersion in the early, infantile phantasy of British Kleinian psychoanalysis. What I wish here to emphasise is the extent to which French psychoanalysts who have absorbed the profundities of early mother child relations—largely but certainly not exclusively through Winnicott, as early object relations have a place in French psychoanalytic theory (Bouvet, Lebovici, Diatkine, etc.)—nevertheless discipline themselves to attend to the Oedipal significance of any transference expression. The *après coup* of early experience is always filtered through an Oedipal encounter however rejected or distorted, and with respect to this understanding, most French analysts are Lacanian.

Après coup

In Lacan's return to Freud, he resurrected the concept of "*Nachträglichkeit*" that had almost been lost in English interpretations of Freud: "The credit for drawing attention to this term must go to Jacques Lacan" (Laplanche & Pontalis, 1967). It is now generally acknowledged that the Strachey translation of *Nachträglichkeit* usually but not consistently as deferred action, contributed to the fading of this concept in the English Standard Edition. In French psychoanalysis, thanks to the deep impression made by Lacan's intervention, the notion of "*après coup*"—the French translation of *Nachträglichkeit*—has come to be understood by most French analysts as fundamental to a psychoanalytical understanding of neurosis, psychic development, and the psychoanalytic process itself. Indeed, the notion of "*après coup*" appears ubiquitously in French psychoanalytic thinking, and it includes an appreciation of the moment to moment evolution of any psychoanalytic situation. This would be a generalised and less specific version of what is sometimes called the dynamic (Perelberg, 2007) interpretation of the meaning of *après coup*, for which Freud's early theorisation of hysteria provides a basis. Freud initially (1895) hypothesised that early sexual trauma, childhood exposure to adult sexuality, is reawakened in the context of sexual development at puberty, flooding the adolescent ego with overwhelming drive related excitement and anxiety. The trauma in adolescence produces the symptoms. The trauma lies in the retrospective linking of the early experience and the reawakening of the drive, now bound to a signifier, in the context of sexual changes after puberty—this linkage is the *après coup*. After 1897, the trauma was linked to infantile sexuality itself, the process of development, successive reawakenings, phantasied interpretations and re-interpretations of drive experience. In 1918, Freud describes the experience of the Wolfman, first as an eighteen-month-old baby witnessing a primal scene which the child later reinterprets, *après coup*, at the age of four, when the Oedipal conflict has set in, and when the issues of sexual identity and castration colour and structure previous experience (Laplanche & Pontalis, 1967). Lacan, who followed Freud in his emphasis on retrospective structuring of sexuality and identity, differs from Freud in that Lacan links the logic of the development specifically to the linguistic notion, the Name-of-the-Father, the acquisition of language. Non-Lacanian French psychoanalysis has generalised the concept, following Laplanche and Pontalis who see *après coup* at the heart of Freudian theory of sexuality, development, trauma, as well as in the structuring function of the Oedipal conflict. And retroactive signification is not limited to the word, though attention to the word remains paramount. As discussed earlier, it is almost universal that in hypothesising the conflicts and identifications of their patients, the French generally refer to their patient's material as having passed through the encounter with the Oedipal conflict, and take it as retrospective organiser.

In a study of why the process of baby observation, a central feature of most psychoanalytic trainings in Britain, has failed to catch on in France, the heritage of Lacan has been convincingly invoked. Houzel shows the marshalling of major French theorists in the rejection of baby observation, amongst them Pontalis (Houzel, 2012; Pontalis, 1979), the very man so pleased to have the *infans*, the child without language, released from the exile to which the theory of Lacan had sent it. Pontalis rejects infant observation on the grounds that the interiority of the baby cannot be observed from outside, the implication is that meaning can only be gleaned in analysis itself, retrospectively, or *après coup*, in the analytic situation, through the words of the patient which are directly linked to the patient's historical evolution. The triumvirate of Pontalis, Laplanche, and Green, have constructed an implacable defence against the seductions of baby observation. They all challenge the usefulness of baby observation, all cast a cold eye on the apparent positivism of the use of observation, all are critical of a model of thinking which "pulls the child in the direction of psychology, pedagogy, relations with the law or medicine [...] tends, ultimately, towards 'family planning'". (Houzel, 2012). This language echoes the criticism of American ego psychology made so convincingly by Lacan in the post war years. Houzel thinks the powerful critics of baby observation in psychoanalytic training base their thinking on the notion of the *après coup*, the retrospective and interior remodelling of early traumatic experience, and he holds Laplanche and Pontalis responsible for elevating this conception to the highest rank of Freudian theory, keeping Lacan alive within the mainstream (Houzel, 2012) (there are, of course, many facets to Lacanian influence; one of Lacan's greatest contributions to psychoanalytic thinking, *le stade du mirroir*, is based on a baby observation by Henri Wallon).

An appreciation of the development of any particular psychoanalytic session is informed by the concept of *après coup*, in the observation of the retroactive trajectory in the free associative and interpretive sense of any given session, Haydee Faimberg, for example, has highlighted the process of "listening to listening". To illuminating effect, she focuses on the changes that are evident in the patient's own reflection of analytic meaning, as it moves within the session. She emphasises the patient's own capacity to listen, to associate or reflect on his own utterance, *après coup*. She theorises the analytic process, and what the French call the cure, in this development of the patient's listening (Faimberg, 1961). Donnet, addressing the function of interpretation in his treatise on the analytic session, writes: "interpretation, when it is mutative—whether it originates from the analysand or the analyst—comes when it wants: it is a matter of *après-coup*, and its emergence is uncertain and unpredictable" (Donnet, 2001). Rather less mysteriously, Green links it specifically with the development of insight, when the patient, in principle, says "I now understand the meaning that I have to give to what happened before" (Green, 2005, p. 229).

In conclusion

There can be no conclusion to this meditation, based as it is on the understanding of an outsider to a large body of work which is by its nature heterogenous, a product of years of historical evolution, reactions, splitting, political and theoretical disagreements, and misunderstandings, accommodations, and syntheses. Nonetheless, what I have highlighted here are some points at which I think, in France, the Lacanian heritage has influenced the non-Lacanian, and in the work touched upon in this essay, in a creative way. I think it is because of Lacan's originality, daring, even fanaticism, that the French analysts remain so committed to and attuned to the unconscious as it is disclosed in the analytic session, and link this unconscious representation with the drives which Lacan first identified as a key to psychoanalytic understanding of the mind, though he later moved away from emphasising their centrality.

In addition to an enriched and liberated exploration of what Lacan relegated to the Imaginary, to the mysteries of affect, to preverbal phenomena, the non-Lacanian French analysts have never lost the grounding in the Oedipus (Kristeva, 2007) and have understood this linking as related to the speech which is the vehicle of analytic work. The limitations of the word as well as the significance of the word informs the stance of the French analysts. Language still represents the fundamental element of the psychoanalytic field, and respect for this fact lies behind the care and precision and minimalism of many interpretations which have come to be understood to be French, in a common understanding of what Widlöcher calls the "culture" of French analysis (Widlöcher, 2001). I think an appreciation of Lacan's contribution can only illuminate the particularity of the non-Lacanian French psychoanalysis which has developed around and *après* his radical intervention. I suspect that just as some knowledge of Lacan helps to understand French preoccupations in psychoanalysis, so does knowledge of French psychoanalysis drive the curious back to Lacan.

References

Aisenstein, M. (1993). The Man from Burma—psychotherapy of a case of haemorrhagic recto-colitis. *Int J Psychoanal, 74*: 371–381.

Anzieu, D. (1989). *Le moi-peau*. Paris: Dunod [The Skin Ego. New Haven, CT: Yale University Press, 1989].

Aulagnier, P. (1975). *La Violence de L'interpretation*. Paris: Presses Universitaires de France [(2001) *The Violence of Interpretation: From Pictogram to statement*. London: Routledge].

Bailly, L. (2009). *Lacan*. Oxford: One World Publications.

Bick, E. (1968). The Experience of the Skin in Early Object Relations. *Int J Psychoanal, 49*: 484–486.

Birksted-Breen, D. (1993). *The Gender Conundrum*. New York: Routledge, 2007.

Birksted-Breen, D. (2003). *Time and the après-coup. Int J Psychoanal, 84*: 1501–1515.

Botella, C., & Botella, S. (1984). L'homosexualité inconsciente et la dynamique du double en séance. *Revue Francaise de Psychanalyse, 48(3)*: 687–708. Revised and reprinted as Working as a Double in *The Work of Psychic Figurability: Mental States without Representation*, (2005) A. Weller & M. Serbib (Trans.). London: Routledge.

Botella, C., & Botella, S. (1995). La Dynamique du Double en séance, *Monographies de la Revue Francaise de Psychanalyse*, reprinted as Working as a Double in *Reading French Psychoanalyse*. Breen, Flanders, Gibeault (Eds.) (2010), p. 378. London: Routledge.

Botella, C., & Botella. S. (2001). *La figurabilite psychique.* Paris/Lausanne: Delachaux et Niestle [A. Weller & M. Serbib (Trans.) (2005). *The Work of Psychic Figurability: Mental States without Representation.* London: Routledge].

Diatkine, G. (1997). *Jacques Lacan.* Paris: Presses Universitaires de France.

Denis, P. (1982). Homosexualite primaire, base de contradiction. In: *Revue Francaise de Psychanalyse, 46(1)*: 35–42 [Primary Homosexuality: A foundation of contradictions. In *Reading French Psychoanalysis.* Birkstead-Breen, Flanders, Gibeault (Eds.). London: Routledge, 2010].

Donnet, J. (2001). From the Fundamental Rule to the Analysing Situation. *Int J Psychoanal, 82*: 129–140.

Duparc, F. (2001). The Countertransference Scene in France. *Int J Psychoanal, 82(1)*: 151–169.

Faimberg, H. (1961). *Listening to Listening* in *The Telescoping of Generations.* New Library of Pychoanalysis, Hove: Routledge, 2005.

Faimberg, H. (1987). *The telescoping of the generations: A geneology of Alienated Identifications in The Telescoping of Generations.* New Library of Psychoanalysis, Hove: Routledge, 2005.

Fain, M. (1971). Prelude a la vie fantasmatique. *Revue Francaise de la Psychanalyse, 35*: 291–364.

Freud, S. (1900a). *The Interpretation of Dreams. S. E., IV & V.* London: Hogarth.

Freud, S. (1905d). *Three Essays on the Theory of Sexuality. S. E., VII.* London: Hogarth.

Freud, S. (1915e). The Unconscious. *S. E., XIV.* London: Hogarth.

Freud, S. (1916–1917). *The Introductory Lectures on Psycho-Analysis.* The Paths to the Formation of Symptoms. *S. E., XVI.* London: Hogarth.

Freud, S. (1918b [1914]). From the History of an Infantile Neurosis. *S. E., XVII.* London: Hogarth.

Freud, S. (1920g). *Beyond the Pleasure Principle. S. E., XVIII.* London: Hogarth.

Freud, S. (1923b). *The Ego and the Id. S. E., XIX.* London: Hogarth.

Freud, S. (1950a). Project for a Scientific Psychology. *S. E., I.* London: Hogarth.

Green, A. (1986). The Dead Mother. In: *On Private Madness.* London: Hogarth Press.

Green, A. (1993). *Le Travail du Negatif.* Paris: Editions de Minuit [The Work of the Negative. A. Weller (Trans.). London: Free Association Books].

Green, A. (1999). *The Fabric of Affect in the Psychoanalytic Discourse.* The New Library of psychoanalysis, London: Routledge, Keegan and Paul [*Le Discours Vivant, la conception psychanalytique de l'affect,* Paris: Presses Universitaires de France 1073].

Green, A. (2005). *Key Ideas for a Contemporary Psychoanalysis.* The New Library of Psychoanalysis, Hove: Routledge.

Houzel, D. (2012). Infant Observation and the French Model. *Int J of Psychoanal, 93(1)*: 181–201.

Kestenberg, J. (1984). *Astrid ou homosexualite, identite, adolescence. Quelque propositions Hypothetiques in Adolescence a vif.* Paris: Presses Universitaires, 1999.

Khan, M. (1974). The Use and Abuse of Dream in Psychic Experience. *The Privacy of the Self.* London: Hogarth.

Kristeva, J. (1974). *La revolution du langage poetique.* Paris: Editions du Seuil [Water, M. (Trans.) (1984). *Revolution in Poetic Language.* New York: Columbia University Press.]

Kristeva, J. (2000). *Le Genie Feminin, Melanie Klein.* Librarie Artheme Fayard [Guberman, R. (Trans.) (2001) *Melanie Klein.* New York: Columbia University Press].

Kristeva, J. (2007). La Cure de Parole. *Revue Francaise de Psychoanalyse. 71, No. 5* [*Speech in Psychoanalysis,* in *Reading French Psychoanalysis,* (2010). Birksted-Breen, Flanders, Gibeault (Eds.). London: Routledge].

Lacan, J. (1949). Le Stade de Miroir comme formateur de la fonction du Je telle qu'elle Nous est révélée dans l'expérience psychanalytique. In: *Ecrits* (1966). Paris: Editions du Seuil. [A. Sheridan

(Trans.) (1977). The Mirror Stage as Formative of the Function of the I as Revealed in Psychoanalytic Experience. In: *Ecrits*. London: Tavistock].
Lacan, J. (1954a). Discourse Analysis and Ego Analysis. In: *The Seminar of Jacques Lacan Book I* (1988). Miller, J.-A. (Ed.). Cambridge: Cambridge University Press.
Lacan, J. (1954b). The Topic of the Imaginary. In: *The Seminar of Jacques Lacan, Book I* (1988). Miller, J.-A. (Ed.). Cambridge: Cambridge University Press.
Lacan, J. (1973). *Le Séminaire, Vol XI*. Paris: Editions Seuil.
Laplanche, J. (1989). *Towards a General Theory of Seduction*. In: *New Foundations for Psycho-analysis*. D. Macey (Trans.). Oxford: Blackwell, pp. 104–116.
Laplanche, J. (1997). The Theory of Seduction and the Problem of the Other. *Int J Psychoanal, 78*: 653–666.
Laplanche, J. (1999). *Essays on Otherness*. London: Routledge.
Laplanche, J., & Pontalis, J. B. (1964). Fantasme originaire, fantasmes des origins, origine du fantasme [Fantasy and the origins of sexuality]. *Int J Psychoanal*.
Laplanche, J., & Pontalis, J. B. (1967). *Vocabulaire de la Psychanalyse*. Paris: Presses Universitaires [Nicholson-Smith, D. (Trans.) (1973). *The Language of Psychoanalysis*. London: Hogarth & Institute of Psychoanalysis].
Lewin, B. D. (1946). Sleep, the Mouth and the Dream Screen. *Psychoanalytic Quarterly, 15*: 419–434.
Marty, P. (1958). La relation objectale allergique. *Revue Francaise de Psychanalyse, 22*: 5–29.
Marty P., & M'Uzan M. de (1963). La pensée operatoire. Intervention sur le rapport de M.Fain et Ch David: *Aspects fonctionnels de la vie onirique Revue francaise de psychanalyse, XXVII*: 345–356.
de Mijolla, A. (2004). Quelques particularites de l'histoire de la psychanalyse en France. In: Gibeault & A. Rossokhin. *Anthologie de la psychoanalyse contemporaine* (In Russian) [Breen, Flanders, and Gibeault (Trans. & Eds.) (2010). Some distinctive features of the history of psychoanalysis in France. In: *Reading French Psychoanalysis*. London: Routledge].
M'Uzan M. de (1994). *La bouche de L'inconscient*. Paris: Galimard.
Perelberg, R. (2006). The Controversial Discussions and Apres coup. *Int J Psycho-Anal, 87*: 119–2220.
Pontalis, J. B. (1979). La Chambre des Enfants. *Nouvelle Revue de Psychanalyse, 19*: 5–11.
Pontalis, J. B. (2005). Notable Encounters. Paper presented at the British Psychoanalytic Society.
Roudinesco, E. (1990). *Jacques Lacan and Co: A History of Psychoanalysis in France, 1925–1985*. London: Free Association Books.
Roussillon, R. (2010). Sexualisation and Desexualisation in Psychoanalysis. In: *Reading French Psychoanalysis*. Birksted-Breen, Flanders, Gibeault (Eds.). London: Routledge.
Rosenberg, B. (1982). Masochisme mortifiere et masochisme gardien de la vie. In: *Les Cahiers de Pscyhoanalyse et Psychotherapie, 5* [Birksted-Breen, Flanders, and Gibeault (Trans. and Eds.) (2010). In: *Reading French Psychoanalysis*. London: Routledge].
Sechaud, E. (2008). The Handling of the Transference in French Psychoanalysis. *Int J Psycho-Anal, 89(5)*: 1011–1028.
Widlöcher, D. (2001). Que sont devenues les voies de la psychoanalyse: L'evolution des pratiques en France (2001). In: A. de Mijolla (Ed.). *Evolution de la Clinique psychanalytique*. Paris: L'Esprit du Temps [Breen, Flanders, Gibeault (Trans. and Eds.) (2010) What has become of the lines of advance in psychoanalysis: the evolution of Practices in France. In: *Reading French Psychoanalysis*. London: Routledge].
Winnicott, D. W. (1971). *Playing and Reality*. London: Tavistock.

CHAPTER THREE

Editors' introduction

S. Bailly

There exists a tension between the solitariness of the psychoanalyst at work, where each faces the analysand alone with only the understandings, strengths, and weakness of his or her own psyche as their tools, and the gregariousness of the psychoanalytic movement, with its many societies, associations and groupings. The link between connectedness and creativity has been much discussed, and Lacan's contribution to the process and structure whereby psychoanalytic advance could be made is one that has not received much attention since his death. Cormac Gallagher's paper is a fascinating stroll through the part of the history of the Lacanian movement in which the issue of working in groups was brought to the fore by Lacan's ambitious Founding Act. Gallagher charts the fate of this Act from its inception in the storm in which Lacan was stripped of his accreditation as a training analyst, to the dissipation of the cartels after his death, and in doing so resurrects the important question of what kind of social structure is most conducive to the advancement of psychoanalysis.

CHAPTER THREE

The Founding Act, the Cartel and the Riddle of the Plus One*

Cormac Gallagher

> When, after passing through a narrow defile, we suddenly emerge upon a piece of high ground, where the path divides and the finest prospects open up on every side [...] we find ourselves in the full daylight of a sudden discovery. (Freud, 1900a, p. 200)

For Freud, this sudden discovery was that his method revealed the dream as the fulfilment of a wish and, upon the notion that it was the first in a series of formations of the unconscious, he constructed the whole of psychoanalysis. For Lacan, the sudden discovery was that psychoanalysts could work together in a school held together by a new social bond founded on the psychoanalytic discourse, and that the cartel was the basic organ that would allow such a body to be established.

The strange fact is that in neither the Ecole Freudienne de Paris during his lifetime nor in any of the schools and associations that lay claim to Lacan's inheritance has this basic organ of the cartel functioned in the way that he envisaged. In particular the element that he described as "PLUS ONE"—in capitals in his text—has been volatilised, so that Guy Le Gaufey, who organised the 1975 EFP debate on the cartels, can say that Lacan accepted that it was a "latent infinitude" and Christian Fierens who presides over an association based on cartels can say that "I have heard a lot about it but I have never come across a genuine +1".[1]

What if the dream came true?

There is very little in the rhetoric of the Founding Act that is not familiar to readers of the Lacan of the 1950s and early sixties, covering as it does his grievance against Anglo-Saxon

*A version of this paper first appeared in Issue 44 of *The Letter, Summer 2010*. We thank the editor of the Letter for permission to produce this version.

psychoanalysts and conviction that their way would lead to a "complete regression to pure and simple psychologism"; nor is there much originality in the three broad themes proposed for investigation: the nature of a training—for Lacan didactic—analysis, the clinical applications of psychoanalysis, the assessment and criticism of what passes for psychoanalysis in learned journals. And the idea of working in small task-oriented groups was very much in the spirit of the anti-authoritarian sixties.

Yet Lacan seemed to believe that he was taking a new and unprecedented step forward in his own engagement with the psychoanalytic cause and in what he was demanding of potential followers. The theatrical gesture that had him record his text and then have it played to his pupils and colleagues in his absence had more than an echo of General de Gaulle's 1940 radio broadcast calling his defeated countrymen to arms. And the opening words: "*Je fonde ...*" seems to give credibility to the proposition of a Belgian analyst that Lacan felt that while Freud had invented psychoanalysis, he himself had "founded" it. For Lacan's constant reproach to Freud was that he was ultimately responsible for the pitiful state of analysis by his failure to isolate a specific psychoanalytic discourse and in having left his momentous discovery in the hands of masters and academics.

But is there any justification for such a belief? If we look for what is radically original in Lacan's Founding Act, we are brought back to the paragraph in which the structure and function of the basic organ of the school is declared:

> For the execution of the work, we shall adopt the principle of sustained elaboration in a small group. Each of these (we have a name to designate these groups) will be composed of three people at least, of five at most, four is the right measure. Plus One charged with the selection, with the discussion and with the outcome to be reserved to the work of each.

Two initial remarks. First, the insistence on a range of four to six people to constitute a small group is not usual in group work—even when it is inspired by analysis. Second, the Plus One is *Plus Une* in the text and thus agrees in gender with the French *personnes* who make up the rest of the group. This will be central to the later acrimonious discussions on whether Lacan intended the Plus One to be incarnated in a real individual or simply saw it as referring to some imaginary or symbolic presence.

In the years that followed the Founding Act there is little trace of a discussion on the structures it lays down. But when the place of the cartels in the school does come up in the mid to late 1970s, most debate and disagreement came to centre not on the notion of the small working groups, but on the nature and role of what had initially seemed to be the clear, if radical, insistence on introducing an additional active agent—the *Plus Une*—to steer the work of their participants.

From directing an analysis to directing a school

Lacan does not simply found a school. In the opening sentence of the Founding Act he promises to personally direct it for the next four years. It is hard not to see in this choice of words a reference to "The Direction of The Treatment" (Lacan, 1966a) written six years earlier, which contains a rebuke to psychoanalysts who had forgotten Freud's basic recommendation—that of the application of certain fundamental rules. Freud had insisted that the effective use of the psychoanalytic method "involves some psychological preparation of the patient. We must aim at bringing about two changes in him: an increase in the attention he pays to his own psychical perceptions and the elimination of the criticism by which he normally sifts the thoughts that occur to him" (Freud, 1900a, p. 175).

Lacan's view was that neglecting this fundamental rule has led analysts into the error of seeing themselves as educators and models of the normal behaviour they hope to produce in the patient. But if the analyst "must not direct the patient" in the sense of making lengthy interpretations according to ideological models, Lacan insists that the treatment is nonetheless given its direction from the start by the analyst making clear the fundamental rules and ensuring their application. Lacan felt to be "a pretext" the idea that somehow the analysand would apply the rules better without thinking about them or perhaps even without having them made clear at the start.

It was perhaps with this in mind that Lacan laid out his Founding Act: the direction of the school also required some psychological preparation of those who want to commit themselves to the re-conquest of the Freudian field from those who illegitimately dominate it. What stands out here is that this notion of "training" seems to be more akin to the preparation of workers in the field of spirituality, rather than for a scientifically based profession. What it means in practice is nailed down by what reads at first sight as a shockingly doctrinaire prescription:

> Those who come to this School will commit themselves to fulfilling a task submitted to both internal and external supervision. In exchange they are assured that nothing will be spared so that everything valuable they do will have the repercussions it deserves, and in the appropriate place. (Lacan, 1964a, paragraph 4)

If you want to be part of this enterprise it is not enough to work—you have to work under supervision (the French *contrôle* sounds even more restrictive!) which is further qualified as "*both internal and external*" and your recompense will be that what you produce will be assured of an "*appropriate*" fate. There are of course profound psychoanalytic resonances here that recall the twin mechanisms of prohibition and promise crucial in the dissolution of the Oedipal crisis. But on the face of it, this is an outrageous interference with scientific investigation and academic freedom and goes way beyond the prescriptions of the IPA which simply required adherence to the easily understood professional norms of an approved training and a respect for the patient's right to acceptable standards of treatment in terms of time and money.

"Denouncing deviations and compromises ..."

Lacan's wish that his school would serve to "expose the deviations and compromises that deaden the progress and degrade the use" (Lacan, 1964a, paragraph 2) of psychoanalysis raises issues that have plagued psychoanalysis from its beginnings—"who has a right to be called an analyst?", or even more fundamentally "what is psychoanalysis?" In Freud's early circle Jung, Rank, Adler, and Ferenczi, to take only the personalities who have left prominent movements behind them, each had their own version of the crucial features of the theory and practice of the new science of the unconscious. Freud, as Lacan repeatedly pointed out, had despaired of ever forming a coherent body based on his own idea of analysis and after an abortive attempt to protect his teaching through a secret committee had confided this task to an international organisation inspired more by ideas of professionalism than by doctrine. And so it was that at the International Congress in London, after reporting the shock of some IPA colleagues that the secession of the French group was not based on a scientific disagreement, Lacan records the reaction of the "penetrating Mr Walder [...] that if we were to confront the principles on which each one believed his experience was founded, our walls would very quickly dissolve into the confusion of Babel" (Lacan, 1966b, p. 239, my translation).

Lacan saw his return to Freud as a return to the fundamental truths of his doctrine. Although "truth" and "doctrine" are notions that scandalise the scientific community, he argued that they are essential reference points to ward off a psychological relativism which is completely inadequate to ground psychoanalysis as the science of desire.[2]

I believe that it is in this context that the central role of supervision is to be understood and that the Plus One—even though his role seems to be advisory—is part of this attempt to ensure a purity of doctrine without which the whole Freudian discovery is "degraded". The Founding Act was after all produced at the end of a year in which Lacan had put forward the view that the fundamental concepts of psychoanalysis were not to be found in the stages of developmental psychology, nor in the cultivation of ego strengths based on the reality principle, but in the largely neglected fundamental foursome of the Unconscious and Repetition, Transference, and the Drive[3] (Lacan, 1977).

"What guides me ..."

It is at the end of the adjoining note to his Founding Act that we discover Lacan's motive in founding a school. Many of his pupils and colleagues had accepted the demand of the IPA that Lacan be removed from any position where he could influence the training of new analysts. But it was only as a "training analyst" that he had, against considerable opposition, been able to adequately train a certain number of pupils, and his restriction to a strictly teaching role, without undertaking the accompanying didactic analyses and supervision, would have rendered him no more than an interesting and eccentric academic performer.

> To those who may question themselves about what guides me, I will unveil its reason. The teaching of psychoanalysis cannot be transmitted from one subject to the other except along the paths of a work-transference. The "seminars", including my lectures at Hautes Etudes, will found nothing, if they do not refer on to this transference. No doctrinal machinery, and especially mine, however auspicious it may be for the direction of work, can prejudge the conclusions that will remain from it. (Lacan, Founding Act, 1964b)

And the "school" itself "is to be taken in the sense that, in ancient times, it meant certain places of refuge, indeed operational bases against what could already be called the malaise of civilization" (Lacan, 1964a, preamble).

This dense apologia meant in practice that a place now existed where those who wanted to restore the cutting edge to psychoanalysis, could find in the company of others, direction and support for their efforts.

But there is a novel condition for entry: "People will join the School by presenting themselves to it in a working group constituted as I have said" (Lacan, 1964a, section 3).

Is the Founding Act a practical proposition?

In fact, the condition of entry to the school—belonging to a cartel—was almost never fulfilled and indeed Christian Simatos, who was Secretary of the EFP throughout most of its existence, is reported as saying that J.-A. Miller and some colleagues from the Ecole Normale Supérieur were the only ones who initially applied for admission as an already functioning working group. In addition, the "school" itself failed ever to cohere, as we shall see later. So, did the whole grand project really hang on the charismatic position of a unique personality? And does the failure effectively to implement it over the past fifty years, and the abandonment of the numerical limits and the Plus One, simply confirm that fact? Before we can answer this, let us look at the practical details proposed by Lacan.

Directorship: Setting a time-limit of four years to his own involvement as director strongly suggests that Lacan assumed that others would assume that post once the school had survived the current crisis. The functioning of the school was intended to be "*easy to program*" and it seems to have been designed to ensure that all the members would be able to get on with their analytic work without being bogged down by bureaucratic procedures. In addition, even though there is provision for a committee and a general meeting, the "*circular organisation*" and the permutation of the membership of the groups would guard against the setting up of individual "*fiefdoms*" that would obstruct the work.

Training: The modification of subjective positions, in particular one's ethical stance with regard to desire,[4] through the experience of personal analysis, is what most distinguishes the analyst from other specialists in mental health. But the way in which the small group was to be set up also involves a serious personal involvement and one that is designed to have an ongoing formative effect. Even though one would join the school in a group "constituted by mutual choice", the permutation of its elements was designed to ensure a constant challenge to the Imaginary, narcissistic bonds that unite a band of brothers or sisters. The limitation of four to six members avoids the traps of both the one-to-one mirror relationship and the escape into a large group where patriarchal leadership figures can emerge to spare the individual the anxiety of having to take up her or his own position.

Supervision and criticism of work: For an analyst, consulting a supervisor is an ongoing requirement in learning the trade, but in the school founded by Lacan, the school itself and the model it used was to be scrutinised. Lacan specifically invited the small groups he had created to submit his own work to examination and criticism:

> What I suggest should be studied are the features whereby I break away from the established standards of didactic analysis, as well as the effects that my teaching is said to have on my analyses when my analysands attend my courses as pupils. If it is really necessary in this teaching, I will include the only dead-ends borne of my position in such a school, that is to say the ones that the induction of my teaching will engender in the work of the school [by which he means the dead-ends or contradictions that arise out of his position of opposition to the idea of didactic analyses]. (Lacan, 1964a, section 1)

The criticism and supervision is envisaged as running parallel to the role of the instructions and interventions of the analyst in the course of a treatment, and will bring to those who accept it an ever-keener awareness of the way in which their own complexes interfere with their analytic work and allow them to achieve what they really desire.

Why Plus One?

"Plus One charged with the selection, with the discussion and with the outcome to be reserved to the work of each" (Lacan, Founding act): In later years, a suspicion arose that some of Lacan's successors saw the Plus One as an instrument to be used in the ideological control of a quasi-military organisation, modelled along French Revolutionary lines. In 1789 the Revolution appointed supervisory officers to its forces to provide political education and ensure loyalty to the revolutionary cause, and this notion of a commissaire politique was adopted by the Russian Provisional Government in 1917 to ensure the same ideological conformity.

But the original emphasis on the non-hierarchical, circular nature of the organisation argues against the notion of the Plus One as an instrument of centralised control. Philippe Girard, in an intervention praised by Lacan, admired the concept of the cartel but questioned its effectiveness. His remarks are worth quoting at some length:

> Is the cartel not a way to avoid two types of groupings or of regroupings, let us say a totalitarian type with phenomena of identification etc., and a type which is currently that of liberalism. In other words the Plus One functions as an instrument to avoid what one could call mass psychology with all the effects that one knows, and on the other hand not to sink into a republic of egos which is obviously equally fictitious. Under what conditions can we escape from these two modes of social institution of social bond? If we had to define the function of cartels, it would be with respect to this; by taking into consideration the dominant forms of the past like the army, the church, more recently the party [...]. (p. 238)[5]

How does the choice of the three functions delegated to this Plus One contribute to this goal? It seems to me that they can be best viewed as editorial. You come to the school with the title of the work that you intend to pursue, but Lacan was aware that good intentions have a habit of remaining just that: "let us remember that the worst objection that can be made to Societies in their existing form is the drying up of work, manifest even in the quality, that they cause among the best of people" (Lacan, Founding Act, 1964a).

The Plus One in an editorial role would do the sort of things that good editors do when they are offered a piece of work—sharpen the focus and select the best line of approach, discuss ways of approaching the task, find the best medium in which the work can be communicated. And when all is said and done, Lacan insists: "the success of the School will be measured by the production of work that is acceptable in its proper setting" (Lacan, 1964a).

A final point is that the responsibility of the Plus One is limited to the production of this work: she or he is not a group analyst and is not concerned with the internal dynamics of the group or with the direct creation of the new kind of social bond that is envisaged. But Lacan's insight seems to be that without the Plus One the bond linking the members to one another and to the school would be different as would the quality of the work that is produced.

The "cartel"

When hearing the word "cartel" for the first time one may think of its resonances of political and business combinations or even international drug-dealing. How could this word be fit for purpose to describe the basic unit of a school of psychoanalysis? At best, one may think that the word may not have the same connotations in French, but in fact, "cartel" in French has pretty much the same sense as in English. However, in both languages these popular meanings appeared only in the twentieth century. *The Concise Oxford Dictionary* defines it as a "written challenge to a duel" but it also means "a written agreement as to an exchange of prisoners". A duel is after all involves not just the two combatants but their seconds and a referee—four plus one as in the ideal cartel. And just as in a duel—as in any serious analysis—the stakes are high. However, Guy Le Gaufrey, on reading a longer version of this paper, remarked that the meaning of cartel as "challenge to a duel" was a rather unknown meaning for French people. He suggested that it was not present in Lacan's choice of this term.

The cartel study days, 1975

The spirit without the form

One way of summarising the fate of the cartels after the Founding Act is that while the signifier remained, the signified was forgotten. Nowhere does this appear more clearly than in the three set-piece discussions on the 12th and 13th of April 1975 in which large numbers of the school participated and in which Lacan was pushed to express his own position on the crucial issues of the Plus One and the three-five restriction on members.

Guy Le Gaufrey had begun the morning session by pointing out that the study days had been organised by a cartel comprising Eric Laurent, Erik Porge, Juan David Nasio, and himself under the "impulsion" of Solange Faladé, but the afternoon plenary session began with the chairman, Pierre Martin, striking a rather pessimistic note and feeling it necessary to remind his audience of the basic proposals of the Founding Act regarding the cartel:

> It is in effect interesting, sometimes even a little bit disturbing, to note how these cartels are constituted most of the time. The cartel, in the perspective of the Freudian school, is not a meeting of people who simply want to meet to exchange ideas, still less is it a locus for direct or magisterial teaching, in a small group. What the cartel is concerned with is to be found very explicitly and in a very clear fashion in the Founding Act of the school in 1964 eleven years ago. What we want to encourage among you, is in some way to resurrect a text and its implications which remain, we have to admit, completely under a veil [...] it is not in this spirit, I believe, or rather in this form that most of the cartels that I know about are constituted and work. (p. 219)

He goes on to specify that his concern regarding the constitution of the cartels he has come across is precisely the Plus One. His question to his colleagues is:

> What place have you given in the creation and the organisation of your working group to this little word: Plus One? It is not a matter of un en plus (an additional one), of three plus one equals four, or four plus one equals five, it is: *plus une;* there is something here that was, I am convinced, put in that way to give rise to a whole problematic.

The lure of the Borromean knot

And Lacan, in his first contribution to the debate, agrees:

> Martin was quite right to intervene on this point. I mean that this Plus One would have deserved a better fate …

This might have lead to a debate on the practical aspects of the cartel but Lacan is in the full sweep of his discovery of the Borromean knot and its possible role in the ultimate attempt to mathematicise psychoanalysis, and the Plus One he is concerned with is no longer that of Founding Act but the much more enigmatic additional ring that he is exploring in his current seminar on the *R.S.I.*

> [...] since to the best of my knowledge it does not seem that this thing which truly, I don't want to be boasting about having anticipated in that something that I am trying to articulate in the form of the Borromean knot. One cannot fail to recognise in this Plus One the something which I obviously did not tell you the last time because I do not always manage in a seminar to say everything that I have contributed but anyway which is to be referred strictly to what I would write as X+1 it is very precisely what defined the Borromean knot, starting from the fact that it is by withdrawing this 1, which in the Borromean knot is any one whatsoever, that one obtains from it a complete individualisation, namely that what remains—namely in terms of the X in question—there remains only the one by one. (p. 220)

This intervention was to leave the field open to those who wanted to theorise about the Plus One and eventually culminates in Daniel Sibony—who admits that he has never been in a cartel—proposing the term "latent infinitude" which Lacan accepted, justifying a shift from the "problematic" of the real Plus One to its mystification. He is delighted to find someone who has worked in a group of mathematicians:

> When mathematicians get together, there is incontestably this plus one. Namely that it is quite striking that the mathematicians, I could say, they don't know what they're talking about, but they know who they are talking about, they are talking about mathematics as if it were a person. One might say up to a certain point that what I might call my wish was, in the functioning of groups, that they would function like any group of mathematicians function. (p. 224)

But how can this Plus One of the mathematicians perform the tasks the Plus One of the Founding Act is charged with?

Imaginary and absent presences

Lacan goes on to inquire into the concrete experience of those present, since whatever the logico-mathematical reasons for the way he has structured the elements of the school "it is first of all necessary that the thing should be put to the test" and on current evidence "[…] the School has perhaps not really yet begun to function. We could say that. Why not?"

Colette Soler is the first to be called to testify to her experience of the cartel and her answer will set the tone for the pattern of avoidance that will follow. What does she make of the notion of a real agent to supervise and criticise, to select, discuss, and determine an outcome for the work produced?

> […] the question that I have asked myself is whether in fact the Plus One should necessarily be a person […] the element which made the connection was perhaps the idea that we were attached to the School by means of the cartel or perhaps to your name, I don't know. But I don't see, at the level of a person, who had a role in the group of the Plus One. (p. 222)

This is followed by another exchange:

Jacques Lacan:	What is it that fulfils this role according to you, in your group?
Maurice Alfandari:	I don't know. I think it is because I don't know that it functions.
Jacques Lacan:	Yeah … [laughter].

Alfandari argues his position by suggesting that the role of the Plus One is most effectively held by whoever happens to be absent from a particular meeting. This is not what the Founding Act says but Lacan is determined to cut his interlocutor as much slack as possible:

> There is no trace of a signal by absence in my "Plus One" of the text, but why not question oneself about this; there is perhaps a certain angle from which this person can be focussed in the absent person, your experience of a cartel may suggest some answer to you on this point. (ibid)

There is much, much more along this line—"That's the Plus One …? The one who doesn't understand anything? Why not? [laughter]"—with Lacan being extraordinarily tolerant with whatever was being said. Here is Pierre Kahn, speculating on whether the Plus One being a real person would have affected his work:

> The question that I am posing after what Martin set out earlier is the following: this work which was satisfying for me, what difference would have been introduced into it if the Plus One which was there imaginarily had been not an imaginary person but a real person. Without being able to advance very far on this I want simply to express my conviction that there would certainly have been an influence on the work if the Plus One person had been something other than the imaginary person that each one put there, certainly. (pp. 223–224)

There is one real person that Lacan warns against and that is the one who assumes the mantle of leader. The cartel must function in a psychoanalytic way, one which he is exemplifying by his patient questioning and his refusal to adopt the role of master:

> [...] habitually, make no mistake, it is a habitus, habitually it is always the same person and this is what people resolve on without measuring the consequences of it, I mean that everyone is very happy that there is one who acts as what we currently call the leader, the one who leads, the Führer [...] this Plus One is always present in some form or other that can be absolutely incarnated, the case of the leader is manifest but analysts can notice that in a group there is always a Plus One and adjust their attention to that. (pp. 224, 226)

"We had never really read the Founding Act ..."

In the discussion, Jacques Crépin honestly stated what appears to have been the situation of most of the members present:

> Currently and from the beginning there are nine of us; I must admit that it is only since yesterday evening and since this morning that we have begun to pose the question about the three and six. I would also say that we had not reflected on the question of the Plus One, probably moreover because at the time we set up the cartel we hadn't really read the Founding Act of the aforesaid cartels. (p. 243)

Lacan's clarification of his reasons for constructing the Founding Act in the way he did may be taken as a direct response. As regards the Plus One:

> I wanted to make of it by this text, something altogether nodal for the formation of a small group. The fact that it is small is altogether essential, it is essential for its functioning; if I said that it can't go beyond six, it's for the best of reasons, it is for theoretical reasons that are very profound. Taking on a very large group involves such limitations, this is what I think at least, that there is not much to be expected from it in terms of real progress on the effects of analysis. This is what inspired me when I produced this Founding Act and to which after all I have no reason for thinking that you should in principle be resisting. I absolutely cannot see what could justify this resistance, especially if what I was trying to get from a certain number of you, all of whom I thank, what I tried to get from a certain number was: to put it on the agenda. (p. 228)

The exchange with Safouan

Possibly because so many of the senior members of the school—Clavreul, Leclaire, Dolto, etc.—had not thought it important enough to be present, Lacan is anxious to engage those who were. His questions to Jenny Aubry did not lead very far but, once he had given Moustafa Safouan time to reflect over lunch, he was luckier.

Safouan: I had time to read the Founding Act. I noticed that I had forgotten this text.
Lacan: You're not the only one!

He has an obvious question that has not been clearly put before: "Why is the term Plus One underlined? It is even the only term that is underlined in the text. Why were you concerned to underline this term?"

And he is rewarded with an answer that shows that Lacan had been deliberately provocative but that it had taken a long time for people to react: "First of all so that people would notice it, which in fact has only happened recently [...] this Plus One which has become such a riddle [...]."

Safouan's quick read of the Founding Act has left him with some interesting ideas of his own about this riddle. His first thought is that "it is a function like the Socratic maieutics" but then he decides that this is too pretentious:

> I don't know why I had made such an exaggerated idea of it that I went so far as to talk about Socrates, but as I can glimpse it here I see the function would be completely comparable to the function of tutor in an English college; I want to stress everything that relates not to a theoretical direction but an arrangement which has an empirical character; I repeat the style appears to me to be that of a tutor in Cambridge or Oxford charged with the selection, the discussion and the outcome of the work of each individual. It is not his function to knot the relation between him and the other members of the cartel, but to support the relationship that each one may have in his work to what he has to say. That seems to me to constitute the essential of the function.

Lacan seems very happy with this way of putting things and goes as far as to say that this was why he had wanted Safouan to speak. But there is one further point that he has picked up on: "Has it happened effectively after a certain time of functioning that the elements of a group are permuted into another? Because it seems to me that precisely without this permutation, the rest has no value. But has that been done?"

Again he elicits an important remark, reflecting Lacan's dismal assessment of how his plans for the School have been implemented: "It has never been done ... There is no kind of veritable realisation of a cartel" (pp. 248–251).

The Plus One and mathematics

Daniel Sibony's dialogue with Lacan is the most substantial of the study days both in the sense that it occupied most of the Sunday afternoon session and that it seems to have changed Lacan's position on the nature of the Plus One and led him to accepting, despite his immediately preceding approval of Safouan's remarks, that it did not have to be incarnated in a real person. The *R.S.I.* seminar, with its complex formulations on the Borromean knot, is nearing completion and it is within this context that Sibony situates his argument.

The mathematical abstractions he develops are beyond me, as indeed was the case with Nasio, Nassif, and Safouan. But they delighted Lacan and indeed help him to develop his idea that the model for the cartel was the group of mathematicians who made progress in their field by addressing themselves to a personification of mathematics which for them took the place of the Plus One.

Here is something of the tone. Sibony:

> By reason of the effects of speech, human sets however small they may be, know both the sensible determinations of their manifest finitude—there is no infinite meeting of individuals—and, in addition to this manifest finitude, the paradoxes of what one could call their latent infinitude which comes there as an extra imposition, which comes to overdetermine in a crushing and plural way the individuals who are present. Thus the effect by which such a set flees the fact that there are leaks [...].

It is here that Lacan makes his fatal response: "Latent infinitude, that is precisely what the Plus One is."

And Sibony replies: "Precisely, that was what I was trying to articulate. Therefore, the effects by which such a set is closed or is opened, that of its pulsations finally is the effect by which there is traced its frontiers and its limits" (pp. 251–252).

The cartel with its Plus One is there to support the individual subject in his relationship to psychoanalysis just as the mathematician is sustained in his work by his relationship to mathematics.

> A mathematician in mathematics is dealing with a person [...]. It is not the mathematical community which is the final judge. The proof is when Cantor put forward his whole machine, there were some mathematicians who spat in his face, and at the same time he felt that he was mad. But all the same he held on and he continued. He was dealing with mathematics. It is not at all the same thing for analysis because analysis is still to be created [...]. (p. 256)

And so, for now at least, the psychoanalyst needs an interlocutor to whom he can address his work. It is not the IPA or any other of the conventional groupings that can provide this support. It required the subtle genius of Lacan to develop the kind of group that could. But as he surveys his school, eleven years on, he seems to be taking the view that his message had not been heard.

A further discussion on cartels took place in November 1975 and Lacan, though he was not present during it, took the opportunity, in his closing remarks, to reflect on the report he had received. Here, Lacan's position on the "*un en plus that I formulated*" seems to amount to a definite repudiation of the Founding Act: "Nothing indicates in what I wrote that the *un en plus* should be incarnated".[6]

However, this did not settle the matter, and instead we entered into a period of confusion. For as the cartels were resurrected there was no doubt that the form they took and the pronouncements attributed to Lacan in his final seminars point very distinctly to a real live Plus One who "if he may be anyone at all, must be someone", charged once more with very specific tasks (Lacan, 1980).

Let us now turn to this difficult and contradictory phase in the history of the cartels.

The revival of the cartels and the dissolution of the school

The neglect of the cartels

In the 1975 discussions, Lacan's disappointment at the fact that the Founding Act had not been implemented is palpable and he seems driven to cling to theoretical abstractions about numbers and the Plus One as a way of getting at least some return for his current reflections on the Borromean knot from a program of training that had once been pragmatic and centred on stimulating the work of his followers.

To some extent he had only himself to blame, but events too played their part. The publication of the *Ecrits* in 1966 brought him worldwide recognition; the 1968 revolution turned some of his closest associates away from analysis towards direct political action; the reform of the universities in the early 1970s opened up a new forum for his teaching. And all the time, the numbers at his seminars and the demand for analysis and supervision grew and grew. The 1967 Proposal on the analyst of the school shifted the focus away from the small working cartels to the identification of those who could do the best theoretical work—the Analystes de l'Ecole—and those who could best represent the school as clinicians—the Analystes Membres de l'Ecole—to the extent that the first document the newcomer to the school was presented with was not the Founding Act but the Proposal, and a cartel became any group of Lacanians who came together to study a text.

The bureaucratisation of the cartels[7]

The Department of Cartels was introduced by an undated letter signed by Eric Laurent and Jacques-Alain Miller in which they set out "the spirit in which we are tackling the task confided in us by J. Lacan". It reminded us that the creation of cartels was contemporaneous with the foundation of the school and that in the first Directory in 1965 "the list of members was preceded by that of the 27 cartels then active" and that "the name of each member was followed by the mention of his cartel and the work in progress". Laurent and Miller proposed to methodically update the existing lists and to hold a meeting in November-December to consult with the cartels on desirable innovations.

Extracts of this meeting on 10th November 1979 were circulated in December and January in numbers one and two of *Plus-Un*. It seems to have begun quietly enough with presentations on the nature of the cartels and their link with membership of the school—there is the rather curious fact that even though the cartel is the basic organ of the school you did not have to be a member of the school in order to join a cartel recognised by the school. However, the tone began to change when Philip Girard among others began to question what was behind the organisation of a department, with the bureaucratic control this implied, and Miller's seeing this as an extension of the accusation of tyranny that had been made against Lacan at the general meeting the previous September.

What begins to surface at this meeting is the suspicion that the members of the school are being organised into cartels so that those who are behind Lacan can be clearly distinguished from those who want to use his name—and the locale of the school—to promote their own agendas. Two aberrant tendencies in particular are targeted: the Catholics and the feminists. Denis Vasse, a close friend of Francoise Dolto, had been sacked from his post as vice-president because of his ecumenical advances towards non-Lacanian groups, and Serge Leclaire and Michele Montrelay had been refused the use of the school premises to promote their views on psychoanalysis and feminism. The vote on Vasse's dismissal at the September meeting had shown an amazing 110 votes against the proposition out of a total of 350, indicating substantial support for the view that Lacan was now a capricious old man who no longer had the best interests of the school at heart.

Whether or not this was the purpose of the creation of the department of cartels is a matter for speculation, but in the short term at least the appeal to the Founding Act and the call to rally behind Lacan against those in the school who were calling for his head was successful. An impressive catalogue of the cartels that had declared themselves before mid-November was drawn up as if to show that the work of the school as originally envisaged by Lacan was going to continue in a new and vigorous way. But on 8th January 1980, the members of the school received a letter dissolving the EFP and calling for all those who wanted to join Lacan in a new association to write to him within the next ten days.

More than a 1000 responded and received a formal acknowledgment announcing the establishment of La Cause Freudienne. In the months that followed, Lacan returned again and again in his seminars to the cartels and to the text of the Founding Act. The statement on 11th March 1980 is the most explicit. With those who have written to him he intends to restore:

> [...] the basic organ taken up again from the foundation of the school, in other words the cartel, the formalisation of which I am refining, with the experience that has been gained. Firstly—Four choose one another, to pursue a work which must have its product. I specify: a product proper to each one, and not collective.
>
> Secondly—The union of the four takes place around a Plus-One, who, if he can be anyone at all, must be someone. He is charged with overseeing the internal effects of the enterprise, and to provoke its elaboration. Thirdly—to guard against stickiness, permutation must take place, at a fixed term of one year, two maximum.
>
> Fourthly—No progress is to be expected, unless there is a periodic opening to public view of the results as well as crises in the work.
>
> Fifthly—The drawing of lots will insure the regular renewal of the reference-points created in order to vectorialise the whole.
>
> To this can be added two further remarks on 18th March and 23rd October: Is the Plus-One to be drawn by lots? No, the four associates choose him.

Apart from the neologism "vectorialise", these are the clearest statements that Lacan has ever made on the importance he accords to the cartels and how he intends them to function. There is only one problem. It seems very likely that, even though they were read out by a now visibly failing Lacan at his seminar, they were written by those he had put in charge of the department of cartels. But whether they were or not, there is no doubt that the emphasis put on the cartel with its Plus One as the basic organ of the school he founded, dates from a time when he was at his most dynamic and creative and there is nothing inconsistent between the prescriptions of the Founding Act and these extracts from his final seminars. What is doubtful, especially in the light of the exchanges at the cartel study days, is whether in his later years he would have been fully satisfied with the unambiguous five-point plan outlined above.

In any case the vast majority of "the 1000" had by now "cartellised" themselves, so that when the new catalogue appeared in early 1981 it listed no fewer than 279 cartels, almost all with their very real Plus Ones, organised under eleven different areas of work: neurosis, psychosis, perversion, clinic, the unconscious, repetition, the drive, concepts and mathemes, technique,[8] ethics, and practice. The cartels contained the names not only of newcomers but of the grandees of the EFP: Clavreul, Conté, Dumézil, Melman, etc., though not those of the dissidents mentioned earlier. So, the stage now seemed finally set for the realisation of the dream.

But on 9th September 1981 Jacques Lacan died. By the beginning of the new year the consensus around the cartels had shattered and different personalities and groups emerged to found new associations and schools while many others simply drifted away to work as psychoanalysts as far as possible from the pressures and supports of the group.

The cartels after Lacan

The Parisian scene

Claude Dumézil was able to draw up a list of eight Lacanian associations set up in 1982 and 1983 alone. They would be followed by many more but the striking feature of their statutes is that none of them give a major role to the cartel. The exception is the Ecole de la Cause Freudienne which requires candidates to apply for admission through a cartel and reproduces the Founding Act as well as a number of the seminars of 1980.

Some of the new groupings do mention the importance of working in cartels but the structure of these and particularly the role of the Plus One is not modelled on the Founding Act. My own impression is that those who were mourning Lacan's loss felt that Miller and Laurent had hijacked the cartel by bureaucratising it under cover of carrying out Lacan's wishes. They regretted the naiveté with which they had joined the rush to cartellisation in Lacan's dying days and decided to go forward rather than taking what appeared to be a regressive step back to an idealistic dream of analysts working together in a new social bond based on the analytic discourse.

The cartel today

On 6th and 7th June 2009, the Inter-Associatif Européen de Psychanalyse held a seminar on The Training of the Psychoanalyst in Brussels under the auspices of Le Questionnement Psychanalytique (QP). The position papers prepared for the meeting give a valuable account of the current state of thinking about cartels and the usual small discussion groups were set up as cartels drawn by lot.

QP had been set up in 1984 by eight Belgian psychoanalysts who had explicitly chosen the cartel in order to reflect together on the questions that preoccupied them after the dissolution of the EFP. They were determined to resist the lure of the hierarchical organisation and even though they were Lacanians, also rejected the *passe*. Their innovations in the practical use of cartels in recruitment and formation would merit an extended reflection but I would simply like to give a brief quotation to highlight how even after twenty-five years of cartel-based work the Plus One remains an enigma:

> Another question, that of the Plus-One which, in QP, seems to remain in suspense, never really posed. We work essentially in cartels but we abandon the question of the Plus-One. To it we prefer [...] to welcome a "cartelliser" outside the association. His presence is precious. His acceptance is quasi-universal. But does he correspond in the contrivance to the function of the Plus-One? Could it be that the old haunting memory of the master is still producing its effects? (Debar, 2009)

It is hard not to hear in this an echo of the suggestions made in the 1975 debate. Now it seems the solution is to invite someone outside QP to join the cartel presumably to prevent it becoming too cosy and inward-looking. But once again the tasks the Plus One is charged with in the Founding Act have evaporated and we are left with someone who seems to have been chosen in order to introduce a stranger into the dynamics of the group rather than to ensure a criticism and supervision of the work of each member. Neither do the notions of the four-six limit and the permutation so highlighted in Lacan-Safouan exchange play a part.

In short, the contemporary evidence from the association that has most explicitly made the cartel the centre of its thinking and practice is that the structure and functioning of this device still defy implementation.

Conclusion

Nothing, since I first encountered his work almost forty years ago, has changed my conviction that in our time Lacan is the best available interlocutor in any attempt to promote a style of psychoanalysis that is theoretically rigorous and relevant to our contemporary clinical and social concerns.

But as the English-speaking world has struggled to come to terms with the obscurities and mistranslations of the seminars and the *Ecrits*, it has been easy to overlook the importance Lacan accorded to the cartel as an instrument of on-going formation in psychoanalytic theory and practice. This oversight has been encouraged by the fact that, for various reasons I have tried to outline in this paper, it was shared by many of the francophones who have taught and inspired us.

However, the experiment the ISLP has been carrying out, with psychoanalysts and other specialists, of attempting to implement the prescriptions of the Founding Act has shown that Lacan's project is not utopian. Perhaps it may persuade colleagues to mobilise the resolution required to tackle in this innovative and productive way a task imposed on us by our duty to those who are still waiting for the enlightenment that Freud's discoveries can bring.

Notes

1. I have no direct knowledge of the fate of the cartel in the Ecole de la cause freudienne which was launched in Lacan's dying days with a great display of catalogues of cartels and their Plus One's. Its website contains some interesting material, but the vast bureaucratic structure it has developed is very far from the easily managed, circular, non-hierarchical, cartel-based association envisaged in the Founding Act.
2. These are views expressed in Lacan's seminars on *The Freudian Thing* (1955) and *Science And Truth* (1965).
3. Both the French establishment of the text and the English translation are deeply flawed but it is worth noting that the Founding Act was produced in the week between the penultimate and the final sessions of the seminar.
4. Editor's note: See Khoury's chapter on the "Desire of the Psychoanalyst", seen by Lacan as underpinning the ethical position of the analyst, both in terms of motivation and countertransference.
5. The page numbers refer to the report of the 1975 Cartel Study Days available on the website of Lettres de l'Ecole Freudienne de Paris and translated at www.lacaninireland.com under "Other Works".
6. www.ecole-lacanienne.net, Pastout Lacan. Christian Simatos links the Plus One to the notion of *"y a d'l'un"* ("there is something of the one"). An insistent reminder that our individual work contributes to the realisation of this "one".
7. I am unaware of any publication dealing with the link between the focus on the cartels in the late 1970s and the dissolution of the school. Therefore, much of what follows is based on letters and circulars issued at that time.
8. Among the thirty-one cartels listed under this heading we find a cartel on "The logic of the phantasy" comprising Russell Grigg, Bill Richardson, and myself. Our Plus One remained to be determined!

References

Debar, A. (2009). Le cartel d'association en questions. IAEP, June, 2009.
Freud, S. (1900a). *The Interpretation of Dreams. S. E., IV*, p. 200. London: Hogarth Press.
Lacan, J. (1964a). Founding Act. 21st June, 1964.
Lacan, J. (1964b). Adjunct to the Founding Act. 21st June, 1964.
Lacan, J. (1966a). La direction de la cure et les principles de son pouvoir. In: *Ecrits*. Paris: Seuil.
Lacan, J. (1966b). Function and field of speech and language. In: *Ecrits*. Paris: Seuil.
Lacan, J. (1977). *The Four Fundamental Concepts of Psychoanalysis*. London: Hogarth Press.
Lacan, J. *Dissolution*, 11.03.1980. Unpublished.

PART II

SOME CENTRAL CONCEPTS

CHAPTER FOUR

Editors' introduction

S. Bailly

It has been said that Lacan brought fathers back on the psychoanalytic scene at a time that it was enthralled by the Mother, but this is a formulation about which we have some reservations. It seems to pit fathers against mothers in some kind of competition for status; it allows critics of Lacan to say that he wasn't interested in mothers and so on and so forth. Mostly, it fosters non-comprehension of his important work on the paternal metaphor and the structure of the signifying function by reducing it to being about the "importance of fathers".

For Lacanians, the place of the mother in the development of the human subject is so utterly central that she is even equated with the Thing—the Real that escapes signification, the beyond-of-the-signified that operates as the desire-generating lost object (Lacan, 1992). She is the ineffable reality around which and in response to which the psyche of the *parl-être*—the being of speech—in fact the human subject, is constituted. That being the case, the question then becomes that of examining in detail how this happens.

It is interesting that Lacan's attempts to do this began with his seminar on the psychoses, the condition in which the human mind is at its least social, its least intersubjective. His line of thought was to try to understand phenomenologically the difference between this kind of mind and the "ordinary neurotic" mind: how did the being discernible in the disordered or non-existent speech of the psychotic come about, as compared with the being to be found in the speech of the neurotic? It is not immediately obvious why his intuition should have led him to seek the answer in object relations, but it was out of this that he came to see the Oedipus complex and its resolution as the key structural element upon which 'normal' speech and the ordinary neurotic psyche could develop.

The paternal metaphor is perhaps Lacan's most useful insight; it renders the construction of the Oedipus complex more credible and demystifies the mechanism of its dissolution. It situates the beginning of the Oedipal problematic very early in infant life (in agreement with

Melanie Klein), makes the sexuality inherent in it compatible with the sexual and cognitive development of a baby, and results in the formation of a structural element that allows the subject to enter into the world of human language and the social universe, both of which are metaphorical in structure in the sense that all human interactions and thoughts are edifices of infinitely substituting elements that code for meaning (any clinician who has ever made an interpretation will know what we mean). These are difficult concepts but once grasped, of great clinical relevance.

Because of Lacan's excommunication, his paternal metaphor failed to gain currency in the mainstream of psychoanalysis and it has taken half a century for any other analysts to come close to theorising the importance of the "third" or paternal element in the psyche. Perhaps even more regrettably, Lacan himself dropped the ball—his planned seminar on the Name-of-the-Father coincided with his expulsion from the IPA as a training analyst, and after just one session on the subject he switched courses abruptly and did not return to this line of reflection for another decade.

In this paper, Lionel Bailly picks up the thread of the unfinished story and traces it back to its origins in Lacan's reflections on psychosis, through his preoccupation with early object relations and finally to his consideration of metaphorical and metonymical substitutions and their structuring function in the psyche. This clarification of a central concept of such significance should be of value to clinicians of any persuasion.

Reference

Lacan, J. (1992). *The Seminar, Book VII: The Ethics of Psychoanalysis, 1959–1960*. D. Porter (Trans.). London: Routledge, p. 54.

CHAPTER FOUR

Lacan's version of the Oedipus complex

Lionel Bailly

Both Freud's and Lacan's thoughts about the Oedipus complex grew out of their preoccupation with the Object: one of Freud's earliest preliminary discussions of it is to be found in a chapter entitled "The Finding of an Object" in the *Three Essays on the Theory of Sexuality* (1905d). Likewise, Lacan provides the foundation of his revision of Freud's views on the Oedipus complex in his fourth seminar (1956–1957) entitled *Object Relation and Freudian Structures*. Freud (1905d) points out that in the child "the sexual instinct has a sexual object outside the infant's own body in the shape of his mother's breast". Later, the instinct loses that object at the time "when the child is able to form a total idea of the person to whom the organ that is giving him satisfaction belongs", but there are "good reasons why a child sucking at his mother's breast has become the prototype of every relation of love. The finding of an object is in fact a refinding of it". This initial object, lost and re-found is at the heart of human sexuality. In connection with this, Freud points out that "anxiety in children is originally nothing other than an expression of the fact that they are feeling the loss of the person they love". After the breast, the genital zones will be involved as "a child's intercourse with anyone responsible for his care affords him an unending source of sexual excitation and satisfaction from his erotogenic zones". Here too the provider of these excitations is primarily the mother according to Freud, but this is not without difficulties as "by the postponing of sexual maturation, time has been gained in which the child can erect, among other restraints on sexuality, the barrier against incest, and can thus take up into himself the moral precepts which expressly exclude from his object-choice, as being blood-relations, the persons whom he has loved in his childhood". However, "the simplest course for the child would be to choose as his sexual objects the same persons whom, since his childhood, he has loved with what may be described as damped-down libido". This is a source of conflict but eventually this conflict will have not only a structuring role for the psyche but also at a social level: "as these plainly incestuous phantasies are overcome and repudiated, one of the most significant, but also one of the most painful, psychical achievements of the pubertal period is completed: detachment from parental authority, a process that alone makes possible the opposition, which is so important for the progress of civilization, between the new generation and the old".

Thus, Freud laid the foundations of the Oedipus complex, but despite later refinements of his theory some questions remain unanswered. Why does the child move from the breast to the genital object? What is that genital object? Who has it? How is the incest taboo enforced? What role does the father play in the Oedipal drama? Lacan's work provides a model that can answer these questions in a clinically meaningful way.

Frustration, deprivation, and castration

Lacan's fourth seminar (1956–1957) was entitled *The Object Relation and Freudian Structures*. Aware that object relations was becoming "the first theoretical element in the explanation of Psychoanalysis" (Lacan, 1957), Lacan wanted to revisit Freud's views on what an object was, but came to argue a more complex form of object relations than anyone had done before or has done since. He followed the development of the infant's relationships from relating to an object through relating with another subject (other, who may also be an object) *in relation to* an object, and finally relating with a subject/object *in relation to another subject/object and an object;* and in charting this course of development he sought to elucidate what each step required and brought in terms of psychic structure and functioning. It is this close look at how structure develops from the interplay of subject and object, and how each new configuration facilitates and imposes a style of functioning that makes Lacanian object relations unique.

To begin with, Lacan suggests that any imaginary relationship is "modulated from a certain fundamental intercourse, the mother–child intercourse [...]." This initial position is often called dyadic today, but for Lacan, it always involved three elements: the mother, the child, and in between them, the phallus. This triadic relationship is made of unequal elements, two are objects in relation to the other and are also subjects, whereas the phallus is only an object. However, before the phallus can be constituted in the baby's mind, there have to be some preliminary steps in psychic development which take place around the experience of lack, and the coming into being of the three psychic registers of the Real, Symbolic, and Imaginary.

Lacan suggests that it is important to distinguish three types of qualitatively different experience of the lack of an object: deprivation, frustration, and castration. Lacan calls these three elements "the three reference terms of the lack of the object". He clearly states that he is talking of "a lack of the object" and not of an "object lack". It is not that the subject does not have an object to cathect but that the cathected object is at some point absent. Lacan points out that in the imaginary triad of mother-child-phallus, it is also necessary to introduce the concept of *agent*, the one who causes the object lack, for example in the case of frustration, the mother. Lacan summarises all this in a table, first drawn during the seminar of the 12th December 1956. For didactic reasons the table can be modified in the following way:

Reference terms of the lack of the object	*Agent*	*Type of lack*	*Type of object*	*Object*
Frustration	Symbolic mother Symbolic father	Imaginary prejudice/harm	Real	Breast Penis
Privation	Imaginary father	Real hole	Symbolic	Child
Castration	Real father	Symbolic debt	Imaginary	Phallus

The question now is how do these relationships operate structurally?

Ontologically speaking, frustration comes first. Frustration is linked with pre-oedipal experiences, which does not imply that it is unconnected with the Oedipus complex but that it constitutes "its preparatory terrain, its basis and foundation, modelled in a such way that already certain inflexions are prepared which will provide the slope towards which the Oedipal conflict will lean [...]." By "inflexions", Lacan means the particular attitude and position adopted by each subject towards frustration; this positioning of the subject *vis-à-vis* object lack forms the basis of all subsequent evolution of object relating, and give us the "imaginary anatomy of the development of the subject".

In frustration, what the child or more generally the subject becomes frustrated about is a real object: the "object of frustration is, while frustration itself is imaginary, in its nature a real object [...]." Frustration should be seen as being based on real impressions, experienced in a period when the subject's relation to the object is centred on the primordial image of the maternal breast. Frustration contains the notion of prejudice (in the legal sense of something that causes harm)—of an imaginary harm:

> Frustration is in essence the domain of claims, the dimension of something desired and which is not kept, but something which is desired without any reference to the possibility of satisfaction, of acquiring this object. Frustration is in itself the domain of unbridled demands, the domain of lawless demands.

It is interesting that in his seminar, to refer to the notion of legal prejudice associated with frustration, Lacan uses the French word *dam*. It is an obsolete word in French (although the equivalent English damned is not) from the Latin *damnum*, meaning prejudice as well as damage but is also used in a religious sense to describe the chastisement of the damned, the eternal privation of the beatific vision of God. This double meaning suggests both the imaginary harm conceived by the frustrated subject and the hypothesis of having been harmed by the lack of the object and also directs the reader towards the idea of a beatific vision, that of the object which would satisfy the subject's "unbridled demands".

The real object of frustration is the breast, while the frustrating agent is the mother, who "is called when she is not there and rejected when present under the same modality of a vocalisation [...]." This elaboration through vocalisation of presence and absence is for Lacan the "priming" of the Symbolic order, something that allows us to "extricate as a distinct element of the relation to a real object, something other that [...] offers the possibility of a link between this real relation and a symbolic one". The moment when the mother-child relationship becomes more complex and opens onto new developments is when the mother stops responding to the child's call. When the mother stops responding, "she becomes real, she does not answer, she only responds at her will [...] she becomes a power".

From the moment the mother becomes a power, it is only through her that the child will get access to objects that until then were only objects of satisfaction. The maternal object moves from being the one that is present/absent to one "that can refuse itself and has everything the subject may need, even if he does not need it"—she becomes another subject and the baby can begin to develop a form of relating not of subject and object but subject and other (subject). Concomitantly, the breast, a real object linked with the satisfaction of needs and once the ultimate desired object, becomes symbolic of the goodwill and potency of the mother—a gift. Where before the object, breast, was real and the mother symbolic, a reversal has occurred: "The mother has become real and the object is symbolic; the object more than anything testifies of a gift bestowed by the maternal power [...] the object has now two types of properties [...] it satisfies the need and symbolises a friendly power [...]." The experience of frustration (lack experienced in the Imaginary of a Real object) can become an experience of deprivation (lack experienced in the real of something symbolic).

Deprivation is "something that in its nature as a lack is a real lack, a hole" and refers to an object that is not where it should be. It cannot therefore be something belonging to the Real as "anything real is always necessarily in its place, even when disturbed, the Real has the property to carry its place under the sole of its shoes, you can disturb the Real as much as you want, it remains that our bodies will be, after having exploded, still in their place, in their place as bits". The absence of something in the Real is purely symbolic in as much as a law states that the object should be there. To illustrate this, Lacan uses the following metaphor: a book in a library is not in the place on the shelf where it should be, there is a hole there. It might be misplaced and in fact wrongly stored a few spaces away but it is from the point of view of the library "missing". "When we are talking of deprivation, it is only about symbolic objects". In other words, for a subject to experience deprivation, she or he has to have a notion that the object *should be there*; there has to be a sense of a law that decrees it, and the other side of deprivation is entitlement. Also with deprivation, the imaginary father comes into play—the father that keeps mother away; but to explain this new element we have to go back a little to considering the impact of the baby's realisation that the mother is the possessor of the breast.

With this realisation, the notion of power once invested in the breast passes to the mother; but the baby cannot help but notice that mother's power resides in far more than the ability to provide or withhold the breast; there is the whole gamut of interactions that constitutes maternal care: she modulates the world. And because she modulates the world very often according to the baby's wishes and needs, it is not unreasonable for the baby to think at times that she or he is also possessed of the same power. Infantile omnipotence therefore arises out of identification with a mother perceived as omnipotent, but it is important to remember that sometimes the baby just feels helpless. Lacan does not posit the breast or any physical object as the original symbol of mother's power and this leaves open the possibility of the baby forming the question: in what does power reside? His answer is the phallus.

The imaginary triadic relationship mother-child-phallus is the "prelude to the introduction in the game of the symbolic relationship, that will be only when the quaternary function, which is that of the father, will be introduced by the Oedipal dimension". While the infant is in the process of forming hypotheses about the mysterious power of the mother, the presence on the scene of another subject—for now the imaginary father—introduces the possibility of another level of conceptualisation.

The final experience of object lack, castration, can only be experienced when the imaginary father who is already in the child's mind at some point intervenes in the Real. Castration was introduced by Freud, says Lacan, in a way fundamentally linked to "the notion of a primordial law, that there is something of a fundamental law in the prohibition of incest and in the structure of the Oedipus complex". Castration is "something that can only be classified in the category of a symbolic debt". In castration, the consequence of a symbolic debt, what is missing is something that underpins the law and its lack is justified punishment for the transgression. It is not an object belonging to the Real, for Lacan, the object of castration is always imaginary—the phallus.

The Name-of-the-Father

In his seminar on Psychosis, Lacan had introduced the concept of the Name-of-the-Father through a careful examination of the Oedipus Complex:

> [...] in order for the human being to be able to establish the most natural of relations, that between male and female, a third party has to intervene [...] there has to be a law, a chain, a symbolic order, the intervention of the other of speech, that is of the father. Not the natural father, but what is called the father. The order that prevents the collision and the explosion of the situation as a whole is founded on the existence of this name of the father. (Lacan, 1993)

Lacan separates clearly the father of the family from the Symbolic dimension carried by his role, which is the key of its power as a function. Working on the case of President Schreber, Lacan continues his elaboration of the concept and points out that the only element that can stop the emergence of aggression from an Oedipal relation that has been reduced from a triangular relationship to a dual one is "a signifier that is primordial but excluded from the subject. I named this signifier [...]. Thou art the one who is, or who will be, a father" (Lacan, 1993). This fundamental signifier is from here onwards written as one, with capital letters and hyphens: Name-of-the-Father.

The paternal metaphor

Lacan's version of the Oedipus complex involves a young child and focuses in a first phase on the dealings of the mother and the child. The child is aware that the mother is coming and going. This awareness comes from the fact that when she is present, the world of the child changes and changes again when she leaves, something that the baby senses even before being able to fully symbolise it. This leads, Lacan suggests, to a theoretical reflection about the mother's comings and goings and her motivations: "What does she want? I'd like it to be me that she wants, but it is clear that it's not just me, there is something else on her mind [...]. What is on her mind is the x, the signified. This signified of her comings and goings, it's the Phallus" (Lacan, 1998).

With the first symbolisation of the mother, something is instituted which is subjectified at a primitive level. This "subjectification consists simply in positing her as the primordial being who can be there, or not be there" (Lacan, 1998). The first symbolisation of the mother leads the child to separate out the idea of its dependence on her desire from the lived experience of that dependence. More importantly, "what the subject desires, is not simply the craving for her care, for her contact, even for presence, it is the craving for her desire" (Lacan, 1998). What the child seeks is to be able to satisfy his mother's desire, to be the object of the mother's desire and to do so will identify with this object that is the satisfying object for the mother. Lacan calls this the primitive phallic stage.

Until now the description was that of a mother and a child but for the next step, the father, who had been in the background, already constituted as symbol outside the subject, needs effectively to intervene as a real person clothed in the symbol. The father intervenes despite the fact that the baby is not a credible seducer and although "the mother is quite sufficient to show the child the extent to which what he offers, is insufficient, and she is also sufficient to prohibit his use of the new instrument". He intervenes because the issue is that of the *desire of the mother* and not of the baby's attributes. In reality, the father is not in a caricatural way a herald of the prohibition of incest: "no one has ever dreamt of putting in the forefront of the castration complex, the fact that the father, effectively, promulgates the law of the prohibition of incest [...]" (Lacan, 1998). He intervenes simply as bearer of the law, as the guarantor of a prohibition: the mother is not to be enjoyed without limits by her children.

In a second phase, the father intervenes in the Imaginary realm. The child's demand to the mother is that she stays. This demand, addressed to the Other comes back to the child as the law of the father "conceived imaginarily by the subject as depriving the mother". She is not free to stay, she "must go". Lacan sees there a crucial aspect of the process where "something that detaches the subject from his identification attaches him at the same time to the first appearance of the law in the shape of this fact: that the mother is dependent on it, dependent on an object, on an object which is no longer simply the object of her desire, but an object that the other has or does not have". At this point the other to whose law the mother refers appears as also having the object of her desire. This is central in the understanding of the Oedipus complex as the mother "has a relationship not to the father, but to the word of the father". Lacan points out that the father intervenes by virtue of his rights and not as a real person, "even if he is not there, if he calls the mother on the telephone for example, the result is the same. It is the father here qua Symbolic who intervenes in a frustration, an imaginary act concerning an object that is real, who is the mother, to the extent that the child needs her".

The third and last moment in the development of the paternal metaphor, is when the father can give the mother what she desires because he has it, restoring the relation of the mother to the father in the Real. "Here intervenes the fact precisely of power in the genital sense of the word, let us say that the father is a potent father, that, in this third moment, there is produced the restitution, if you like, of, that the relation [...]." Without this credible potency, without an ability to satisfy, it is likely that the mother would not take the word of the father seriously. In the last phase of the Oedipus complex it is what supports the mother's desire that has to be strong enough to satisfy her. As we will see this could be the sexually potent man with whom she made the child but it could be anything potent to which the object of her desire is connected.

Lacan moves away from a literal interpretation of the role of the father in the Oedipus complex by stating that in the Oedipus complex the father is not a real object even though he must intervene as a real object to embody castration. As we know this principle applies independent of the presence of a father, the point is that *a real object with a known signifier* must intervene to embody castration. The father is symbolic; more precisely says Lacan, the father is a metaphor. "The function of the father in the Oedipus complex is to be a signifier substituted for the signifier, that is for the first signifier introduced into symbolization, the maternal signifier" (Lacan, 1998). The mother being the first object to be symbolised is at the centre of the baby's preoccupations and the need to "secure" her is paramount. However, as we have seen above, in the dialectic of the presence/absence the child has to think about what takes or keeps her away and faces the question of the mother's desire. Having been able to symbolise its first object, it is logical for the child to postulate an object that the mother is after, even though from the point of view of the child "it should be me that she wants". This imagined object, something the mother desires more than the child, therefore by his lights more than anything else, is the phallus.

The Oedipal drama in its first phase rests on an impossible exchange: "prove to me, by your behaviour, that I have it" is the child's demand; "how can I tell him/her that he/she's not everything for me?" underlines the mother's non-response. The mother anticipates that the whole truth would be devastating in its raw form: "you don't have it, you can't fully please me and I will leave you because of this"; or maybe worse: "you have it, I don't need anything or anyone else and we will stay forever enmeshed". A subterfuge is in the best of interest of both the baby and the mother to avoid the baby's narcissistic collapse and the damage to the mother's ego ideal and maternal identifications. The disguising of the truth is made possible through a metaphoric process, which precisely substitutes and hides signifiers.

In linguistics, a metaphor is a figure of speech in which one object is ascribed the attributes of another without the attributes being mentioned, by a substitution of signifiers; but although all signifiers for the attributes themselves disappear in the process, it is precisely this that is at stake—e.g., "you're a star"—what is important are the bright and high-up qualities of a star, not its physical reality; "Jane is a lamb"—the unmentioned idea here is one of docility, etc.

In Lacan's view of the Oedipus complex, the mother's object of desire is something that has a symbolic representation that is represented in her unconscious by a signifier. This signifier of the mother's desire (the symbolic phallus, Lacan's φ—small phi) is associated with a signified, the idea of the mother's desire (the phallus as an imaginary object). In the baby's life, there is a real father (even if he may be absent or a sperm donor), who has a name and is an object—he is a signified with a signifier. This is what is going to be used in the substitution process of the paternal metaphor, leading to what Lacan calls the Name-of-the-Father. In this process, the Name-of-the-Father (signifier) associated with the idea of the father is connected with the idea of the mother's desire (phallus). The signifier of the mother's desire is removed by the metaphoric process and both child and mother are freed from having to face it. The child wants his mother to stay and she says "sorry, but your dad is back". If the child accepts her statement, he or she does submit to the metaphor: he or she accepts that he or she does not have what would make the mother stay but furthermore recognises that the mother too lacks something, because if she had it she would not be looking for it. By accepting the metaphor the child uses a symbolic device to find a satisfactory solution to a potentially overwhelming issue: that of his or her need for love and of the unreliable quality of the one on which the satisfaction of this need rests; worse, that the absence of the mother could be caused by the absence of his mother's desire for him or her which would constitute an unbearable narcissistic wound.

In accepting the paternal metaphor, the child gains the ability to use substitutes and symbols, to move away from concrete thinking. At the very moment of acceptance of the metaphor, the child seals its entry into the Symbolic realm, becomes the castrated neurotic subject and submits to the law of the prohibition of incest. The Name-of-the-Father is "the signifier which in the Other, as the place where signifiers are to be found, is the signifier of the Other, as the place where the Law is to be found" (Lacan, 1958). From this new position, the child can move away from a dual relationship with his or her first object and engage his desire, as a subject, towards substitutive objects in a hopeless but eventful and enjoyable quest for the lost object.

Lacan proposed a formula of the paternal metaphor that is not without ambiguities. He introduced first a general formulation of "the signifier's substitution or formula of metaphor" that represents a move away from classic linguistic formulations:

$$\frac{S}{\not{S}'}\cdot\frac{\not{S}'}{x}\rightarrow S\left(\frac{I}{s}\right)$$

The capital S's are signifiers, x the unknown signification, I the unconscious and s the signified introduced by the metaphor. The metaphoric process substitutes S to S´.

He then presented on the same model "the metaphor of the Name-of-the-Father, that is the metaphor that substitutes this name into the place firstly symbolised by the operation of the mother's absence".

$$\frac{\text{Name-of-the-Father}}{\text{Desire of the mother}}\cdot\frac{\text{Desire of the Mother}}{\text{Signified to the subject}}\longrightarrow\frac{\text{Name-of-the-Father}}{\text{Phallus}}\{\text{O}\}$$

As Lacan in his seminars and subsequent writings does not say how he arrived at the formula in this precise form, it has been the object of many interpretations. From the point of view of the clinician it can be understood in the following way: in the discourse of the mother what is signified to the subject (the child) is that the mother's absence is caused by the symbolic Name-of-the-Father and not by her desire which has been deleted in the metaphoric process. This was, before the metaphoric process took place, an unknown signification. The right part of the equation shows that when the metaphor is successful, the subject is consciously aware of the Name-of-the-Father but despite the disappearance of the mother's desire, in the child's unconscious lies its true cause: the phallus, which as signifier is to be found in the Other.

Further elaborations of the phallus

This paper being devoted to Lacan's view of the Oedipus Complex, the text focuses on the phallus as object of castration, an imaginary object lost through the symbolic metaphoric process.

Many other aspects of the phallus are to be found in Lacan's work. First, let us mention the fact that the phallus has a symbolic dimension to be found in the phallus as signifier of the mother's desire. In his paper "The Signification of the Phallus" (1966a) Lacan points out that as signifier of the mother's desire, the phallus is to be found in the Other where all signifiers are to be found. This allows a logical shift from the mother to the Other, the subject making the hypothesis that the phallus is not only what the mother has on her mind but what the Other is after. The phallus becomes the signifier of the desire of the Other. Lacan uses the notation φ small phi) for this symbolic aspect of the phallus, signifier of desire and $-\varphi$ to represent the phallus as the imaginary object lost in castration. Continuing his theoretical elaborations, Lacan describes how $-\varphi$ can move "to the other side of the equation, from the imaginary to the Symbolic, being in any way turned positive [...] becoming Φ (capital phi), the symbolic phallus, impossible to negativate, signifier of enjoyment" (1966b). From the symbolic phallus, signifier of enjoyment, Lacan continues his elaborations of the concept in his seminars between 1967 and 1973. He uses mathematical logic to explore the role of the phallus in gender differences and in enjoyment. This leads to the conceptualisation of the Phallic Function also represented by Φ. In mathematics a function is a relation between a set of inputs, called the arguments, and a set of permissible outputs. Every subject (x) is the "argument" of the phallic function; Lacan denotes this relationship as Φ. The subject's structural outcome of its phallic functioning would therefore be $\Phi(x)$. This means in particular that the distinction between men and women is not to be based on having or not having the phallus or not even on being or not being the phallus for someone, but on the logical modality through which one is the argument of the phallic function.

Impact on non-Lacanian Psychoanalysts

Even where Jacques Lacan has been forgotten, hidden or misrepresented, the radical reframing of the Oedipal triangulation offered by the Lacanian model does seem to have had a lasting impact on the way psychoanalysts think about the phallus, castration and the paternal function. André Green who attended Lacan's seminars from 1961 to 1967 said in a 1992 interview with Catherine Clement:

> Lacan wanted indeed to restore the paternal function, at a time when psychoanalysis was drifting towards the mothers, a drifting that has not ended [...] and towards the primary relationship between mother and baby: as if the father only appeared later, following an allegedly "genetic" point of view. A total aberration, Lacan was right: for it to be a child it is necessary that the father plays his part and the father has also to be in the mother's head in the company of a few others. (Green, 2012)

In his paper "Thirdness and Psychoanalytic Concepts", Green (2004) explores Lacan's view of Oedipal triangulation, stating:

> I do not think that one has to wait until the child is capable of conceiving of the third person (through language, for instance) before acknowledging that the child can be influenced by fantasies in the mother's mind about the father. I propose to call this phenomenon the other of

> the object (that which is not the subject). The element of the third is not restricted to the person of the father; it is also symbolic.

Green's contribution clarifies that as the paternal metaphor is linked to the object of the mother's desire, it is legitimate to wonder "Who is the true father for the mother? Is it her own father, her mother, a brother, an earlier lover?" Curiously over the years, authors quoting Andre Green seem increasingly to have forgotten that the bulk of his views on the paternal function were not new concepts but directly derived from Lacan's.

Laplanche and Pontalis, authors of the highly influential Language of Psychoanalysis, were both analysands of Lacan. Perhaps because of the controversy he aroused and their choice in remaining analysts of the IPA, they kept references to him to a minimum while still remaining highly influenced by him. In their explanation of the phallus, they seem to be trying to present a Lacanian view of it, but explaining it for a non-Lacanian audience: they say the phallus:

> [...] **underlines the symbolic function taken on by the penis in the intra- and inter-subjective dialectic** [...]. How are we to understand "symbolic value" here? First, it would be mistaken to assign a specific allegorical meaning to the phallus-symbol, however broad it might be (fecundity, potency, authority, etc.). Secondly, what is symbolised here cannot be reduced to the male organ or penis itself, in its anatomical reality. Lastly, the phallus turns out to be the meaning—i.e. what is *symbolised*—behind the most diverse ideas [...].

This insistence on the Symbolic is very Lacanian and Laplanche and Pontalis end their article with Lacan's views, neatly summarised:

> In France, Jacques Lacan has attempted a reorientation of psycho-analytic theory around the idea of the phallus as the "signifier of desire". The Oedipus complex, in Lacan's reformulation of it, consists in a dialectic whose major alternatives are to be or not to be the phallus, and to have it or not to have it; the three moments of this dialectic are centred on the respective positions occupied by the phallus in the desires of the three protagonists.

Dana Birksted-Breen (1996) developed the concept of penis-as-link, a concept written in a way reminiscent of Lacan's hyphenated Name-of-the-Father. In this work she opposes penis and phallus: "I will argue that phallus refers to one specific symbolic aspect only and that there are other symbolic aspects for which the word phallus is not appropriate. In particular, I want to make a distinction between the phallus on the one hand and the penis as representing the mental function of linking and structuring on the other". However, she does not actually make an argument as to why "phallus" should refer only to one aspect or why it is inappropriate for others. Birksted-Breen attributes to her new term penis-as-link the mental functions of linking and structuring, saying that this "involves the knowledge of difference and by the same token the recognition of incompleteness and need for the object". Crucially "as opposed to the binary aspect of the phallic vision along the lines of presence and absence, the structuring and linking function of the penis of the tripartite world of mother, linked with but different from father, and child in relation to the parents, makes for a more complex world. In this position, good and bad, powerful and powerless, masculine and feminine are encompassed rather than being mutually exclusive". The phallus on the other hand is seen as the agent of many ills and Birksted-Breen describes analysands engaging in "a compulsive search for the phallus in the erroneous belief that it will provide an internal structure, while the introjection of the penis-as-link enhances mental space and thinking. The absence of this structuring function is particularly clear in borderline and perverse pathologies where there is often a compulsive attempt at organisation along phallic lines". It can be argued that this paragraph would remain identical and faithful to its meaning if the words *introjection of the penis-as-link* were replaced by *submission to the paternal metaphor*. For a Lacanian reader it is indeed difficult not to see that what Birksted-Breen calls the "penis-as-link" as the agent for clinical outcomes identical to those resulting from what Lacan calls the submission to the Name-of-the-Father. She describes the penis-as-link as an "instrument of Eros whereas the phallus is instrument of Thanatos in so far as it aims to destroy that link". For Lacan, the penis has very little part in the argument and the phallus is not a symbol but an object, imaginary in castration, symbolic as the signifier of desire or enjoyment; it is neither directly an instrument of Eros or Thanatos but could indirectly be either depending on the subject's submission or non-submission to castration and therefore entry into the Symbolic realm. However, it is a *precondition* of Eros, in that without its existence somewhere in the mind of the subject, there can be no castration, no entry into the Symbolic, no support for language and the Law, and no neurotisation of the subject.

Conclusion

Lacan's work restored the paternal function in analytic thinking as a concept that needs to be taken into consideration beside the primary relationship between mother and baby. His model clarifies the place and function of the phallus in the development of the psyche. As an object, the phallus is not as easy to understand from the point of view of the baby as the breast is. Using the word "penis", which refers also to a real object, may lead to either a phallocentric and simplistic view of sexual relations and psychic development or to a rejection of the conceptualisations involving it in the name of gender equality. The phallus, on the other hand, is clearly an imaginary object that compels the mother to engage in a complex process of dissimulation and the child to access the metaphor and accept incompleteness. The reservations and incredulity of social scientists and the non-analytic world in response to Freud's formulation of the Oedipus complex should be addressed by the Lacanian version, which does not depend directly on concrete sexual realities or indeed on hypothesised universal fantasies. Castration being the symbolic loss of an imaginary object, the father's role is not any more to incarnate a threat of physical retaliation but to be the one that at some point the mother desired enough to have intercourse with and also proves that mother and her desire pre-existed the child and are independent of it. Alternatively, the place of the father can be occupied by something or someone who is not a man, as long as it is the object of the mother's desire and therefore acts as a third party between the mother and the child and guarantees that the mother is not omnipotent or the maker of all laws. It also opens onto a different understanding of gender identity, that Lacan bases on the subject's attitude towards the place and role of the phallus, the Phallic function, defining the feminine and the masculine as consequences of this function and not of biological determinants.

References

Bailly, L. (2009). *Lacan: A Beginner's Guide*. Oxford: One World Publication.
Birksted-Breen, D. (1996). Phallus, penis and mental space. *Int J Psychoanal, 77*: 649–657.
Freud, S. (1905d). *Three Essays on the Theory of Sexuality. S. E., VII*. London: Hogarth.
Green, A. (2004). Thirdness and Psychoanalytic Concepts. *Psychoanal Q, 73*: 99–135.
Green, A. (2012). Interview of André Green by Catherine Clement (recorded in 1992), *Le Magazine Litteraire, 26/01/2012*.
Lacan, J. (1998). Le Séminaire de Jacques Lacan, livre 4, *La Relation d'Objet, 1956–1957*. Paris: Seuil.
Lacan, J. (1966a). La Signification du Phallus. *Ecrits*, pp. 685–695.
Lacan, J. (1966b). Subversion du sujet et dialectique du désir. *Ecrits*, pp. 793–827.
Lacan, J. (1993). *The Seminar of Jacques Lacan Book 3, The Psychoses 1955–1956*. Russell Grigg (Trans.). London: W. W. Norton.
Lacan, J. (1998). *Le Séminaire de Jacque Lacan, Livre V, Les Formations de L'Inconscient*. Paris: Seuil.
Lacan, J. (2006). On a question prior to any possible treatment of psychosis. In: *Ecrits*. Bruce Fink (Trans.). London: W. W. Norton.
Laplanche, J., & Pontalis, J.-B. (1973). *The Language of Psychoanalysis*. London: Hogarth Press.

CHAPTER FIVE

Editors' introduction

S. Bailly

"Object lack" remains a concept full of deliberate ambiguity. Does it only mean an object that is absent for the subject? Or an object that is in itself lacking in something? Is what the object lacks the subject? This last is an idea explored in detail by Maria Torok and Nicholas Abraham in their paper, "L'Objet Perdu: Moi" (Torok & Abraham, 1978); but Vanier reminds us here that Lacan had already made the same propos: "We mourn people of whom we could say 'I was his lack'."

The idea of the trace is ubiquitous in Lacanian writing—here, Vanier mentions the "trace of gratification"—and it might help to think of a "trace" in the terms in which Freud explained how psychic structure is created by the formation of favoured neurological "pathways" in his "Project for a Scientific Psychology". This favouring comes about by means of a lowering of the resistance in the contact barriers between the ends of neurones. The lowering of resistance is brought about by application of a stimulus that raises the electrical current in the nerve—a supercharging of the neurone. Freud abandons such biological speculation when he turns to psychoanalysis and in his metapsychologies, the idea of electrical energy within the nervous system is replaced by a more generalised idea of "drive" or libido, but one can easily hear the echo of the Project in his formulation of libido flowing in channels carved out by highly-cathected past experiences. Cathexis means charge in the sense of an electrical charge or load—a cathected object is an object or a way of relating with an object that is highly charged—the pathway (or train of thoughts/fantasies around it) is easily activated and indeed may be "live" at all times in the unconscious. For Lacanians, signifiers are the carriers of the charge, in much the way electrons are of electrical current. The "trace of gratification" mentioned by Vanier in this paper may be thought of as the signifying pathway in which drive is channelled.

References

Abraham, N., & Torok, M. (1978). *L'Ecorce Et Le Noyau, part 4 chapter 5*. Paris: Flammarion.
Freud, S. (1950a). Project for a Scientific Psychology. *S. E., I*, pp. 298–302. London: Hogarth.

CHAPTER FIVE

Object *a*

Alain Vanier

Lacan argued that this object was his only true invention. He kept reworking it, and it runs as a common thread throughout the entire body of his work. He indicated to us several sources that inspired his invention—two of Freud's papers, *Three Essays on the Theory of Sexuality* and "Mourning and Melancholia", but also Winnicott's concept of the transitional object. At the time when Lacan began teaching his seminar, the entire field of psychoanalysis was focused on the object-relation. The question was, how does one manage, by moving through a series of developmental stages, to eventually form a stable relationship with the genital object. Lacan immediately reversed this perspective: starting from his seminar *La relation d'objet* (Lacan, 1998) where he discussed Freud's case of *Little Hans*, he emphasised the fact that the object in question was necessarily an absent object. By doing so, he was only staying true to the Freudian discovery—for Freud the object is always fundamentally lost. The drive aims at an object that has been lost and whenever it is found, it is always only rediscovered. Moreover, we might say that its rediscovery is always a failed encounter because the satisfaction we derive from it never matches our expectations. In *Three Essays* (Freud, 1905d), Freud emphasised something that Lacan, like Melanie Klein before him, was later be able to take advantage of: namely that when the child becomes able grasp the other as a whole person, he loses the fragmentary objects. Still, Freud left us no precise definition of the object—the object is contingent. It was only really theorised by Karl Abraham, with his notion of partial object-love, and later by Klein and her partial object, which nevertheless implies an idea of wholeness that is incompatible with analytic experience. In the mirror image, from which the child's idea of wholeness derives, the drive's objects do not appear. They are in fact missing from it, while the continuity of body image disguises their absence.

Lacan considers Klein's part objects—the breast, the penis—to be real objects. But the breast, an object of pure gratification, depends on someone, namely the mother, who has the power to either give or refuse it. And the only reason this object assumes its real status is precisely the fact that it can be missing. This lack creates *frustration*. Such objects quickly take on the role of objects of exchange, of gifts, which introduces another register—the Symbolic. By the same process by which objects become symbolic, the mother, who is entirely symbolic at the outset—a pure alternation of presence and absence—too becomes real because she is perceived as omnipotent, because she has absolute power to either give or withhold the object.

As I have said before, Freud does not emphasise the particularities of either the first object—which is always already lost—or the substitutes that we think we rediscover in its place. Instead, he underlines the trace of gratification set down at this early time, which will then guide each new attempt at finding the object again. Whichever object takes the place of the object lost, the encounter is necessarily a failed one. Repetition involves a radical but essential difference since there can be no true reunion with the object. Any encounter with it takes place against the backdrop of this radical lack; it is lack that underpins its discordance, not simply in terms of the object's inadequacy to satisfy desire, but of inadequacy as such, since the very fact that the object is caught in the network of signifiers makes it unsuitable for its satisfaction. From the analytical perspective that this idea opens up, the object is a constructed object, except that it is constructed by the effect of signifiers.

At that moment, the object has a symbolic dimension, associated with a real mother who is all-powerful, and this object is inscribed on a background of lack. The lack is real and corresponds to the absence of the penis in women. Clearly, in the Real, a woman lacks nothing in order to be a woman. But it is precisely because, on the symbolic level, this can be inscribed as a lack that the very notion of woman can exist. Being a woman proceeds from a symbolic determination, not a real one.

What is lacking is the phallus *qua* symbol, in other words a signifier of what is not there. The phallus as imaginary is before all else the maternal phallus, a pre-eminently imaginary object which assumes, through the paternal metaphor, the form of a signifier—the signifier of lack. Its function is two-fold: it is an object on the imaginary level, and a signifier on the symbolic level.

In mourning, the subject has lost an object, but although he knows that he has lost something, he does not know what it is. Lacan is even able to write: "We mourn people of whom we could say 'I was his lack'" (Lacan, 2004). In other words, we lose something or someone for whom we were this object-lack. This kind of loss can become conscious, Freud (1917e) tells us, but it is still an ego-loss. "The shadow of the object falls upon the ego", which is now "judged [...] as though it were an object, the forsaken object". In this way, "an object-loss [is] transformed into an ego-loss"—the ego treats itself as an object and this can in fact also result in suicide.

However, at the beginning Lacan forges the *a* with the initial of the little other (*autre*). The *a* therefore initially belongs to the register of the Imaginary—a dimension which refers to the mirror stage and to the fundamental alienation that pervades any relationship with the other. Later in his teaching, the *a* is still connected to the small other, but Lacan writes the following formula: $d \rightarrow \$ <> a \rightarrow i\,(a) \leftarrow m$ where d is desire, $\$ <> a$ is his formula for fantasy (the divided subject in a certain relationship with the object cause of desire), i(a) is the image of the other and m is the ego. This becomes the first line of what he then theorises as the dialectics of desire and demand. We should note that there is a gap between desire (d) and demand. This gap is the effect of what the demand, always necessarily articulated in language, produces in addition to satisfying a need. There is a remainder which demand cannot satisfy. Lacan links what later becomes his formula for fantasy ($ <> *a*) with desire. However, the *a* is already detached from the other's image as it appears in the mirror—i(a). In a certain way, Lacan illustrates this first approach to the *petit a* in his seminar *Le désir et son interpretation* (*Desire and Its Interpretation*, 1958–1959), in which he refers to a passage in Augustine's *Confessions*: "I have *myself observed* a *baby* to be *jealous*, though it could not speak. It was livid as it watched another infant at the breast" (Saint Augustine, 2002, p. 7). Here, Lacan stresses the idea of rivalry, of the *alter ego*, in other words the child's imaginary rivalry with the other, who occupies the coveted position regarding the mother.

In this first elaboration of the object *a*, it plays a role in the subject's desire as connected to the question of the phallus. Faced with the threat of the possible suspension of desire—the loss of which is experienced in the register of castration—and in order to ensure its permanence, the subject relies on a certain number of objects. These, although they are caught in phallic signification, are not themselves the phallus and cannot be reduced to it. For Lacan, the signifier rules out the possibility of the subject's direct relationship with the object; however, by means of a displacement the subject can rely on a series of objects that lend themselves to the phallic function most obviously and easily. By displacement he therefore constitutes a number of objects that serve as a guarantee against the loss of desire. Lacan illustrates this with the example of Moliere's *Miser* and his famous casket, in which the miser's riches are kept. In this case, desire subsists through the withholding of an object, one that provides no other jouissance but that of being the support of desire, of being its token and even its hostage. Through this valorisation—which is also a volatilisation—the object is torn away from the domain of pure and simple need. Hence at first, the object is what appears in order to keep phallic signification in place; in other words, a number of imaginary objects come to embody, to take the position of the phallic signifier. At the same time, we spend all our time mistaking various things for the object *a*—because it is never "that". This is even the reason, Lacan later said, why the phallus is constructed in the first place—as a privileged object that does not deceive us.

However, it is no doubt Winnicott's (1953) notion of the *transitional object* that comes closest to Lacan's object *a*. Winnicott discerns this object in the bit of cloth, the feather, or the stuffed animal that interests the child at one point in its development. This may seem to be a nondescript object and yet it is not quite so because it is not easily replaceable. It must have certain characteristics of texture, softness, and the like, and it keeps the child company at special moments such as falling asleep. Winnicott emphasises that, although it represents the mother or a part of her, it is not the mother. This is something that the child knows. The transitional object is neither a part nor a whole, Winnicott says, nor the part of a whole. Now, this object is the beginning of object relatedness, the first external, not-me possession: "At the same time that it is neither the one nor the other of these two it is also both." (Winnicott, 1968). And it is the framework in which all future relations with others and with the things in the world will take form. It brings about a delimitation and produces transitional space, the space of play and creativity that will remain after the disappearance and abandonment of the object. But the privileged sphere of the relation of the subject to these objects is also a space of disjunction, since it impedes any direct, congruent relation of subject to object.

Lacan himself argued that it was Winnicott's transitional object that allowed him to articulate the notion of his object *a*. Lacan at first identified it with the *fort-da* spool, meaning that he does not locate it as directly linked to weaning which, in his view, is traumatic for the mother only. He identifies it with the thumb—the first object of jouissance which is not the breast—an object which is not "in-house", but it remains within reach. A subject, as such, functions first of all at the level of this transitional object, which commands the subject and, in this sense, is neither real nor illusory.

We should note that Winnicott insists less on the object itself—a piece of cloth, etc.—than on the intermediate area, the potential space. It covers the hollow space which must one day appear. As opposed to Lacan's concept, Winnicott's transitional object is not an object already lost—yet being lost is its fate. It is made to be lost. Hence all the little tragedies when it is misplaced, something mothers try too hard to keep from happening. The transitional object is the commemoration of a lack. We could even go so far as to say that it is something that gives lack the meaning of loss.

Winnicott stresses that what he is interested in is not the object itself but "the use of the object". We should note here that the word "use" in English can be very well translated into French not only by "*utilisation*" but also by the legal term "jouissance". And, in the same way, Winnicott wrote that the child is "*addicted*" to it, that precisely "most mothers allow their infants some special object and expect them to become, as it were, addicted to such objects" (Winnicott, 1953, 1971). The idea of addiction suggests that the object is linked to jouissance. The transitional object is not an additional partial object—it is neither a Kleinian object, nor a fetish.

This object, initially situated as the object of the mother, soon changes its position. Lacan draws the line between the breast and the mother's body, between the object and the mother; the child always loses something of himself. Once the object has fallen away from the mother, it belongs, as the transitional object, to neither one nor the other. Right after the seminar on *Desire and its Interpretation*, Lacan tackles another loss, which is more radical and fundamental because it comes earlier—the loss of the primordial other, of the other as the first, real stranger, whom he calls, based on Freud's "Project" (Freud, 1950a), the Thing (*das Ding*). The Thing remains at the centre of the subject's representations—it is neither inside nor outside and both inside and outside—and it is radically lost when the subject enters language. The Thing therefore remains as a kind of vacuole at the heart of the subject's being and the object *a* as a fragment can take its place. Lacan first identifies this fundamental and original loss with the placenta, with the envelope that the subject loses at birth and which had separated him from the other in a fundamental way. This is where he places the Freudian objects: the breast and the faeces, as well as the gaze and finally adding the voice. Initially he also situates the penis here. But ultimately, the object *a* becomes—occasionally—embodied only in four substances: the breast, the faeces, the gaze and the voice.

Going back to Saint Augustine's observation in *Seminar XI* on *The Four Fundamental Concepts of Psychoanalysis* (Lacan, 1973), Lacan points out that in addition to the aspects of rivalry, which are of course part of the mirror image, the object *a* is derived from an image of wholeness. In 1920, Freud became interested in what seemed to be a difficulty in analytic treatment. In traumatic neurosis, he found, the subject repeatedly dreams of a painful situation that he experienced, just as the child, in the *fort-da* game (Freud, 1920g), repeats an experience of unpleasure. Observing the game of his one-and-a-half-year-old grandson, Freud noted that the little boy, though very attached to his mother, did not cry when she left him for a while but instead threw various objects across the room while she was gone. As a rule, when he threw these objects, he uttered a long sound like "o-o-o-o", which the mother and Freud understood as the German word *"fort"*, "gone." On another occasion, Freud observed the complete game, in which the child threw a spool attached by a string over the edge of his crib while making the "o-o-o-o" sound, then pulled on the string to make the spool appear once again, joyously exclaiming "*da*!" ("there!")—a game of disappearance and return.

Freud interprets this game as progress on the cultural level: a renunciation of the drive, which enables the child to endure his mother's departure. At the same time, the question that arises for Freud is to know why the child repeats a game that reminds him of an unhappy situation. What the *fort-da* game introduces is primal symbolisation. This symbolisation of the mother's comings and goings, presences and absences, occurs by means of language. In connection with this game, Lacan emphasises two things. Firstly, what is at stake is the constitution of the subject: the person who utters the signifiers *fort-da* is speaking from a subjective position that is separate from the Other, the primal mother. Secondly, the spool is not only an object representing the mother, but also an object that the subject sees as torn away from himself. Hence in this operation the subject is "de-completed" of this object, and the object, separated from the subject, functions to plug an absence, a lack, at the same time that (although it is absolutely contingent) it incarnates that absence or lack as closely as possible. The spool, Lacan says:

> [...] is not the mother reduced to a little ball by some magical game worthy of the Jivaros—it is a small part of the subject that detaches itself from him while still very much his, still retained [...]. If it is true that the signifier is the first mark of the subject, how can we fail to recognize here—from the very fact that this game is accompanied by one of the first oppositions to appear—that it is in the object to which the opposition is applied in act, the spool, that we must designate the subject. To this object we will later give the name it bears in the Lacanian algebra—the little *a*. (Lacan, 1973)

Thus the repetition of the mother's departure is the cause of the subject's division, a division bound up with a signifying opposition as the only way to establish the signifier as pure difference. This first loss, which occurs with symbolisation, establishes the divided subject and, at the same time, the object *a*. Lacan writes this operation with the help of the following formula, in which S_1 and S_2 are signifiers, $ the divided (castrated) subject and this process of symbolisation produces a remainder: object *a*.

$$\begin{array}{ccc} S_1 & \rightarrow & S_2 \\ \$ & & a \end{array}$$

At the end of *Seminar IX* (Lacan, 1962) and throughout *Seminar X* (Lacan, 2004) Lacan carries out a fundamental reversal, which gives the object *a* its true function, making it no longer the object aimed at by desire, but instead its *cause*: an object fundamentally lost, lacking, connected to castration. From now on, it is therefore not an empirical object, an object of this world, but *"the index finger raised toward an absence"*. It is no longer imaginary, absent as it is from the mirror image; it is what the libido subtracted from the narcissistic image invests. Neither is it only symbolic because it cannot be reduced to a signifier, it cannot be symbolised. It is a residue of the very operation of symbolisation, of the subject's capture in the signifying chain, of his division. It is even outside the Law, which nevertheless remains, on the one hand, its connection to jouissance and desire, outside meaning, but also its constitutive limit. It causes desire, but is not desire's aim. It is not an empirical object, but instead an object of logical consistency that only occasionally becomes embodied in the partial objects, yet it is not *only* them. The Symbolic gives the object its functional coordinates—as we see in the four discourses Lacan later elaborates—but these again are *not* what it is, because as such, the object *a* cannot be an object of knowledge. It provides access to the Real, while simultaneously screening it out. It is not really a lost object—that is only one of its aspects. For the neurotic, it is polarised by the phallus, "which is the whole weight of the function of the object *a*. It is impossible to articulate the object *a* without this reference" (Lacan, 1972). To say that the object *a* is the cause of desire in fact refers to its relationship to castration, which is the result of an act of language, and it is also an act of language that turns the absence of the penis in the mother into a lack. The object thus becomes essential as the subject's support, insofar as it is his fantasmatic relationship with object *a* that defines him.

Seen from another angle, object *a* is elaborated through jouissance, if only as a drive. It represents the object of the partial drive as completely contingent. The object is always fundamentally missed by the drive, which thereby continuously reactivates itself. Lacan will coin the term *plus-de-jouir* ("surplus enjoyment"—an expression forged on the basis of Marx's surplus-value) by making use of the equivocation inherent in the French expression, which means both a lack of enjoyment and its return through fantasy. Jouissance can return via fantasy, which becomes one of the crucial issues of psychoanalytic treatment. Fantasy acts as a screen against the Real of the sexual non-rapport. The object *a* therefore regulates jouissance. Fantasy is not a grammatical sentence from which the subject has completely disappeared; nor it is an agency of the Imaginary. Instead, it harbours within itself something real—the object *a*—and through its writing becomes a way of binding the signifier and jouissance together. It is in this movement towards the object's bareness that it can be situated as a hole in the Real and an effect of language. The object is therefore lodged in all three registers, yet belongs to none of them. It is the effect of the subject's cut—the "fallout" from his separation from the other.

When Lacan comes to theorise the Borromean knot, the object *a* is placed at the unique point where the three registers—the Real, Symbolic, and Imaginary—are tied together. Here, it becomes a letter—*a*—of the Real. The object *a* is in a sense irretrievable. In Lacan's final way of writing the relationship between the three registers, *a* is identified as a place to which "all jouissance is connected". In the Borromean knot it holds the three rings together, but nevertheless presents a difficulty in the Real: what *is* an "object in the Real?" What is a "hole" in the Real? In this sense, it is also external to each of the knot's intersections. Lacan said that the effect of science was to produce an object *a* for everyone, simply because the object *a* as such, i.e., truth as a cause, is excluded from it. While science "only proceeds by plugging all the holes", the excluded truth nevertheless returns in the products of science. Science, Lacan says, always gives us something to chew on: we get gadgets instead of what we are lacking in terms of the sexual rapport. If, as he argues, "the future of psychoanalysis depends on the Real, [it is a question] namely of whether, for example, gadgets will indeed get out of hand, if we ourselves will become animated by them". Yet he thinks this to be unlikely: "We will never be really able to prevent gadgets from being our symptom."

References

Freud, S. (1905d). *Three Essays on the Theory of Sexuality. S. E., VII.* London: Hogarth.

Freud, S. (1917e). Mourning and Melancholia. *S. E., XIV.* London: Hogatrh.

Freud, S. (1920g). Beyond the Pleasure Principle. *S. E., XVIII.* London: Hogarth.

Freud, S. (1950a). Project for a Scientific Psychology (1950 [1895]). *S. E., I.* London: Hogarth.

Lacan, J. (1962). Séminaire livre 9, L'Identification. Unpublished.

Lacan, J. (1972). Intervention sur l'exposé de S. Leclaire: « L'objet a dans la cure », *Lettres de l'École freudienne, n° 9*: 445–450.

Lacan, J. (1973). *Séminaire livre 11, Les quatre concepts fondamentaux de la psychanalyse.* Paris: Seuil.

Lacan, J. (1998). *Séminaire livre 4, La relation d'objet.* Paris: Seuil.

Lacan, J. (2004). *Séminaire livre 10, L'Angoisse.* Paris: Seuil.

Lacan, J. (2013). *Séminaire livre 6, Le désir et son interpretation.* Paris: La Martinière.

Saint Augustine (2002). *The Confessions of St. Augustine.* A. Cook (Trans.). New York: Courier Dover Publications.

Winnicott, D. W. (1953). Transitional Objects and Transitional Phenomena—A Study of the First Not-Me Posession. *Int J Psycho-Anal, 34*: 89–97.

Winnicott, D. W. (1968). Playing: Its Theoretical Status in the Clinical Situation. *Int J Psychoanal, 49*: 591–599.

Winnicott, D. W. (1971). *Playing and Reality.* London: Tavistock (Routledge, 1991).

CHAPTER SIX

Editors' introduction

L. Bailly and S. Bailly

This chapter will introduce the reader to exciting but complex developments in Lacanian child psychoanalysis. The work, strongly anchored in Lacan's writings, goes beyond explaining Lacan's use of the old psychiatric concept of transitivism. It innovates and leads to new understandings of the chemistry at work between a mother and a baby that changes both the baby's thinking and his subjective place in a radical and necessary way. Unusually, these conceptual developments were the result of a Socratic dialogue that went on for more than a decade from the early 1990s between Jean Bergès and Gabriel Balbo, with the two authors taking turns to confess to the other that they had little knowledge, pushing the other to demonstrate and clarify his views. The outcome is a consistent and powerful model of early interactions leading to a more general understanding of psychic mechanisms. Babies in Bergès' work are, like Lacan's, little philosophers, but they also have a body. More precisely they are bodies, whose functioning they enjoy and which therefore make them think. Examining this thinking in all its complexity led Jean Bergès to develop the conceptual importance of the hypothesis—hypotheses formed both by the baby and by its interlocutors. He wrote:

> Speaking of the clinical workings of the hypothesis is in reality expressing the hope that it is possible to approach children in other than in an Imaginary way [...]. When one talks about clinical matters it is important to point out that the clinician has to see things—he points at things, notices things, looks for distinctive signs or indicated meanings. Experience makes me feel that it is not by signs or meanings that one makes progress in child analysis; this is why I put the emphasis on hypothesis. (Bergès, 2007)

Like Winnicott, Bergès and Balbo think that "there is no such thing as a baby", but for them it is not just the mother and possibly the father that need to be introduced into the system but a multitude of small others—siblings, fellows, the alter ego of the baby, as well as the mother, the Other and more originally following Balbo's suggestions, the Other *of* each protagonist, baby, mother, father etc. This has led to a model of psychic complexity capable of dealing with the large effects of minute incidents, and the differences of structure between individuals apparently exposed to the same environment. It does to dyadic interactions what relativist physics did to Newtonian observations.

An interesting difficulty arose in the translation of this paper because of the authors' use of a French neologism, *s'identifier* followed directly by a noun rather than a preposition, to denote a mechanism that is has not been adequately described or defined in psychoanalysis and is to do with the process of identification. The English *"to identify* with *someone"* corresponds to the French *"s'identifier* a *quelqu'un"*; likewise, the English *"to identify"* (as in *"to identify a new species of parrot"*) corresponds to the French *"identifier"*. However, Bergès and Balbo deliberately use the grammatically incorrect *"s'identifier le discours de la mere"* (omitting the use of a preposition between verb and object) to force a distinction to be made between what they mean by this and the usual use of the reflexive verb *"s'identifier"*. There is no possible English translation for this, as there is no reflexive form of the verb *"to identify"*, and its reflexive quality in such sentences *"he identifies with his father"* is conveyed simply by the addition of the preposition *"with"*.

The question thus became, what did Bergès and Balbo wish to convey with their neologism? It is clear that they wish to highlight a mechanism at play in the construction of the child's subjectivity, and that this mechanism involves the child's taking in of the discourse of the mother so that it becomes his own. An understanding of this depends on the view that psychic structure is defined by the signifying chain, and that the insertion of discourse into this is constitutive of the subject. It is also important to emphasise that Bergès and Balbo use "identification" to mean the constitution of the subject that experiences and is mostly unconscious, rather than constitutive of the self-conscious ego.

The processes of identification have been and still are a matter of continuous exploration and this paper belongs within that body of work. Most authors agree that identification involves "taking in from an other" or (in the IPA) "taking in of an object" and the most important term used to denote this mechanism is introjection, or introjective identification. Gabriel Balbo clarified in conversation with us that the mechanism denoted by their neologism could be understood as introjection or introjective identification, but emphasised that he and Bergès had avoided using these terms in order to avoid any connotation of objects and imaginary relations between subject and object. They wished to emphasise that it is the mother's *discourse* that is taken in and becomes the baby's own and contributes towards his evolving subjectivity. We have decided that for this translation, we would use both the terms introjective identification or identificatory introjection; where this has felt clumsy, we have used the very simple concept of *acquisition*—making something one's own—which we feel conveys the authors' meaning with little risk of adding a penumbra of unwanted connotations. It is our hope that the understanding of introjective identification as a mechanism involving discourse and not imaginary objects might in the end prevail, and we think it is not an idle hope, as there are authors within the IPA mainstream whose views on introjective identification "coincide with Lacan (1953–1954) when he maintains that projection and introjection are not of the same type, since introjection is always symbolic: *what is introjected is the words of the other, while projection belongs to the imaginary order*" (Etchegoyen, 1985, p. 133).

The text here makes no direct reference to Lacan's late concept of *lalangue*—the very early linguistic experience of the child, when speech is still experienced as material and when its distinguishing point from other phenomena perceived by the baby is that it is uniquely laden with the affects of others: "*Lalangue* affects us first of all by everything it brings with it by way of effects that are affects" (Lacan, 1972–1973). However, we feel that the authors' do here clarify two important aspects of *lalangue*: firstly, how by acting as a vector for affect, the spoken phoneme brings into being for the child a full experience, full in the sense of existing in all three psychic realms (RSI); and secondly, how the very act of transitivism, imposed by the mother and accepted by the child, creates the template for the complex intersubjective exchanges typical of our species. We also feel that if read with an open mind, this paper could provide a bridge between the Lacanian tradition and that of the various object relations schools in thinking about mechanisms of identification.

References

Bergès, J. (2007). *Le corps dans la neurologie et la psychanalyse.* Paris: Erès.
Etchegoyen, R. H. (1985). Identification and its Vicissitudes. *IJPA, 66*: 3–18.
Lacan, J. (1972–1973). *Seminar 20—Encore.* C. Gallagher (Trans.). Unpublished.

CHAPTER SIX

An essay on transitivism*

Jean Bergès and Gabriel Balbo

Transitivism in the mother

It is a common observation that at the sight of her child at risk of falling, or who has just fallen and makes no particular display, the mother is affected and does not hesitate to express her affect of pain, perfectly articulated and demonstrated in speech. What she experiences and expresses is a certainty, because her affect is supported by a Real. It is because her affect is supported by the Real that the child finds reason in what she has experienced and therefore said.

Transitivism is not only what the mother experiences and demonstrates, it is also the process she initiates when she addresses her child, because she makes the hypothesis of a knowledge in him—knowledge around which her speech is going to circulate as around a pulley, to return to her in the form of a demand: a demand she supposes to be that of the identification of her child with the discourse she holds about him. This circulation describes a very general process which has to do with the access to the Symbolic. In the particular case of transitivism, this process necessarily involves the body as it is engaged in an experience which affects the subject in a manner different from the way in which a purely affective experience would affect him, as the latter can only be moral. The body here is for the child the receiving place in which the world takes form and consistency. This access to the Symbolic represented by the child's acquisition/introjective identification[1] of the mother's discourse involves the body as not only the imaginary body but also the body of language, signifiers and letters.

The transitivism of the mother towards the child can be considered as a *coup de force*. By holding a transitivist discourse the mother forces the child to integrate himself in the Symbolic.

---

*Extracts from: Jean Bergès and Gabriel Balbo, (1998) *Le Jeu Des Places De La Mère Et De l'Enfant—Essai sur le transitivisme.* Paris: Erès. With thanks to Erès. Translated from the original French and abridged by Lionel Bailly.

She obliges the child to take into account affects that she names to designate his experiences in reference to hers. She therefore obliges him to evaluate what he experiences in reference to a masochism which is only hers. The characteristic of transitivist thinking is to negate the real experience of the other in order to force him to experience. It makes the child experience in reality and in a mirroring effect what has been supposed by another and that he has to experience.

The transitivist forcing anticipates and conditions that which later pushes the child to enter, whether he likes it or not, the field of speech and language and then that of written language. This *coup de force* is not of the magnitude of a trauma but has a connection with the Real, a Real necessary for access to the Symbolic and for the knotting of the three registers of Imaginary, Symbolic, and Real. This *coup* forces the child towards the Borromean knot, no more but no less.

Why is this *coup* not a trauma? It is not a trauma because the child and the mother elaborate a discourse about the forcing, something that supposes anticipation and a hypothesis, and because transitivism depends upon the knowledge that it supposes in the child and that it solicits. The acquisition of experience through transitivism opens access to the Symbolic, while trauma is purely disruptive due to its character of pure, unthinkable Real, which is impossible to knot. Where trauma leaves the subject overwhelmed by unbearable pain, in transitivism the pain is the object of a remarkable symbolic elaboration. This elaboration involves a double negation: a child hurts himself without reaction (first negation) and it is another who complains of it without suffering (second negation). This double negation results from the effect of a double splitting and a double repression. The *coup de force* requires these three terms—double negation, splitting and repression. Traumatic effects on the contrary deprive the subject of the capacity to be forced as he can only be overwhelmed.

If the child takes up the baton from his mother and becomes transitivist, clinical experience shows that other people also will take up this baton—teachers and masters in particular who will demand of the child that he acquires the discourse of knowledge that they hold because they make the hypothesis that what they transmit to the child is connected with a knowledge that the child already possesses. Clinically, failures of learning cannot be properly understood or tackled if one does not take into account deviations in transitivism.

Transitivism is a forcing process far from tender maternal care such as holding, but this process has its roots in the maternal hypothesis that the child asks her to read to him the knowledge that is within himself. Through this reading, the child can make an identificatory introjection of the knowledge, and take possession in the Symbolic of something that he already possessed in the Real.

Implications in the direction of the treatment

What an analysand experiences—is it not the analyst's function to return it to him? And in particular in saying it so that he will introjectively identify with the knowledge. One can recognise there a whole sympathetic practice founded on the empathy of the therapist, which uses the experience and their sameness to make patient and therapist complementary. This practice leads to a classic transitivism which goes only in one direction.[2] There is here an aspect of the conduct of the treatment that needs to be thought about in a new way, from a different form of transitivism.

Transitivism was first studied in classical psychiatry with psychotic patients, particularly by the German school of the nineteenth century. It was elaborated by Wallon in 1934 in particular in chapter 5 of *Les Origines du Caractere Chez l'Enfant* (Wallon, 1949) and was used by Lacan (2001) in his article on "Family Complexes" in 1938, in *Ecrits* in 1966 and particularly in *Seminar 11*. From the beginning of the twentieth century until the 1930s, following its initiator Wernicke (1906), the notion of transitivism is used by psychiatrists who tried to differentiate a real transitivism from a process of appropriation. The merit of Henri Wallon is to have pointed out in 1921 that morbid transitivism is close to normal transitivism as observed in children between the ages of two and three. From that date onwards, transitivism became not only a psycho-pathological concept but also one used to describe the normal development of the personality of the child. As was typical of the time, a genetic dimension was prominent: "transitivism precedes immediately the moment where the child will know how correctly to attribute to himself or to others, the states or the acts that he perceives" (Wallon, 1949). At the same time, Lacan in his article on "Family Complexes" (Lacan, 2001), takes up in a Freudian way the evolution of the concept of transitivism and its linking function. He highlights its insufficient psychoanalytic elaboration and its close connection with identification and therefore with the relationship between the subject and everything that is other. However, in his seminar on *Identification* (1961–1962) Lacan did not take up the question of transitivism. In British psychoanalysis, Winnicott (1965) mentioned a clinical case which for us evokes transitivism, while the author himself doesn't mention it: "in the excitement of an experience linked with a good object, it happens that the child bites: the object will then be experienced as an object that bites". In 1968, Castoriades-Aulagnier in her paper "Demande et Identification" describes what she calls primary identification, putting emphasis on its relationship with demand; but she defines this relationship as purely univocal (having only one correspondence) and makes no reference to transitivism. In the same issue of the review *Inconscient* in which this articles appeared, J.-L. Donnet and J.-P. Pinel (1968) tried to distinguish between the identification in a dream and hysterical identification through an analysis of Freud's ideas of identification. We feel that their omission of the concept of transitivism has limited their success.

All these different approaches in transitivism seem without exception to end up reducing the observed phenomena to a univocal relationship—subject-object, ego-object, object-object, subject-subject, etc. The authors often try to get away from this bipolarity using the concept of primary narcissism, which is however itself marked by the issues of doubleness, ubiquity and ambivalence; in what they theorise of what they observe, their over-investment of the object and the relation to the object keeps bringing them back to a dead-end. We are grateful to Lacan for giving primary importance not to the object but to discourse, in describing and explaining psychic phenomena and the characteristics of a case. Discourse allows the intercalation of the Other and the unconscious between the agent of the discourse and its effects.

From this point, the phenomena observed are not bipolarisable but will always be related to at least three terms. This minimal threefoldness obliges us to think of subject and object, but to think of them in reference to the Other, and therefore of the splitting function it commands and by which they are marked. Without this, a bipolarity would insist, which excludes non-specularity. This insistence is also exclusive of psychoanalysis itself, of all theorising of subject-object relations, relations that are often reduced to affronts to the ego.

Transitivism as we conceive of it, is in contrast exclusive of bipolarity as it introduces the third term of the demand, attributed to the child in the hypothesis formulated by the mother in her discourse.

The game of changing places in transitivism

When the mother has put herself in the place of the child, she expresses to him that he should have felt a pain, and without this, he would not have felt pain. The child then takes the mother's place and says, "ow". And having taken the mother's place, which she vacates for him, the child attributes to himself the mother's hypothesis, taking it to be his own. In a way, he puts himself in the skin of the mother who, having felt nothing, said, "ow"; in short, he not only takes his mother's hypothesis as his own but he also ratifies it. In acquiring through identification the "ow" of his mother, he authenticates her utterance. In this place in which he is affected, in both senses of the word, what is in operation is not hysterical identification; he doesn't suffer because she would have suffered but because he took upon himself the hypothesis that she made and according to which he would have suffered. It is a symbolic way of involving affect, which has nothing to do with imaginary hysterical identification. It is not the contamination of affect of which Freud speaks with regard to hysterical identification but the appropriation of a hypothesis. Properly speaking, this is about a game of affectation.[3]

This game of affectation, which is as primordial and important as that of identification, is to be distinguished and retained as a fundamental process by which the infant will access affect. Here, we clarify the difficult concept of affect by examining the mechanism that produces it: affectation.

In taking the mother's place, the child does not, however, take the mother's splitting upon himself as well, only her hypothesis. It is only the mother who is divided and this splitting is the basis of the mother's transitivist function, in the measure that she speaks the pain for the infant *while* he showed no reaction. What can one say about this splitting effect in the mother in this game of places? Already, in taking the place of her child she is split, in that she is both in his place and in her own.

a) In the case of the child who says "ow" upon seeing a fellow receiving a bump and not reacting, the child isn't split: he is only being his transitivist mother. In this case, it is about *identifying* with a transitivist mother and a consequence of this is that the child is led to turn the love of his mother into hate—so that the effect produced by this sort of transitivism is by nature sadistic. A common example: someone falls over and I burst out laughing. Can we explain this turnaround? It seems to operate by a double negation, which this time does not only apply to the absence of the experience but also to the love of the mother. Otherwise, the effect of the negation of the affect, in its consequences upon love as an affect, perhaps allows one to suggest that the negation of love comes first, determining a lack that the infant just parries with another affect.

In this place that permits the child to reverse the affect of love into one of hate, we could argue that he is repeating the primal scene, at the heart of which for him love is absent: Father is doing violence to Mother. The child supposes his mother to suffer, transitives and repeats this pain: the primal scene is for him a secondary fantasmatic erotisation that allows him to preserve, inscribed in him by its repetition, the memory or the signifier of the original transitivism. From this, one can better understand that violence emerges through the diverse actualisation of the primal scene. And where transitivism is usually produced by the sustaining of an utterance that expresses a painful affect, in the case of the primal scene there is no speech to sustain transitivism, which is instead produced by the unsaid that the act implies. Violence could well originate, be produced, in this kind of speechless transitivism.

b) In the case of a child victim of aggression, transitivism allows him to substitute for his real masochism a symbolic masochism which will limit the real masochism. These limits are produced by repression. How? It seems due to the fact that the symbolic masochism of the mother's discourse will order the child's pain to the phallic function. What we are trying to do here is to translate into metapsychological terms the common clinical observation that the mother's speech, in substituting itself into what she supposes the child to have suffered, renders this suffering and its experience symbolic, this is how the mother's speech represses and imposes limits.
c) In the case of a child who telephones a child abuse helpline to disclose having been abused, this child can only have made the hypothesis that whoever takes his call herself harbours a wish to be rescued from some past maltreatment, which doubtless drives her towards a repetition. In fact, she is not only concerning herself with a battered child but with the battered child that she was, either in reality or in fantasy. This is why she can be interested and the way in which her interest is captured does bring to mind Freud's elaboration on masochism in his text, "A Child Is Being Beaten" (Freud, 1919e). In this text, he distinguishes 3 stages:
   1. My father beats the child that I hate.
   2. My father beats me, therefore my father loves me.
   3. A Child is being beaten: who is doing the beating and who is being beaten are both unknown. This is the phase that appears in the course of treatment: "It often comes into my mind, and this affects me, that a child is being beaten […]."

Freud holds that the second stage—that of the blows of love—is totally unconscious and must be reconstructed in analysis. It is by this reconstruction that Freud makes his hypothesis about unconscious knowledge in the analysand, which allows us to approach a transitivism similarly in three stages.

What are these in transitivism? Firstly, a child receives a blow without reacting and it is another child, who hasn't been hit, who reacts. In this first stage, the transitivism is a product of the maternal function. Which one? The function in which she separates the child from its hallucinatory object of desire; therefore, there is a necessary transitivism that allows a child to react to a real object!

What is the second stage? It is that by which hate, which made the child force another child to suffer what he had not experienced returns implicitly to the love the mother could have only for he who transitivises and not he who has to suffer. In other words, it is always because my mother loves me that the other has to suffer a blow that he anyway did not experience.

This love brings us back to the transitivism of the mother:

- In the first phase, an infant cries, experiencing something. The mother, because of love, gives him hunger or thirst or otherwise thinks about his needs.
- Secondly, she feeds him, or waters him or otherwise cares for him.
- In the third phase, her further hypotheses about her child's experiences will tend to fall back upon and verify the initial hypothesis. This is what she will express in phrases such as: "When he cries like that, I know it's because …" followed immediately by the hypothesis of that demand. This third phase is decisive. It is never infantile, it is always maternal; it never belongs to the child, who in no case ever attributes to himself either by reflection or introspection hunger, thirst etc. There is therefore no tolerable gap between what she anticipates of the functioning experienced by the child (hunger, thirst etc.) and the functioning really experienced by him. However, this gap does exist and it is because of this that the mother never really responds truly to the demand of the child: she responds only to what she supposes to be his demand.

While there is necessarily a gap in the first and the third phases, this gap does not exist in the second: if it did, it would effectively cause the failure of transitivism by invalidating in one blow the anticipatory hypothesis of the mother.

In a general way, transitivism turns a subject into a "new subject", to the other, a double; it also makes possible reversals of object-subject positions and reversals of aim. More precisely, there is no new subject without anticipatory transitivism.

Does the one who hurt himself do it because the other, who saw it, transitivises? Is he not led to do it? This would mean that he who hurt himself found with his fellow what his mother found with in him at the beginning: not everything is lost of the primary transitivism. Also, as we have seen, it is the witness who arrogates to himself all maternal love.

Let's look at the case of the child who hurts himself, cries and just as quickly produces a discourse (quite simply, he hurts himself and verbalises immediately what he has done). This time, it's not about assuming the pain of the other, it's about assuming his own; and as by imitation, as by identification with a maternal trait, he doesn't repress this suffering but lets it happen, appending his discourse to it, exactly as does his mother; in short, he identifies himself with his mother and renders her present. This absence-presence repeats and recalls the splitting that produced the mother's discourse, when she was present to speak it. In short, he has introjected this dialectic of absence and presence.

The birth cry anyway is a demand addressed by the infant. It seems, however, more important to us to underline the cries of the mother while giving birth. Those in effect anticipate the infant's cry, not only in the sense that they are pain cries but perhaps and especially because they show the mother's waiting for the cry of her baby, as if the mother's cry announces the baby's, as if she is already in the game of hypothesis that the baby will require her to cry, so that he can appropriates this cry and cry in his turn. By the pain she experiences, the mother can try to limit that which her child expresses in his birth cry: he appropriates her cry of alarm and with this identification, she will have to respond. With this identification, he is at once split because of a suffering that his cry has to symbolise.

The introjection of the transitivist function of the mother by her child appears thus to take its full meaning, determining eventually the relationship that a subject will have with the pain of his body. Here, one could evoke the insensitivity to pain of the psychotic, a typical pathology of transitivism: if he bumps into the wall, he strokes it; he takes the place of the mother, who never allowed him to, and who never made possible the introjective identification of her transitivism. One can also evoke the relationship of psychosomatic patients with their bodies. They suffer from an excess of transitivist discourse, to the point they have to defend themselves against this excess. They do this by casting doubt upon transitivism, or rather by putting between their mothers and themselves a need that caused Lacan to say of desire: "It is in the measure to which need becomes involved in the function of desire that psychosomatism can be conceived of as something other than by the simple adage that consists of saying that there is a psychic lining to everything somatic" (Lacan, 1973). So that for example, it is the eczema that is itching, the subject, exiled from his own symptom cannot say, "it makes me itch". And the subject frees himself by aphanisis. One can suggest that for these patients with transitivist excesses, their mother never addressed them with a discourse adequate to limit their suffering and their masochism.

It is a function of transitivism to make suffering positive, rendering, by this process, absent objects present. One could suggest that in this process, there is a double affirmation in operation that is implied in the double negation characteristic of transitivism. This double affirmation shows how much *Bejahung* is inscribed in this process: the suffering of the mother comes to make present what was only virtually present.

By this particularity of the mechanism of transitivism, the subject also sometimes renders the absent present using a substitute that is present and not only in an imaginary or symbolic way. This substitute can be a persecutor, which is quite real; it is an other, which becoming real, not only produces pain but also authenticates it. This persecutor can be chosen to be the original transitivist mother that the child wants to re-find and with whom he wishes to repeat his jouissance: it is the new object that the ego adopts. It is this mother who says, "careful, you're going to hurt yourself", not as an interdiction but as an injunction to jouissance.

In this order of ideas, for the mother herself, the fact of having a child may be therapeutic. In effect, the ability to make transitivism work will allow her to modify sensibly the paranoid relationship that she established with her own body. As far as the body of the child is differentiated from that of the mother, this introduces a gap that constitutes a lack. It is this lack that in the mirror stage is not specularisible. So that from this, one can see that lack can be considered the negative of affect: hate, like pain, cannot be specularised.

Transitivism and voice

(The voices of transitivism)

It is because I say "ow" in the place of the Other in transitivism that this "ow" is heard to be coming from the Other, and this voice affects the other and makes him cry.

The voice is what transfers an affect from the Other to the subject, who is sensitive to the voice that carries the message; not only can transitivism be sadistic but it is equally by the voice that displacement takes place and that affect is invested.

By what metaphorical circuit is the transfer of affect produced by the one who says, "ow"?

a) From the one who is hit to the one who says "ow" there is the introjective identification of a trait.
b) From the one who says "ow" to the one who is hit and is now going to cry, having heard this "ow", the voice is the vehicle of affect and what releases the affect is identification. The function of transitivist identification consists in giving birth to and experiencing an affect.

At the exit of a Metro station, a woman had her hand painfully caught between a door and its jamb. She talked about this in her session, almost in a whisper, as if she was talking to herself. "I make no sound when I am in pain, I never cry out. It just doesn't come out. I walked on fifty metres and it went straight to my heart—when the pain took hold, I felt I was tottering. I waited for it to pass. As if it were nothing. I think it is nothing. I hope that it is nothing because I need that hand. Anyway, there's nothing to be done—it's inside. One has just to wait. It's a bit crushed."

There was no transitivism between herself and her mother around pain: no voice had ever really echoed her sufferings. There is a soundless hole of introjective identification of the trait in which pain is the signifier.

Her analyst said to her: "You must have experienced an intense physical pain, no?"

She responded: "I have no idea. I don't remember."

What follows the identificatory hole is a memory hole: no memory, no meaning.

She added: "I'm not hardened to suffering. I am capable of complaining, of being in pain everywhere."

Suffering is therefore for her not of the order of the impossible, the Real: she has not excluded all transitivism, but by a narrow margin.

"There is something about immediate exteriorisation that doesn't come out. Once, I burned my whole arm with hot soup. Nothing—no sound came out of me. Something gets held in all the time."

There is no hypothesis of a demand being made with regard to this on the part of the Other: a demand dwells unformulated, it doesn't emerge, she can't find her voice.

"There is really a difference between the me that is boiling inside and ready to explode all the time, and the exterior with which I give the impression of being someone calm and poised. I listened yesterday to a radio recording of Roland Barthes about the body, and it was quite beautiful: you are the one you never see, the one you know the least well, at least when it comes to the body."

Her psychoanalyst then said: "You would be a dancer and it is your body that you know the least?"

She thought for a moment and then declared: "I know it from the inside. It's mostly that …" then fell silent. After a while she spoke again: "I know it from the inside, yes. What is it inside and what image does it give? Why do these things never match up? Also, what does one believe others expect of us?"

All these questions are as much calls to the transitivism of the Other as they are calls and expectations that a demand will at last be hypothesised of her. There is no voice to convey affect and lacking an identification with the voice, an affect is not released.

She moves on to a dream: "I dreamed the other night that I was planting a bomb in a market-place ... no, in a carpark. A very simple bomb, bought in a shop with its packaging and its user's manual: you just had to press a button and run away quickly to seek shelter. It was market day. It was crowded. Why have you done this? I thought: there are lots of people here, you must be mad!"

If there were such a thing as transitivism by narcissistic withdrawal, in place of a real mother-child transitivism, we would have to see it here in response to the question the subject puts to herself about the madness of the Other (the world).

"Because everyone could see me, it was as if I was condemning myself out of hand, as if I was doing everything possible to get caught."

And so that, even if it meant being found guilty, there would at last be transitivism.

"So I tried to change my appearance, my clothes ..." That is, she tried to change her experience, her bodily affect. Alas: "And the bomb just wouldn't explode! And the emergency services arrived—surely called by people suspicious of the device. They told me to get out of there."

And here is the desire of which the dream is the realisation: the desire for transitivism, in which the emergency services are evidently the signifiers for saving the dreamer from the worst ... what follows in the dream confirms the accomplishment of this desire.

"In fact, it was on the Esplanade de la Défence—that's where the market was. The bomb wouldn't explode. I absolutely had to set it off."

Her analyst asked a question: "You had to—were you ordered to do this?"

After a silence, she replied: "If you like, yes. It was what had to be done, yes. Like something very every day and banal, in fact. The bomb only had value when triggered."

One recognises from these words what a *coup de force* sustains transitivism.

"And in that moment—it has to be done really quickly, leave, protect yourself, think fast, understand fast too ..."

This is how the child is dragged along by the *coup de force* of transitivism: everything happens very quickly, as much from the point of view of motor function as that of thinking, and as much in its masochistic element as in the escape this allows.

"It should have exploded!"

The analyst asked: "Why should it have?"

After a long silence, the analysand replied: "Because it had to explode ... there had to be a before and an after ... a trigger, something violently released, which explodes in me ... there is something violent in me that doesn't come out, which is there. There cannot be change in my life without me doing some violence—physical violence, not verbal. Verbal violence—that would never come out."

From the desire from which the dream is constructed arises a demand for transitivism, the only *coup de force* that can mobilise, make a cut and bring about change.

"Indeed, you did some violence to yourself this morning, at the very start of your analytic session, to mark or to write on your own hand how you sometimes have to do it, in order not to forget—a before and an after?"

"Yes, that's true ..."

"But you have been able to speak about it, no?"

"Yes, that's also true, that's fair: but it astonishes me."

"Looking after your body, all the same—is that not how you earn your living?"

"Exactly that, yes—exactly that."

After this inaugural session—the third from an ordinal point of view—the analyst could engage: the discourse of the analysand was from here on hallmarked with transitivism.

Regarding representation consequential to identification (representation of the word, where the "ow" is the representative of the representation, that is, the signifier), it is on the side of that which is identified and entails repression by the voice, which can only transmit affect. It is the inverse mechanism of negation: the affect is preserved while the representation is available for repression. We can see here how and why it is the inverse process at play, while negation has yet to take its place.

Bejahung[4] is indeed the process by which representation is repressed and the affect transferred.[5] The one towards whom the mother holds a transitivist discourse receives the affect, and will preserve the representation of a pain that from this point onwards, he would have experienced.

Here, one could separate out the lines of research that permit the posing of hypotheses about the relationship between the hazards of the lack of transitivism and the voice in auditory hallucinations. If we take into consideration Lacan's view that a hallucination is the return in the Real of what has been foreclosed in the Symbolic, we could suggest that what was missed, is missing and will be missing, in the knowledge about pain, hunger, thirst, etc., transitivised by the mother from her own experience, and which will come to appear, by her voice, in the Real. The impossible would be overcome—the experience of feeling cold or thirsty when I'm not. It is important here to draw the fundamental link between transitivism and negative hallucination: I hear in the Real the voice of my mother experiencing what I have not experienced, what pain or cold have of the Symbolic—while the voice of the mother is Real—"be good, oh my pain and behave yourself".[6]

The child who almost burns himself, or who is about to hurt himself, is in full negative hallucination, which is primary and normal: the Real of the mother's voice deprives the child of the satisfaction of this type of hallucination and obliges him to take into account the real object of which he is in danger, and which she doesn't want him to think is just an object of jouissance. In this way, the mother also attempts to negate the negative hallucination that the child therefore has to give up. However, in this negation, the mother can only transitivise the measure of her experience—in a positive hallucination—what she is convinced the infant could suffer. It is indeed she who is persecuted by the hallucinatory object she experiences (cold, hot, diverse dangers). It is by means of a paranoid relationship with her own body that the mother transitivises into the child's body the negative hallucination in its positive form, obliging him to lose an object that would persecute the body. By this loss, she renders the child competent of depriving himself of the negative hallucination.

Psychotic transitivism (like that of the patient who cries out upon hearing a rug being beaten) gives the subject a body, which is always necessary: the negative hallucination of his body, which explains his transitivism, comes to be substituted with a positive hallucination that temporarily gives him a body. But what he hears is not a voice; and not hearing a voice makes him return to the negative hallucination. It is the voice of the mother that fleshes out the child in such a way that the positive hallucination of the mother is not properly one, as first, she speaks it and therefore she represses it and becomes divided. This explains that transitivism between the mother and the child is not a *délire a deux*. Maybe we could conceive of the maternal hallucination as being in the register of the Imaginary as she speaks it to the child, while the child renounces a negative hallucination which is Real.

Notes

1. The authors' concept of identification has led them to coin the neologism *"s'identifie le discours de la mére"*, which is untranslatable in English. They insist it is not "to identify *with*" as it is not about identification with an *object*. It is in simple terms the taking in of someone's discourse and the assimilation of that within the signifying chain that makes up the developing subject. It is an introjection that refers specifically to signifiers. In other places we have used the simple word "acquire" to denote a mechanism that results in the ownership of the discourse by the subject.
2. This form of "transitivism" is much closer to a simple mirroring and its weakness lies in taking at face value what the analysand is able to say about himself. Transitivism as elaborated in this article rests upon what *isn't* felt and remains uninscribed in the Symbolic—and which therefore cannot be uttered by the analysand.
3. "Affectation" is also a neologism that may suffer in translation because of the English *faux ami* and its connotations of falseness. The authors mean "the bringing into being of affect", and their conceptualisation of how this occurs through the game of hypothesis can be seen as a clarification of Bion's notions of beta elements and their transformation by alpha functioning.
4. *Bejahung* is translated in the Standard Edition as "affirmation" but Laplanche and Pontalis suggest as an alternative, "postulation". In this context, we prefer the latter.
5. The representation is presented to the child, linked with the affect, and he can then repress the representation while experiencing the affect.
6. From Charles Baudelaire's poem "Meditations".

References

Bergès, J., & Balbo, G. (1998). *Jeu Des Places De La Mére Et De l'Enfant—Essai sur le transitivisme.* Paris: Erès.

Castoriadis Aulagner, P. (1968). Demande et identification. In: *L'inconscient, 7*: 23–65, Paris, PUF.

Donnet, J.-L., & Pinel, J.-P. (1968). L'identification. In: *L'inconscient 7*. Paris: *PUF.*

Freud, S. (1919e). A Child is Being Beaten. *S. E., XVII* (1917–1919). London: Hogarth.

Lacan, J. (1973). *Séminaire XI, Les Quatre Concepts Fondamentaux*. Paris: Le Seuil, p. 207.

Lacan, J. (2001). Les complexes familiaux dans la formation de l'individu. In: *Autres Écrits*. Paris: Le Seuil, pp. 23–84.

Lacan, J. (2006). *Ecrits*. B. Fink (Trans.). New York & London: W. W. Norton & Company.
Wallon, H. (1949). *Les origines du caractère chez l'enfant*. Paris: PUF.
Wernicke, K. (1906). In: Jaspers (1946) *General Psychology*. Manchester: Manchester University Press, 1963.
Winnicott, D. W. (1965). *The Maturational Processes and the Facilitating Environment*. London: Hogarth Press.

CHAPTER SEVEN

Editors' introduction

S. Bailly

This paper is about more than the title suggests: it is a reflection on the nature and function of the symptom in the structure of the subject and provides a road-map for the clinician confronted with it in analytic treatment—moreover, one with a zoom function that allows for the minutiae of a session to be situated within the largest possible view of the Subject within the Other. Nobus eases us into his way of thinking by means of Lacan's reflection upon how an analyst might experience the puzzle presented by an analysand in his intriguing paper on "Logical Time", but then reviews the meaning of the symptom as a survival strategy and goes on to map its contours within the registers of Symbolic, Imaginary, and Real. While as clinicians we may be used to thinking about the metaphorical structure of the symptom and indeed pushed by the need to diagnose into trying to decipher this quickly, Nobus reminds us that it is composed equally in metonymy and that the elaboration of this will determine the logical time both for diagnosis and of its treatment.

When addressing the vexed question of working through, he focuses on the liberation of the drive from the fantasy in which it has been bound up, and reminds us of how preciously guarded fantasy may be, and how long it may take for it to appear in clinic. Fantasy is largely unconscious to the subject but lurks in his speech and language, which by their logical nature allow it to emerge. Fantasy is what is accessible to the analyst of a symptom with a real dimension and has first to be painstakingly assembled in analysis before it can be decomposed and emptied of jouissance.

CHAPTER SEVEN

The logical time of diagnosis: terms and conditions of the symptom in the Lacanian tradition

Dany Nobus

I

Health care practitioners generally agree that a correct diagnosis—literally a "discerning knowledge"—of a sick person's condition constitutes the essential clinical basis upon which a specific treatment programme can be implemented. Despite the fact that, on occasion, clinicians rely on interpretations of outcome causation to formulate a diagnosis—the patient suffers from bipolar disorder *because* he or she responds positively to lithium—in most cases the diagnosis provides a rationale for the treatment, and it ensures that the therapeutic intervention is adapted and adjusted to the clinical specificity of the patient's symptoms. Straightforward as this may seem, the purpose of a diagnosis, which always epitomises a targeted process of knowledge-production against the background of established socio-cultural beliefs about health and disease, has nonetheless been questioned by medical sociologists and critical theorists working within a Foucaultian paradigm, on the grounds that diagnostic categories are often not at all indicative of clinical realities, but rather a clever means for medical and health authorities to exercise power, either with a view to pathologising and stigmatising those conditions which cannot be recuperated as "desirable" within existing configurations of ideological acceptability, or with a view to capitalising on the creation of new lucrative opportunities for the production, sale and consumption of drugs. Diagnosing persistent shame as social anxiety disorder endows the sufferer with a new label of pathology, and excludes him or her from the mentally healthy section of society, but it also allows pharmaceutical companies to profit from the administration of Seroxat/Paxil®, Zoloft®, and other psychotropic substances (Lane, 2007). In cases such as these, the psychiatrically sanctioned diagnosis also has the secondary benefit that it removes the patient's accountability, so that sufferers no longer need to look for personal answers to the question as to what caused the condition.

Within the framework of psychotherapy and *a fortiori* within a psychoanalytic setting, diagnosis also informs the way in which the clinician directs the treatment, and as such it conditions the position he or she will adopt during the treatment process. Here, much more than in mainstream medical (psychiatric) approaches, the diagnosis is the epistemic foundation upon which the clinician orients him- or herself within the treatment. The diagnosis is held to predict the nature (quality) of the patient's transference, and it helps clinicians to modulate their interventions (interpretations, constructions) in such a way that the treatment process can be sustained in light of the projected outcomes. It is common knowledge that psychiatric classifications of mental disorder, such as the newly released *DSM-V* (American Psychiatric Association, 2013) do not appeal to psychoanalysts. The reason for their discomfort, which sometimes explodes into a full-blown attack on the psychiatric establishment, has nothing to do with the idea of classification *per se*. Psychoanalysts themselves have always entertained nosological distinctions and continue to operate with conceptual categories of psychic dysfunction, despite their emphasis on the clinical preservation of the patient's subjective reality. From the inception of psychoanalysis, Freud himself argued in favour of a basic nosological differentiation between the psychoneuroses and the actual neuroses (Freud, 1898a), subsequently refining the category of the psychoneuroses with a supplementary division between narcissistic and transference neuroses, depending on the patient's ability to establish an emotional tie with the analyst (Freud, 1916–1917). Nowadays, some psychoanalysts maintain a basic threefold distinction between psychosis, neurosis and perversion, whereas others employ slightly more sophisticated, yet equally categorical taxonomies, including borderline personality disorder, narcissistic disorders, neo-perversion, etc.

The main reason why psychoanalysts reject diagnostic classifications such as the *DSM-V* is that these nosological systems rely on a conception of the symptom which contravenes some of the fundamental principles of psychoanalytic doctrine. First and foremost, despite its explicit neutrality, allegedly devoid of theoretical and explanatory paradigms, the *DSM-V* embraces a traditional medical viewpoint, in which symptoms operate as signs, and particular associations (clusters) of symptoms constitute distinct patterns (syndromes) of mental disorder. The psychiatrist considers an observed or reported symptom in the mental or somatic sphere to be a reliable (and valid) index of a specific form of psychopathology and, pending an evaluation of the symptom's onset and duration, proceeds to formulate a diagnostic statement which also includes information on the nature, the course and the outcome of the disorder. Just as much as a sore throat, swollen lymph nodes and an increased bodily temperature serve as pathognomonic indications of laryngitis, persistent hallucinations, social withdrawal and depersonalisation reportedly function as clear, reliable manifestations of psychosis.

Throughout his career, Freud expressed his profound reservation concerning the accepted practice of deducing a patient's state of mind via a consideration of his or her symptoms. In the *Studies on Hysteria*, for instance, he averred that patients are all too often diagnosed as hysteric purely on the basis of allegedly characteristic traits such as anaesthesia and convulsions, a collection of sensory and motor symptoms (Breuer & Freud, 1895d, pp. 258–259). Freud did not believe that the *singularity* of the hysterical entity could be grasped through the appreciation of the symptomatic tableau, no matter how consistent these symptoms may appear. As his own rudimentary distinction between psychoneurosis and actual neurosis already suggests, Freud attempted to construct a nosological system on the basis of distinct etiological (predisposing) and precipitating factors, thus moving away from epidemiological relationships between clusters of symptoms and particular psychic disorders.

The important issue, here, is that psychoanalytic clinicians (and by extension all mental health professionals) should not zoom in on their patient's symptoms when formulating a diagnosis. This guideline does by no means imply that diagnosis becomes less important. On the contrary, it is precisely because symptoms lose their value as unambiguous semiological elements that diagnosis requires a less straightforward and more nuanced, a less categorical and more subtle approach. And for Freud, diagnosis remained of fundamental clinical importance, because he regarded it as a condition of possibility for the psychoanalytic treatment. At a time when mental illness was dealt with mainly by the patients' confinement and restraint, and the only treatments aimed at curing patients were those attempted by the practitioners of various alternative "therapies", Freud expressed his contempt for clinical psychiatry in no uncertain terms: "To make a mistake [when formulating a diagnosis] [...] is of far greater moment for the psycho-analyst than it is for the clinical psychiatrist, as he is called. For the latter is not attempting to do anything that will be of use, whichever kind of case it may be. He merely runs the risk of making a theoretical mistake, and his diagnosis is of no more than academic interest" (Freud, 1913c, p. 124). For the psychoanalyst, misdiagnosing a case of neurosis as psychosis implied, at least according to Freud, withholding psychoanalytic treatment from a patient who would most certainly benefit from it. Mistaking psychosis for neurosis entailed embarking on a clinical process that is bound to run aground on the psychotic's inability to develop a solid relationship of transference.

II

Before I explore the tortuous path of diagnosis further, it is worth lingering on the vexed issue of the symptom and its clinical status within psychoanalysis. If the symptom is not a clear-cut sign of a particular type of disorder, and can therefore not be used as a criterion for setting up a nosological classification and for formulating a diagnostic statement, which, if any, function does it still have within the course of a psychoanalytic treatment? If psychoanalysts need to guard themselves against viewing symptoms as signs, to what extent does this affect the way in which they operate with and on the symptom? The question is by no means gratuitous, for if the semantic relationship between the symptom and the disorder is broken, there is no guarantee that the latter (the disorder, the underlying conflict) has been resolved if the former (the symptomatic pattern) has disappeared, nor is there a means of gauging the progress of the treatment through an assessment of the symptoms (and this is unfortunately where much of the clinical outcome research, and many therapeutic effectiveness studies demonstrate their limitations). In addition, psychoanalysts cannot satisfy themselves with treating their patients' symptoms, if "treating" means working towards their disappearance, and then consider the therapy a success if the patient is symptom-free.

In keeping with Freud's argument that, given the endless variety of clinical situations and the enormous plasticity of psychic processes, it is much easier to formulate guidelines for the beginning and the end of the treatment than for the clinical process as a whole (Freud, 1913c, p. 123),

I shall first of all concentrate on the significance of the symptom within the analytic opening and endgame. By no means do I want to claim that my account is representative of the entire field of psychoanalysis, nor that my position is the synthetic distillation of the various clinical viewpoints on the symptom that have been advocated within the psychoanalytic schools since Freud. My outlook is merely a reflection of my own reading of Freud's work, and that of his most controversial follower, Jacques Lacan, who claimed to be working strictly within the Freudian tradition, and it should therefore be situated within a specific personal, theoretical, and clinical context. Its value needs to be judged not only in confrontation with mainstream psychiatric conceptions of the symptom, but also in light of alternative psychoanalytic approaches, such as those advanced within Kleinian, object-relations, neo-Freudian, modern psychoanalytic, relational and self-psychological traditions.

How are we to conceive of the symptom during the initial stages of a clinical consultation, that is to say before the psychoanalytic process *strictu sensu* starts, during what Freud would have called the "trial period" (*Probezeit, Erprobung, Sondierung*) (Freud; 1913c, p. 124), and what psychoanalysts within the Lacanian orientation tend to designate as the "preliminary conversations"? Whatever the patient's social and psychic landscape, regardless of age and gender, the symptom appears first of all as a *complaint*, that is to say as a more or less coherent verbalisation of a psycho-social and/or bodily "malfunction": something does not work properly, or there is a suspicion on the part of the patient that something isn't as it should be. As such, the patient arrives with a more or less disturbing problem, defined as such by him- or herself and/or by others, and thus presents the analyst with something that interferes with the continuation of his or her daily activities, and reduces the quality of his or her life and/or that of others. Put differently, the patient talks about something in her social, professional or personal life that gives cause for concern, and which cannot be resolved without the help of a professional. It should be noted, here, that the patient does not necessarily suffer from his symptom, nor that he necessarily demands that the psychoanalyst help him in overcoming it. Sometimes a patient makes clear that she only decided to seek professional help because *others* suffer from her "problem", whereas she herself does not experience any serious trouble at all. This is what Theodor Reik sometimes designated as a "garlic neurosis": the patient does not notice that he has a problem, but everybody in his immediate environment is affected by it. Many drug-related problems fall into this category, yet any type of symptom can in principle acquire "garlic" qualities. When this is indeed the case, the patient may ask the practitioner for advice on how to keep the others happy, and redress the stability in his environment, without making any changes to the alleged problem. It should also be noted that the symptom is not necessarily represented as a lack, deficit or absence; it may equally appear in the patient's life as an excess, a super-abundant presence or overwhelming fullness. A symptom, in other words, may appear in one of the two distinct forms that we generally attribute to "monstrosity": either *in defectu* (literally, as a "defective form") or *in excessu* (as a manifestation of excess). And in some cases, the symptom may effectively appear simultaneously as *in defectu* and *in excessu*, which is the case, for example, in problems of addiction, whereby patients regularly complain about "it being never enough and always too much", and which poses particular challenges to the clinician's therapeutic acumen.

At the very beginning of the treatment, during the preliminary conversations, before the treatment has effectively started, the symptom appears as a complaint, a concern, a worry, an expression of pain and suffering. This may seem obvious, if not to say banal, yet by contrast with the traditional approach to symptomatic phenomena in Western medicine, psychoanalytic theory emphasises the verbal rather than the visual component, here. Indeed, however conspicuous a patient's symptom(s) may be, the psychoanalyst is primarily attuned to the way in which these symptoms appear in the patient's speech. Or, to put it more provocatively, for a psychoanalyst the symptom does not really exist beyond the form and content it receives within the patient's narrative account of the circumstances of its emergence, its historical development and its current significance.

III

At this point, I want to introduce Lacan's 1945 paper on "Logical Time and the Assertion of Anticipated Certainty" (Lacan, 2006c), because it will provide me with a first step for articulating the precise challenges that the diagnostic process poses for the psychoanalytic clinician who takes it seriously. The article in question takes its starting point from what Lacan describes as a logical problem, but is essentially a puzzle designed to trick the power of reason, and which can therefore deservedly be called a sophism. A prison governor explains to three prisoners that he is forced to set one of them free, but rather than he himself deciding who shall be released he will put the prospect of freedom into the hands of the prisoners themselves. He informs them that he has three white disks and two black disks (five disks in total), and that he will attach one of these five disks to each of the three prisoners, between their shoulders, so that each of them will be able to see the colour of the two other prisoners' disks, without being able to see their own. With no reflecting surfaces on site and the men being prohibited from communicating with each other, the challenge is to deduce one's colour, the first prisoner who is able to do so correctly "upon logical and not simply probabilistic grounds" (Lacan, 2006c, p. 161) being led through the prison gate. When attaching the disks to the prisoners' backs, the governor gives each of them a white disk, so that all three of them see exactly the same pattern appearing when inspecting their fellow inmates' colours: in seeing two whites, and having been told that there are three whites and two blacks, they thus know that they themselves can be either black or white. Which colour is it, and how can they arrive at a logical conclusion?

In his analysis of the sophism, Lacan defines the moment when the prisoners detect the colour of the disks on the backs of their companions as the "instant of the glance" (*l'instant du regard*).[1] It is a moment of visual examination and communication, yet because within this very moment two white disks appear, it is also an instance of bewilderment, hesitation and confusion. For, on the one hand, there is the visual certainty that something (two white disks) is there to be seen, is offering itself to the eye, yet on the other hand it is not immediately clear how these "data" should be interpreted, what this observation means, and what conclusion should be drawn about the colour of the disk between the shoulders of the observer. The colour of the observed disks may be unambiguous, the way in which their combined appearance should be read and used as a basis for making a reliable judgment about one's own colour, and upon which—let us not forget—one's freedom depends, is not at all clear, and does not reveal itself in the mere blink of an eye.

I will return to the puzzle and its solution later on, but already here I would like to suggest that the psychoanalyst's confrontation with the symptom (as a complaint) during the initial phase, or the pre-phase of the treatment, is similar to the prisoner's observation of the two white disks in the sophism, with the caveat that it is no doubt less his own freedom than that of the other (the patient) which is at stake, and with the added proviso that the complaint is situated in the auditory rather than the visual field, which changes the "instant of the glance" into an "instant of the ear", a "moment for hearing". Rather than the visual nature of the symptom, it is the auditory structure of the narrative account in which the symptom is set which may give the psychoanalyst a clue as to which diagnosis is indicated, yet much like the two white disks it is a clue which generates as many questions as it answers, and which should at least be recognised as a complex message about the precise clinical structure in which it is embedded. I am involuntarily reminded here of Freud's technical recommendation—one of the very few—that the psychoanalyst should always approach a patient "free from any presuppositions" (Freud, 1912e, p. 114), by which he meant that clinicians should deliberately avoid the instantaneous identification of a presenting problem as a known clinical issue. No matter how much experience one has accumulated, and no matter how advanced one's clinical skills, it is better to allow the absolute singularity of the complaint to deploy itself, in all its ambiguities, before pinning it down as the manifestation of a certain case. Acknowledged in its appearance as a complaint, the symptom loses its status as a sign, then, and starts to operate as a *signifier* (S_1) an acoustic image or verbal (symbolic) utterance, whose relationship with the patient's general code of knowledge (S_2) reveals something about his or her particular *modus operandi* without this "reference" being immediately clear, so that no immediate conclusions can be drawn.

Let me illustrate this with a concrete clinical example. A man in his mid-thirties comes to see me because he suffers from what he describes as a pervasive lack of self-confidence, which undermines both his professional aspirations and his love life. At work, he cannot cope with the demands that are imposed upon him by the senior management, and the more he gets the impression that the company expects him to perform the more he fails in reaching his target. Every time an appraisal interview is imminent he falls ill because he knows that he will have to provide evidence of his achievements. The same mechanism presides over his relationship with his girlfriend. Every time they have sex, he feels that she expects him to demonstrate his virility, to show her that he is a man's man, and so he becomes impotent. He does not experience any erectile dysfunction when he is with a lover or with a prostitute, simply because these girls do not demand anything from him. When describing the nature and extent of his problem, the man adds that it may have something to do with his now deceased mother, who was extremely demanding and who always scorned him as a complete failure, even when he believed he had succeeded in fulfilling her wishes. He also points out that before seeking the help of an analyst, he was in psychotherapy for a couple of months, which did not really resolve the problem but somehow relieved his suffering. He stopped going to his weekly session when his therapist suggested that he increase the number of sessions from one to two a week, because he thought the therapist became as demanding as his bosses and his girlfriend, and moreover showed a propensity for greed, which only a "bad therapist" could do.

What does this brief case vignette show? First of all, it demonstrates that the symptom, in its appearance through the patient's narrative complaint and verbal utterances, does not constitute a locus of ignorance. The man knows something about his problem and he makes clear that he has thought about its possible origin and its vicissitudes. Yet in his address to the analyst he also admits that he himself does not know how to solve this problem, and that he expects help from a qualified professional. In his critique of his previous therapeutic experience he moreover defines the type of position he expects the analyst to adopt. Basically, he demands the analyst to be non-demanding, and warns him that the intervention will fail if he tries to impose a rule or display his authority. In this way, the patient tries to construct the situation along the lines of his complaint; his relationship with the analyst is defined in accordance with the problem and his expectations of the treatment are fully dependent upon the mechanism of the symptom.

It is also important to recognise, here, that the symptom does not only express itself in and through the patient's narrative, but also in his relationship with the analyst. The patient presents his symptom as a significant disturbance whose meaning continues to escape him, and he expects the analyst to possess sufficient expertise to come up with an acceptable resolution, yet the analyst is only allowed to act upon this knowledge as a non-demanding other. In terms of diagnosis, the analyst has good grounds to believe that the patient's symptom is structured according to a neurotic, perhaps obsessional mechanism. Doubting the value of his own knowledge, imbuing the analyst with therapeutic expertise, yet simultaneously neutralising his power and authority, the patient's discourse is self-effacing and manipulative, obsequious and controlling, respectful, and passive-aggressive—features which the analyst may use to ponder the influence of an obsessional neurotic structure, yet without being absolutely sure that this is indeed the clinical backdrop against which the symptom *qua* complaint expresses itself.

It should also be noted that, once the patient has formulated his or her symptom, and the latter has received a certain, albeit ambiguous signifying status within language, speech and discourse, the analyst generally avoids substituting his or her own knowledge for the patient's ignorance, even when the symptom seems to be quite painful and debilitating. The reason for this ostensibly cruel strategy is that the symptom is not merely the physical and/or mental outcome of an unconscious psychic conflict or, if one prefers, the indelible hallmark of a pathogenic process, but also an indemnifying structure, which serves an organising, pacifying and "curative" function. Following Freud's assertion, in his Schreber-study, that the delusion is always already part of the healing process (Freud, 1911c, p. 71), I wish to take up the point that the symptom, apart from constituting a disruptive force, also brings the patient a certain form of relief. A phobia, for instance, can paradoxically protect someone against anxiety, and thus enable him to live a relatively anxiety-free life, because the anxiety is attached to a concrete constellation, which can actually be avoided. Because of the phobia's protective function, a patient is more likely to seek help when the symptomatic organisation has been disturbed, and the anxiety can no longer be situated and warded off, than when the mechanism is firmly in place, unless the symptom interferes too negatively with other aspects of life, or there is a pressing conflict between the symptom and current forms of satisfaction. The symptom is a peculiar type of survival strategy, and the solidity of this strategy is inversely proportional to the degree of suffering it entails. The more consistent and encompassing the symptomatic strategy, the less suffering it is likely to induce, and vice versa. As I will demonstrate further on in my text, this conception of the symptom has important consequences for the nature of the psychoanalytic action.

IV

Given this particular function of the symptom, it is crucially important that the analyst does not set out with the goal of helping the patient get rid of his problem as quickly as possible. The symptom is an integral part of the patient's being and cannot be excised (or exorcised) without peril. Instead of attacking this "being", the challenge is to map the contours of the symptom within what I would designate as the patient's "psychic body". At this point, I need to embark on a small theoretical excursus in order to clarify what this "psychic body" entails and how it relates to the symptom. From a Lacanian perspective, the psychic body participates in the three constitutive registers of human experience: the Imaginary, the Symbolic, and the Real. The imaginary body is a recognisable, coherent shape that appears as an organised totality and which equips the human being with a relatively well-integrated self image. The symbolic body coincides with the consistent, yet incomplete structure of language, which human beings employ to talk about and defend themselves as social bodies, governed by basic duties and entitled to fundamental rights. This symbolic body incorporates and corporealises the imaginary body, inasmuch as it grants meaning and status to the self image. Finally, the real body is synonymous with the involuntary physiological processes of the human organism. It is the Lacanian equivalent of Hegel's innate, originally animal nature and it maintains itself as an independent, strange and unfathomable remainder, the signature of a "foreign body". Taken separately, each of these three registers of the body sustains a specific mode of self-preservation. The imaginary body gravitates towards the self-conscious unity of the ego, the symbolic body catalyses the social authority of the citizen, and the real body follows its selfish course of infinite reproduction via the genome.

The analytic procedure of mapping the symptom within the patient's psychic body is tantamount, then, to trying to determine how the symptom partakes of the three aforementioned bodily conditions. First, the analyst working in the Lacanian tradition will establish during the preliminary conversations how the symptom relates to and affects the patient's self-image. Does the patient use his symptom as a source of identification or not? Is the symptom in any way attached to the image that the patient has developed about him- or herself? In the case of the aforementioned patient who suffered from a lack of confidence, it was clear that his self-image was somehow tarnished by his experience of professional and sexual impotence, yet by no means did he identify himself as an impotent man, the less so as he realised all too well that his impotence was restricted to specific social and amorous circumstances and did not constitute a core aspect of his personality. Sometimes, however, a symptom can take over someone's entire identity, so that the patient's self-image is transformed into an essential image of pathology. When, in *The Birth of the Clinic* (1973), Foucault criticised the medical establishment for implementing their diagnostic systems in such a way that patients would become identified with their illness—thus referring, for instance, to fever-patients instead of patients having a fever-attack—he forgot to mention, in a sense, that patients themselves regularly engage in this process of reification, for the simple reason that it allows them to re-establish their identity and to use the label of pathology as a new source of power. It is therefore not unusual for a patient to present himself as an insomniac, an alcoholic, a sex-addict, a fetishist, etc. Here, the symptom (insomnia, alcoholism, sexual compulsivity, fetishism) has monopolised the patient's imaginary body, and it is important for the analyst to establish the extent to which the patient's identity is connected to the problem he is suffering from. Without wanting to formulate a general rule, I can say that it is frequently the case that the identificatory value of the symptom is directly proportionate to the intensity of the anxiety and/or the trauma it conceals.

As I pointed out earlier, the symbolic body gives meaning to the human condition, whilst simultaneously opening perspectives on social identity and role. Assessing the impact of the symptom in this area implies an evaluation of the significance the patient accords to the problem, and of its importance for the patient's social relationships and his or her position within the social field. With reference to the case-vignette mentioned earlier, it became clear from the first session that the man situated his lack of self-confidence and the associated professional and sexual difficulties within a socio-political discourse on the essential qualities of masculinity—ambition, mental and physical strength, endurance, etc.—which made him feel uncomfortable and insecure, as well as commendable and triumphant. Indeed, whereas his lack of self-confidence elicited on the one hand strong feelings of failure and resentment, on the other hand it induced a sense of superiority and detachment, which consolidated his social position as an insolent isolated character. Also, as could be seen from the way in which he tried to manipulate the treatment, he definitely did not lack the self-confidence to demand that the sessions be organised according to his wishes and to threaten with his immediate departure if the analyst were to impose his own rules. Mapping the symptom according to this component of the psychic body thus comes down to an assessment of how the patient relates to the Symbolic order (the Lacanian Other) or, better still, to an assessment of how the symptom affects the patient's position within the social fabric—its legal principles, discursive practices and ideological systems as well as its representations at the level of the patient's psychic economy.

Finally, the symptom needs to be mapped in its real dimension. Here, the focus is first of all on how the problem affects the patient's basic bodily functions. In my case-vignette, the real impact of the symptom did not seem to be very extensive, yet the patient did indicate that he fell ill every time he was about to have an appraisal meeting, and that the illness was not just simulated, but a generalized bodily disturbance characterised by nausea, migraine headaches, and extreme tiredness. Every time he expected his girlfriend to want sex with him, he tended to experience palpitations and a painful sensation in his legs which would often persist long after they had (not) had intercourse. It bears repeating, here, that it is not the analyst's task to ascertain the real existence of these phenomena, and even if a patient were to go so far as to show the analyst the physical presence of the symptoms on her body the analyst is only concerned with the way in which these physical aspects are represented at the level of speech. One of the basic rules of the analytic profession is that the treatment ought to take place through words, and that words suffice as therapeutic tools for obtaining the desired effect.

V

Thus far, I have concentrated on how the analyst "receives" the patient's symptom during the so-called preliminary conversations, prior to the start of the actual treatment. This has enabled me to situate the symptom along two distinct, yet interrelated axes: the axis of speech and the axis of the psychic body. Although it is crucially important that the symptom is acknowledged as a signifier rather than a sign, the analyst's intervention is basically restricted, here, to a process of auditory observation, registration and nomination, that is to say to acknowledging what the patient is presenting in all its semantic ambiguity. As such, the analyst does not immediately formulate a diagnosis, in the sense that he or she does not immediately infer the precise clinical background against which the symptom *qua* complaint presents itself. Suspending his own knowledge, and encouraging the patient to explore the nature, origin and impact of his complaint, the analyst attempts to generate a detailed cartography of the symptom, which will inform the diagnosis and his subsequent approach during the treatment. It is less important for the analyst to know what the symptom means, or to use the symptom as a reliable indicator of a certain clinical structure, than to know how the symptom interferes with the patient's life and how it conditions his relationships. Owing to the essential semantic ambiguity of the symptom, formulating a diagnosis requires time, notably the time it takes to assess how exactly the symptom manifests itself in the patient's speech, how it is embedded within a symbolic narrative (of knowledge and truth) and how it is presented to the analyst (within the transference) as a disturbing and disruptive point of conflict.

I can now return to Lacan's discussion of the sophism of the three prisoners who are trying to regain their freedom by solving a challenging logical puzzle. Let us assume, for a moment, that the prison governor had attached the two black disks to the backs of two of the three prisoners. In this case, the third prisoner—let us call him "Prisoner C"—would almost immediately draw the conclusion that his own disk must be white, on the basis that he had been told that of the five disks that were available for distribution only two were black. In this case, Prisoner C's "instant of the glance" would practically coincide with what Lacan designated as the "moment of concluding" (*le moment de conclure*) (Lacan, 2006c, p. 168), that is to say the prisoner's judgment about the nature of his own colour. What is reduced to almost nothing in this situation is what Lacan called the "time for comprehending" (*le temps pour comprendre*) (Lacan, 2006c, p. 168), because very little understanding is required for Prisoner C to deduce which colour he has or "is". For the prisoner who sees two black disks attached to the shoulders of his fellow inmates, there is no semantic ambiguity in the instant of the glance: two black disks convey unequivocally that "I am white". But let us, for the sake of the argument, consider the possibility that Prisoner C is a total idiot, does not manage to conclude anything meaningful from his observation, and does not immediately walk towards the prison gate. In this case, prisoners A and B will have time to contemplate and ruminate over what they see: one black disk and one white disk attached to the shoulders of respectively prisoners B and C, and prisoners A and C. In this case, for prisoners A and B the instant of the glance is unlikely to coincide with the moment of concluding, because a longer time for comprehending is required to "diagnose" one's own colour on the basis of the assessment "black and white". Basically, in order to reach a conclusion, Prisoner A (and, of course, Prisoner B is in the same position) will need to reason as follows: given the fact that B is black and C is white, if I were black, C would see two blacks and run to the gate; since C is not doing anything, I must be white. Although this is an acceptable logical inference, and the only way to arrive at any type of conclusion, it is at the same time not a type of reasoning that can generate a statement about one's own colour of which one can be sure, for the simple reason that the key criterion in support of the "diagnosis" is one of the prisoners' hesitation. Yet it may very well be the case that Prisoner C is just stupid, or so overwhelmed by the challenge that he cannot bring himself to acting upon what he sees. The more Prisoner A realises during his time for comprehending that there are no solid criteria for drawing a conclusion about his own colour, the more he himself may start to feel nervous, anxious and confused, which may result in his action being delayed, or which may prevent him from acting altogether.

In the actual situation of the three prisoners each being given a white disk, the moment of concluding is even more difficult to arrive it, because the time for comprehending that is required for the prisoners to grasp what they see is likely to be much more extended, and because the criteria for arriving at a solid conclusion are even less reliable. The prison governor creates a situation in which all three prisoners see two white disks. In order to establish the colour of their own disk they all need to make the same inference: if I were black, the two others (who are both white) would see the same thing, i.e., a black and a white disk, and so both of them would think that if they themselves were black, the prisoner with a white disk would see two blacks and immediately draw the conclusion that he is white and walk towards the gate, but because the prisoner with the white disk stays put, it must mean (both of the other two prisoners will think) that they themselves are white and walk towards the gate, yet since none of the other two prisoners make a move, it can only be because I am not black in the first place, and so I must conclude that I am white …

Considerations of intelligence aside, this reasoning will no doubt take some time to materialise, if it happens at all, but it is the only way in which some form of conclusion can be reached. And until the prison governor has effectively confirmed the accuracy of the conclusion, it will never be certain, because the criterion informing it is everything but reliable—an interpretation of the others' hesitation on the basis of an attribution of reasoning. And again, the confusion, bewilderment and anxiety elicited by the mere observation of two white disks may stop the prisoners from engaging in any kind of reasoning at all or, if they do, their realisation that the conclusion they arrive at will be one of "anticipated certainty"—as Lacan calls it—may in itself exacerbate their own hesitation, through which they may inadvertently put their competitors in the "game of freedom" at a serious advantage. Nonetheless, in the absence of certainty, the moment of concluding needs to be expedited, that is to say the time for comprehending needs to be reduced as much as possible if a prisoner wants to safeguard his chances of regaining his freedom, because his fellow inmates are in exactly the same position, and the longer he waits the more the others will take advantage of his hesitation, or the more he will have to admit that his freedom is slipping away.

I want to argue, here, that the same principle of what Lacan defines as the three components of "logical time"—the instant of the glance, the time for comprehending, and the moment of concluding—applies to the diagnostic enterprise as it governs the direction of the psychoanalytic treatment within the Lacanian tradition. Ideally, the instant of the glance (or the instant of the ear) should coincide with the "diagnostic" moment of concluding, yet despite what many psychiatrists continue to believe, symptoms as complaints are semantically ambiguous and may be associated with a great many different underlying clinical conditions. A patient who refuses to eat because he is convinced that he carries the planet on his tongue and he categorically refuses to take responsibility for creating a global catastrophe in case he accidentally swallows the world when eating his food does not express the same clinical condition as a patient who refuses to eat because she believes that, despite being fairly thin, she is nonetheless massively overweight. In both cases, the symptom is the same (refusing to eat) but the psychic hinterland is completely different. Diagnosing this psychic hinterland takes time, requires a certain time for comprehending on the part of the analyst and, much like the prisoner who is confronted with two white disks on the backs of his fellow inmates, the analyst is likely to have to rely on clues, indicators and criteria that are not strictly reliable, or that are at least open to ongoing revision, which implies that any diagnosis will only ever be preliminary, uncertain and incomplete, dynamic, iterative, inchoate and rudimentary.

This, in a sense, is also what Freud tried to convey towards the end of his life, in a little-known text entitled "Explanations, Applications and Orientations", which forms part of the *New Introductory Lectures on Psycho-Analysis*. Reiterating his belief that only patients with a so-called "transference neurosis" (hysteria, obsessional neurosis, phobia) qualify for psychoanalytic treatment or, *mutatis mutandis*, that psychoanalysis is unlikely to be successful (and is therefore not indicated as a form of treatment) in cases of so-called "narcissistic neurosis" (schizophrenia, paranoia), Freud voices his concern over the clinical rigour with which a differential diagnosis can be made. The passage deserves to be quoted in full:

> Our diagnoses are very often made only after the event [*Nachträglich*]. They resemble the Scottish King's test for identifying witches that I read about in Victor Hugo. This king declared that he was in possession of an infallible method of recognizing a witch. He had the women stewed in a cauldron of boiling water and then tasted the broth. Afterwards he was able to say: "That was a witch", or "No, that was not one". It is the same with us, expect that we are the sufferers. We cannot judge the patient who comes for treatment [...] till we have studied him analytically for a few weeks or months. We are in fact buying a pig in a poke. The patient brings along indefinite general ailments which do not admit of a conclusive diagnosis. (Freud, 1933a, p. 155)

Ordeal by water, pig in a poke, buying a puppy—fact of the matter is that one is never entirely sure of what is going on "in advance" and it is only "with hindsight", when in a sense it is already too late, that one can establish the validity of what has been said and done. Much like the prisoner who is trying to regain his freedom on the basis of a spurious type of reasoning, the analyst who acknowledges the fragility of the diagnostic enterprise may delay his judgment in an attempt to acquire more and better knowledge about the patient's condition, yet in doing so he is effectively acting upon his own insecurity and anxiety not to make a mistake, and fools himself into thinking that a prolonged time for comprehending will result in a more reliable diagnosis, all the while postponing the direction of the treatment and depriving the patient of certain clinical interventions.

VI

For the last sections of my text, I wish to move to the other side of the psychoanalytic treatment, addressing the thorny issue of what, in the Lacanian tradition, can be expected from a psychoanalytic process in terms of the resolution of the symptom. This perspective will allow me to introduce two additional axes—the axis of enjoyment (jouissance) and the axis of the fantasy—and it will also enable me to formulate some ideas on what exactly the analyst is supposed to do with the symptom during the course of the treatment. Moreover, I shall approach the question of the symptom and its relation to the end of analysis through a reading of Lacan's later seminars, those of the mid-1970s, in which he developed a radically new theory of the symptom, less faithful to the letter of Freud's work and more idiosyncratic in its theoretical inspiration. I should also emphasize that any discussion of the symptom from the perspective of the end of the treatment must necessarily include some considerations on the ethics of psychoanalysis (Lacan, 1992). Whereas the analyst's handling of the symptom during the preliminary conversations is primarily, although not exclusively, a technical matter, and the same is true for the way in which the symptom is approached during the course of the treatment, its status during the psychoanalytic endgame cannot be dissociated from the cardinal question as to what the analyst is trying to achieve with his clinical interventions. This is indeed how Lacan conceptualised the ethics of psychoanalysis: not as a psychoanalytic theory of ethics, even less as a theory of the analyst's mandatory code of conduct or, for that matter, on the moral value of his therapeutic influence, but as a doctrine on the actual goals of the treatment.

Conceptualising the symptom as a figure of enjoyment may seem bizarre, if not to say outright paradoxical. Isn't the symptom something that disrupts the patient's bodily integrity and psychic harmony, and therefore by definition a source of suffering? How is it possible to maintain that patients derive satisfaction from what essentially disturbs their mental and physical economy? To be fair, it took Freud himself a good twenty years to understand the aspect of enjoyment in the symptom, and the same can be said of Lacan, despite the fact that he had Freud's texts at his disposal and did not have to invent everything from scratch. Freud as well as Lacan initially conceived of the symptom as a coded message, formulated in a language unbeknownst to the patient and to the analyst, but decipherable by virtue of the materials provided by the patient's free associations and the analyst's tactics of interpretation (Lacan, 2006d, p. 215; Lacan, 2006e, pp. 495–503). Much like the dream and other formations of the unconscious, the symptom appears here as an obscure semantic construction of the mind whose concealed meaning can be discovered through a careful process of translation, which undoes the complex network of mechanisms that has led to its emergence. Whereas for Freud the meaning of the symptom always resides in the unconscious (repressed) wish supporting it, for Lacan meaning always coincides with a desire. Put differently, in Lacan's account of Freudian psychoanalytic practice, the meaning produced through the interpretation of a symptom reveals the expression of the patient's desire (Lacan, 1998, pp. 319–320; Lacan, 2013, pp. 566–573), and meaning *qua* desire is by definition metonymical: it shifts, escapes fixation, resists identification, is always "fleeting from the cask of language" (Lacan 1975, p. 11).

This paradigm of the symptom as a decipherable message built on the remnants of a repressed (sexual) wish informed Freud's clinical practice for many years, yet from the mid-1910s he gradually acknowledged the destructive power of an extraordinary clinical phenomenon. In the crucial text "Remembering, Repeating and Working-Through" (Freud, 1914g) he conceded that some patients fail to recall, actually refuse to remember the circumstances presiding over the birth of their symptoms and prefer to repeat their symptomatic constellations instead. In 1920, he conceptualised this unconscious force as the repetition compulsion, a corollary of the death drive (Freud, 1920g), and the main engine behind primordial masochism (Freud, 1924c) and the so-called "negative therapeutic reactions" (Freud, 1923b, p. 49), whereby patients are effectively getting worse during the course of their analysis.

From the 1920s, Freud started to realise that something makes the patient want to hold on to his symptom, despite the pain and suffering it induces. Beyond the antagonistic dynamics of the pleasure principle, the symptom is animated by a force which fuels the patient's satisfaction. This is exactly what Lacan tried to capture with the notion of jouissance. Jouissance functions beyond the pleasure principle; it is not incompatible with pain and is not necessarily pleasurable. As Lacan put it in an oft-quoted line from *Seminar VII*: jouissance is pain and pleasure in a single packet (Lacan, 1992, p. 189). This mixture of pain and pleasure is often already noticeable at the level of the complaint. On the one hand, the complaint is rooted in an experience of suffering, yet on the other hand patients may find it quite pleasurable to complain about their ailments. One of the main tasks in the Lacanian approach to psychoanalytic treatment consists in bringing this satisfying mixture of pain and pleasure, which pervades the texture of the symptom, to light. This does not mean that a symptom ought not be interpreted, yet beyond its interpretation, and the concurrent crystallisation of meaning (desire), another assignment awaits, which is much more delicate and onerous. The entire endeavour even seems to be intrinsically futile, for the satisfaction which the symptom incorporates operates beyond the boundaries of the Symbolic, which is precisely why Lacan referred to it as Real, whereas the psychoanalytic process is entirely embedded in language. How could we possibly use language to reach what remains fundamentally beyond it? In a programmatic paper from the mid-1980s, Jacques-Alain Miller phrased the issue as follows: "[T]he symptom is not all signifier, and what this formal envelope of the symptom evokes as negative is what it envelops of jouissance, of jouissante matter. Thus, what is carried out in analysis, in some way naturally, that is to say logically, is a labour on the formal envelope [...]" (Miller, 1991, p. 20). What Miller, with reference to Lacan (2006b, p. 52), terms "the formal envelope of the symptom", is nothing but the narrative structure the symptom acquires in the patient's account of his problem. Yet Miller argues that this narrative structure is wrapped around jouissance, and that psychoanalytic treatment should be geared towards emptying out the container, or at least towards separating the symptom from the satisfaction it contains.

As I pointed out earlier, this process engages the analyst in an ethical as well as a technical endeavour. Ethically, the analyst's operation on the symptom reflects a particular theory on the goals of psychoanalytic practice. If the end of analysis consists in opening the symptom's envelope and liberating its content of satisfaction, separating the juice of jouissance from the symptomatic receptacle, reducing the symptom to an empty container, then this achievement does not signal the disappearance of the patient's symptoms, the restoration of happiness, and the installation of a care-free existence. At the most, it epitomises a simplification of the symptom, its transformation into a less ponderous and swollen structure, no longer bursting at the seams by the self-generating mass of deadly satisfaction. In one of his later seminars, Lacan even suggested that at the end of analysis the symptom emerges along the lines of a new identification: "What does one identify with at the end of analysis? Might one identify with one's unconscious? I don't believe so, because the unconscious [...] remains Other. Might it be identifying with one's symptom, or not?" (Lacan, 1977, pp. 6–7). Lacan's suggestion of an identification with the symptom, here, is evidently not of the same order as the patient's identification with the symptom I referred to earlier on, within the context of the mapping of the symptom along the three constitutive lines of the psychic body. At the end of analysis, the symptom does no longer fulfil the same function, and no longer has the same structure, as it did at the beginning of the treatment. When the patient arrives with his complaint, the symptom is saturated with meaning, orchestrated by an imbalance in the pain-pleasure equilibrium, and pervaded by the dark power of satisfaction. At the end of analysis, the symptom has become purified, exfoliated and exhausted to the point of becoming a naked trait, a formal letter with which the patient can identify as a new kind of name.

Technically, with regard to the enjoyment that is hiding in the creases of the symptom, the analyst is faced with the problem of how to access the patient's "non-sensical" satisfaction, the so-called "Real of the symptom", through interventions that are intrinsically symbolic and therefore permeated with meaning. Freud himself struggled with this problem on numerous occasions, and the only solution he managed to formulate was the process of working-through (*Durcharbeitung*) (Freud, 1914g). This rather peculiar term appears on no more than three separate occasions in Freud's entire oeuvre, an observation which has prompted historians of psychoanalysis to argue that the notion and the process have no conceptual status in Freudian theory at all (Roudinesco & Plon, 2006). Furthermore, Freud's minimal glosses on the nature and function of working-through are quite remarkable, given the fact that he regarded it, and deservedly so, as the most important aspect of psychoanalytic labour—a process bringing about the greatest transformation of the patient's state of mind, guaranteeing psychoanalytic effects beyond those obtained through the power of suggestion (Freud, 1914g, pp. 155–156), and epitomising the only effective response against the infernal resistance of the id, i.e., the compulsion to repeat (Freud, 1926d, pp. 159–160). The only indications Freud gave as to how exactly we need to understand the mechanism of working-through relate to the patient's necessary immersion in the radius of psychic resistance, in order to discover the drive on which this resistance is feeding itself, and in particular how the drive is bound up in the unconscious. Working-through therefore requires the most intensive of labours and its operation can be neither anticipated nor accelerated. "One must allow the patient time" (*Man muß dem Kranken die Zeit lassen*) (Freud, 1914g, p. 155), and the psychoanalyst can only wait. Hence, if working-through is a mental test for the analyst's patients, it is therefore simultaneously a test of endurance (*Geduldprobe*) for the analyst's patience.

VII

Rather than taking on board one of the numerous, often contradictory interpretations of Freud's term that have been advanced since the 1950s, I will single out one minute comment on working-through by Lacan in the final session of his *Seminar XI, The Four Fundamental Concepts of Psychoanalysis* (Lacan, 1994). Lacan's comment will enable me to introduce the fourth axis of the symptom, namely that of the fantasy. At the end of *Seminar XI*, Lacan underscored that the end of analysis occurs "after the mapping of the subject in relation to the *a*, [when] the experience of the fundamental phantasy becomes the drive" (Lacan, 1994, p. 273). This statement is immediately followed by the idea of the "traversal" of the fantasy, which has gained momentum as one of the most significant of Lacan's contributions to a theory of the end of analysis (Attié, 1983; Harmand, 1993; Liart, 1996). Yet Lacan launched this idea by means of an open-ended question: "How can a subject who has traversed the radical phantasy experience the drive?" (Lacan, 1994, p. 273) And he simultaneously deplored the fact that this question had only been investigated from the viewpoint of an analytic treatment with training effects. At this precise point, Lacan rekindled Freud's notion of working-through, which he employed to designate the process whereby an analysand runs through the cycle of analytic experience a sufficient number of times for the fantasy to give way to the drive, that is to say for the drive to be liberated from the fantasy with which it has been bound up. Hence, in Lacan's reading of Freud, working-through chimes with the traversal of the fantasy, conditions the emergence of the drive as "de-cathected" from the fantasy, and it is also a necessary precondition for the crystallisation of analytic training effects, whereby the analysand moves towards the position of the analyst. During the late 1960s and early 1970s Lacan did not hesitate to qualify this transition from analysand to psychoanalyst as a specific act (Lacan, 1967–1968), so that working-through may also be conceived, here, as the psychic force that clears the path for this act to take place. Similar to the process of *Bahnung* (facilitation), which Freud adduced in his "Project for a Scientific Psychology" (Freud, 1950a, p. 300), working-through involves pathbreaking—not of the neurones, but of the mental logic of the fantasy, in view of the crystallisation of an act—notably the act of a patient relinquishing the very position of "patient" within a clinical framework, and possibly adopting the counter-position of the one who treats. The latter point is fully consistent with Freud's outlook in "Remembering, Repeating and Working-Through", where the effect of working-through is compared to that of an "abreaction" (*Abreagieren*), with the caveat that the latter tends to occur suddenly whereas the former requires a long(er) time (Freud, 1914g, pp. 155–156; Starobinski, 2003, p. 182).

I will not enter into a discussion, here, of how the traversal of the fantasy functions as a precondition for analytic training, but bring this text to a close with a brief exploration of the relationship between the technical procedure of working-through, the associated traversal of the fantasy, and its effect on the status of the symptom. The link between the symptom and the fantasy seems to be of fundamental importance, for if working-through is a necessary operation within the analytic process of disentangling the symptom and its heavy load of satisfaction, and working-through is a pre-condition for the traversal of the fantasy, then the separation of symptom and jouissance must depend on this traversal of the fantasy or, vice versa, the fantasy must somehow be responsible for keeping symptom and jouissance together.

How is the relation between the symptom and the fantasy conceived in the Lacanian tradition? How does the symptom feed on the fantasy, and how can the fantasy constitute a bridge between the symptom in its narrative form of complaint and the non-sensical satisfaction perpetuating it? These questions open up onto some of the most complex and advanced developments within Lacanian psychoanalytic theory, and I shall therefore only be able to scratch their surface. As a basic rule, it can nonetheless be said that the symptom, by virtue of its indebtedness to the fantasy, is never purely an individual accident, but something which follows a logical trajectory that allows the subject to adopt a particular position *vis-à-vis* the Other.

Relying on clinical experience, it is much easier to differentiate the symptom and the fantasy than to pinpoint the areas where the two forces meet. In general, if most patients enter the treatment with their symptom as a complaint, the fantasy is rarely complained about, even when it includes scenes of sexual debauchery that are strictly illegal, and has acquired a high degree of fixity. If patients complain about their symptom, they generally comply with their fantasy. Partly because of this compliance, or even complacency with the fantasy, patients do not even tend to talk about it—a silence which is often exacerbated by feelings of guilt or shame at the perverse nature of this "private theatre".

What is the function of the fantasy? For Lacan, the fantasy is an answer to the mysterious desire of the Other. It is an answer to the question, forever puzzling and unresolved, as to what the Other wants, as to which place one occupies in the desire of the Other, as to the Other's intentions, which Lacan captures with the Italian phrase *Chè vuoi?* (What do you want?) (Lacan, 2006g, p. 690), taken from Jacques Cazotte's 1772 novel *Le diable amoureux* (Cazotte, 1925). In this sense, the fantasy constitutes the subject's most intimate *Weltanschauung*, a subjective ideology which guarantees psychic continuity, regulates our inter-subjective space, and provides stability and reassurance. The fantasy governs our so-called 'object-relations' and sustains our desire, which is precisely why Lacan defined it as "*désir de*" (desire of/for) (Lacan, 2006f, p. 653). Yet the fantasy is also the psychic architecture which allows us to experience an event as a source of satisfaction, and which may therefore prompt us to actively seek its continuation or return. The classic example is the sexual act, whose satisfaction crucially depends on the consistency of the fantasy. Whether practiced alone, with a partner or in group, human sexual activity is never intrinsically satisfying, inasmuch as satisfaction only ensues if a particular fantasy, which may be very different from the sexual act itself, is operative. One does not need to be a psychoanalyst to understand this function of the fantasy. Behavioural therapists working with sex offenders know very well that the criminal behaviour may become extinct if the satisfaction-generating fantasy with which it is paired is altered or replaced.

The fantasy also connects the button of jouissance to the fabric of the symptom. As such, the symptom's jouissance is dependent upon the fantasy; without the fantasy, the symptom would not be enjoyable. Therefore, disconnecting the symptom from its jouissance relies on a decomposition of the fantasy, which is responsible for keeping the contents into the envelope. Rather than operating directly on the patient's enjoyment, the Lacanian analyst thus works with the fantasy, with a view to facilitating its "traversal", which should be understood in the sense of a crossing, a passing through or the embarkation on a journey to the other side of a territory. This analytic labour is difficult, yet it is by no means impossible because the fantasy does not live beyond speech and language. In Freud's most elaborate contribution to a psychoanalytic theory of the fantasy, his 1919 paper "A Child is Being Beaten" (Freud, 1919e), he made it perfectly clear that the fantasy exercises its power according to precise linguistic rules. Yet unlike the symptom, the fantasy is not a coded message but an intricate circuit of interconnected components. Because of this, it cannot be interpreted and needs to be re-constructed. Hence, before the fantasy can be decomposed, traversed, worked-through, it needs to be assembled first, and this constitutes the most advanced aspect of the Lacanian psychoanalytic treatment. Its effect is not that the fantasy disappears, but that it loses its grip on the subject's symptom and the latter's *jouissance* is being emptied out. The rest may not be total silence, nor a subjective state of cathartic happiness, but nonetheless worthy of what Lacan, in his early text on the "mirror stage", described as the "ecstatic limit of the '*Thou art that*', where the cipher of [...] mortal destiny is revealed [...]" (Lacan, 2006a, p. 81).

Note

1. The French "*instant du regard*" sounds much more common and prosaic than the English translation of "instant of the glance" suggests. "*Instant du regard*" quite simply refers to the moment of looking, an instantaneous visual inspection, a momentary glimpse.

References

American Psychiatric Association (Ed.) (2013). *Diagnostic and Statistical Manual of Mental Disorders, Fifth Edition—DSM-5*. Washington DC: American Psychiatric Association.
Attié, J. (1983). Sur la traversée du fantasme. *La lettre mensuelle, 21*: 3–4.
Breuer, J., & Freud, S. (1895d). *Studies on Hysteria. S. E., II*. London: Hogarth.
Cazotte, J. (2011). *The Devil in Love*. J. Landry (Trans.). Sawtry: Dedalus.
Foucault, M. (1973). *The Birth of the Clinic: An Archaeology of Medical Perception*. A. M. Sheridan Smith (Trans.). London: Tavistock.
Freud, S. (1898a). Sexuality in the Aetiology of the Neuroses. *S. E., III*: 261–285. London: Hogarth.
Freud, S. (1911c). Psycho-Analytic Notes on an Autobiographical Account of a Case of Paranoia (Dementia Paranoides). *S. E., XII*: 1–82. London: Hogarth.
Freud, S. (1912e). Recommendations to Physicians Practising Psycho-Analysis. *S. E., XII*: 109–120. London: Hogarth.
Freud, S. (1913c). On Beginning the Treatment (Further Recommendations on the Technique of Psycho-Analysis I). *S. E., XII*: 121–144. London: Hogarth.
Freud, S. (1914g). Remembering, Repeating and Working-Through (Further Recommendations on the Technique of Psycho-Analysis II). *S. E., XII*: 145–156. London: Hogarth.
Freud, S. (1916–1917). *Introductory Lectures on Psycho-Analysis*. Lecture XXVI: The Libido Theory and Narcissism. *S. E., XVI*: 412–430. London: Hogarth.
Freud, S. (1919e). A Child is Being Beaten—A Contribution to the Study of the Origin of Sexual Perversions, *S. E., XVII*: 175–204. London: Hogarth.
Freud, S. (1920g). *Beyond the Pleasure Principle. S. E., XVIII*: 1–64. London: Hogarth.
Freud, S. (1923b). *The Ego and the Id. S. E., XVIIII*: 1–66. London: Hogarth.
Freud, S. (1924c). The Economic Problem of Masochism. *S. E., XVIIII*: 155–170. London: Hogarth.
Freud, S. (1926d). Inhibitions, Symptoms and Anxiety. *S. E., XX*: 74–175. London: Hogarth.
Freud, S. (1933a). *New Introductory Lectures on Psycho-Analysis*. Lecture XXXIV: Explanations, Applications and Orientations. *S. E., XXII*: 136–157. London: Hogarth.
Freud, S. (1950a). Project for a Scientific Psychology. *S. E., I*: 281–397. London: Hogarth.
Harmand, C. (1993). La traversée du fantasme. *Letterina—Bulletin de l'ACF Normandie, 5*: 21–27.
Lacan, J. (1967–1968). *Le Séminaire XV: L'acte psychanalytique*, unpublished.
Lacan, J. (1975). Introduction à l'édition allemande d'un premier volume des Ecrits. *Scilicet, 5*: 11–17.
Lacan, J. (1977). L'insu que sait de l'une-bévue s'aile à mourre. *Ornicar? 12/13*: 4–16.
Lacan, J. (1992). *The Seminar. Book VII: The Ethics of Psychoanalysis*. J.-A. Miller (Ed.). D. Porter (Trans.). New York NY-London: W. W. Norton & Company.
Lacan, J. (1994). *The Four Fundamental Concepts of Psycho-Analysis*. J.-A. Miller (Ed.). A. Sheridan (Trans.). Harmondsworth: Penguin.
Lacan, J. (1998). *Le Séminaire. Livre V: Les formations de l'inconscient*. Texte établi par J.-A. Miller. Paris: du Seuil.
Lacan, J. (2006a). The Mirror Stage as Formative of the *I* Function as Revealed in Psychoanalytic Experience. In: *Ecrits*. B. Fink (Trans.), pp. 75–81. New York NY-London: W. W. Norton & Company.
Lacan, J. (2006b). On My Antecedents. In: *Ecrits*. B. Fink (Trans.), pp. 51–57. New York NY-London: W. W. Norton & Company.
Lacan, J. (2006c). Logical Time and the Assertion of Anticipated Certainty: A New Sophism. In: *Ecrits* (B. Fink, Trans.), pp. 161–175. New York NY-London: W. W. Norton & Company.

Lacan, J. (2006d). The Function and Field of Speech and Language in Psychoanalysis. In: *Ecrits*. B. Fink (Trans.), pp. 197–268. New York NY-London: W. W. Norton & Company.

Lacan, J. (2006e). The Direction of the Treatment and the Principles of Its Power. In: *Ecrits*. B. Fink (Trans.), pp. 489–542. New York NY-London: W. W. Norton & Company.

Lacan, J. (2006f). Kant with Sade. In: *Ecrits*. B. Fink (Trans.), pp. 645–668. New York NY-London: W. W. Norton & Company.

Lacan, J. (2006g). The Subversion of the Subject and the Dialectic of Desire in the Freudian Unconscious. In: *Ecrits*. B. Fink (Trans.), pp. 671–702. New York NY-London: W. W. Norton & Company.

Lacan, J. (2013). *Le Séminaire. Livre VI: Le désir et son interpretation*. Texte établi par J.-A. Miller. Paris: du Seuil.

Lane, C. (2007). *Shyness: How Normal Behavior Became a Sickness*. New Haven CT-London: Yale University Press.

Liart, M. (1996). La pulsion après la traversée du fantasme. *Quarto, 60*: 55–57.

Miller, J.-A. (1991). Reflections on the Formal Envelope of the Symptom. J. Jauregui (Trans.). *Lacanian Ink, 4*: 13–21.

Roudinesco, E., & Plon, M. (2006). *Dictionnaire de la psychanalyse*, troisième edition. Paris: Fayard.

Starobinski, J. (2003). *Action and Reaction: The Life and Adventures of a Couple*. S. Hawkes & J. Fort (Trans.). New York, NY: Zone Books.

PART III

SOME CLINICAL REFLECTIONS

CHAPTER EIGHT

Editors' introduction

D. Lichtenstein

The concept of the borderline as a clinical diagnostic category in psychoanalysis has in fact had a long history. As Nestor Braunstein indicates, there is good reason to think it was addressed in Vienna in the 1920s, which would make it not in fact a discovery of recent decades but instead one whose nosology was described at the origins of the field. This earlier dating would make its clinical significance quite different than that which is sometimes proposed. The borderline concept would cease to appear as an aberrant form that calls for alternative modalities of thinking and practice and instead be recognized as a dysfunction of the border to which all subjective structure might be vulnerable—the designation of borderline would then be seen as a matter of degree than a matter of absolute difference.

This perspective allows Braunstein to explore Lacan's ideas about the structure of the psyche and in particular his distinction and examination of the three registers: Real, Symbolic, and Imaginary in new and interesting ways. Lacan was not only interested in defining these three registers and their differences as representative of psychic life, but was increasingly interested in how they functioned or failed to function together. For what links the three registers and what allows them to come apart holds great importance for what constitutes pathology and treatment from a psychoanalytic perspective. Lacan introduced the logic of the Borromean knot, a way of linking three rings so that cutting any one of them frees the other two, as the logic of psychic function. However, once he discovered this logic, he also became interested in its impossibilities and its fault lines. Indeed, the logic of this structure is directly relevant most notably to the distinction between psychosis and neurosis and hence to conditions typically called borderline.

As in most psychoanalytic thinking about slips, the slippage in the Borromean knot, the failures and the means of restoring those failures became more generative and important than the model of its smooth functioning. Braunstein's essay introduces the idea of a cotter pin, i.e., a smaller loop that secures the larger loop, as a topological representative of both slippage and repair in the Borromean ring. In introducing this idea and in exploring what might be the relevant cotter pin for each of the Borromean rings, Braunstein is able to further elaborate the meaning and the dynamics of the Real, Symbolic, and Imaginary registers and to point out their relevance for the notion of the borderline, and for thinking about clinical psychoanalytic treatment as an act that always traverses borders.

This exploration of the uniquely psychoanalytic perspective on psychic structure and its borders also allows Braunstein to locate the interpretive character of psychoanalytic thought in relation to the more descriptive nosology of psychiatry and, in effect, to indicate a border there.

CHAPTER EIGHT

The borderlines between psychiatry and psychoanalysis

Néstor A. Braunstein

It is an appealing metaphor: limits in the field of subjectivity. From infancy, we learn that there is a territory which we consider as our own, where our thoughts navigate and where the other cannot penetrate, the ambit of "privacy". We cannot know what happens in the mind of our neighbour and, not being paranoiac, we believe that we are also opaque to him. Speech can widen or narrow the space of that which the other knows about us: therefore we have an *interior* and an *exterior* domain. They are separated by the function of speech (*parole*). The idea of a topology of the subject and its relations to the Other implies that boundaries exist and that it even may be dangerous to trespass them, to invade the space where the other dwells.

The father receives a command from society: he must draw the borders for his offspring in the same way as he received the message of the Law preceding him. From this viewpoint, a father is the one transmitting the Law to his descendants indicating to them the field of the legitimate and the forbidden. Limits, what limits? The limitations to the satisfactions allowed to the drives, to the use that can be made of the body as a substance of jouissance and of the "tolerance" or consent that the subject can expect from his counterpart, the Other. The drive, as I have said before (Braunstein, 1992) and now I repeat, is a dialectic category. It deals with the exchange of demands ($ <> D). From the beginning Freud said that the drive was a *Grenzbegriff*, a concept dwelling in the limits between the psychic and the somatic; we should say, also, that drives stay always in the bordering zone separating the subject from the Other, between their respective demands. The erogenous zones are the privileged spaces for exchanges, for the commerce between one and one another.

Without limits the child would live in a situation of omnipotence in relation with his mother. We must always keep in mind that the paternal function is a limit imposed also on the mother insofar as she must obey the prohibition of reintegrating her product. I do not need to remind you of the devastating effects that the discourse of the Other may have when it goes overboard with its limiting function and spread the stain of prohibition on many or all the acts of the nascent subject. When everything is forbidden nothing is forbidden; that happens when the subject crosses the border and acts out or "passes to the act". The command given by the Other to both parents of the new-born is that of "setting the limits" and of transmitting to her the norms of the culture. Without them, the subject lives on the outside, in an unlimited space, in psychosis, exiled from the regime of exchanges, with no gauge. On the other hand, enclosed in a suffocating ambit of rigid norms (exterior or superegoic) she will be prey to neurosis and varied symptoms.

The object is always in the limit of subjective experience, involving at the same time jouissance (*plus de jouir*) and desire (as being caused by it). The frontiers are unstable and it is supposed that the Law and the laws are destined to outline their respective jurisdictions. Limits between the interior and the exterior; between ego and non-ego; between wakefulness and sleep; between the instances of the soul; between one and the other; between man and woman; between one generation, the preceding one and the next; between life and death; between sanity and madness; between the paternal and the maternal inside each one; between the Real, the Imaginary, and the Symbolic; between two deaths; limits, limits everywhere. The life of the beings marked by language unfolds in topological spaces whose frontiers usually are diffuse and have to be negotiated with the Other.

"Identity", a concept less psychoanalytic than socio-political, is the feeling of knowing who one is. It depends of the possibility of being able to answer according to the expectations to certain questions: "Who are you, what is your name, who your parents are, where are we, what day is today, do you hear voices, who am I and why am I asking you to answer these questions, are you aware of the problems you represent for the others, do you think that they know what you think or do you know what the others are thinking of without talking to them, etc.?" The difficulty for the subject to give the expected answers attests for the physician the subject's loss of his sense of reality and an identity disorder which will be classified as diffuse in a patient who has not a clear consciousness of the limits separating him from the Other. If the answers leave the doctor with doubts, undecided about the integration of the patient as a subject in the kingdom of the Other (which is the kingdom of the doctor himself) and if the subject lives in a world where is no clear-cut distinction from the Other, she draws the conclusion that the patient resides in the frontier, in the border zone at times psychotic, at times not. If the *psy* technician cannot definitely assess his subject's sanity or madness, he puts an end to his or her hesitation opting for the label of *borderline state or condition or personality disorder*, which is, finally, a compromise. It is a dubious case … that of the patient or that of the doctor, the ambassador of the Other?

Is there any relation between those limits set, established, as it is said, through the action of the paternal function, and the presumed and much publicised contemporary proliferation of borderline cases, states and experiences where the distinctions between neurosis and psychosis are erased? Is in this "world with no limits" where the "subject with no limits" is produced, a subject who, without a precise demarcation of what is her own and what does not belong to her, of what is allowed and what is forbidden, of the masculine and the feminine, would be sentenced to live in an unbound frontier, in a no man's land belonging to multitudes, always unsure about her rights and duties, unable to accomplish with the "expectations of her culture" (*DSM-5*)?

Some of the authors facing the subject of these conditions (psychiatrists according to *DSM-5*, Kohut, Kernberg) distinguish between narcissistic pathology and borderline conditions, some deny the convenience of this distinction (e.g., André Green). There are the ones who keep the label "borderline" for cases in which is impossible to affirm whether the patient is psychotic or neurotic, while others pretend to name "borderline" a very definite kind of patients, different from classical neurotics and from manifest psychotics, with characteristic personality traits permitting an independent and permanent diagnosis of conditions belonging to a "third world" of psychopathology. It seems difficult to draw the borders of the area to be considered as limit (no-body's land). Limits are unlimited and the corresponding zone has blurred contours. Phenomenological descriptions concur in the vividness of cases and authors, and a unified agreement between them is out of the question. In official, non-Lacanian, psychoanalysis, while everybody accepts the convenience of the label, there is no clear-cut definition enjoying general acceptance. This is a highly sensitive point in the contemporary psychoanalytic clinic. The way of facing the clinic of borderline conditions may be in itself the sign separating the domains between psychiatry and psychoanalysis, and, inside psychoanalysis, between the different schools of theory and practice, between the analytic and the therapeutic, etc. The way of dealing with the questions of borders and its lines may be essential to define the identity (diffuse or not) of whoever ... resorts to the notion.

As psychoanalysts we are driven to reject the idea of clinical tableaux portrayed as definite entities with a clear delimitation. This nosological frame belongs to a psychiatry that we contest. However, we recognise certain subjective positions and clinical structures that are specific in the relations of the subject with the Other, such as they appear, in a singular and unstable way, in the analytic situation. Our marking points are not the "symptoms" grouped in syndromes but the manifestations of the subject under transference (*positions subjectives*). While going through the analytic cure the analysands cross through different border lines and we are not the customs or migration agents asking them for passports in order to avoid their passing from a certain clinical area to another or asking them to keep a constant identity.

Freud set some criteria to differentiate neurosis as an alliance between the ego and exterior reality with disavowal of drives coming from the id, and psychosis as psychic reality taking sides against exterior reality and the reality principle under the exigencies of the pleasure principle. However, analysts received patients with well-established clinical neuroses, who, after some insightful and "hot" sessions developed open and exuberant psychotic manifestations. Everyone had to accept that, before the outbreak of psychosis, sometimes for long decades, the patients never showed any indication of a reality loss. Lacan, in his seminar on psychosis, approached the question saying: "Nothing is so similar to a neurotic symptomatology than a pre-psychotic one." Later he asked: "From when should we decide that the subject has trespassed the limits and he stays in delusion [*il est dans le délire*]?" The sentence and the question imply that Lacan acknowledged, without speaking specifically neither of cases nor of borderline structures, the likeability of a diagnostic doubt between two similar clinical presentations, that of neurosis and that of pre-psychosis and justified the psychoanalyst's hesitation before taking sides in favour of one or the other of the options. He also admits that the psychotic comes into delusion after going through a frontier that is both temporal and spatial. In Schreber's case Lacan is ready to accept that the structure is psychotic since the beginning but it doesn't manifest as such until a certain moment of juncture in which the delirium (delusion) explodes.

Every clinician knows cases of men and women who go on with their lives in a seemingly normal way but are vulnerable to suffer decompensations and precipitate in states of true madness when certain links of dependence with somebody or something are broken. Those cases lead us to think about situations of extreme stress and pathological mourning that take the appearance of psychotic episodes. Thus, we may suppose that the subject was previously dwelling in an intermediate region between psychosis and neurosis and that her symptom (*sinthome*) was held and incarnated in the mirroring function of the other. Facing the absence of this other, the subject loses her shield against the psychotic breakdown. In many other cases, the diagnosis of borderline is supported by the more typical hysterical revolt against the other's efforts to set limits to her whims.

The borderline condition is considered one of the most frequent forms of "mental pathology" in the contemporary world. Rare is the author who avoids the temptation to begin his paper by emphasising the increase in the amount of these cases and evoking the good old times in which the boundaries between psychosis and neurosis were precise and clear-cut. When contemporary authors confront the fact that Freud never resorted to this diagnosis, that Klein seldom did it, and that Lacan only once spoke about a "borderline" case and then was referring to a Freudian case, that of the Wolf-man, is for them a strong argument in favour of the idea that this "pathology" was formerly uncommon. They insist on this as a new actual "morbidity", often mentioned as an "epidemic". However, this is impossible to prove inasmuch as there are no data from the past, a past that did not know of this signifier of a clinical condition. This is why we consider useful to follow an historical inquiry.

Nobody considers himself the inventor of the entity or of the word signifying it. The first reference published in English appears in a paper signed by Robert Waelder (1976) in 1925. It is interesting to note that for him, and since these early days, the cases are considered as not accessible to the analytical method as it applies to psychoneuroses. The rather shy introduction of the expression allows us to advance the idea that the notion already had a citizenship card in Freud's circle in Vienna. An additional proof is that in 1929 in the Vienna Psychoanalytic Clinic, Paul Schilder (1886–1940) took the initiative of opening a "Department for Border-Line and Psychotic Cases".

The first American analysand Freud ever had was Adolph Stern. Is it only by chance that the first author who dedicated papers specifically dedicated to the border line patients had to be Freud's first American patient? Stern insisted from the very beginning in the necessity of changing the conventional setting for dealing with these cases. In the first of his papers, Stern (1938) published a clinical description of this group of patients which is like the ones we can find in the most modern books specifically devoted to the subject. He acknowledged the fact of the frequent failure of the traditional method and insisted in the remarkable increase of its frequency … "in the last three or four years" (!!!)

Every author of today echoes not only his descriptions and his reserves concerning the eventual success of analytical treatment but also his ideas on the causes of these conditions: he stressed the importance of the traumatic factors ("as in Freud's early theories") and the insufficiency of maternal care, with no mention related to the figure and authority of the father.

Nevertheless who inaugurated the fashion of the borderline diagnosis was not Stern but another American analyst, Robert P. Knight (1906–1966). Knight (1953) starts with the adequate remark that the syntagm "borderline conditions" has no official existence and does not contribute any further diagnostic information about a case other than that of the patient being ill enough, although not overtly psychotic ... Thus, the label of "borderline state" tells us more about the incertitude and indecision on the part of the psychiatrist than about the patient's condition. Knight refers to more or less 10 papers already published, but his most important quotation is one from ... 1932! His author, Ernest Glover, says that he "finds unsatisfactory, as they are usually employed, the terms 'borderline' and 'pre-psychotic'. If we find evidences of a psychotic mechanism, we should give it a precise denomination. If we merely suspect the possibility of a crumbling of the repression, the situation may be understood as a potential clinical psychosis. In regard to 'larval psychosis', we are all larval psychotics and have been such from the age of two". Wise words. Their fall into oblivion is to be deplored!

We shall not deal here with the overwhelming literature produced on this subject. Suffice it to say that analysts enjoyed a tremendous success in introducing the label into the psychiatric vocabulary and practitioners of all schools fervently embraced this new label of "*borderline*" as a hard-felt necessity. We even have an interesting book now, written from a Lacanian perspective, whose title is *Le sujet en état-limite* (by J.-J. Rassial, 1999).

Subjects satisfying the criteria set for borderline patients undoubtedly exist. In our analytical practice, we often find patients who, under transference, present episodes of transitory madness that in time usually disappear. Nevertheless, we cannot accept the idea that a subject can be at times neurotic and at times psychotic. In structural terms, it is difficult for us admit the existence of a no man's land between neurosis and psychosis and I'll venture to say—setting a difference with André Green's considerations—that such a "vast region" would be an empty set. Most of French psychoanalysts, beginning with Bergeret, following with Green himself, and ending, for the moment being, with Rassial (1999), prefer to speak about *états limite* and not about *borderline conditions*. We fully agree with them. How can we accept that these cases exist and at the same time be reluctant to admit them in structural terms? What then is their clinical reality and how can we conceptualise it?

It is a frequent experience for any of us to see subjects who are structurally neurotic (with symptoms and character traits (hysterical, phobic, or obsessive-compulsive) fall into transitory states of loss of reality and of confusion about their own identity. In these cases we ourselves become disoriented and cannot decide if we are confronted with a transitory condition or if a psychotic outbreak has been produced with the perspective of an ominous development into a chronic state. I am quite certain that Freud, Klein, and Lacan had similar cases in their practice and if they did not speak about a specific structure for these situations it was because they obeyed the rules of the parsimonious procedure they themselves had invented, that of a test period in the case of Freud, and of a set of potentially indefinite preliminary interviews in Lacan. They considered it necessary to wait for the evolution of the case to dissipate the doubts concerning the structure behind the anecdote, even while facing analytically the danger of the subject's eventual passages to the act. Lacan found patients with structural deficits due to the foreclosure of the Name-of-the-Father (an idea that André Green finds *stimulating*) who could, through treatment, be kept from trespassing the limits that separate them from the unchaining of psychosis.

If such cases have become more and more usual in psychoanalytic practice (epidemics?) and if these patients are refractory to psychoanalysis or even directly unanalysable within the

Freudian setting, what are we to do with them, how do we propose to deal with them? Must we consider analysis obsolete because of supposedly recent (social) changes in subjectivity? Has psychoanalysis become an anachronistic procedure fitting an old-fashioned model of human beings, apt for an imperiled species, i.e., neurotics? Would it be convenient to modify the fundamental rule and other technical devices such as even and free-floating attention, use of the couch, high frequency of the sessions? Shall we stop giving importance to infantile sexuality and Oedipal constellations and requiring transference as the soil of interpretation? Should we accept the emergence of a new clinic where the perverse, the neurotic and the psychotic mingle inextricably in unforeseeable sequences leading us to a "new" borderline practice lacking of definite contours? I cannot accept this diagnosis of *our* condition.

We well know that Freud took the rejection of reality as the essential trait constituting psychosis and differentiating it from neurosis. It is not necessary to wait for the arrival of Lacan to acknowledge that exterior reality is shaped by language, and more specifically, by discourse. Exterior reality for the subject results from discourse, defined as "*social link*". What we want to emphasise is that psychic structure cannot sustain itself by itself. It needs to be hooked, hitched to something exterior, to reality (*Wirklichkeit*) in order to avoid dissolution. This *Wirklichkeit* is the opposite pole to psychic reality: in Lacanian speech, it is the reality of the Other, created by discourse. For Lacan, the Freudian name for this "psychic reality" is: Oedipus complex. Lacan's intervention is not necessarily a rejection of the Oedipus complex, even though he ends by considering it a dream dreamt by Freud and requiring interpretation. His own proposal is the substitution of the mythical complex by a signifier: that of the Name-of-the-Father.

From the beginning, Lacan also had the idea of a structure linking three elements—the famous three registers—but, like Freud, he ended by recognising that he needed a fourth element and had to transform the triplet into a quaternary. The new element was the symptom. At first, he writes *symptôme*, as usual, but later on he changed the spelling to *sinthome*, and that was the title given to the seminar of 1975–1976 dedicated to James Joyce. What is the conceptual content of *sinthome*? I will sum up the long development by saying that the *sinthome* is precisely the fourth *ring* that keeps as a consistent set the three others, avoiding the dissolution of the Borromean chain. In the first session of that seminar he stated that "the father is a symptom, a *sinthome*, or whatever you like". The father is, of course, the Name-of-the-Father, neither a person nor the character playing his role in the Oedipus complex. Thus, the Name-of-the-Father becomes, as a *sinthome*, the element dissociated from the Symbolic that guarantees the stability of the structure for the subject. Thanks to its function, the unchaining of psychosis is prevented and the Imaginary, the Real, and the Symbolic keep their distinct places.

I know that this summary is transgressive and I would like to have the time to be more exact, but I do not, so I shall only underline this: in Freud as in Lacan, the consistence of the three elements constituting the structure is given by the psychic reality (Freud) or through the *sinthome* (Lacan), and both of them are references to the paternal function—oedipal or naming signifier. If the Freudian psychic reality or, in Lacanian words, the *sinthome* fails, psychotic breakdown would or could be, the clinical consequence.

When the paternal metaphor is not accomplished, when the foreclosure of the Name-of-the-Father takes place, a lack is revealed in the subject's position regarding the Other. It is a symbolic defect. However, the fall into psychosis due to the absence of the inscription of that signifier in the Borromean structure is not automatic. Lacan tries to exemplify this with the case of James Joyce, which is probably, as we posed elsewhere, a disguise of his own case and a result of his auto-analysis. The *sinthome* (in Joyce's case, his writing), taking many different aspects, can offset the failure of the paternal metaphor. As early as 1976, Lacan would enlarge the scope of the *sinthome*; for example when he said: "for every man, a woman is a *sinthome*".

Now, armed with the concept of *sinthome* widened to cover different aspects of reality, we can come back to the clinic of borderline states. We can understand the outbreak of the episodes that drive the clinician to doubt whether they are real psychotic situations or transient decompensations of a psychoneurotic structure, moments of vacillation of the stabilising *sinthome*. A remedy for this situation can be brought about by restituting the old *sinthome* or through the introduction of a new one that will correct the structural mistake in the knotting of the structure. Every subject "invents" his mode of "being-in-the-world". This is why Lacan proposed in April 1976, "every invention is reduced to the *sinthome*".

It was in February of that same year when Lacan uttered a surprising statement. He said that "in the majority" (*dans la plupart*) the Imaginary, the Symbolic, and the Real become so confused that they reach a point where, unless an operation distinguishing them in the Borromean chain is accomplished, they melt into each other. This idea of confusion, of an absence of precise limits among the three registers, reminds us of Freudian statements (1932) about the gradual changes in color among the "provinces" of his psychical apparatus, among ego, id, and superego.

We must conclude that the situation in which the subject is driven to invent *sinthomes* able to hold his pieces together must be extremely frequent. The cornerstone of this framework is the name-giving father who bestows the subject with a semblance of identity, a base from which the ego can function, assuring his linkage to the Other through discourse and through the Unconscious. The subject is hooked to reality by means of her inventions which can be the producing of art works, a sexual partner, a profession, an identification with some master signifier offered by her culture, a *Weltanschauung*, a hobby, an institution promoting any kind of nuttiness, a perversion, a religious or political creed, even (why not?) a psychoanalyst. In many (most, *plupart?*) of the cases that best illustrate what are called limit-states (borderline states), the outburst of "madness", or destabilisation of the structure, is due to the subject's suffering the physical or imaginary absence of the object of his dependence. This can be seen in the paradigmatic separation from the analyst in the almost experimental setting of analysis itself. Absences that throw subjects into madness are paradigmatic of these "*transitory states of the structure*" as we propose to call them.

The Borromean knot requires, at least, four elements. Thus, the *sinthome* is not contingent but necessary. We are therefore faced with the possibility of anyone being able to suffer a psychotic breakdown (or at least, "the majority"). It this were true, the borderline state would be the "normal" state of the structure and the puzzle would not revolve around the emergence of psychotic episodes but about the relative rarity of these disturbances. For us, the question is: what is the subject's *sinthome*, this artifact or invention that plays the role of preventing precipitation into madness?

In an important lecture delivered in 1965, Edith Jacobson (1976) set forth the idea of *psychotic conflicts* as the strenuous fight that the psychotic puts on before losing contact with reality and his reconstruction of it in a delusional way. Once this happens, the psychiatrist or analyst no longer has any doubts about a diagnosis of psychosis. Jacobson speaks of the importance that we must concede to these intra-psychic conflicts *before* a break with reality takes place. Jacobson reasonably objects to the extreme simplification of limiting psychosis to a loss of reality followed by reconstructive phenomena. She argues the frequent existence of "potential" or "ambulatory" psychotics who often modify external reality in order to keep their contacts, adapting it to their special needs and goals. In doing so they strongly resemble … "normal human beings". These patients do not arrive at a total break with reality; first they try to appeal to the exterior world, to consolidate their links with it and to seek help from it to solve their conflicts. This kind of "potential psychotics" abound. How often do we hear people say: "I would go crazy if I couldn't go on with my writing" or: "I would not be able to live without him or her"; or "I won't be able to make it if my analyst takes a vacation"? Lacan was peremptory when he said and underlined: "The psychoanalyst cannot be conceived in a different way than as a *sinthome*. It is not psychoanalysis which is the *sinthome*; it is the psychoanalyst".

Sinthomes pullulate through the social fabric. They can also be little nothings: a tic, a certain queerness, an eccentricity, but they must be strong enough to keep in place the links of the Imaginary, the Real, and the Symbolic. Otherwise the three registers will fly apart and the subject can lapse into an unchained psychosis. When Klein says that everybody is potentially psychotic inasmuch as the beginnings of life imply a psychotic origin he is making a similar proposal, as does Winnicott when he proposes that the subject is saved from psychosis through the construction of a transitional space not belonging to him or her but also not belonging to the mother, an intermediate (border?) area between them.

The social link is kept in place by the *sinthome* and the subject constitutes him/herself in the link that exists between the appeal coming from the Other and his or her answer as ego, which is a *sinthome*—the necessary cotter pin if the subject is to avoid falling into madness. This mechanical image of the *cotter pin* (*chaveta, clavette*) is more than a device. A cotter pin is the brace that is placed at the end of an axle that impedes the loosening of the wheel and the possible wrecking of the vehicle. In colloquial Spanish, "*perder la chaveta*" (losing the cotter pin) means going crazy; it is the topological invention of Lacan in the last session of his seminar on Joyce when he draws on the blackboard the ego, *Lacanian ego*, as a bar that impedes the dissemination of the pieces held together by cotter pins. The subject is the effect of the security device, which is the ego, something that holds the wheel fast to its axis and assures the connection to the propelling motor of discourse. Lacan assigns the role of cotter pins to the ego, to the name-of-the-Father and to the *sinthome*: the cotter pin is an element that helps the subject to maintain the social link and his contact with the Real.

The stability of the ternary structures proposed by Freud as well as by Lacan is extremely precarious because the three rings are neither clearly defined nor neatly organised in a chain, therefore the absence of boundaries separating them makes *every subject* (the mysterious "*plupart*" alluded to by Lacan) *a "borderline case"*. The cotter pin's reliability changes according to the different psychic structures; its effectiveness usually being stronger in perverts; maintained in neurotics through "true" symptoms as an after-effect of repression; and precariously in the wide band of "potential psychotics", often "normopaths", who are linked to the world by hitches, acting-outs, and sometimes—*helas*!, not many— through genial inventions that change the horizon of humankind. Two examples of the latter could be Joyce's writing and Lacan's teaching.

The Name-of-the-Father, the one and only, traditional and religious, has been the guarantor in the constitution of the subject's sinthomatic "ego", allowing him to articulate with the Other and with his unconscious knowledge ("the unconscious is the discourse of the Other"). The Name-of-the-Father is the condition that makes possible the social link and the transference, in its generic as well as in its specifically psychoanalytic sense. The instability of the Name-of-the-Father, a common situation in our ultra-neo-liberal times, removes the support of the *sinthome* that we call "ego" from the subject and pushes him to live on the border of disintegration of his structure, on the border of the delimitation of what is proper and what is alien to him.

The proclaimed unlimited freedom reigning in our times is a false ideology that erases the bonding power of words and makes uncertain and revocable all contracts, weakening all performativity. There is no stability in the relation between the worker and his job, between the partners in a couple, between parents and children, between living human beings and the ground they stand on. When the Symbolic, the Imaginary and the Real form a disorderly tangle, the *majority* (again Lacan's expression) experiences a real uncertainty concerning its limits; it needs to constantly test its relation with the Other, this Other upon whom the subject can no longer rely and simply enjoy his *sinthome*. The dearth of the guarantees that the subject expected from the Other drives her to live on the border, on the frontier of structural dissolution.

The cotter pins of James Joyce: a borderline case?

Lacan uses the colloquial term "*jaspiner*" ("jabber") in relation to the way he reflects on "Joyce's case" and the writer's clinical condition. Having to determine whether Joyce was crazy or not he sustains that this was not Joyce's privilege since "*in the majority*" the registers are tangled and they fuse into one another *without precise limits*. Furthermore, he adds, being crazy is not a privilege. He never says that Joyce was psychotic or perverse, and in spite of the writer's many phobic and hysterical symptoms, which could substantiate such a diagnosis, Lacan never refers to him as neurotic. At most, he is taken as someone "unsubscribed from the unconscious" seeking to compensate through his art the fact that "his father meant little to him". We will leave this comment aside since we know that the opposite was much closer to the truth and that this consideration really applies to Lacan whose own father never counted as such. We can, however, ask ourselves what the expression "a factual *Verwerfung* [*forclusion de fait*] as a result of the paternal desertion" means in Joyce's (or in Lacan's) case?

Lacan's expression, "the majority", when speaking of the tangled registers, lends itself to confusion. Are there beings with the three registers well demarcated and others not? Lacan substitutes the exact (rather stiff) Borromean chain and its three distinct rings painted in three different colours with the clover knot, but Joyce's case forces him to contemplate the errors that can occur in the knotting and the need of inventing a fourth element to compensate for these errors.

During the first nine classes of *Seminar XXIII* Lacan maintained that the separation of the Symbolic register from the other two (Real and Imaginary) was Joyce's structural defect and that Joyce strove to compensate for this with his writing, understood as a *sinthome*. However, in the last lecture (May 11th, 1976), he made a surprising twist on the Joyce case. Basing his conclusion on a single line of a novel ("Portrait ..." p. 57), he said that the register that had come loose and needed fixing, was the Imaginary. Joyce, therefore, had had to construct an ego that enabled him to repair the unknotting of the Symbolic and the Real that had allowed the Imaginary to come loose. The ego is then drawn on the blackboard (p. 152) in the same way that the *sinthome* had been drawn before (pp. 94, 97), as a fourth ring making fast one of the registers.

If we project these drawings in the third dimension, we see that the small rings constitute a simple mechanical artifact: the cotter pin previously described. Lacan assigns the role of cotter pin to all kinds of *sinthome*: the real father; a woman (for every man), the psychoanalyst for his analysand; for Joyce and many other writers, writing itself; etc. The cotter pin is an element that helps the subject maintain the social link and his contact with the Real.

It is convenient now to remember Lacan's teaching beginning in 1974 (*Seminar XXI*: *Les non-dupes errent*) when he states that he will speak to convince his audience that *the sinthome belongs to the Real*. However, on February 11th, 1975 (*Seminar XXII*, *R.S.I.*), he says: "only the Name-of-the-Father can make a Borromean knot that holds together the Symbolic, the Imaginary and the Real". On April 15th, he adds: "four are needed since the fourth is the one that holds the Symbolic inasmuch as it produces it, in other words, the Name-of the-Father". On May 13th, 1975, in the last class of *R.S.I.* he announces the title of next year's seminar as "*4, 5, 6*" giving to understand that each one of registers 1, 2, 3, (*R.S.I.*) had to be divided in two: the register itself and *the name of the register*, a signifier that does not belong to it. The idea then was that each register had to be duplicated because the name itself implied an unfolding; this forced him to raise from 3 to 6 the number of elements in the Borromean knot.

At the beginning of the following *Seminar XXIII* (*Le sinthome*), Lacan felt overwhelmed by the project and was driven back by the magnitude of the work. On November 18th, 1975, he confessed: "I have let myself drift from the project I announced last year, the one with the title '*4, 5, 6*'. I am reconciled with four and that makes me happy since with '*4, 5, 6*' I would have surely succumbed. And that does not mean that this 'four' which I will deal with will be less burdensome." The announced fourth would be the *sinthome*.

Now I propose to come back to the original Lacanian "*4, 5, 6*" without succumbing, with the utmost clinical and topological rigor and without straying from the sayings of Lacan and his discoveries. Each cotter pin, one for the Symbolic, one for the Imaginary and one for the Real is the way of representing in a graphic manner the unfolding of the three registers and their keeping at bay without losing their differentiation and specificity. It is a way of conceptualising the concrete clinical discoveries corroborated in every analyst's practice. If there is a failure in the knotting of any two of the registers (articulated one to the other in the Olympic manner instead of being merely superimposed), the third will come loose and need fixing. In the case of the fourth ring that Lacan worked on at the beginning of 1976, referring in an equivocal way to Joyce, this supplementary element is the ego that impedes the Imaginary from coming loose. In performing this operation on the knot, he was definitely adding a new element but leaving aside what he had put forth all along *Seminar XXIII*, concretely, that the supplementary stabilising element was the *sinthome*. At this point it is important to remember that he had already postulated the need for a fourth element when he insisted in the convenience of unfolding the Symbolic in two: the Symbolic itself and the Name-of-the-Father.

In the first and most extensive part of Lacan's itinerary, beginning on June 6th, 1953, his teaching was centred on the three registers and nothing but three: the Imaginary, the Symbolic, and the Real. Then, in 1974, he introduces the Name-of-the-Father as a fourth element. In 1975, he incorporates the *sinthome* calling it the fourth when in reality it was the fifth. In 1976, he adds one final element, the ego, which he again calls the fourth as if he had completely forgotten the first two. The ego is properly the sixth that closes the series: *I, S, R* (1, 2, 3), *Name-of the-Father* (4), *sinthome* (5), ego (6). I propose to consider these three new rings as cotter pins that assure the stability of the structure of each *parlêtre*. The cotter pins are indispensable but do not have the hierarchical status or the transcendence of the three classical registers. The cotter pin lacks the dignity of the wheel—it is a mere accessory—but the wheel needs it so as not to fly off its axle. In the same way, the subject needs the ego, the Name-of-the-Father and the *sinthome*, so that the Imaginary, the Symbolic, and the Real remain hitched.

The precariousness of the welding of the cotter pins to the corresponding registers is the key to understanding the so called borderline cases that are *not* different structures from the classic ones recognised by Freud and Lacan. These *states* do not present a specific different *structure;* they are situations of subjective emergency that may manifest as psychotic when the subject loses one of the cotter pins and is faced with the need to restore it or substitute it for another. At this moment, the direction of the analytic cure requires that the analyst serve as the *sinthome* that will aid the subject in hitching back to the Real.

The ideas I am putting forth can be read in Lacan in three consecutive *Seminars XXI, XXII and XXIII*. I believe Lacan failed to place in sequence the three cotter pins we have been talking about, the ones that evidence the continuity of the theoretical elaboration he was proposing and drawing on the blackboard. That 4, 5, 6 where "he would have succumbed" had been realised behind his back, as a job of the unconscious.

> In synthesis:
> The ego is the cotter pin of the Imaginary
> The Name-of-the-Father is the cotter pin of the Symbolic
> The *sinthome* is the cotter pin of the Real

Coming back to Joyce and using him as an example: a) the Name-of-the-Father (the Joyce family and their emblems, the two generations prior and the two generations following, the rejection of the maternal signifier "Murray", Ireland and Dublin, his proper name confirmed by the authorship of his books) is the cotter pin that binds him to the Symbolic; b) the *sinthome* (Nora until approximately 1917, his writing ,and Lucia from then on) is the cotter pin binding him to the Real; c) the ego (the feeling of having a body of his own, the making of a name for himself) is the cotter pin that hitches him to the Imaginary. The moments of "madness" come when he is separated from Nora by his travel to Ireland, when he submits himself to dangerous surgical procedures and when he is sees his writing threatened by the possibility of losing his protectors (wife, brother, friends). A phenomenological, not structural, clinic would call these transitory failures of the structure "psychotic episodes" and would term the subject's state as "borderline". Robert P. Knight, the psychoanalyst that in 1953—the same year that the Imaginary, the

Symbolic, and the Real saw the light- put into vogue the term borderline specified: "The term 'borderline-states' [...] implies not only that the patient is quite sick, but also that he is not frankly psychotic [...]. So the term borderline-states [...] gives us more information about the doubts and indecision of the psychiatrist than on the condition of the patient."

The nodal clinic of the last Lacan, can accept Joyce's case as paradigmatic in explaining why the badly termed concept of borderline-states came into being. It also moves us to rephrase the question, why is this subject neurotic? The more appropriate question is, how is the subject able to maintain his or her sanity? Which are the cotter pins that keep him, her, us, in contact with the Other and under what conditions could we *perder la chaveta*?

[Translated from Spanish by Tamara Francés]

References

American Psychiatric Association (Ed.) (2013). *Diagnostic and Statistical Manual of Mental Disorders, Fifth Edition—DSM-5.* Washington DC: American Psychiatric Association.

Braunstein, N. A. (1992). *La jouissance. Un concept lacanien.* Paris: Point Hors-Ligne (and 2006, Erès).

Braunstein, N. A. (2003). *Desire and Jouissance in Lacan's Teaching* in *Cambridge Companion to Lacan.* Cambridge: Cambridge U. P., pp. 102–115.

Jacobson, E. (1976). *Depression: Comparative Studies of Normal, Neurotic, and Psychotic Conditions.* New York: International Universities Press.

Knight, R. (1953). Borderline States. *Bulletin of the Menninger Clinic. XVII.* pp. 1–12.

Lacan, J. (2005). *Le séminaire de Jacques Lacan: Livre 23, Le sinthome.* Paris: Seuil.

Rassial, J.-J. (1999). *Le sujet en état-limite.* Paris: Denoël.

Stern, A. (1938). Psychoanalytic Investigation of and Therapy in the Border Line Group of Neuroses. *Psychoanalytic Quarterly, 7*: 467–489.

Waelder, R. (1976). *Psychoanalysis: Observation, Theory, Application. Selected Papers of Robert Waelder.* Ed. S. Guttman. New York: International Universities Press.

CHAPTER NINE

Editors' introduction

D. Lichtenstein

The place of emotion in Lacan's approach to psychoanalysis has not been sufficiently appreciated. His attention to theories of speech and language, to mathematical and topological models, and to a certain intellectual rigor in his formulations have contributed to the tendency to overlook the fact that throughout his seminars and papers there is a consistent concern with affect and its role in the psychic life of the divided subject. His early work on the mirror stage is, among other things, a reflection on the feeling of joy that accompanies the self-image of wholeness, the feelings of rage that accompany the first awareness of the other, and anguish in the encounter with lack. In the appreciation of these fundamental affects and their role in both early narcissism and object relations Lacan was close to Freud's thought and was well aware of the elaboration of these processes by Melanie Klein and others. That he then sought to bring the affective dimension into his overall conceptual framework of psychoanalysis and to subject them to the rigor of his inquiry is consistent with Lacan's general effort.

Later (1962–1963), Lacan devoted a full year of his seminar to an examination of anxiety. The conceptual and clinical significance of this affect and its importance in Lacan's subsequent elaboration of the object *a* and the function of the Real is fundamental. There is a continuing debate within the Anglo-American literature as whether anxiety is in fact the best translation of the French *L'Angoisse* or the German *Angst*. It is a debate that reveals how important the nuances of affect are to Lacanian thought. We use anxiety in the translation that follows but call attention to the fact that some scholars recommend anguish or even the Anglicised angst as better renderings.

This paper by Colette Soler is an examination of Lacan's ideas about Love and Hate. More specifically it takes up some of the ideas that Lacan developed in his later work especially about the role of the Real, the materiality of language, and experience rooted in the body. Soler has made a significant contribution to the literature on Lacan's theory of affects with her book

Lacanian Affects: The function of affect in Lacan's work (2015). The essay published here develops some of the ideas in that work. Soler focuses closely on those aspects of the unconscious that have not been captured by the representational functions of the Symbolic register or been represented in the Imaginary—what she calls the real unconscious.

How speech in the analytic setting affects bodily experience has always been a central question for psychoanalysis. Lacan's reworking of this question in his later teaching occasionally involved the creation of neologisms and portmanteau words to convey the elusive dialectic of speech and being. *Lalangue* is one of those creations, derived from *la langue* [language], it is meant to convey the materiality of language, the effects of sound and phonemic play that go beyond or alongside the effects of meaning. *Parlêtre* is another, combining *parler* and *être* to suggest the unique status of being that comes about through speech. It is a conception of the human subject not simple as a speaking being but as a being made up of or derived from speech.

We do not translate these terms but use them in the French as quasi technical terms in Lacan's exposition.

Unarité is another such term formed by the joining of *unité* and *unaire* that each have a distinct significance in Lacan's work. Here we have chosen to render the term as an English neologism, *unarity*, signifying a quality of the individual subject as simultaneously singular and contingent, not singular as a logical necessity but as a contingent effect of formation.

Soler's style of exposition presumes a certain familiarity with Lacanian thought that some readers may find challenging. However, it yields the opportunity to think with Lacan, in the terms of his own development. While there may be value at times in rendering Lacan's ideas into more familiar terms for Anglo-American readers, there is also value in seeing how the ideas work in their own framework. Soler's essay is an invitation to do this even as she breaks important new ground in exploring their implications.

Acknowledgement

The editors wish to thank Manya Steinkoler for her invaluable assistance in the translation of this chapter.

References

Lacan, J. (1962–1963). *Anxiety, Seminar book 10*. C. Gallagher (Trans.). Unpublished.
Soler, C. (2015). *Lacanian Affects: The function of affect in Lacan's work*. London: Routledge.

CHAPTER NINE

Two affects: love and hate

Colette Soler

The subjective affects that are experienced and attested to are actually effects. Lacan called them "*effects*" [not a French word, *trans.*] in a calculated and perspicacious neologism. This idea did not originate with Lacan but was also Freud's[1] and is consistent in both of their work (Freud, 1914d). We must nevertheless ask: effects of what? To start with, obviously, they are the effects of what happens in life, of life's events. But what occurs in reality is already directed and perceived via the filter of common discourse and of the unconscious proper to each subject. It is this last point that is of particular interest to psychoanalysis: how and to what extent in deciphering the unconscious using Freudian technique is one able to modify affect and alter the mood that accompanies the symptoms the subject complains of?

Let's not forget that the affects experienced are most meaningful for the patient who confuses them with his own truth. In the technique we've inherited from Freud, the compass used to approach the unconscious is the signifiers deciphered in the analysand's words and not the affects that displace themselves in the patient's speech and which consequently deceive. Freud's case of the Rat Man is paradigmatic in this regard. The case lets us see that the analytic approach to affect strictly depends on our conception of the unconscious.

Under transference, the unconscious can be deciphered like a language, and we obtain effects of the subject's symptomatic suffering. Before we interrogate it in analysis, the unconscious "ex-sists". In this sense, at the end of his teaching, Lacan was able to call the unconscious "Real". It has effects on the living individual, and specifically on the jouissance of the speaking being. These effects express their impact in diverse subjective affects. The elements, the signifiers of the real unconscious that initiate the process of bodily jouissance, come from *lalangue*. This is what Lacan calls "the knowledge of *lalangue*"; only *lalangue* is incommensurable. I cannot know either its extent or the magnitude of its effects. In this sense, *lalangue* is inexhaustible insofar as it constitutes me. It is a knowledge that remains unknown even if it determines me as a speaking being (*parletre*), another Lacanian neologism. This knowledge that comes from *lalangue* exceeds me, manifesting in certain specific affects that, as effects, are the signs of what I am not able to articulate in signifying terms.

"The unconscious evinces knowledge that, for the most part, escapes the speaking being. That being provides the occasion to realise just how far the effects of *lalangue* go in that it presents all sorts of affects that remain enigmatic. Those affects are what result from the presence of *lalangue* insofar as it articulates things by way of knowledge (*savoir*) that go much further than what the speaking being sustains by way of enunciated knowledge" (Lacan, 2000).[2]

Thus, Lacan completed his conception of the affects from the real unconscious.

Prior to this, he had already determined an exceptional affect, one not produced by unconscious language, but as a sign of a Real, namely anxiety. Anxiety is the sole phenomenological manifestation of the object *a*, this object cause of desire that has no image and no signifier which makes a hole in the Other. Anxiety is the only affect that doesn't deceive since it does not slip in the signifying chain. It is indexed in the experience of the Real that is the object *a*.

Later in his seminar, *Encore*, Lacan will speak of "enigmatic affects". I have developed this point: "all affects are not enigmatic" (Soler, 2011). Those determined by common discourse are not mysterious because they are understood by everyone. Those affects, however, that are particular in that they articulate the fantasy of each individual subject often surprise others who may find them enigmatic. For the subject himself, however, they are very familiar, indeed identical with the feeling he has of his own self. These should be distinguished from the true enigmatic affects: those affects that do not surprise others, but the subject himself. Here, the subject does not recognise himself at all. These, like anxiety, are signs, no longer of the object *a*, but the *unknown* effects of *lalangue*, the first among them being love. We recall that this unknown carries with it the shadow of hate, and we pause here to consider this classic couple.

Two passions of being

Lacan discussed the passions very early on in his teachings and continued to develop his formulations right to the end help us think about them in new ways. At the beginning, he situated them as "the passions of being", as the effects of the lack of being that generates language. Well before his theorisation of the Borromean knot, Lacan places them in the three dimensions Imaginary, Symbolic, and Real. As early as *Seminar 1* (Lacan, 1954), he posited a thesis: "It is only in the dimension of being, and not in that of the Real, that the three fundamental passions can be inscribed at the junction of the Symbolic and the Imaginary." These passions respond to the primary effect of language, and refer neither to unconscious knowledge nor to the Real, but to the question of Being. For the speaking being, being presents itself as a question. This is not the case for the Real, however. Lacan continues: "This fault line, if you will, this ridge line called love—at the junction of the Imaginary and the Real—hate—and at the junction of the Real and the Symbolic—ignorance" (ibid). Some twenty years later, in *R.S.I.* (Lacan, 1973–1974), Lacan would alter these formulations in these same intersections. Between the Imaginary and the Symbolic, he places not love but meaning, more precisely—*joui-sense*. Between the Imaginary and the Real, he places not hate, but anxiety. And between the Real and the Symbolic, he places not ignorance, but the letter of the symptom. Obviously, the three categories of 1954 are not exactly those of the Borromean knot, but it is interesting to note that love, as it is grasped in 1954 as disconnected from the Real, differs from both hate and ignorance. At that moment, love is differentiated from the libido, and from desire. Lacan says in this regard: "Love, as human reality, is a reality of words. We can only speak of love when the symbolic relation exists as such—where the aim is not satisfaction, but being" (Lacan, 1954., p. 304). What he called at the time the symbolic relation is the relation to the Other, not as a simple place of language, but as marked by a lack, one that we write as the barred A. At this level, love is established as a relation of lack from the subject to the Other; it has nothing in common with positive virtues of either of the partners or with their imaginary or real qualities; it has nothing to do with any of their merits. We understand why then, Lacan would say at the time that in psychosis, love is a dead love since in psychosis, two lacks do not intersect. One is left only with specular competitiveness and an imaginary relation to the other that could only be a sacrificial one. This thesis of course, should be reconsidered in light of his later work. Love is a quest to be for a lacking being. Love addresses the lack in being; hate aims at it in order to destroy.

Correlatively, all through his work to his late seminar, *Encore*, Lacan engaged in a veritable trial of love and for love. He denounced love's falsehood, its illusions and its impotence. Love claims to be a gift, and in fact, to love *is to give what we do not have*, i.e., our lack—Being. But love lies, since it demands; to love is to want to be loved, to look for one's complement in the lack in the Other, in the hopes of making One.

The notion of a pure or disinterested love has traversed centuries. In Christian theology it returns with Madame Guyon in the debate on a supposed "pure love" that would demand nothing in return for its offering, not even one's own salvation. Thus, the cowardice of an affect that does not want to know the destiny language makes for us, a destiny that condemns us to the One all by ourselves, in solitude. Isn't love a comical delusion (psychotic in kind) about the one and only object that uniquely responds to our being, one equal to the miser's coveted chest of gold? And we could add to this—that if to speak is a jouissance, as Lacan advances in his seminar *Encore*, then love itself rivals the beloved. The words of love are not true, rather they satisfy the jouissance the subject takes in the *blablabla*. Conclusion: Love is impossible.

"I don't love him", Freud said, to situate the rapport of the psychotic to his object in erotomania and persecution. In *Television*, (Lacan, 1980) Lacan generalises this "I do not love him" of psychosis to both neurosis and perversion. He liked to cite the statements at the end of the Masked Ball: "It wasn't him. It wasn't her." Such are not merely statements of fact. They are ethical judgments of a type often found in the work of Freud and Lacan. These judgments reveal that Love defends against the Real. Love is a friend of the passion of ignorance that does not want to know anything.

Love and the Real

The last lesson of *Encore* introduces a totally unprecedented thesis: love is an enigmatic affect, that is an effect of the Real unconscious.

Psychoanalysis revealed that unconscious knowledge is a fatal destiny for the speaking being: it confronts him with the impossibility of the rapport of sexuated jouissances, establishing the subject's structural exile from union. At the same time, it fixates him to the compensatory jouissance of the fundamental symptom, an opaque positivity that imposes itself and allows us to speak of "the being of jouissance", as the opposite of a lack. These real effects of the real unconscious are translated in the subject by all types of affects and symptoms, love, being one of them. Its definition is now known: "All love is based on a certain relationship between two unconscious knowledges" (Lacan, 1998, pp. 144, 131) It concerns a "recognition—via signs that are always punctuated enigmatically—of the way in which being is affected qua subject of the unconscious knowledge" (ibid, p. 144).

We might as well say that love, far from being situated as an effect of unconscious language hollowing out the lack in being, comes from the Real, in a double meaning: the Real of the impossible rapport, of the exile, of the curse, but also the Real of the unconscious *lalangue*, affecting the body of jouissance by way of the symptom. Enigmatically, love answers as the detector of the way a being cohabits with its unconscious Real. Suddenly, in love, the sexual rapport that is lacking, *stops not being written.*

Let me insist a bit. Lacan says "cohabitation": the speaking being *cohabits with* the knowledge of *lalangue.* This cohabitation is utterly particular to each person. The way one person cohabits is not the same way that another person does. And yet, neither can be stated about it in terms of knowledge. Nevertheless, this cohabitation with *lalangue* becomes manifest, but only by the affects aroused by the sexual non-rapport and the symptoms that love recognises in the other. Recognising, however, does not mean knowing. Indeed, this ability of love to recognise is in itself an enigmatic effect; the mystery of love that has perplexed us for centuries, is not reduced by this notion of cohabitation, but rather returned to its unconscious origins. Lacan hesitated a bit on the nature of that recognition.

In *Encore*, Lacan invoked a historically known type of love, the Greek *philia.* He stated: "Regarding one's partner, love can only actualise what, in a sort of poetic flight, in order to make myself understood, I called courage—courage with respect to this fatal destiny" (Lacan, 1998, p. 144). Love would then become an ethical detector of a subject affected by solitude and by jouissance, which he is not master of, one that is beyond him. "But are we really speaking of courage? Or of a way of recognition?" (ibid, p. 144). Interestingly, he concludes by barring the word courage. "There is nothing else there but a meeting between two *lalangues* or rather the meeting in the partner-symptom of the affects (I underline) of all that in each, marks the traces of his exile, not as a subject, but as speaking, of his exile from the sexual rapport." And he adds: "It's only by affect, I underline, that from this gap, something is encountered." In other words, love is between two beings—the affect that answers to the gap of the sexual rapport—this Real, proper to the unconscious *lalangue.* Witness to this "fatal destiny", as Lacan said, it is not simply the effect, the ideal images, nor the fantasm that covers the gap of the sexual rapport. Lacan isolates there for the first time, regarding love, a dimension of rapport to the Real, making of it a sign, indeed an index of this Real. This is why I had ventured the formula: "A love that knows" (Soler, 2009, p. 180). It is a love that knows, but it cannot say what it knows. This begs the question, insofar as it responds to the Real—does love give access to the Real being of the Other?

Despite opposing hate to love Lacan does not make it the other side of the same coin. True hate is not of the register of which Lacan writes *"hainamoration"*, or "love-hate". There is, in fact, a whole side of detestation that results from disappointed love. Strangely, of the three passions named by Buddhism, i.e., love, hate, and ignorance that Lacan made a big deal of, it is his concept of hate—the only passion that we say is lucid—that has changed the least. Lacan maintains the same formula as with love: Hate is addressed to being. But what is this being of the other? This does not concern his being of lack, as it did with love, but his being of jouissance as symptom or the being of his speech. Thus, he underlines the lack of symmetry with love. In this regard, I will cite the end of *Encore*: "Hate does not stem from the plan articulated by the capture of unconscious knowledge. Unlike love, hate is not induced by unconscious knowledge and its effects of non-rapport." Hate is not part of the enigmatic affects that reveal what language does not reveal, as are anxiety and love.

That hate has no rapport with unconscious knowledge is propitious to renew what we have called the negative transference. I have developed it: hate is not transferential, but rather de-transferential. After all we may have said about negative transference, hostility towards the analyst certainly exists, but it is the effect of transferential disappointment it is no more than *"hainamoration"*, i.e., a return of love as its opposite. This does not stop it from being virulent and loud, but it also has dramatic, and somewhat fluid, highs and lows. That is not the case with hate; Lacan speaks of a "solid hate", one that targets the speech of the other.

This is because the speech, and here I cite, "is what comes closest to being that I call ex-sisting. Nothing concentrates more hatred than an act of saying in which ex-sistence is situated" (Lacan, 1998, p. 121). It is definitely true if we think of Freud and Lacan. I ask myself, anyhow, at times, about this strange hate that is so tenacious, and so venomous that it takes the form of a passion in certain followers of Lacan. This is especially the case in those who had left him at one time of another and sometimes even pass this hate on to their analysands. Insofar as hate aims at the very existence of *the saying* of the other, hate can only be radically murderous; it can only aim at the disappearance of the other. This being that Lacan calls "to ex-sist" is not a lack in being; it is just the opposite. It is the *sinthomatic* being which knots, in a borromean way between Symbolic and Imaginary, the enjoyment of meaning (*joui-sens*), and between Symbolic and Real, the enjoyment of the letter in its opacity. In this sense, hate can only obscurely target someone's style of jouissance. It is often what can be impossible to tolerate for others, or what can simply be found grating.

Let's go back to love. Love connects itself to the Real of the non-rapport. Does it erase its illusory side, the subject's affinity with the "not wanting to know anything" that makes us call him blind? If love recognises in the other the effects and symptoms of the unconscious knowledge that condemns it to being alone, we could imagine that love is able to recognise the *unarity*[3] of the other, precisely where hate harbours nothing but destruction.

In 1977 in the unpublished seminar "L'insu que sait de l'une bevue, s'aile a mourre", Lacan had recourse to other formulations. He says: *"There is such a thing as the One*. I repeated it just a moment ago, to say that, that there's such a thing as the One and nothing else."

When we hear this in 1977, we're not surprised. It's an allusion to the non-rapport of jouissance and to the solitude of the I who knows "that he is alone; it's horrible". I follow the citation: "There's such a thing as the One but it means that there is nevertheless feeling. This feeling that I have called, according to the unaritiés, that I have called the support, of what I must recognize as hate [...]." There, we find a surprise for the reader. The reader of the end of the seminar *Encore*, could have been mistaken and have expected that this feeling would be love because at the end of *Encore*, Lacan had said that the stigmata—if I can use this expression—of unconscious knowledge—and of the exile of the sexual rapport which results—could generate a rapport of affect between two subjects, but a rapport of love.

Did Lacan change his mind? I don't believe so. And I would like to demonstrate how love and hate do not refer to the same point of the structure. We are in the frame of what I've developed—a knowledge that the affect responds to what either inscribes itself, or to what does not inscribe itself, as a consequence of *lalangue*. The "there is such a thing as the One" goes in tandem with the "there's no" of the rapport, but these are not at the same level. It does not designate what is lacking but the contrary, the status of jouissance that exists for the one who speaks despite the exile that I spoke of. Hate responds to "there is" of jouissance or of another's *saying*. Here Lacan indicates something like a rapport of hate that poses the symptomatic existence of the other, recognising it by the affect—but this time, with the affect of hate. In fact, there is, in hate, a perception of the *other* being of the other—of the other's singularity. It is why undoubtedly, we say that hate is more lucid. Hate enters in an affective rapport with the other and its *unarity*: a rapport of execration. Hate is paradoxical, since it doesn't aim at a union that would compensate for the disunion of the sexes, but at *disunion itself, at* destruction. So, hate redoubles the absence of rapport rather than trying to compensate it, as love would. It is hate's first difference from love.

Love, conversely, certainly approaches the real being of the other, but it misrecognises it and misses it. The being approached by love, and I cite here, "is only sustained by the fact of being missed. and *that* is the verdict". Love is therefore, not a means of knowledge, but only of an obscure recognition. I cite: "It is impossible for the subject not to want not to know too much on the subject of this eminently contingent encounter with the other" (1975, p. 145). Long ago Lacan had advanced the idea that amorous encounters participated in the logic of *tuche*, i.e., of chance, of a repetition of a missed encounter. Love then, doesn't want to know too much about the repetition of the "One" alone. Love involves the perception of the gap of the non-rapport but at the same time, love denies the correlate of the non-rapport, i.e., the singularity of the jouissance of the other. Love remains the illusionary power that dreams of the "always or forever" of the love union, in order to ignore the absolute disparities of jouissance.

On the other hand, we see that hate does not want to live forever. Neither does hate harbour any illusion of a rapport. It is *an* affect, adjusted to the irremediable character of its absence. It's an affect poised on the fact that the speaker is a *unarity*. And that's precisely why hate is more adjusted to the Real. We love since it flatters the "I don't want to know anything". Let's just hope that it doesn't flatter the "I don't want to know anything" of the psychoanalysts! We have often seen this as a rehabilitation of love in Lacan's theorisations. This is not mistaken, but this was understood incompletely.

Thus, when Lacan says, (Lacan, 1998, p. 146): "True love gives way to hatred", one must not read this too fast. He does not say that hate is the other side of love, but rather that hate is love's successor, i.e., it follows. One could think that it is logical, that it is the impotence of love that brings hate about, because when the illusion of the possible rapport fails, then the singularity of the other appears—both that of the other and that of the subject with its accompanying dimension of solitude. While this is not false it should be elaborated.

To understand better how much each of these two affects responds to a different aspect of the structure, we must return to the statute of the "One" of Lacan. It is not simple. To go from *"il y a de 'l'Un"* (There is such a thing as the One) to the term *unarity* is a leap that adds something. The *"y a de l'Un"* has different meanings, but in all cases, Lacan says that there is solitude, the lack of the soul-mate, the lack of the "two" of sex. It is a formula of the curse on sex of which love registers the affects. The term *"unarity"* says another thing. It does not deny the solitude—*"il y a de l'Un* and nothing else" but it indicates that despite the lack of rapport, there is the One of the metabolism of jouissance that is valid for each speaking being. This is the One of the *sinthome* of substitution.

At the end of the *Encore* seminar, Lacan writes down the "swarm of S ones" (1975, p. 143). of enjoyment, which are deciphered "without ever depleting the knowledge of *lalangue*". I remind you of the formulation:

S1 (S1, (S1, (S1 ———> savoir))). Lacan specifies that this swarm, *essaim* (which in French "sounds like" S1, the master signifier),[4] "assures the unity of the subject's copulation with *lalangue*" It presupposes that the One of the swarm is distinct from the multiple ones that constitute the swarm; in the same way that the One of a set is different from the one that is an element of the set. "The signifier One is not any signifier, it is the signifying order itself, as established by the wrapping around[5] by which the whole chain remains." This *unity* characterises the metabolism of enjoyment. That is to say that the cohabitation with *lalangue* is not fluctuating but constant. There is no correlation between sexual enjoyments, but singular enjoyments, without any rapport with each other, yet which are stable and that Lacan designates at the end of his text as *the being of the other.*

To sum up: love is an encounter of two subjective solitudes, a result of the non-rapport that hopes for a rapport. The coincidence, if we may say so, of two exiles, of two suffering beings, of two curses. Hate, on the other hand, is a meeting not of what doesn't work but of what is present in the gap of the rapport, the being of *jouissance-sinthome*, even with the autism of such jouissance. The 1977 thesis does not then contradict the thesis of *Encore*; it insists on another side of the experience that hate is a more lucid affect that at least does not deny the subject's exile and recognises the suppletive function of *jouissance*. Lacan recalled, referring to Empedocles, that he who ignores hate would be the most ignorant of men. In fact, he would know nothing of the singularity of jouissance precisely where love misses the mark. We certainly can't wish for an elegy to hate, but hate nevertheless is a form of homage given in the negative to the consistent singularity of the other.

I can write this opposition of both aspects of the structure:

Negativity (Y a pas)	Positivity (Ya)
Curse	Unarity (singularity)
Foreclosed sexual rapport	There is (Sigma: Symptom)
Love	Hate

Love approaches the being of the Other but misses it; hate buries it.

It bothers us to think that loves misses something that hate gets, but it's essential to understand why this is the case. Why would love not recognise more than in the exile of the other, the being of the other and his proper mode of jouissance? Why would he not love this being of the other and his proper mode of jouissance as much as himself?

We've known for centuries that this is not the case, from whence the biblical precept, "love thy neighbour as thyself". The reason is that love aims at a union even a fusional one, and this union can only be founded on what both have in common, namely, a destiny of solitude—the famous history of soul-mates. Even if both respond to this destiny, each in his own way, it is what makes conjunction of coordination between the two: you and me, the same destiny, the same exile, two poor errant souls! On the contrary, the metabolism of jouissance is not shared between the two. It produces the difference between the two: the real kernel of narcissism, indifferent to the other. You and me, has nothing to do concerning jouissance, especially when it concerns a sexuated couple: man/woman. Love is not able to supplement the rapport because it misses the mark of the being of the other, the *unarity* of its jouissance. Lacan specified: "the rapport of a subject to a subject". He did not say "rapport of a *parlêtre* to a *parlêtre*". Even without passing by way of Lacan's text, if love could recognise this difference, there would not be the "drama of love" and perhaps we would not need psychoanalysis and its ever-so-particular desire so expensively acquired, the desire of the analyst—the desire of the Real of the absolute difference that has not much to do with love and that supplants hate.

In conclusion: these two affects have in common the fact that they are binding affects that take the other into consideration. This can be well perceived if we think of their difference with indifference or disdain. Indifference to the other that consists in ignoring the other, seems softer than hate, but brings much more negativity to the mix. And, we know well for example, that an indifferent parent is more de-structuring for a child than a hateful parent. A noticeable fact that the analysis confirms: certain subjects on the paranoid side hold on to being hated, even inventing the hate of the Other when they are unable to inspire it. I showed this trait in regard to Rousseau. When he is really persecuted, he is enchanted, but when he thinks that he is forgotten, he becomes totally crazy.

No elegy for hate, however. As hate is not at the level of unconscious knowledge, it cannot reveal anything of it. Hate concerns what the other, the neighbour, shows: the other's image as well as his discourse and actions. I couldn't speak of a hate that knows as I've spoken of a love that knows. I could only speak of a hate that sees, that takes account of the being of the other but without indicating its unconscious source and is indifferent to its origins. Let us not confuse the lucidity of hate with a larger concern of knowledge. We can reproach love for its illusions that disavow the non-rapport; I insisted upon this. But in this regard, hate is worse. It would even be too much to say that hate doesn't want to know that it is indifferent to knowledge. It's happy enough to execrate whatever appears short-circuiting any question about an unconscious cause. On this point it is love that has the superiority in the eyes of psychoanalysis because there is a rapport to unconscious knowledge even though it doesn't go so far as to form the foundation of a desire to know. For this, one needs a psychoanalyst.

Notes

1. In section III (Unconscious Emotions) in his metapsychological paper, "The Unconscious", Freud writes: "[…] affects and emotions correspond to processes of discharge, the final manifestations of which are perceived as feelings." (p. 178) Thus "affects" are the perceived *effects* of discharge of drive, which has been cathected in ideas.

2. (Bruce Fink Translation, p. 139/Lacan Encore, p. 127).
3. (An untranslatable neologism of Lacan's that combines two French words: *unité* and *unaire* that have a distinct significance in Lacan's work. Their combination thus suggests something uniquely psychoanalytic in the formation of individual subjects, Ed.)
4. Lacan makes a poetic use of the homophony, perfect in French (Ess=S; aim=1)
5. Wrapping around refers to Lacan's work on topological sequences.

References

Freud, S. (1914d). On the History of the Psycho-Analytic Movement. *S. E., XIV.* London: Hogarth.

Lacan, J. (2000). *The Seminar of Jacques Lacan: Bk. 20: On Feminine Sexuality, the Limits of Love and Knowledge (1972–1973).* J.-A. Miller (Ed.), B. Fink (Trans.). New York: Norton.

Lacan, J. (1988). *The Seminar of Jacques Lacan: Bk. 1: Freud's Papers on Technique.* J. Forrester (Trans.) New York: Norton.

Lacan, J. (1973–1974). *The seminar of Jacques Lacan: Book XXII: R.S.I.: 1973–1974.* Gallagher, C (Trans.).

Lacan, J. (1980). *Television.* New York: W. W. Norton & Co. Inc.

Lacan, J. (1998). *The Seminar of Jacques Lacan Book XX: Encore.* Fink, B. (Trans.). New York: W. W. Norton & Co. Inc.

Soler, C. (2011). *Les Affects Lacaniens.* Paris: Presse Universitaire de France.

Soler, C. (2009). *Lacan, L'inconscient réinventé.* Paris: Presse Universitaire de France.

CHAPTER TEN

Editors' introduction

S. Bailly

Perhaps the two clinical matters about which there is the greatest divergence of views between Lacanians and the psychoanalytic mainstream are the use of variable duration sessions and of counter-transference. For clinicians in the IPA tradition, adherence to the analytic frame and the use of counter-transference as an analytic tool are shibboleths that set psychoanalysis apart from other forms of psychotherapy. For Lacanians, the rejection of these practices is equally defining, and remains the greatest impediment to rapprochement. However, in my view the divergence on these matters stems not from differences in metapsychological understandings but from the ideas of *how* best to take these into account and manage the problems inherent in them.

In the IPA, the ideation around the analytic frame is premised upon the need to represent in practice an Oedipal third—in Lacanian terms, the paternal metaphor is concretised in a set of rules that both analyst and patient have to respect (or disrespect, as the case may be). Lacanians on the other hand expect that the metaphorical father should be firmly enough established in the mind of the analyst to be able to govern his or her practice (including regulating boundaries, phantasies of omnipotence, or defensive or indulgent enactments) and that adherence to a literal frame is equivalent to what Kleinians would call making a symbolic equation. This is not the place for a discussion of the relative merits of either view, and I mention it here mostly as an illustration of how the same metapsychological understanding (that of the importance of the Oedipal third in psychic space) and the concern arising from it (that of holding boundaries in an analysis) can lead to quite different practical strategies for dealing with it.

Counter-transference is the other important area of controversy, and here again we feel that the differences in view are not fundamental but contingent upon a set of understandings (and misunderstandings) that existed at a particular historical moment. The metapsychology of counter-transference is not in question: there is agreement on both sides that it exists, that it is dependent upon both conscious and unconscious elements in the psyche of the analyst as well as in the analysand, and that it is important in practice to note it. There is disagreement, however, on its usefulness as an instrument of analysis and whether or not it should be acted upon; it can be argued that this disagreement arose in part because of the conflict between Lacan and the IPA in the late 1950s and early 1960s, and may also be due to some misunderstandings within French circles (Lacan included) of the writings of Margaret Little on the subject. His rather caricatural view of Little's clinical practice (Little, 1957) has led his followers still to talk of counter-transference only in terms of "mastering" it in order to avoid acting in. And while many Lacanians today are aware that the theorisation and use of counter-transference by mainstream analysts today has moved a long way from that pilloried by Lacan, it is still an under-researched phenomenon in the Lacanian tradition. In our view, there have been excesses on both sides—the elevation of counter-transference to the place of primary therapeutic tool in certain clinical traditions has promoted "imaginary-to-imaginary" dialogues that concretise the phantasies of both analyst and analysand, while the Lacanian view of it has verged on the phobic.

In this paper, Maurice Khoury looks at the theoretical construct that Lacan set up as a response to the interest in counter-transference that was developing in the 1950s and early 1960s: the desire of the analyst. He shows how this can be more than just a talismanic way of surviving counter-transference difficulties and opens up a different framework within which the analyst can relate to the analysand and help him or her arrive at their truth. Here, desire may be understood as the channel, established by object cathexes, in which the drive flows and therefore the motivating force in any and all human activity. Lacan's formulation that the desire of the subject is the desire of the Other leads to the possibility of a system in which in order to access the truth of the analysand's desire, the analyst must enter into the Other of the analysand without seeming to embody it.

There is a curious congruence of ideas in Lacan's formulation of how the desire of the analyst arises (see Khoury, paragraph 14) and Little's writings on what is meant by counter-transference. Lacan writes about "what remains in the order of the ambiguous, the enigmatic, the unanalysed, in which is based the persistence and permanence of desire" and "that which posits itself as a conquest over the unconscious as the source of inexhaustible desire"—formulations not a million miles away from Little's definitions of:

> The analyst's unconscious attitude to the patient; repressed elements, hitherto unanalysed, in the analyst himself which attach to the patient [...]. Some specific attitude or mechanism with which the analyst meets the patient's transference; and the whole of the analyst's attitudes and behaviour towards his patient. This includes all the others, and any conscious attitudes as well. (Little, 1951)

However, Lacan's desire of the analyst also explicitly includes "the central place of the relationship between the question of origins in the desire of Freud and the Name-of-the-Father". It is this attention to the Oedipal third in the mind of the analyst that gives the desire of the analyst its protection against a form of relating in which the analyst may be engulfed by or may abandon himself to the seductions of the patient's transference fantasy.

References

Little, M. (1951). Counter-transference and the Patient's Response to it. *Int J Psychoanal, 32*: 32–40.

Little, M. (1957). "R"—the Analyst's Total Response to his Patient's Needs. *Int J Psychoanal, 38*: 240–254.

CHAPTER TEN

The desire of the analyst and counter-transference: from the mirroring analyst to the desiring analyst*

Maurice Khoury

The Lacanian notion of the desire of the analyst reached its apogee in the 1960s, during the period in which the decision of the IPA's executive committee to withdraw Lacan's status as a Training Analyst was in play. Above all, the idea appeared to be a response to developments made by the British school in the concept of counter-transference—the affects solicited in the analyst by the transference of the patient that would be reutilised in the analytic process; Lacan felt that these should not obscure the fundamental position of the analyst in directing the treatment, an enigmatic position that comes into play from the first moment that an analysand decides to become an analyst. This text examines the principal axes that brought Lacan to forge the idea of the Desire of the Psychoanalyst, in reflecting also, in light of these axes, on what had stopped Freud from writing his essay on counter-transference.

The desire of the psychoanalyst is a notion that was not fully conceptualised in either the seminars or *Ecrits*. Although Lacan spoke only conjecturally about it, this notion nevertheless found its way over the course of the seminars, notably *On Transference* (1960–1961), *Anxiety* (1962–1963), *The Four Fundamental Concepts of Psychoanalysis* (1963–1964), the chapter in the *Ecrits* "Of Freud's 'Drive' and the Desire of the Psychoanalyst", as well as in diverse interventions, to becoming a mainstay of psychoanalytic practice. The desire of the psychoanalyst is borne out of the general concept of desire which constitutes the platform of his theory of lack as an element that creates subjectivity and structures the psyche. This concept emerged as emblematic around the events that shook French psychoanalysis in the early 1960s. In large part, it also owes its *raison d'être* to the changing conceptualisation of counter-transference by the British school in the 1950s. Attention to the desire of the psychoanalyst reached its height in the years

*Translated from the original French by Lionel and Sharmini Bailly.

that followed the decision of the executive committee of the IPA to strip Lacan of his training functions while he was still in the French Society of Psychoanalysis in 1963. The day after this decision was announced, Lacan decided to interrupt his seminar on the Name-of-the-Father after only one session, and replaced it, having also changed location, with a seminar on the fundamentals of psychoanalysis (Lacan, 1964b).

This rupture in the affiliative link in the training of analysts—a rupture in the process of transmission for Lacan—was therefore contemporaneous with another rupture, that of the suspension of his seminar, and this was at once interpreted by some as giving a particular value to his silence, which became loaded with meaning This discourse placed him in direct conflict with the Freudian orthodoxy, while he simultaneously announced a "return to Freud" by way of Descartes. As Eric Porge said:

> In proceeding with a return to Freud which depended on a Cartesian subject, Lacan called into question a tradition of interpretation of Freud and also the texts of Freud himself. What appeared to him as the obstacle to this questioning was nothing other than the Name-of-the-Father, on which rested the crisis of 1963.[1] (Porge, 1996, p. 66)

The desire of the psychoanalyst in relation to the Name-of-the-Father—here in its relationship with the Freudian text as transmitted by the IPA–was to take on a different meaning, that of "the ethic of desire" advocated by Lacan against a so-called traditional ethic, an ethic of "fathers", in the transmission of the Freudian work.

At the same time, the notion of the desire of the psychoanalyst had began to develop in contrast to the Freudian concept of counter-transference which gained importance in the work of British analysts towards the end of the 1940s (Heimann, Money-Kyrle, Low, Little, Tower, etc.). With certain post-Lacanians, the desire of the psychoanalyst and the concept of counter-transference began a relationship of stormy rivalry and complementarity, although never of complicity. Lacan, who contested the idea of an affective and mirroring dialogue between the transference of the patient and the emotional response of the analyst, put counter-transference in a category of suspect ideas. For him an inter-psychic, indeed inter-subjective, dialogue could only support the needs of a relationship of imaginary reciprocity, a sort of symmetrical communication of "persons" and of unconscioues which reduced the place of the analytic third, of the symbolic function and of the neutrality required of the analyst in the deployment of unconscious processes. Ultimately, this position was to prove rather simplistic: all counter-transference cannot simply be reduced to a dual relationship in which any tertiary elaboration is absent.

Upstream of any conscious or unconscious "dialogue" in the session, Lacan places the fundamental question, "what does the analyst want?" when he decides to become an analyst. This question *Chè vuoi*? What do you want? was inspired by the eighteenth century fantastical novel *The Devil in Love* by Jacques Cazotte (1991). This question is kept up along the entire course of an analysis and guides the way in which the analyst listens, supporting his desire to analyse throughout the treatment. Counter-transferential states, are seen as something that again puts into question the initial desire of the analyst and their function is seen as something that could correct and restitute the desire to analyse, moving therefore the question of counter-transference beyond the concept of counter-transferential "resistance" or counter-transference neurosis, as Racker called it (Racker, 1968).

Where in the Freudian tradition, the notion of neutrality with all its implications is central, the very expression "desire of the psychoanalyst" attributes desire to the analyst as a keystone of his practice. But close observation would force us to agree with Lacan that we owe first and foremost to Freud this path animated by a passion for origins. Freud's demand of the hysteric was to "remember" and reveal the contents of an unconscious scene, and this never ceased to stoke his desire, nor that of those who followed him. Freud's use of pressure on the forehead would, according to Cottet, be "less a technical artifice having the place of a provisional measure before he came to a more mature understanding of the dynamics of transference and resistance, as a permanent sign of Freud's desire to discover a secret, to obtain an avowal" (Cottet, 1982, p. 30). Freud used the metaphor of sexual intercourse to illustrate the work of the analyst in suggesting that:

> The analyst's power over the symptoms of the disease may thus be compared to male sexual potency. A man can, it is true, beget a whole child, but even the strongest man cannot create in the female organism a head alone, or an arm or a leg; he cannot even prescribe the child's sex. He, too, only sets in motion a highly complicated process determined by events in the remote past, which ends with the severance of the child from his mother. (Freud, 1913, p. 130)

In this allegation, Freud guides us on a paradoxical trail where "the sexualising power" of the analyst upon the foundation of the analytic situation is all the while marked by a sort of impotence to determine in advance the process, which remains unpredictable, mysterious and random in its path (Canestri, 2004). Besides, he reminds us in the same text of the response of the philosopher in Aesop's fable: "when the wayfarer asked how long a journey lay ahead, the philosopher merrily answered, 'Walk!' and afterwards explained his apparently unhelpful reply on the grounds that he must know the length of the wayfarer's stride before he could tell how long his journey would take" (Freud, ibid, p. 128).

In this major article on technique, Freud focuses on how the initial disposition of the analyst marks the analytic path thereafter, and describes the problem in terms of a primary investment in the bringing together of desire and method, expectant belief and technique. In contrast, the question of counter-transference which began to be posed several years before always had a more accidental flavour, as shown by the misadventures of the first analysts in their practice (e.g., Jung & Sabina Spielrein, and Ferenczi & Elma Pálos), which led Freud to plan an essay on counter-transference, which he never wrote.

Here then is a first major difference: the desire of the analyst would be of the order of the primary motivation which incites an analyst to conduct analyses, where the counter-transference by definition is limited to what an analyst experiences when faced with transferential affects of the analysand. Even if this schematic distinction appears obvious, there is a lot of overlap between the two concepts. As an illustration, just think about what analysts are recommended to do when experiencing problematic counter-transference: they should talk to their peers, go into supervision or even go back into analysis themselves. In other words, to re-examine their desire to analyse or their transference onto analysis (Donnet, 1995)—inaugurated in their personal analysis—a desire usurped for a while by the shackles of listening, emotional overload or even the urge to act-in in the face of hostile or sexual transference.

When I talk about counter-transference in this paper, I will limit myself to the understanding of the term as it was in the 1950s and from which arises in part the concept of the desire of the psychoanalyst in Lacan. I am aware that the concept of counter-transference has been considerably developed since then, both in clinical practice and for its value as a research tool.

The desire of the analyst in its various forms

Many definitions attempt to circumscribe the concept of desire of the psychoanalyst and the specificity of this concept might be grasped through the complementary of these definitions and their dynamic interaction. The concept appears nonetheless impossible to fully define as it involves the enigmatic desire to spend time with the unconscious. On this point, Lacan shows himself to be as firm as he is perplexed. On the one hand he wonders about "this madness that pushes someone who knew what happened to the analyst at the end of the analysis, to in turn practice analysis", and on the other, he thinks that "what the subject achieves as a 'pacific' victory over his unconscious is priceless" (Safouan, 1983, p. 68). Having won a victory over his own unconscious, the analyst takes on other unconsciouses, which makes Safouan say that it "is therefore conceivable that a desire to practice analysis could be born out of a training analysis and not as some of Lacan's formula suggest, despite it". In a training analysis, this desire is born out of the future analyst's commerce with his own unconscious, which led Lacan to question the sources and the paternity of the Freudian desire in its primary relationship with hysteria.

The "original sin of analysis" and the Names-of-the-Father

As a concept, the desire of the analyst could be seen as an "unanalysed remnant", an incontrovertible element in the discovery of psychoanalysis as it was for Freud. With regard to this, Lacan spoke of the founding desire of the first historical figure in psychoanalysis, "namely the fact that something in Freud was never analysed" (Lacan, 1964b, p. 21). It is noteworthy that twelve years later, when Lacan looked at the literary work of James Joyce, it is precisely also at something in the category of the unanalysed and indecipherable upon which is founded the enigmatic writing of the Irish creative genius, a writing that would act as a "substitutive ego" that compensated for Joyce's paternal lack. Lacan also pinpointed this unanalysable element as that which inspired Freud to invent his economic view of the psychic apparatus.

It would be wise to point out here the parallel and almost synchronic course taken by Lacan on the question of the unanalysable, what cannot be articulated about primordial desire, and what would crystallise in the expression "desire of the analyst"—alongside the Name-of-the-Father, the seminar which he felt compelled to give up—"aimed at nothing else than to question the origin, to know, through what privilege Freud's desire had found, in the field of unconscious experience, the entry point" (Lacan, 1964b, p. 21).

This is when Lacan questions the aspects of the father of religion and sacrifice (the sacrifice of Isaac) that are revealed to him as "the original sin" in the desire of Freud in relation to the origins of psychoanalysis. After the interrupted seminar, the notion of the Name-of-the-Father will go astray for ten years before returning in the 1970s, this time illustrated "topologically" with the analyses of Joyce's work (Porge, 1996, pp. 59–60). The shadow of the interrupted seminar hovered over Lacan's teachings with occasional reminders without altogether being reprised and conceptually developed (Porge, 1996, pp. 59–60). To return to the beginnings of the discovery of psychoanalysis, Freud's entry point was in seizing the relationship between the hysteric and language, a relationship that enabled him to discover the unconscious. But despite his genius, this discovery would have remained incompletely elucidated for Lacan, except that he himself was seized by the desire of Freud, by the unanalysed in him: if for curing the hysteric, the best way was to satisfy the hysterical desire (which is to show her desire as being unsatisfied), Lacan suggests that the question remains of "why she sustains her desire only as unsatisfied".

In his response to M. Tort towards the end of the introductory seminar about the *Four Concepts*, Lacan states that the "Freudian field of the practice of analysis remains dependent upon a certain original desire which continues to play an ambiguous but prevalent role in the transmission of psychoanalysis" (Lacan, 1964b, p. 22). In this original desire, Lacan attempts to examine the origin by revisiting the fundamental concepts of psychoanalysis: the unconscious, repetition, transference, and drives, which he was to develop over the course of that year. Lacan posits the existence of a desire as the basis of all creation, the desire of the analysis being the end product of multiple phenomena:

- what remains in the order of the ambiguous, the enigmatic, the unanalysed, in which is based the persistence and permanence of desire;
- that which posits itself as a conquest over the unconscious as the source of inexhaustible desire;
- the central place of the relationship between the question of origins in the desire of Freud and the Name-of-the-Father.

In his single seminar of the 20th of November 1963 on the Name-of-the-Father, Lacan considered that Freud put the myth of the father at the centre of his doctrine because of the inevitability of this question and that if the theory and the psychoanalytic praxis appeared to be stalling, "it is because of not having dared to go further than Freud on this question" (Lacan, 1963, p. 85). In "daring" to go further, Lacan declared that "he who researches truth can supercede all the opinions of specialists" (p. 86). He returns to the animal father of the horde, to the subject "before the question", putting forward that "mythically [...] the father can only be an animal. The primordial father is the father before the interdiction of incest, before the appearance of the Law, of the order of structures of alliance and of kinship, before the appearance of culture. This is why Freud is the head of the horde, in conformity with the animal myth, the satisfaction is without brakes" (pp. 86–87). The evolution would have been in the passage to totemism and the access to the function of proper names. Afterwards, this name, which is read in all languages, will find media on which to be printed, human media or Phoenician characters on potteries, beyond any possible speech. This is where Lacan introduces the relationship between law and desire, this "co-conformity" being born "of the assumption of the pure enjoyment of the father as primordial" (p. 89).

The desire of the analyst therefore reunites both jouissance and law, from the supposition of this pure, primordial jouissance of the father. This could mean that the law banning incest and (incestuous) desire would together be constitutive of the notion "law and repressed desire [being] one and the same thing" (Lacan, 1966, p. 782). A few months before, in his seminar on *Anxiety*, Lacan put forward that "what constitutes the substance of the law, is the desire for the mother, and conversely, what is normative in the desire itself, what makes it desire, is the law known as the prohibition of incest" (Lacan, 1959–1960, p. 176).

Desire is therefore in an intrinsic relationship with the law, and the primordial father would become the Name-of-the-Father, a symbolic function that operates in the desire of the analyst, the analyst who becomes himself in some way his own father, an "authorising" father and having ethics as desire. The Name-of-the-Father would be at the same time a symbolic, separating and differentiating function that makes a metaphor of the prohibition of incest and the advent of language. These considerations show the close links between notions of the desire of the analyst and the Name-of-the-Father, as well as the trap in which Lacan was caught—and the Lacanian movement after him—in transforming itself paradoxically into the defender of Freudian texts but also into the challenger to Freud (E. Porge). André Green said it well in a colloquium of the Paris Psychoanalytic Society, the return to Freud meant for Lacan, going towards Lacan (Green, 2008). The desire of the analyst is a desire for the knowledge of origins, marked by the law and therefore by renunciation. Furthermore, Lacan argues that desire does not come into being because of secondary repression, which operates in a metaphorical structure, but of primary repression, which can be understood as the result of the incapacity of language fully to signify. Desire is therefore inarticulable, it is "desire for nothing".

The desire of the psychoanalyst as "desire for nothing"

Lacan gives "desire" the responsibility of bearing his theoretical edifice about lack and one may conceive of the difficulty in making out the horizons of such a notion. Nevertheless, the meaning of such a concept gradually becomes clear in the course of the evolution of Lacan's thinking and one notes that his attempts at elucidation detract from the precision of its definition. His definition often came by default, or arose from other notions by a metonymic approximation. So, it is of desire with regard to drive, of desire in its relationship with lack or again of desire defined by the nature of its objects; both objects cause of desire (the lost object, the evanescent object of desire,) and objects as vehicles of the drive and its satisfaction. Overall, desire was not conceptualised but could be approached as would a movable "gaseous" state around which gravitate slightly more concrete concepts which in return define it.

Lacan distinguishes the desire of the analyst from good intentions, moral high ground and the "most Samaritan help" (Lacan, 1966, p. 98) raising the concept of an end of analysis that is beyond the scope of treatment and from which it has to be distinguished "when it is about the 'making' of an analyst" (Lacan, 1966, p. 854). It is this dimension, beyond the treatment, that helps us understand what the desire of the analyst is, this indestructible force allowing an analyst "to remain an analyst … once past the initial enthusiasm, the freedom and the opening granted by the end of its own analysis, all through a professional life" (Guyomard, 1992).

Guyomard tries to develop Lacan's explanation of desire in general and also of the desire of the analyst. This is an "absolute point" (Lacan, 1967), a "power of a pure loss" from which "the value of desire cannot be raised higher" (Guyomard, 1992), which remains impossible to articulate. Opposing desire in Lacan to desire in Freud, Guyomard suggests that for Freud, desire can be named, unlike Lacan for whom desire does not rest on secondary repression and therefore remains impossible to name, being prey to a sort of continuous unbinding. This unspeakable nature of desire, which lacks a clearly defined object, brings Lacan to a theory of the end of analysis in opposition to the accepted view that the end of analysis was synonymous with identification with the analyst. The end of analysis for Lacan is a trial in which the subject faces its own impotence when confronted with what makes its condition and makes him desiring. The future analyst experiences a form of helplessness (*Hilflosigkeit*), as a "man in this relationship to himself that is his own death [...] cannot expect help from anyone" (Lacan, 1959–1960).

The desire of the analyst is therefore born of this "Unbeing", this inarticulable distress at the end of the personal analysis of the future analyst. This desire will leave an indelible mark in his practice: he will learn to accept his own removal as a transference object at the end of the analyses he will undertake with his future analysands.

In Lacanian theory, this "desire for nothing" in the analyst will meet a similar outcome in the analysand, as long as the analyst allows himself to fall from his place as a transference object, of his place as the Subject supposed to Know. But upstream of this "crowning", a "dialectic of desire" (Lacan, 1966, p. 793) leads the dance between analyst and analysand, a dialectic that causes the intervention of the (unknown) Other as the place of desire. Thus, desire finds its roots according to Lacan in the desire of the Other. "To what should the desire of the psychoanalyst respond? To a necessity that we can only theorise of having to make the desire of the subject like the desire of the Other, or to make it the cause of this desire" (Lacan, 1967). How can we locate this dialectic of desire in the concept of the desire of the analyst?

The desire of the analyst as the desire of the Other

Guided by Hegel's formula according to which the Desire of Man is the desire of the Other (Lacan, 1966, "Propos on Psychic causality", p. 181), Lacan refers to Jacques Cazotte's fantasy novel *The Amorous Devil* in order to illustrate the paradoxical nature of the desire of the subject and its articulation in fantasy, starting from the desire of the Other. In "The Subversion of the Subject and the Dialectic of Desire in the Freudian Unconscious" Lacan tries to show that desire can be desire for recognition, how the subject "discovers that he is the instrument of the jouissance of the Other", how he even becomes the object of the demand of the Other. The dialectic of need and demand is as we know, marked by the inability of the signifier to symbolise the lack, and desire appears from the mismatch between need and demand. The subject is alienated to the Other of language and the issue of "what does he want?" (*Chè vuoi*?) or "What does he want of me?"[2] will fill the question of the neurotic subject ("Who am I?") in addressing a demand for recognition to the Other (Lacan, 1966).

In the treatment, this demand is addressed to the analyst as a demand to know, as a demand for truth, demand played out in the transference. Where Freud saw transference as the affective enactment of a past experience, Lacan sees it as a demand addressed to the Other *supposed to know*: "as soon as there is somewhere the subject supposed to know [...] there is transference" (Lacan, 1964b, p. 258). This demand to know is an aspect of the desire of the analyst: "It is he who knows [...] I desire his knowledge and his desire to know". For the patient, the question will also be: "What does he want of me?" and will expand to questions reflecting fantasies: "What does he know of me?" or "What does he desire?". These fantasies in the analytic treatment, are constructed around the desire of an Other who is after all, wounded, like scaffolding both supporting and hiding the Subject Supposed to Know. These questions can be seen as fulfilling a fetishistic function, hiding what the analyst's lack, like the hypothetical maternal phallus comes to fantasmatically fill the missing phallus of the mother.

Mustapha Safouan pointed out that "desire, once linked with the desire of the unknown Other can only be constituted as a question to which the response, whatever it be, always brings, with a part that is light, a part that is shadow; since the being of the subject arises from a basis of non-being. It is in the maintenance of the hole of non-being that the being of the subject resides [...]" (M. Safouan, 2001, p. 258). The signifiers of these primitive demands would essentially be the breast and the faeces. This question with regard to the Other (the analyst) will have the character of being continually in search of the lost object, that part object, the remains of the primitive body. And the analyst, supported by his desire to keep open this questioning (the lack which cannot be filled except very partially), will not respond to the demand by a response to need: "Should the analyst also know his limit to be the space in which resonates Chè vuoi?" (M. Safouan, 2001, p. 158). The analyst therefore defines himself always by this function that continually returns the demand of the patient to a desire, that of the Other who will be confused with the desire of the analyst.

The analytic function of having constantly to leave open the space of the *Chè vuoi* calls into question the place of the "being of the psychoanalyst" (see Lebovici in Shentoub, 1955) and his presence in the here and now of the session, beyond his function of incarnating the patient's infantile past objects. The view was that counter-transference puts the analyst in a conscious and unconscious oscillation, which connects with the transference representations and affects of the patient to the point where this connection becomes the linchpin of interpretative technique in the treatment. Lacan railed against this tendency, which according to him, "called into question even the concept of the unconscious" to the advantage of the intersubjective dynamic within the session; a criticism that Lacan was right to address, according to the analysts who followed him, as shown by the development of the so-called interpersonal schools.

The hunt for counter-transference

A new conceptualisation of counter-transference was formed by British authors towards the end of the forties and throughout the fifties. If it was the work of Little (1951) that developed the idea of effects produced by the analyst and the person of the analyst upon the patient. Paula Heimann (1950) began to take the measure of what the patient activated in the analyst and after Heimann, Money-Kyrle presented counter-transference—the feelings of the analyst—as a displaced manifestation of the transference of the patient (Cottet, 1982).

In her 1949 article, "On Counter-Transference", Paula Heimann develops the idea that makes the analysis of counter-transference the instrument of interpretation in the treatment (Heimann,

1950): the conscious or unconscious affects solicited in the analyst by the transference of the patient would constitute a precious tool for understanding the psychic movements of the latter. These counter-transference affects would be used as a lever in psychoanalytic interpretation.

Rejecting this theses in his text of 1951, "Intervention on transference", Lacan launched a war against the tendency that makes of the analytic relationship a relation of "dialogue" in the here and now of the session. For him, this tendency reduces the place of something "beyond" transference (the transference object that is the analyst always returning to a past object, and Other from the past), and consequently of something "beyond" counter-transference. We recall Freud's position towards transference as resistance against the emergence of traumatising and repressed unconscious representations—the presiding transference resistance paradoxically indispensable to the analytic process and its engine. It is from this conception of transference that Lacan starts his war against counter-transference. If transference resistance as described by Freud is a lure (tool), then what would be counter-transference but the response of the analyst to a trick? What makes counter-transference doubly deceptive if one allows oneself to be taken in by it, is the "illusion" of using counter-transference in the technique of interpretation. In using this "dialogue" of transference/counter-transference, "what presents itself as a situation is a false situation" (M. Safouan, 2001, p. 157).

If Lacan never stopped reiterating in his seminars the illusory nature of the demand and its articulation in contrast with desire, it is in his seminar on *Transference* (1960–1961) that he calls up the desire of the analyst (as the desire of the Other) as the mainspring of transference, after criticising theories of counter-transference as implicitly responding in kind to the demand.

The seminar on *Anxiety* (1962–1963)—concomitant with the elaboration of the Lacanian conception of anxiety in relation to that of Freud—was to be a chance for Lacan to examine more closely the British work on counter-transference, an examination which has clarified further the concept of the desire of the analyst. He also looked at the clinical examples and the theory brought by these authors.

Lacan's commentary on the clinical example of Margaret Little

In 1957 Margaret Little published a paper about the total response of the analyst to his patient's needs. While in agreement with the author's position regarding the commitment and responsibility of the analyst in the treatment, Lacan insists that the lack in the Other, governed by the anxiety of the analyst, leads her to provide a counter-transference interpretation. Margaret Little gives the clinical example of a kleptomaniac patient whose analysis, despite all possible varieties of interpretation during a session when she was very upset, started to take off when the analyst showed her that she was completely at sea and that seeing the analysand like that made her sad. Little suggested that it was "the positive, the Real, the liveliness of a feeling which gave the analysis its movement back". For Lacan it was the anxiety that appeared in the analyst, together with the place of the lack in analysis, which contributed to it: "This insertion [...] opens a dimension which allows this female subject to grasp herself as lacking, when this was never possible in her relationship with her parents" (Lacan, 1962–1963, p. 169).

Lacan's opinion shows the importance of the theorisation of the lack of and in the parental Other in the psychic construction, and how this contrasts with the "liveliness of feeling" in the here and now of the session. In other words, a Lacanian point of view on the question would suggest an analyst in this case signifies to the patient his incapacity to fill an impossible demand through his lack of response, as a response to the demand would have to be found in a "beyond" of the analyst (desire is the desire of the Other). It doesn't stop the analyst from showing himself to be present, as the object of containment which would partly fill the lack: a framing of primitive representations not yet bound by tertiary processes (Green, 1972).

Following on from these developments, M. Little could in her interventions say things like, "listen, stop that, because literally, I can't listen to any more, you are putting me to sleep" in response to the same patient who never stopped rehashing her stories about money and her mother. Or again, listening to the patient telling her about the changes she had made to her consulting room, and having conceded, about these modifications, the remarks of patients that day, Little retorted: "Listen, I don't care what you think of it" (here she is well beyond liveliness of feeling). Shocked, the patient came out of her silence with cries of enthusiasm: "What you did there was amazing …" One may wonder here about the masochistic capacities of patients who defray this type of intervention, capacities which could take the treatment in an unfavourable direction, in particular if this type of intervention became a model of technique in the treatment.

Lacan took up the position of the British authors in returning to the question of the participation and engagement of the analyst in relation to that which is defined as counter-transference. He picked out one of the definitions of counter-transference given by Tower (1956), namely that "counter-transference is all that the analyst represses of what he receives as meaning in the analysis". For Lacan, this statement inadvertently reveals what it is actually about. The question is not that of counter-transference, "for it is in the state of confusion in which it is given to us that it takes its meaning. The only meaning from which no author can escape is precisely the desire of the analyst" (Lacan, 1959–1960, p. 175).

The main question here would be knowing why taking into account counter-transference affects in treatment would discharge the analyst of responsibility for the direction of the treatment and the desire of the analyst in question. The answer may be found in considering counter-transference a generalisable theory, systematically usable, which can indeed explain certain excesses.

In practice, with some patients, we find ourselves brought to play the "liveliness of feeling" card. Think of Ferenczi's experiment of mutual analysis and the consequences analysts might draw after him in paradoxical measure of the importance of these experiments, but also the risk of their effects on the consequences of analysis. We continue to think that interventions that put forward the affect of the analyst constitute only an extreme means and a particular intervention of which the objective is to constitute the weft of later elaborations. But it is their theorisation and their generalisation as theory of technique that would be responsible for the misdirection.

I think here about a patient who had lived through challenging and very violent traumatic experiences and to whom I had at one time proposed some extra sessions to give him enough support and presence in the face of a heavy burden of anxiety which made me fear a suicidal enactment.

In these moments, the experience of frustration that remains at the end of a non-response to the demand for immediate satisfaction—or on the contrary, following an overdose of interventions and of "plugging constructions" of the analyst which are supposed to plug the gaps of impossible demands—can have tragic consequences. On the other hand, and curiously, interventions of the order of a "lively feeling" come as a surprise to the analyst and to the patient.

At a very delicate moment in a session where a patient made me feel the possibility of an imminent enactment, I heard myself say to her: "While trying to understand, to experience this overpowering situation in which you find yourself and to which no response seems to give relief, I realised that, without necessarily being able to fill the void that you feel, you push me to think more and more ..." This intervention, which in the aftermath proved a pivotal intervention, filtering subsequent interventions, had changed the direction of the treatment in aborting a possible enactment.

Clinical example

L is a forty-three-year-old woman who came to analysis for a generalised malaise that affected her social and emotional life. She was married with two daughters aged sixteen and eighteen, and coming from a middle-class family of well-known industrialists in which the family firm was directed by the men of the family. Because of the family's place in society, L's parents, despite their love for their children, were caught up in an endless round of social engagements and public life. Second in a sibling group of four, she found herself "always with the adults" of the family, uninterested in other children of her age. She had always been a mature, studious, self-sufficient child, precocious in comparison with her siblings and with other children her age, and later, a model daughter and above the common herd. Her almost permanent presence in adult social circles forced upon her a high degree of discretion with regard to an overdose of information, family secrets, intrusive events and incidents, at an age at which she did not have yet the psychic means of linkage that would allow their elaboration.

Having spent her childhood in a war-torn country, before returning and settling with her family in her country of origin where she spent the last years of her adolescence and her adult life, she often evoked this long period of permanent fear, of family anxiety and instability. She remembered moments of terror as when a shell once hit the room of her brother, or when upon returning from a period in exile, her father was seized by a heart attack upon learning that their home had been firebombed by militia; or again, when soldiers entered their home and spoke at length with her father who then remained in a heavy silence for days.

During her childhood, her status as a "wise baby" (Ferenczi, 1923), a part that preserved her from the part that was ruled by trauma and terror, tried to preserve her parents, themselves "divided" and often overwhelmed by events. This "baby" had much consideration for others, adults, observing their psychic states and trying to protect them against all anxieties about her; she would look after everything, silence anxieties, in a denial that cost her a part of herself. She sometimes depicted herself as a beggar wandering in dark streets, not knowing if she was coming or going.

I will not dwell further on these first few facts of her life story and come to the subject of interest in this article, in beginning with a counter-transference dream:

> "She and I were at the top of a very tall Roman edifice. A very strong wind was blowing—almost a squall—and threatened to capsize us; the platform on which we stood was small. L. was afraid of falling and clung to my neck; I heard myself say to her not to worry and that she would not fall. In my hand I held a coffee cup containing a red liquid—probably blood …"

This dream intrigued me greatly, despite its quite transparent symbolism. She had often said to me that she was afraid of falling, of collapsing. The Roman edifice had connotations of majesty of an empire which had reigned for a long time, which had been masterly but also a debacle and collapse. The concept of empire often carries an allusion of potential fall. We often speak of the "fall of an empire", of the "end of a reign". The shock and the fall which would destabilise her and myself, often called to me. My desire to see her "let go" and my fear of this desire were often mixed up.

A little later, she herself had a transference dream in which "we walked together in a grand place in a town famous for romantic tourism". Shortly afterwards on a business trip, she experienced an incident that deeply disturbed her. I will not say anything about it for reasons of confidentiality; I will say only that this incident transformed her perceptibly. On her return, she showed a strong anxiety with irrational fears and became very sensitive to apparently insignificant events. My feeling was that she was becoming more "human", her facial expression made her more present, showed her affects more. In her family she was showing signs of weakness not being the invincible mother everybody knew; disconcerted and demoralised she had become unrecognisable to her family.

In the transference she had become more attached to me and was afraid that I would leave her during this phase of intense distress that nothing could soothe. Technically, an intensification of the sessions was required, I offered it and she accepted without hesitation. Through the sessions, it felt that she was stagnating, her anxiety was not diminishing despite my presence and efforts to be containing. This was not without producing some irritation in me but also, and paradoxically, a great tenderness and a strong desire to get out of this hopeless situation. This mixture of emotions I was experiencing was an effect of her state of suffering on me, but also and in great part of the respect and consideration for the adult she placed in me. She was trying to spare me from her anxiety in order to preserve me.

Regression to dependence (Winnicott, 1960) involves the risk of an imaginary reciprocity in which affects from transference/counter-transference may take over elaboration/interpretation in the treatment. This delicate situation can become untenable and force the analyst to operate on an edge, between two potentially overwhelming pitfalls:

- not being present enough, playing the neutrality card and running the risk of the repetition of a trauma with a possible hetero/auto aggressive acting out.
- being too emotionally involved, empathic and flexible with the frame, leading to the possibility of narcissistic seduction and the risk of losing the analytic setting (sufficient neutrality, frame, possibility of interpretation etc.) and of acting out of the analysand but also of the

analyst. In that sort of situation the concept of *Desire of the Analyst* is a great prop. Let us consider three themes that defines it:

1. A "conquest" of the unconscious, an inexhaustible desire to see, to understand and to let psychic truth emerge where repetition, acting out and transference/counter-transference affects prevailed.
2. *Desire of the Analyst* as desire of nothing. A type of representation of the drive with no (sexual) aim, where it is the desire of "analysing" that is cathected and becomes a passion in itself.
3. *Desire of the Analyst* as desire of the Other; desire being located in the Other. The desire of the analyst can be a tool used to "filter" transferential affects to show the analysand what in these is linked to their own story re-written in the present.

I would like to add a fourth theme, an aspect that is technical even if it was the source of great theoretical debates: the place of the analytic frame and the question of the fixed duration of analytic sessions (Khoury, 2006). Lacanian variable duration sessions constitutes a trap in the situation that we have described above. They can easily lead to a counter-transferential destabilisation, the third constituted by the fixed duration of sessions being sacrificed in favour of counter-transferential affects which can acquire an autonomy undermining the analytic process.

Going back to our clinical case, during this regressive period of the treatment, I was sometimes waiting for L's session, being concerned about what she had been experiencing since our last session, increasing the duration of a session or offering the possibility of an extra session, even a telephone session when she was travelling abroad. These variations which can be justified during moments of acute anxiety can become the rule if one does not pay enough attention to it and keep in mind the central place of the "analytic third", defined by Ogden (1994) as "a third subject, unconsciously co-created by analyst and analysand, which seems to take on a life of its own in the interpersonal field between analyst and patient".

During this period, the analytic third remained deeply anchored in me and played its part in an internal personal work underlined by the counter transference. This can be illustrated by two of L's dreams and one of mine.

First dream (L): "It is during a session, I want to tell you something else and the session ends ..."

Second dream (L): "It is during a session, I start to panic when I realise that your wife is present. To comfort me you hug me and kiss me ... we were in your old office."

Two weeks later I have this dream:

We are having a session in the kitchen of the office, the couch is quite high and looks like a bed. Suddenly L sits up to get off the couch and I see that she is lightly clad. We leave the kitchen and I accompany her to the room where I normally see her. She lies down and covers herself with a blanket.

Change of scenery: we are in nature, the colours are beautiful, L wears brightly coloured clothes. Suddenly my wife appears, she is full of energy and nicely dressed, she is humming a song and does dance steps which betray her good mood.

Jean Laplanche coined the term "refusement" (refusal), his preferred translation of the Freudian term *Versagung*, to describe the analyst's refusal "to proceed in the vital or adaptational order" during a session (Scarfone, 2013). Clerc also underlined the importance in analytic technique of "the withdrawal of his own speech that the analyst imposes on himself" (Clerc, 2007). The analytic third and, the "refusal" of the analyst operate for the analytic couple and having opened the space in which regression and its emotional implications play their part, allows the analytic process to continue on its way to symbolisation and elaboration.

This third, "hallucinated" in L's dreams expresses itself in the cut ending the session when she had "more to tell me" or in the presence of the woman who causes her to panic. In my own dream, it is expressed symbolically in the accompaniment from the kitchen to the room where I see her usually but also in the blanket she uses to protect herself. The third seems to appear also in the change of scenery, which introduces a change in the intimate atmosphere that precedes it and in the appearance of my wife, which echoes L's second dream and incarnates for me and L the construction of a primal scene putting things back in order.

The place of the third is an important concept in Lacan's "*Discours de Rome*", "The Function and Field of Speech and Language in Psychoanalysis" (Lacan, 1966) in the context of the 1953 split, when Lacan reintroduces language and its symbolic function at the heart of the analytic experience. In it, he underlines the function of the imaginary, the role of fantasies in the constitution of the object at different stages of the psychic development and argues in favour of a return to symbolisation as the lynchpin of analytic technique which implies a certain type of listening and leads to a move from the Imaginary to a Symbolic structure where the third intervenes.

Counter-transference has always been this unavoidable phenomena that analysts tried to master, from Freud's counter-transference with Dora, synonymous of technical mistake, to the direct unveiling of the analyst's psyche or his or her aggressive words to the analysand. Analysts tried to master it by an understanding of the situation that allowed them to rekindle the analytic process through a use of interpretation. Building upon past and contemporary experiences, Lacan wanted to bring to counter-transference the notion of the responsibility of the analyst in the direction of the treatment, the need to grasp its movements, obstacles and points of weakness and this whatever the size and nature of the transference/counter-transference affects necessarily experienced, as they are contingent on the analyst's commitment to directing the treatment.

In the years following his seminar on *Anxiety*, in particular his interventions following the decision of the executive committee of the IPA to strip him from his training analyst's status, (end of 1963) Lacan reinforces in his work the notion of the desire of the psychoanalyst in key interventions such as the summary of his interventions at a colloquium in Rome, published as "Of Freud's « *Trieb* » and of the desire of the psychoanalyst" (Lacan, 1964a) or the introductory session of his seminar *The Four Fundamental Concepts of Psychoanalysis* (Lacan, 1964b [1973]). In 1967, Lacan revisited the concept in his reflection about the end of analysis and the question of becoming an analyst (Safouan, 2005). In another text (answer to the Proposal of the 9th October 1967) Lacan distinguishes the desire to be an analyst from the desire of the analyst, the first one being "a professional condition" while the second one supports and is supported by the psychoanalytic act. (*Scilicet 2/3*, pp. 9–29).

Freud's essay on counter-transference

The link between the concepts of counter-transference and desire of the analyst and the reflections arising from this linkage leads us to revisit Freud's uneasiness regarding his project of writing an essay on counter-transference. This project was never accomplished despite what Freud said of the necessity of such a work, according to Jung. In an attempt to simplify the Freudian position on counter-transference, it is possible to say that the tone in Freud's letters is that of a warning. He warned his pupils of the risks inherent in drifting towards acting. Freud remained attached to the idea that counter-transference should be mastered:

> What we give to the patient should, however, be a spontaneous affect, but measured out consciously at all times, to a greater or lesser extent according to need. In certain circumstances a great deal, but never from one's own unconscious. I would look upon that as the formula. One must, therefore, always recognize one's counter-transference and be able to cope with it, for not till then is one free oneself. (Letter 20th February 1913 to Binswanger)

Two and a half years after an exchange of letters with Jung regarding Sabina Spielrein, Freud wrote about the essay on counter-transference: "[...] the essay on counter-transference, which seems to me necessary, should not be published but copies should be circulated amongst us" (in Britton, 1993). This "necessary" essay appears for Freud embarrassing and paradoxical as despite being an essay, with the theoretical appearance of that type of writing, it had to be kept within the limited group of his disciples. Why such unease? In the same letter to Jung, and with a previous exchange with Ferenczi who had complained of the repression of counter-transference in mind, Freud wrote: "May I, as a dignified old master, warn you that with this technique one regularly miscalculates, that it is much better to remain inaccessible and merely receive?" This warning showed Freud's wish not go further and to limit the theoretical reflection to the group of intimates. Although recognised in analysis, counter-transference was considered only under its "accidental" aspect, belonging mostly to inexperienced analysts, as the reference to the "old master" suggest. The old master might have understood that despite his project of an essay on counter-transference, the word of a father was needed in a situation so prone to excess. As the Father of his theory, of his discovery or maybe as a father warning younger ones of the risks inherent to his discovery, rather than theorising the counter-transference, Freud chose simply to say, "no". Publishing an essay would also have meant exposing publically something that Freud felt was partly about the excess of the first-generation analysts and he preferred to restrict his comments to their group. In the end this work did not take place and nothing stopped the analysts of further generations trying, after Ferenczi, new developments.

Ron Britton who agrees with the concept of "counter-transference neurosis" that Racker adopted, suggests that if Freud had written his essay he would have probably identified a counter-transference neurosis as a form of resistance to analysis, on the model of transference neurosis (Britton, 2003). He also suggests that in the same way that erotic transference or negative, hateful transference can hamper the necessary condition of analysis, that is positive transference, Freud could have said that "erotic counter-transference and negative counter-transference both hamper positive counter-transference which is a necessary background to analysis" (Britton, 2003).

Rather than imagine what Freud could have added to his first views, we could suggest that the unease that led to his inability to write his planned essay shows the impossibility for him of elaborating on counter-transference (erotic and negative) in any other way than by attributing to it a normative value, that of a precept. At the time of Freud's discussions with his contemporaries the disagreement was less about counter-transference as a tool to interrogate the analyst's blind spots and unresolved problems than about how to sort out situations arising from his pupils' misadventures. For Freud, the elaboration of what was at stake in the counter-transference affects aimed at the attenuation or even the eradication of obstacles to the analytic process. The analyst's reflection about his or her own counter-transference experience is a method that aims to preserve the capacity of the analyst to analyse (his desire to analyse) and not a conceptual frame that can be theorised and can be stored amongst key concepts of psychoanalysis like for example transference. These views go in the direction of development that led Lacan to later construct his notion of the desire of the analyst.

Having in mind Freud's position on counter-transference and Lacan's desire of the analyst, we can underline the following points:

- the desire of the analyst supposes a return to a "paternal" warning coming from a father who is struggling at the same time with the incestuous desire (of the father of the horde) and with the law against desire. The father of psychoanalysis tried to warn Jung and Ferenczi against the miscalculation of giving in to counter-transference. Freud as (omnipotent?) father of his concepts had no choice but to impose limits against the autonomy of his theorisations. A father guarantor of the law is also a father that allows experimenting with desire as Hiltenbrand (1998) suggests when he writes that "the Name-of-the-Father signifies [...] that the subject assumes his desire as assented to the law of the father (symbolic castration) and to the law of language (under the influence of primary repression)".
- *"to institute" the notion of counter-transference as a major axis of the Freudian doctrine would have given it the value of a fundamental concept leading to the use of this concept as an indispensible tool for analysis rather than an obstacle to it. Freud might have been in an untenable position: writing an essay, therefore writing a theory of what was for him an "embarrassing" concept which should at best be mastered. It is possible also that what he feared for was the legitimacy of psychoanalysis itself, if he acknowledged the inevitability of counter-transference.*
- counter-transference is understood by Freud as "counter-transference affect". In an implicit connection with the law of prohibition of incest Freud invites a renunciation of counter-transference fantasies in order to master the affects they would trigger. The fantasies in analysis, created by analysis, are directed in the analyst towards a desire to know the origins of the symptom and for the lifting of repression. This desire to know, this desire for origins become for Lacan a "desire for nothing", an absolute desire which is nothing else than the "desire to analyse" that sustains any analytic enterprise.

To conclude, it is possible to say that both concepts of counter-transference and the desire of the analyst keep a place in the analytic experience and following Guyomard (2003) to suggest that the concept of counter-transference remains pertinent insofar as for the analyst who is exposed to it, "the question is to indulge it or not". For Guyomard (2003) "one does not expect of him [analyst] that he is going to indulge it unreservedly. One expects that he is going to question himself about what is happening in him. This is what is at stake in training and transmission". This position props up the desire of the analyst, guarantor of the direction of the treatment, despite the attacks on the analyst's identity from the transference and counter-transference affects. If the desire of the analyst is what happened "in the beginning" and underpins the direction of the treatment the work on counter-transference is what sustains and constantly rekindles the desire of the analyst all through the analytic work.

Notes

1. Editor's footnote: Porge is suggesting that the main obstacle to dialogue between Lacan and his followers and the IPA executive committee was a rivalry over who were the rightful heirs to Freud—hence invoking the Name-of-the-Father.
2. In the Cazotte novel, the horrible camel-headed monster asks, "*Chè vuoi?*" in the place of the narrator and first person in whom "curiosity is the strongest passion".

References

Britton, R. S. (2003). Le contre-transfert érotique—alors et aujourd'hui. *Bulletin de la Fédération Européenne de Psychanalyse, 57*: 109–120.

Canestri, J. (2004). Le concept de processus analytique et le travail de transformation. *Revue française de Psychanalyse, LXVIII, 5*: 1495–1541.

Cazotte, J. (1991). *The Devil in Love*. J. Landry (Trans.). Dedalus.

Clerc, D. (2007). « L'écoute de la parole ». *Revue française de psychanalyse, 5/2007 (Vol. 71)*: 1285–1340.

Cottet, S. (1982). *Freud et le désir du psychanalyste*. Paris: Navarin éditeur.

Donnet, J.-L. (1995). Contre-transfert, transfert sur l'analyse. *Le divan bien tempéré*, Paris, PUF, le fil rouge, 1995.

Ferenczi, S. (1923). *Psychanalyse III*. Paris: Payot, 1974, p. 203.

Freud, S. (1913). Le début du traitement. *La technique psychanalytique*. Paris: PUF, 1977, pp. 80–104.

Green, A. (1972). Note sur les processus tertiaires. *Revue française de psychanalyse, XXXVI, n° 3*: 407–410.

Green, A. (2008). Un épisode des rapports entre SPP et lacaniens. *Monographies et débats de psychanalyse*, « Avancées de la psychanalyse ». Paris: PUF, pp. 31–37.

Guyomard, P. (1992). *La jouissance du tragique, Antigone, Lacan et le désir de l'analyste*. Paris: Aubier, 1992.

Guyomard, P. (2003). L'ancien et le nouveau—dans les rapports de l'enfance avec l'âge adulte—au cours du travail psychanalytique. *Le travail psychanalytique* (sous la direction de A. Green), Discussion avec P. Denis, Médiateur: M. Ody. Paris: PUF, 2003.

Heimann, P. (1950). Le contre-transfert. In: Heimann, P., Little, M., Reich, A., & Tower, L. Paris: Navarin, 1987, pp. 7–22.

Hiltenbrand, J.-P. (1998). Nom-du-Père. *Dictionnaire de la Psychanalyse*. R. Chemama, & B. Vandermersch (Eds.). Larousse, 1998.

Khoury, M. (2006). Une séance à mille temps. Séances à durée fixe et séances à durée variable: incompatibilité radicale? *Revue française de psychanalyse, t. LXX n° 1*: 83–106.

Lacan, J. (1959–1960). *Le Séminaire-Livre VII, L'éthique de la psychanalyse*. Paris: Seuil, «Champ freudien», 1986.
Lacan, J. (1962–1963). *Le Séminaire-Livre X, L'angoisse*. Paris: Seuil, « Champ freudien », 2004, p. 396.
Lacan, J. (1963). *Des Noms-du-Père*. Paris: Seuil « Champ freudien », 2005, p. 110.
Lacan, J. (1964a). Du « Trieb » de Freud et du désir du psychanalyste. In: *Écrits*. Paris: Seuil, 1966, pp. 851–854.
Lacan, J. (1964b). *Le Séminaire, Livre XI, Les quatre concepts fondamentaux de la psychanalyse*. Paris: Seuil, 1973.
Lacan, J. (1966). *Écrits*. Paris: Seuil, 1966, p. 927.
Lacan, J. (1967). « Discours à l'E.F.P. » *Silicet, 2,3*. Paris: Seuil, 1977.
Little, M. (1951). Counter-transference and the patient's response to it. *I J Psychoanal, Vol 32, 1951*: 32–40.
Ogden, T. (1994). The analytic third: Working with intersubjective clinical facts. *International Journal of Psycho-Analysis, 75*: 3–20.
Safouan, M. (2001). *Lacaniana I, Les séminaires de Jacques Lacan (1953–1963)*. Paris: Fayard, 2001.
Safouan, M. (2005). *Lacaniana II, Les séminaires de Jacques Lacan (1964–1979)*. Paris: Fayard, 2005.
Safouan, M. (1983). *Jacques Lacan et la question de la formation des analystes*. Paris: Seuil, 1983.
Scarfone, D. (2013). A brief introduction to the work of Jean Laplanche. *Int J Psychoanal, 94*: 545–566.
Shentoub, S. (1955). Le rôle de la personnalité de l'analyste dans la thérapeutique psychanalytique. *L'Année Psychologique, vol. 55 no. 2*: 397–399.
Tower, L. (1956). *J Am Psychoanal Assoc, vol. 4 no. 2*: 224–255.
Winnicott, D. W. (1960). The Theory of the Parent-Infant Relationship. *Int J Psycho-Anal, 41*: 585–595.

PART IV

BEYOND THE CLINIC

CHAPTER ELEVEN

Editors' introduction

D. Lichtenstein

When the relationship between literature and psychoanalysis is considered from the perspective of the conceptual origins of each, an interesting resonance between the two fields results. At the heart of both endeavours is a concern with the function of writing, the significance of marks, letters, words, and their agglomeration as occasions of sense and meaning for both writer and reader. If we approach psychoanalysis in terms of the effects of *psychic inscription* as a kind of writing, i.e., the formation of mnemic traces and their expression in the analytic encounter, including the limits and obstacles that appear in that encounter, and simultaneously consider the status of the literary text as an effect of writing that may be similarly in question regarding the locus and boundaries of its meaning, then it becomes difficult and intriguing to say where literary theory ends and psychoanalytic theory begins. The equally elusive subject of writing and authority of the text are current concerns in both.

In the following essay, Jean-Michel Rabaté approaches the relation between literature and psychoanalysis first from the point of suspicion that hovers on the border between the two fields, a suspicion that arises on the literary side from the inadequacy of the psychoanalytic interpretation of literature, its reductive and even laughable predictability. It is a suspicion that arises as well on the other side in the ideal of psychoanalysis as a science, a discipline more grounded in material facts than the arts of textual creation and interpretation.

However, the validity of the *pushback* from both fields against facile efforts to find common ground is just a point of departure for Rabaté. He successfully takes us from this place of mutual suspicion to an examination of the complex roots of theory that link the fields. From these roots emerge more significant dimensions of the interplay between these disciplines, dimensions that allow new discoveries in the critical study of both.

For example, the process of interpretation, the act *par excellence* to be found in both fields, and the act that always puts in question the authority of the text and that of the reader/interpreter, is a process that is still richly problematic for both psychoanalysis and criticism. As Rabaté demonstrates, appreciating the questions surrounding interpretation is one place where literature and psychoanalysis can still enhance one another. It is not a matter of applying one discipline to the other as much as both fields recognising their mutual concern with the status of the text and with the encounters between readers, writers, and texts.

CHAPTER ELEVEN

The letter against literary interpretation: Lacan's critique of literature*

Jean-Michel Rabaté

I

What can the meaning of "critique" or "criticism" be for Lacan? Is Lacan to be taken as a cultural critic (as some readers of Zizek might be tempted to think), as a literary critic (as many students in the humanities see him), or as an author of countless cryptic pronouncements that, despite their obscurity, have impacted the field of literary theory, changing our very way of "doing" theory, and perhaps obliging us to leave "criticism" aside altogether? I will begin this investigation by comparing two statements that bear on the issue of criticism, both made in seminars dating from the early seventies. In the first of these, Lacan explains that one should not analyse (that is, *psycho*analyse) written texts—one should rather criticise them. It is revealing that at this moment in the seminar, Lacan is engaging a critical reading of *Totem and Taboo*: He comments on Freud's fascination with the murder of the father, from Oedipus to Moses. Freud appears in this critique as a neurotic, yet his neurosis was not a hindrance but a productive agency:

> It is curious that I had to wait all this time before asserting that *Totem and Taboo* is a neurotic production, which is undeniable, without jeopardizing the truth of the whole construction. This is why this work can testify to its truth. One does not psychoanalyze a work, and even less that of Freud, does one? One criticizes it, and even though a neurosis may make its solidity appear suspect, it is this same neurosis that solders it together.

*We wish to thank the editors of Umbra for permission to reprint this essay. Portions of the essay subsequently appeared in the *Cambridge Introduction to Literature and Psychoanalysis* (Cambridge: Cambridge University Press, 2014).

> The testimony given by an obsessional subject on the structure that determines him, by which sexual rapport appears as impossible to formulate in discourse, this is what we owe to Freud's myth. (Lacan, 2006a, p. 161, my translation).

Consistent with a life-long quarrel with anything that looked to Lacan like "applied psychoanalysis"—a dominant theme to which I will shortly return—this nonetheless leaves unexamined what exactly is meant by "criticising." Lacan was soon to be the object of a direct "criticism", or of a more general "critique", when, in 1973, Jean-Luc Nancy and Philippe Lacoue-Labarthe published *The Title of the Letter: A Reading of Lacan*. Here indeed was an exercise in close reading, in applying a magnifying glass to a single text—Lacan's "The Instance of the Letter in the Unconscious, or Reason Since Freud"—one that leads them, in the name of philosophical rigor and consistency, to a rather severe critique.

Lacan, who had by 1973 made several attempts to enlist philosophers to read and work with him, does not appear to have been too dismayed by this critique. He counter-attacks snidely, mixing feint-praise (they have produced the best reading so far of any of his texts, one should deplore the fact that no one from his school has done the same work) with several nasty *ad hominem* digs: The two young philosophers are merely "pawns" (*sous-fifres*) in a game that opposes the camp of deconstruction to Lacanian psychoanalysis; they only write so accurately and painstakingly because they want to get "Master's degrees" that would confirm their position of spurious mastery; they have the worst possible intentions because they "love" Lacan with a love that looks very much like hate.

His last direct allusion to their book focuses on one term that Nancy and Lacoue-Labarthe isolate in order to gloss the several meanings of "instance", a key Greek term:

> They investigate the instance so thoroughly, so carefully [...] that they even discover the *ενσταισις*, the Aristotelian logical obstacle that I had reserved for the end. It is true that they do not see where it fits in [*Il est vrai qu'ils ne voient pas le rapport*]. But they are so used to working, especially when something motivates them—the desire, for example, to obtain their Master's, a truly serendipitous term here—that they even mention that in the footnote on pages 28 and 29.
>
> Consult Aristotle and you will know everything when I at last come to this business of the *ενσταισις*. You can read, one after the other, the passage in the *Rhetoric* and the two sections of the *Topics* that will allow you to truly know what I mean when I try to integrate my four formulas, $\exists x\ \overline{\Phi x}$ and the rest, into Aristotle's work (Lacan, 1998, pp. 69–70).

If one turns to the incriminated footnote, one will conclude that the philosophers' remark does not warrant such a scathing dismissal. Nancy and Lacoue-Labarthe merely explore all the possible meanings of "instance", a term that for a long time had been wrongly translated into English as "agency". They provide a philosophical genealogy for the term, finally tracing it back to Aristotle's use of *enstasis*:

> But one will not forget that for Aristotle, *ενστασις*, in the theory of refutation, designates the *obstacle* which one opposes to the reasoning of an adversary [...]. This "agency" ["*instance*"] is, in particular, what the exception opposes to a universal predication. An example of this *topos*

> happens to be the following, to be appreciated according to its most 'proper' meaning: "... it is honorable in some places to sacrifice one's father, for example amongs the Triballi, but it is not honorable in an absolute sense."

Lacan's ire seems to have been triggered by the fact that, at a time when he was elaborating his formulas on sexuation, which rest on a logic of universals whose domain of legitimacy is limited by exceptions, the two young philosophers had, almost by chance, hit upon a powerful tool in Lacan's own appropriation of Aristotelian logic. He also seems to have appreciated their humorous example of an "exception", which looks rather like a remake of the Oedipus myth. The murder of the father should remain an exception, but it is indeed an exception that supports the rule.

Whether he felt that he had exhausted the topic of *enstasis* all at once, or thought that the concept was too obvious, already exposed and given away by the two Derridian readers, Lacan did not return to it in the seminar sessions that followed, even if Aristotle is cited there very frequently. Nancy, perhaps piqued by the accusation that he and Lacoue-Labarthe had not been able to "see the relation [*rapport*]", recently devoted an entire book to examining the Lacanian formula that "there is no" (*il n'y a pas*) sexual relation (Nancy, 1992, p. 24).

What remains missed in this encounter between Lacanian theory and Derridian deconstruction is the fact that the "instance" in "instance of the letter" can take on a critical function. It opposes an objection, often (as Aristotle demonstrates in his *Rhetoric*) by inverting the opponent's *enthymemes* (the incomplete or faulty syllogisms) (Aristotle in Freese, 1982, pp. 335–343). Even though a critical confrontation failed to arise, we can look back to that moment in order to better understand what might be called the critical function of the letter. In this respect, it is tempting to apply to Lacan as he reads Freud most of the epithets he uses for Lacoue-Labarthe and Nancy: He is a devoted close reader whose love for Freud is indistinguishable from hate; he is a reader who aims at something like mastery; he is in the habit of asking untimely questions, posed too either soon or too late.

The critical function of the letter encompasses Lacan's usual critique of applied psychoanalysis. Repeatedly arguing for the centrality of the letter and literature in psychoanalysis, he debunks anything that looks like applied psychoanalysis, especially when applied to the field of literature. What does he mean by "critique", then? In the last meeting of his eighteenth seminar, *D'un discours qui ne serait pas du semblant*, Lacan (2007a, p. 164) puts his cards on the table and names Karl Marx as the true inventor of the notion of symptom. Indeed, his insistence that one's task is not to psychoanalyse a work, but to criticise it, cannot but evoke Marx's famous eleventh thesis on Feuerbach: "The philosophers have only *interpreted* the world, in various ways; the point, however, is to *change* it" (Marx, 1978, p. 145). And it was of course in context of the aftermath of *May '68* that Lacan elaborated, via an articulation of Freud with Marx, his formalisation of social links as discourses, wherein the "discourse of the Master" can be understood as the "discourse of the capitalist." (Lacan, 2007b). Lacan moves between Althusser's influential readings of *Capital* and Foucault's critical historicism, inserting what he called "surplus jouissance" (*plus de jouir*)—a synthesis of Freud's *Lust* and Marx's *Mehrwert*—into a new grid of discursive positions.

In his rehabilitation of the notion of the author (which followed Barthes' announcement of the "death of the author"), Foucault explains that one at least needs authors' names, as beacons in the study of scientific discourses, thereby justifying his use of the author-function. He adds that this function is crucial when dealing with "inventors of discursivity" (or "initiators of discursive practices"), among whom Freud and Marx figure pre-eminently (Foucault, 1977, pp. 113–138). Foucault had Lacan in mind when he stated that it was "inevitable that practitioners of such discourses must 'return to the origin'" (ibid, p. 134). A return to foundational texts would not simply point out lacks or gaps, but transform the discursive practice governing a whole field: "A study of Galileo's works could alter our knowledge of the history, but not the science, of mechanics; whereas, a re-examination of the books of Freud or Marx can transform our understanding of psychoanalysis or Marxism" (ibid, pp. 135–136). Foucault's epistemology entails that, if Marxism and psychoanalysis cannot have the status of hard sciences, it is because they are in debt to the texts of a founder, a founder whose legacy is marked both by future resemblances and future differences: "In saying that Freud founded psychoanalysis, we do not simply mean that the concept of libido or the techniques of dream analysis reappear in the writings of Karl Abraham or Melanie Klein, but that he made possible a certain number of differences with respect to his books, concepts and hypotheses, which all arise out of psychoanalytic discourse" (ibid, p. 132).

By contrast with scientific inventors, "founders of discursivity" cannot be accused of error. Foucault writes that "there are no 'false' statements in the work of these initiators" (ibid, pp. 133–134). It is precisely for this reason that their theories demand a constant reactivation—they are productive because of "constructive omissions" that demand their endless reactivations. The "origin" will not be defined by truth procedures or verification, since it is porous, full of gaps and holes. The "return to—" will not entail respectful imitation but a type of reading that is also a critical rewriting. Should we thus "return" to Lacan as he "returned" to Freud, assuming that both textual corpuses have not yet been sufficiently read? But how can one "return" to a psychoanalytic corpus without applying psychoanalysis to it? In short, can one ever get rid of "applied psychoanalysis"?

II

To the question that serves as the title of Pierre Bayard's book—*Can One Apply Literature to Psychoanalysis?*—one could be tempted to respond with a simple, monosyllabic, and positive answer: "Yes!" (Bayard, 2004). Indeed, one should apply literature to psychoanalysis, and not the other way around. It seems that this is how Lacan always proceeded, given his fiercely literary style. This, however, is not what Bayard has in mind with his provocative title, an ironic inversion of the pattern by which psychoanalysis has typically been applied to literature. Bayard begins by stating that his attempt to create a new school that would apply literature to psychoanalysis has failed, and then offers a post mortem diagnosis of the types of psychoanalytic literary criticism. We tend to agree today that psychoanalytic criticism is a thing of the past. We know that it would be very hard for a candidate to a good American graduate program to be accepted with a proposal to study Hamlet's unconscious inhibitions, or suicidal in term of academic career to plan to assess the consequences of the castration complex in Dostoevsky. Indeed, the "applied" in "applied psychoanalysis" has an ironic ring to it—it calls to mind Bergson's definition of the comic as a mechanical element *plaqué* (i.e., mechanically applied) to the human (see Bergson, 1998). Any "application" of psychoanalysis to literature will thus generally (and rightly) be met with laughter.

While this irony is not dominant in Bayard's case, he is highly critical of the ways in which psychoanalysis has been applied to literature. Surveying Sarah Kofman's *L'enfance de l'art* and Jean Bellemin-Noël's *Vers l'inconscient du texte*, he points out that Freud's theory gives a dubious preeminence to creative writers. They are credited with having hit upon Freud's concepts before he did, though any awareness of the process by which they did so is refused to them; fundamentally, they don't know what they have found, or how. Thus, creative writers need psychoanalytic discourse to make sense of their brilliant but opaque intuitions.

If Bayard distinguishes between classical psychobiography (as practiced by Marie Bonaparte and Charles Mauron, for example) and psychoanalytic readings deployed without any anchoring in the writer's subjectivity or biography (like those of Bellemin-Noël), he does not spare Lacan in his review: "Lacan does not seem to innovate on this issue, alternating critical texts in which the author is taken into account—as for Gide or Joyce—and texts in which the readings are not founded in any privileged manner on the life of the author, as with *Hamlet*" (Bayard, 2004, p. 36). Bayard even states that the manner in which Lacan invents concepts through his readings of literary works brings him closer to "applied literature" (ibid, p. 37). It is hard to deny that Lacan was a "structuralist" with Poe, Shakespeare, Claudel, and Duras, or even that he came close to simple psychobiography when dealing with Gide and Joyce. On should examine this oscillation, and ask whether Lacan was inconsistent—as Elizabeth Roudinesco and others believe—or whether his indifference to the inclusion or exclusion of the author's life may not send us on a different path.

Bayard critiques both the psycho-biographical and the textualist schools for believing in the anteriority and superiority of psychoanalysis to literature. Both schools rely on a hermeneutics of suspicion, which conceals an art of interpretation in which one has to disentangle meanings hidden in works according to a pre-established pattern. As these hidden meanings being, by definition, unconscious, the author cannot know the dark forces that make the work happen. The problem that he sees is that such readings only produce results that confirm an initial theory. They remain within the category of finalist readings. They deploy themselves exactly like religious readings, since what is found in the texts will be less a product of the investigation than an effect of its origins and presuppositions. This point was made forcefully by Tzvetan Todorov when he examined Biblical hermeneutics and pointed out that the Bible always confirms Christian doctrine. Similarly, canonical psychoanalytical readings merely confirm the truth of psychoanalysis about the Oedipus complex, unconscious fantasies, primal scenes, and the determining role of childhood memories. This does not imply that the results are false or the method wrong, but simply, and more damagingly, that they are entirely predictable. It is this type of repetitiveness and predictability that in the end generated boredom and theoretical sterility.

Bayard calls instead for a literature that can be applied to psychoanalysis; he meditates on literary texts capable of reflecting psychic phenomena (ibid, p. 48). Applied literature would focus on moments of emergence, on a new knowledge to be shared by the reader. However, he soon admits that this strategy is not likely to convince anyone; it will sway neither the psychoanalyst who feels contested by it, nor traditional critics from other schools who have no patience with psychoanalysis. To confirm Bayard's misgivings, I have to confess that I haven't been convinced in the least by his examples. The plays and novels that he adduces (by Laclos,

Proust, Maupassant, Agatha Christie, and Shakespeare) simply show that literature "thinks" by itself and that it can, unaided, stage complex psychological problems—hardly news for teachers of literature! What do we gain from the claim that anger was faithfully depicted by Homer in the *Iliad*, at a time when psychoanalysis did not exist? An American take on this observation would tend to historicise the process and point, for instance, to the links between *Madame Bovary* and the invention of hysteria by French medicine, culminating in Charcot's discoveries. We can all agree that the invention of psychology proceeded parallel to certain developments in literature, just as we are ready to see in Maupassant and Stevenson convincing predecessors of Freud.

We know that literature became a field of predilection for psychoanalysis at the time of the latter's invention. Freud, Rank, Ferenczi, and others wanted to test their new hypotheses by applying them to culture, and thus, synecdochically, to literature. Now that this discourse has been over-systematised, the issue is how to continue to be inventive. Assuming thus that a certain hermeneutics of the unconscious has reached a point of exhaustion (ibid, p. 157), Bayard believes that the solution lies in literature. The future task for criticism consists in inventing theoretical forms generated by literary models. Given its riches, diversity, and subversive potentialities, literature both signals the disappearance of psychoanalysis as an interpretive paradigm (ibid, p. 164) and offers new solutions. One chance of success for "applied literature" is to acknowledge its paranoid tendencies, its wish to postulate a new and grandiose system able to replace all previous ones, and a constitutive inability to say "we". Therefore, a good critic should speak in the first person.

Speaking in the first person, I will express my disagreement with the drift of Bayard's argument even if we both agree that, since what is at stake is the function of criticism facing psychoanalysis, it is literature that should be applied to psychoanalysis and not the other way around. We are left to pose the question of exactly how Lacan uses literature; why is he so relentless in his critique of Freud's strategy of "verifying" psychoanalysis by applying it to literature, when he himself uses literature so often? Does he truly manage to consistently avoid this application? These questions are at the core of Derrida's reproach in "Le facteur de la vérité", in which Derrida (1987) cogently accuses Lacan of reducing literary texts to mere examples that confirm a pre-established truth (such a tendency seems to have been generalised by Slavoj Zizek, whose proliferating readings continue to discover examples that prove Lacan's mathemes to be true). Addressing these questions requires yet another detour, one through the debate that opposed Lacan and Derrida in the seventies.

I will suggest that Lacan's theory of the *sinthome*, even where it flirts with psychobiography, aims at pushing psychoanalysis away from the dangers of exemplarity, that is, of the reduction of textual singularity to dogmatic schemas. If a symptom is less what a patient wants to be cured of than the condensed "statement" of her or his individuality, literature, in so far as it leads to the *sinthome*, tends to disclose the element most proper to the human dimension. Joyce's writing thus offers Lacan less a field to be ploughed according to a predictable and repeatable procedure than a model of linguistic equivocation in which the psychoanalysis finds a new youth.

Lacan often advances his own theses by reading Freud closely and then dramatically transforming the perspective. One can observe this process at work most revealingly when Lacan revisits Freud's central insight on Hamlet, that is, that Hamlet is a modern version of Oedipus—an older, starker, more uninhibited Oedipus. It took Lacan some close reading of

Hamlet to find a snag in the usual Freudian reading, namely, its dependence upon an unexamined and questionable psychology (which is yet another reason that it is insufficient to say, like Bayard, that the function of literature is to provide a parallel account of human psychology). Lacan throws into light the dependence of Freud's Oedipal model upon a psychological reasoning that can easily be reversed:

> What does the psychoanalytic tradition tell us? That everything hinges around the desire for the mother, that this desire is repressed, and that this is the cause for which the hero could not approach the act that is requested of him, namely the revenge against a man who is the current possessor, how illegitimate because a criminal, of the maternal object. If he cannot strike the person who has been pointed out for his vindication, it is because he himself has already committed the crime to be avenged. In as much as there is in the background the memory of an infantile desire for the mother, of the Oedipal desire to murder the father, Hamlet would in a sense become an accomplice of the current owner, *beatus possidens*, in his eyes. He could not attack this owner without attacking himself. Is this what they mean?—or he could not attack this possessor without reawakening in himself the old desire, felt as a guilty one, in a mechanism that makes obviously more sense.
>
> Let us not become fascinated by such a non-dialectical scheme. Couldn't we say that everything could be reversed? If Hamlet was to jump immediately on his father-in-law, could one not say that he finds in this an opportunity to quench his guilt? (Lacan, 1982, p. 19, my translation)

In one deft thrust, Lacan punches a hole in Freud's contention that Hamlet cannot kill his uncle in revenge for his father's murder because Claudius has accomplished Hamlet's deepest incestuous wishes. This is, for Lacan, a non-dialectical argument, one that rests on an unquestioned mimetic psychology. Freud's psychologisation of the main characters' "French triangle" (as Joyce would say) is founded on a common-sense view, and hence can easily be turned into its contrary. Indeed, it requires no great stretch of the imagination to suppose that Hamlet would want to punish a successful rival. Lacan addresses this notion in his studies of the mirror stage and of the role of aggression in psychoanalysis. His shift from a subjective genitive (where the "mother's desire" means "desire for the mother") to an objective genitive (where the "mother's desire" is read as "her desire for another man") is a dialectical reversal that refutes mimetic psychology's assumption that one would not want to punish someone who acts out one's deepest longings. Hamlet's inhibition is thus seen to stem from his archaic desire for Gertrude, where the paralysis derives from his fixation on the riddle of her desire for another man, be it an uncle or a father.

In order to avoid relying non-dialectically on common sense psychology, Lacan argues, one has to pay attention to the text's recurrent signifiers, its linguistic nodal points—such as "Ophelia" and "phallus," "foils", and "foil"—so as to dynamically connect them in a phenomenology of the desiring subject. Hamlet's false start as a desiring subject who questions the very source of desire will have to pass beyond the archaic object (the mother) to meet the phallus and death, before reaching an awareness of the place of the Other as determining desire. This complex phenomenology of stages leads, finally, to an ethics of the desiring subject.

From this we begin to understand what Lacan means when he speaks of criticism. His reading of *Hamlet* criticises (and reaches a conclusion totally opposed to) Freud's, while nevertheless remaining within the discursive field that Freud opened.

III

Lacan assigns a similar role to the critical gesture in his "Seminar on 'The Purloined Letter'". As is well known, a salient feature of Poe's story is its logical structure, as it is defined by a pattern of ironic repetitions. Three scenes are superposed. In the first scene, we have a "blind" King, who embodies the Law but is unaware that anything at all is happening, a "seeing" Queen, who suffers but remains impotent, and the daring Minister D—, who profits from the interaction between the first two. The Minister puts his own letter on the table and leaves with the coveted prize, knowing that the Queen cannot ask for it without awakening suspicions.

The second scene details the futile efforts of the police to retrieve the letter for the Queen. This time, the "blind" character is the Prefect of police and, by extension, his men, who cannot find the letter because they assume that it must be hidden from sight. They project their notion of what "hiding" means, never imagining that the letter could be left in full view. The "seeing" character (who cannot do much in this case) is the Minister, who basks in the imaginary security afforded by the letter's possession. The active agent here is Dupin, who identifies creatively with the Minister—who reconstructs his mental process, sees all, prepares an exact double of the stolen letter, and devises the strategy by which he will distract the Minister.

The third scene reverses the first theft. The Minister now turns into a "blind" man, while Dupin acts and, moreover, signs his substitution by quoting lines from Crébillon that will identify him as soon as the Minister decides to check the contents of the missive. Caught up in brotherly rivalry, Dupin is animated less by honour or greed than by the wish to settle an old account. He thus exposes himself to the gaze of the author, Poe, or of Poe's readers, including Lacan. One will have to reconstitute the tale's logic and follow its psychical economy if one is to avoid "stealing" the letter by imposing a meaning or content on it.

The force of Lacan's reading is undeniable, but it may lead to its own undermining. How can it prevent yet another turn of the screw, stop the text's triangular permutations? Such a pattern does not provide for the sort of Hegelian resolution that would bring the dialectic of blindness and vision to the point of absolute knowledge. As Barbara Johnson masterfully demonstrates, when Derrida accused Lacan of translating the contentless letter into a content, a "truth" defined by femininity and castration, it was he himself who saw too much and translated too soon, reducing Lacan's stylistic games and thus misread a seminar no less literary than Poe's story. Derrida repeats Lacan's repudiation of applied psychoanalysis, turning it against Lacan himself:

> From the outset, we recognize the classical landscape of applied psychoanalysis. Here applied to literature. Poe's text, whose status is never examined—Lacan simply calls it "fiction"—, finds itself invoked as an "example" [...] destined to "illustrate", [...] "to illustrate" here meaning to read the general law in the example, to make clear the meaning of a law or of a truth, to bring them to light in striking or exemplary fashion. The text is in the service of the truth, and of a truth that is taught, moreover. (Derrida, 1987, pp. 425–426)

According to Derrida, psychoanalytic criticism cannot but reduce the form of a text to a teleology. Zizek (2007) answers these objections in *Enjoy your Symptom!*, showing that at an imaginary level, a letter always reaches its destination, because whoever receives it retroactively believes (in a movement similar to Althusserian interpellation) that he or she is its addressee. On a symbolic level, the circulation of the letter itself assures that it has already reached its destination, that is, the Other, the Symbolic order itself, birthplace of all desire. This fact is underscored by an important detail, which Zizek fails to discuss: Though the Minister recognises the handwriting of the address and infers from it the real cause of the Queen's embarrassment (he "fathoms her secret" in one gaze), the identity of the sender remains a "cipher": Poe only mention a "small and red seal, with the ducal arms of the S—family" (Lacan, 2006b, p. 19). We are not only deprived of the contents of the letter, but also of precise knowledge of the author's links to the Queen. Not only is the letter always in circulation, but it seems almost impossible that it be returned to its secret sender. The "instance of the letter" at work in Poe's tale does not entail an ideality of a closed economy, as Derrida contends, but rather guarantees that the workings of language displace identities thanks to the constant sliding away of the signifier. For in the end, as Zizek states, the third "destination" of the letter can only be death, since this signifier, seemingly immortal, brings mortality to the fore. This is where Derrida and Lacan meet—where both emphasise the lethal dimension of the letter's endless self-erasure. If the letter always returns to its destination, it returns not to its sender but to its addressee, which implies that such a "destination" is already "destined." Both ends of the letter's trajectory are thus open.

The real clash between Derrida and Lacan revolves around the positioning of the process of interpretation itself—which is where the concept of "critique" should find its true point of application. Derrida accuses Lacan of failing to address the issue of the narrator of "The Purloined Letter" yet this failure is relative. Lacan does mention the "double and triple subjective filter" through which the scenes are narrated (ibid, p. 12). Throughout his seminar, Lacan problematises the act of interpretation in a dynamic manner and at crucial points. The intersubjective triad that he sketches interpellates Lacan as a reader, since the third repetition of the triangular pattern implies that Lacan perceives that Dupin has shifted to the imaginary position. Contrary to what Derrida states, neither in the second nor third triad does the analyst withdraw from the symbolic circuit. The reader-as-analyst tries to inhabit the blind spot of the text, a spot that allows for a perception of the letter, not insofar as its content matters, but insofar as it moves along the chain to impact the very act of interpretation. When he sees Dupin seeing himself, Lacan effectively takes part in the mechanism of the passage of a symptom. Of course, he too will find himself implicated in imaginary delusion if he believes that he likewise possesses some secret knowledge that lies all too visibly on the surface.

Perhaps because he believed that this involved something like the ownership of a secret, or perhaps because he was jealous of such a position of analytic mastery, Derrida strove to adopt the position of the analyst who, by facilitating a repetition with a crucial difference, finds a solution to the subjective problem of interpretation. However, against his strictures, Lacan's reading of "The Purloined Letter" never fully abandons the textuality of the text, neither Poe's nor his seminar's. Lacan chooses to ignore the "scene of writing" insofar as it implies the narrator, in a deliberate effort to avoid the pitfalls of Bonaparte's psychobiographical readings. Against

Bonaparte and against Derrida, Lacan brackets the fact that "The Purloined Letter" was written by Poe in a given historical period with clearly identifiable literary clichés, models, and genres. These are aspects of textuality and literarity that Lacan is not interested in; the text's literality engaged him at the level of a riddle, as the tip of allegory's sunken mass.

To this Derrida opposes the undecidability and infinity of literature; literature, he argues, prevents any idealisation aiming to render itself a model in the name of a pre-established truth. Lacan is a purveyor [*facteur*] of truths. However, no one can produce a reading of a text without reducing, translating or downplaying certain of its elements. The purity of textual plenitude will always have to be sacrificed to arrive at something like a theme, a structure, a plot, or a narrative. We must be ready to account for a certain loss, without which we would not even be able to talk about texts in general; we will, moreover, inevitably need models, examples, and conceptual handles. This need sends us all the more violently back to the question of applying anything to texts. It might be the case that whoever attacks applied psychoanalysis will end up applying it without knowing it—all the more insistently, as it will function as a symptom.

It is in the name of a more balanced critical assessment that Nancy and Lacoue-Labarthe (1992) suggest in *The Title of the Letter* that, because Lacan's theories do not form a totalising system, they avoid reductionism, idealisation, and the illusion of a mastery over truth. Lacan's theses do not exploit literary examples to confirm Freud's insights, since they present themselves as literary rather than as scientific (as Freud hoped his own theories were). This implies that literature plays a more loaded role in Lacanian discourse: it inhabits the theory from the start, so as to make it tremble, vacillate, twist. Literature complicates theory's status; it sullies the mirage of a pure theory neatly fitted with well-chosen examples. In other words, it is important to distinguish an "application" from a pure "exemplification". An application imports some of the dynamism of literary devices into the theory, whereas exemplification merely seeks the confirmation of pre-established truths.

Nancy and Lacoue-Labarthe conclude their critical review of Lacan's elaboration on metaphor in these terms:

> It is certainly not by chance if, along with the usual meaning of the word "metaphor," Lacan also incorporates the literary genre where we seem to find it most often—namely poetry, and more precisely poetry circumscribed by two references: Hugo and surrealism. That is, the poetry that we are able to designate, in its own terms, as that of the Word—of Divine Speech or of speech—and of the "power" or "magic" of words. An entire poetics of this order and an entire poetic practice of this style indeed subtend Lacan's text, here as elsewhere, in its literary references, its peculiar stylistic effects, and finally in its theoretical articulation. (Nancy, 1992, p. 74)

Lacan is reluctant to found his own discourse except in a practice of reading (Freud's texts). Yet he moves strategically between a pragmatics of therapy, on the one hand, and philosophy, linguistics, rhetoric, and anthropology, on the other hand, which, in the end, forces him to appear as a literary theoretician, a *bricoleur* of theory whose conceptual borrowings create a singularly syncretic writing—less the definitive statement of a "founder" of discursivity than the textual experiments of a quester often doubled by a jester.

IV

The rest of this essay will assess the consequence of Lacan's central contention that there is no metalanguage, that truth can never be uttered fully in a philosophical or scientific discourse buttressed upon axioms, basic definitions, fundamental concepts. Even the "four fundamental concepts" of psychoanalysis cannot be articulated in isolation, apart from the dense tissue of Freudian texts. These concepts describe a movement, which, even if it can be stabilised at various points and in various graphs, goes on moving. Lacan staunchly refuses to sum up Freud's "basic terms" in an axiomatic vocabulary. Indeed, in order to avoid a reductive view, he demonstrates the re-opening of Freud's texts, reading them as *literally* as possible—which often also entails reading them as *literarily* as possible, even against the grain of their explicit intentions. If literature is that site in which no intentional fallacy will ever obtain, and if Freud's works are in a certain sense indistinguishable from literature, Lacan then becomes a literary critic, not who applies a knowledge to an object, but who criticises the illusions of mastery inherent to any subjective position.

In "Lituraterre", Lacan (2001) rejects attempts at psychobiography by literary-minded psychoanalysts, whose judgments, he claims, should not carry more weight because of their profession. This rejection is accompanied and sustained by his stress on the letter's lack of content, which distinguishes it from the signifier it carries.

> My criticism, if it can be called literary, can only bear (I hope) on what makes Poe a writer when he gives us such a message about the letter. Clearly, if he does not tell this as such, this is not a defect but an all the more rigorous avowal.
>
> Nevertheless such an elision could not be elucidated by some feature in his psychobiography [...]. No more could my own text be solved by my own psychobiography: as for instance by the wish I reiterate of being at last read correctly. For, in order to think this, one would have to develop what I say that the letter carries so as to *always* reach its destination.
>
> It is sure that, as always, psychoanalysis receives from literature a less psychobiographic conception even when taking repression as its main spring.
>
> As for me, if I propose to psychoanalysis the idea of a letter in sufferance, it is because this shows its own failure. And here is where I bring some light: when I invoke the enlightenment, I demonstrate where it makes a *hole*. This is well known in optics, and the recent physics of the photon is underpinned by it.
>
> This is a method by which psychoanalysis might justify its intrusion better: for if literary criticism could indeed renew itself, it would be because of the presence of psychoanalysis forcing texts to measure up to it, the enigma remaining on the side of psychoanalysis. (Lacan, 2001, pp. 12–13).

Lacan's refusal to reduce the meaning of a text to psychobiography is here coupled with his wish to vouchsafe literature to the domain of enigma, to leave it its cutting edge, its insistent instance. For him, literature insists in a peculiar way, above all through the fact that it is made up of holes and erasures.

This is why Lacan glosses the etymology of "literature" via the Latin root, whose plural form, *literae*, signifies "writing, epistle, literature", while *literatura* in the singular signifies "writing, *learning*, literature". The noun derives from the verb *lino*, whose significations call up "I smear", "I cover", or "I erase". As Freud indicates in "The Antithetical Sense of Primal Words", the oldest roots of any language contain antithetical meanings (Freud, 1910e, pp. 153–161). Literature belongs to the category of antithesis insofar as its roots leave us with a double-image: a hand covers a tablet with wax; the same hand erases the tablet so that it be free to register other signs. Finally, *literatura* brings us closer to *litus* (the act of smearing or covering a surface). *Litus, litoris*, in French, *littoral*: seaside, the edge of the land. "Literature" thus generates a double pun, suggesting both letters and their erasure (a pun that is more obvious in French, in which one can always hear "*rature*"—"erasure" or "crossing out"—in the very signifier) and the limit or border of a territory, be it sea or abyss.

Finally, Lacan argues, such a writing appears as constitutive of the human subject and thus of sexuality as such. His text concludes with an enigmatic reference to the "it is written" underpinning the non-being of the sexual relation; this same "it is written" also refers to the transformation of knowledge into jouissance "through the edge of the hole in knowl-edge" (Lacan, 2001, p. 20). Hence, writing takes the form of a simple knot, which "has all the characteristics of writing—it could be a letter" (Lacan, 1998, p. 122). With Joyce, the letter ends up figuring the trefoil of Trinity; we are hence already in the field of the Borromean knot, whose graceful coils show without words the enigma of the sexual non-relation.

The concept of the *sinthome* was developed in *Seminar XXIII* with Joyce in mind. Having become more interested in thinking the Real, in perversion, in the jouissance of the Other, Lacan deployed the term "*sinthome*" to condense what he had to say about literature. One might say that the *sinthome* deposes the letter; this replacement allows him to bridge the gap between the loop of the letter and the function of psychotic discourse. Joyce was also a good pretext for him to revisit his early essay on psychotic discourse, "Les Ecrits Inspirés", which had already shown how the letter can be inspired by, as well as addressed to, the Other. It would be too great a task to discuss Joyce at length here; there is still today a disagreement as to Joyce's role for Lacanian psychoanalysis. Was Joyce a psychotic like his daughter, since Joyce gave a new model for Lacan to think psychotic discourse, as Jacques-Alain Miller and Colette Soler believe, for instance? Or was he a writer who mimed psychotic discourse so as to confront his daughter's disease and construct a "language of the night", as Nestor Braunstein and Colin MacCabe think? We need to read texts *with* Lacanian psychoanalysis while avoiding simple "applications", because this is the only way to perceive that literature is not only a locus for phantasmatic projections but also offers a critique of life in general.

References

Aristotle (1982). Rhetoric. In: *The "Art" of Rhetoric.* John Henry Freese (Trans. & Ed.). Cambridge: The Loeb Classical Library, Harvard University Press.

Bayard, P. (2004). *Peut-on appliquer la littérature à la psychanalyse ?* Paris: Les Éditions de Minuit.

Bergson, H. (1998). *Laughter: An Essay on the Meaning of the Comic.* Rockville: Arc Manor.

Derrida, J. (1987). Le Facteur de la Vérité. In: *The Postcard.* Alan Bass (Trans.). Chicago: The University of Chicago Press.

Foucault, M. (1977). "What is an Author?" In: *Language, Counter-Memory, Practice*, F. Donald (Ed.), B. & S. Simon (Trans.). Ithaca: Cornell University Press.

Freud, S. (1910e). The Antithetical Meaning of Primal Words. *S. E., 11*. Hogarth Press, London.

Lacan, J. (1982). Le désir et son interpretation. *Ornicar? 25*.

Lacan, J. (1998). *The Seminar of Jacques Lacan, Book XX: Encore*. Jacques-Alain Miller (Ed.), B. Fink (Trans.). New York: W. W. Norton & Company.

Lacan, J. (2001). Lituraterre. In: *Autres écrits*, Paris: Éditions du Seuil.

Lacan, J. (2006a). *Le Séminaire de Jacques Lacan, Livre XVIII : D'un discours qui ne serait pas du semblant*, 1971. Jacques-Alain Miller (Ed.). Paris: Éditions du Seuil.

Lacan, J. (2006b). *Ecrits*. B. Fink (Trans.). New York: Norton.

Lacan, J. (2007a). *D'un discours qui ne serait pas du semblant, Le Séminaire, Livre XVIII*. Paris: Seuil.

Lacan, J. (2007b). *The Seminar of Jacques Lacan, Book XVII: The Other Side of Psychoanalysis*. Jacques-Alain Miller (Ed.), Russell Grigg (Trans.). New York: W. W. Norton & Company.

Marx, K. (1978). Theses on Feuerbach. In: *The Marx-Engels Reader*. Robert C. Tucker (Ed.). New York: W. W. Norton & Company.

Nancy, J. L., & Lacoue-Labarthe, P. (1992). *The Title of the Letter: A Reading of Lacan*. François Raffoul & David Pettigrew (Trans.). Albany: Suny.

Nancy, J. L. (2001). *L' « il y a » du rapport sexuel*. Paris: Galilée.

Zizek, S. (2007). *Enjoy your Symptom! Jacques Lacan in Hollywood and Out*. London: Routledge.

CHAPTER TWELVE

Editors' introduction

D. Lichtenstein and L. Bailly

This chapter illustrates the belief of some psychoanalysts that it is important and worthwhile to apply their metapsychology to society, a tradition that starts with Freud's *Das Unbehagen in der Kultur* [*Civilisation and its Discontents*] (Freud, 1930a). Some of the themes of this paper seem rather obvious to clinicians today but it is to Melman's credit to have laid the foundation of this work fifteen years ago at a time when Facebook did not exist. Clinicians working with young people may observe that the new social media has provided fertile terrain on which his New Psychic Economy has burgeoned.

For the Anglo-American reader, Charles Melman's essay on a New Psychic Economy may bring to mind Christopher Lasch's best-selling book, *The Culture of Narcissism: American Life in an Age of Diminishing Expectations* (Lasch, 1979), itself part of a long line of studies on the interplay of social structures and "psychic economies" dating back to Max Weber. Like Lasch, Melman argues that social conditions and changes in the functions of authority in the family have changed the structure of the subject in contemporary society. Lasch saw these changes as first beginning at the end of the nineteenth century; Melman dates them from the end of the First World War. Both are concerned that in recent years, post World War II for Lasch, perhaps the new millennium for Melman, we have seen an acceleration of these changes.

The outlines are similar for both writers. A weakening of the authority of the traditional father leaves children without the structure, without the paternal interdiction, that allows for the development of the classic neurotic character that Freud viewed as the general outcome of modern civilisation, and indeed the best that can be hoped for. Instead the outcome is a pathologically narcissistic character (for Lasch) and a sort of functionally perverse one (for Melman). For both writers, the new character mirrors new social patterns and indeed is tragically suited to them, while it is profoundly unsuited to certain classic virtues such as the stability of aims and desires.

The arguments appear to be inherently conservative, even reactionary, but Melman argues the reverse. The loss of patriarchy is bemoaned here because it had once held a progressive potential and its loss is in effect a regression. As Melman writes, "Freud remarks that the passage from matriarchy to patriarchy constituted a progress for humanity." Thus, the old patriarchically formed subject of nineteenth century neurosis was anchored to the causes of desire—and thus could work, think, progress—while the new subject is adrift in an ocean of superficial pleasures that can lead nowhere.

Lacan as well tied the emergence of psychoanalysis to a certain diminution of paternal authority in the post-industrial world. But like Freud, Lacan, was perhaps more dialectical in his view of these changes than is Melman here. That the erosion of the paternal function might be the condition for the invention of psychoanalysis suggests that this process might also be an opening to something productive not merely a tragic loss of civilised virtues. We present Melman's piece here knowing that it represents a certain slant on this problematic, a slant that those readers who make a causal link between patriarchy, injustice and destructive social forms, may disagree with.

It is possible however, that clinicians, in particular those working with adolescents and young adults, will be pleased to be offered a metapsychological construct that helps them make sense of clinical manifestations confusingly different from what they are trained to deal with.

References

Freud, S. (1930a). *Das Ubehagen In Der Kultur*. Vienna: Internationaler Psychoanalytischer Verlag.

Lasch, C. (1979). *The Culture of Narcissism: American Life in an Age of Diminishing Expectations*. New York: W. W. Norton & Co. Inc.

CHAPTER TWELVE

A new psychic economy*

Charles Melman

Where in the past most patients came to see an analyst to find another outcome than neurosis to the conflict inherent in desire, today, those who reach the office of the analyst come to talk about being stuck in an excess of enjoyment. It seems that we are moving from a culture based on the repression of desire, and therefore neurosis, to another culture, which encourages a free expression of desires and promotes perversion. "Mental health" today is not associated with being in harmony with an Ideal but with an object of satisfaction. This psychic economy is new. It didn't exist in the past on a social scale but could only be seen under the guise of rebellions, fringe movements. They were mostly attitudes of opposition against firm, established, and apparently unshakable boundaries.

What is this new economy?

It is a mutation in which the psychic economy ceases to be organised by repression and becomes organised by enjoyment—a display of enjoyment. With regard to sexuality, our relationship with sex is moving from being one based on representation to one based on presentation, to a quest for the object itself and not its representation. This cultural mutation is marked by an erasing of the locus where the sacred belongs. With this dimension gone, sex is considered as a need, like hunger or thirst. What is lost in the process is Lacan's object *a*, an object which sustains the quest of our desire. The subject, that was animated by this quest, disappears. For this subject of desire, the relationship with the world is not structured by an object but by the lack of an object. Working through this lack, allows the human being to access a world of representations where

*Translated from the original French and abridged by Lionel Bailly.

desire is both fed and guided. This process of working through is therefore disavowed in the new psychic economy.

The paternal figure is more and more tormented, devalued, forbidden, castrated. This leads to pockets of violent and fanatical resurgence of love for the paternal figure under the guise of nationalist or religious explosions, expressing the vocation of the sons to restore the father at its place. Suburban gangs seem driven by a wish to constitute communities in which the figure of a mythical ancestor is present as a watermark. The mere presence of a religious professional will be enough for it to take shape.

What led to this new economy?

This new economy has been allowed by a considerable progress in human society associated with great threats. People have started to come to terms with a sky empty of God but also of ideologies, references, promises, and prescriptions, which means that the individuals need to be self-determining. The nineteenth and the twentieth centuries have been times of great inventions when limits were explored, the twenty-first century will be a time for the removal of limits: nothing is impossible. The decisive intervention was probably the introduction of contraception allowing the control of fecundity and then the introduction of in vitro fecundation allowing the control of reproduction. Stolen from God, the power to create could lead to the creation of new organisms. In some ways this is the end of an era, a collective dissolution of transference, understood as the crucial process by which a subject supposes that another one knows.

Limits

The absence of limits finds its expression in many social dimensions. The rise of the image is one of them. Images do not signify anymore, they show, unveil, expose. On screen, in electronic media, people expose themselves with complete shamelessness. The gaze has become a tormenter in front of which nothing can be kept private. Language is changing, becoming more iconic than verbal. A neo-language is being created that has the ambition to be exact, to refer to a precise object which unites the speakers—a language without ambiguity, direct, crude, that presents the object.

Enjoyment

Sexual enjoyment, which was the standard with which to compare all enjoyment, is now just one ordinary enjoyment amongst others. It has lost the privilege of being the organiser of all partial enjoyments. Sex can be treated as an instrumental enjoyment, an enjoyment of the body's orifices. People can publicly satisfy their passions and demand that they should be socially accepted, even legalised. This position implies a formidable freedom and the disappearance of thinking. The aphanisis of thinking is the price of that freedom. In this new economy, there is no more phallic enjoyment but only an enjoyment around an object "constructed" from partial objects, the small *a* object.

Father

Without limits, there is no "forbidden" and therefore no object that symbolises this interdiction. The function of the father is to deprive the child of an unlimited access to the mother and therefore introduce the laws of exchange, in place of the beloved object the child will have to deal with a make-believe object. The father today has no authority, he is not the reference, he is alone and everything invites him to renounce his function of interdiction and to join the party.

The aftermath of the First World War saw the emergence of a reclaiming of enjoyment, as if the horrible loss of blood the war entailed was an act of aggression attributable to the figure of the father, and that the sacrifices made had paid any debt to him. What we observe today seems to be the tail end of this process. Lacan, in his seminar on *Transference* (Lacan, 1991) refers to the work of the writer Paul Claudel in which appears the Humiliated Father. There is however a massive misunderstanding about the paternal function. If the setting of an impossible is the obligatory way to access sexual desire, this impossible does not mean that sexual desire is forbidden. On the contrary, far from forbidding sexual desire, the father is the one who makes access to desire possible. There is every reason to think that the enmity towards the father is in fact hostility towards sexual desire. In *Moses and Monotheism* (Freud, 1939a) Freud unfortunately presents the father in the position of a stranger. In logic, the figure of the exception leads to the dimension of alterity, not of strangeness or foreignness. If the father is in the position of an ideal and the sons are separated from him by a cut, the "usual" case, the sons can consider that they are all Other for the father. It is not that the father is the Other but the sons who experience being Others for the father. The One, stranger, would be an obstacle to any happy outcome to the relationship of the subject with his or her parental figures, a relationship becoming organised around their respective autonomies. It would be also an obstacle to any settlement of transference, to a satisfactory end to the analytic treatment.

Desire and enjoyment

Desire today is supported more by envy than in reference to an ideal. In other words it depends on the image of the alter ego as owner of an object that may trigger my envy. Desire, which was organised by a symbolic lack, is in the new economy organised around an imaginary lack. As desire no longer relates to the Other, it becomes fed by envy, provoked by the other's possession of a sign that indicates his or her enjoyment. Desire becomes a social accident, it is scandalous that anyone would have more than I have, a point of view widely represented in the media. The egalitarianism that this system implies and which is promoted by the media is the very image of death, immobility, the victory of entropy.

To maintain the play of desire and avoid that desire would be smothered by the object that satisfies it, it is not unusual that this object is duplicated. I have patients who need two partners in such a way that there is always one that is missing: one introduces the absence that allows to desire the other. But because one partner gets its value from the fact that the other is lacking, the value is therefore on the side of the absent one, leading to a change of partner, and eventually to the repetition of the same sequence of events in a seesaw motion.

In this new economy, we observe a form of identification, which leads to the organisation of communities gathered around a same type of enjoyment. It has always been the case that people grouped together around a type of enjoyment, but in the new economy the type of enjoyment is the only trait that link together the community. This is a very poor social link as it is only based on the support given by the other insofar that the other shares the same enjoyment. Let us note that from the very fact of the similarities between the protagonists this enjoyment is unisex.

Reality

Through a curious shift reality becomes virtual as soon as it is experienced as unsatisfactory. What established reality is precisely that it was unsatisfactory and therefore always representative of the fault that created it as reality. This fault is now considered an accident, a momentary insufficiency and it is the perfect image which has become reality.

One question concerns psychiatrists but also anybody from the point of view of their place in society. Is the world shapeable to our fantasy? Should it follow our legitimate desire to obtain a more complete satisfaction? Should it provide a less complicated, painful, problematic way than the one resulting from education and training. In the last resort does it rest only on our good will? We can imagine that a simple parliamentary majority, a powerful pressure group, could change ethical principles in such a way that boundaries, limits, and interdictions fall. When in society such a valorisation of enjoyment happens history has shown that one should expect consequences, it backfires, often in the shape of authoritarianism, which is supposed to also respond to the wish of the people. This little example raises the question of laws and the Law. That whatever the current laws, there is something that is responsible of the fact that certain boundaries cannot be crossed just because we want it. This something is connected to the laws which are the support of our humanity, of what specifies us within the animal kingdom. There are laws to which we are tributary and the practice of psychoanalysis teaches us that the laws of language are in particular what defines the human species. We cannot, whatever the strength of our wishes modify these.

The subject

The subject is not divided anymore, it is a raw, gross subject. In this new economy there is a place for a subject who has lost its specific dimension: this internal ext-eriority which gave him the ability to question its own ex-sistence, a dialectic, an ability to step back and look at his own life, the world, his relationships. …

Because of the crossing of a limit, the subject of the unconscious has lost its shelter, the place that allowed it to subsist. The subjects we are dealing with now in analysis are not like before, fixed one and for all in a structure, but flexible, changing, engaging in different life experiences. The subject has lost the place from which he could say "no", "I don't accept this", the place from which contradiction could arise. For the ego, one's presence in the world is validated only by our performance within the social field. Without a reference, a milestone, connecting us with our ancestors, from which the subject derives its validity whatever its social destiny, the ego is fragile, exposed to depression as its value is not guaranteed by a fixed, stable reference, a proper noun, it incessantly needs to be confirmed. The ego can therefore find itself deflated, in free fall and this explain the frequency of depressive states. What props up the ego is not a reference to an ideal but a reference to an object and the object keeps demanding to be satisfied.

The changes in the psychic economy have an impact on the process of formation of the divided subject. This is particularly important for adolescents. Adolescents have difficulties finding themselves as subject but often they experience difficulties about finding anything. One of my patients is a young lady who does nothing and cares about nothing. She is not bothered about her place in society, her future, personal or professional. She does not read, does not watch things, nothing interests her. She sleeps most of the day, goes clubbing at night and sometimes suffers from moments of depersonalisation but does not complain of anything. It seems that she owes nothing to anyone, she has no symbolic debt. It is as if the debt in this NEP inversed itself: the debtor has become the creditor. She gets into clubs through friends for free, her mother pays her bills … Her enjoyment is disconnected from the phallic enjoyment, it is not part of an organised totality, her enjoyment appears independent and localised, free, and anarchic. With this young lady one could talk of a deficiency of the subjective dimension, of a failure of the symbolic debt towards the Other.

The unconscious

Is there a place for the unconscious in a world where a total freedom of expression exercised on an entirely lit stage exonerates you from repression? Freud may have rejoiced to see the accomplishment of his hygienic recommendations. However, he would have noticed the emergence of depression replacing defence neuroses. It seems that in this new economy we are going towards not a disappearance of the unconscious but of the subject of the unconscious. It is as if the unconscious having lost that subject has no interlocutor.

A perverse solution

Perversion is becoming the social norm. Perversion, not with any moral connotation but understood clinically as a particular type of libidinal economy. Perversion is observed in the way people use their partner as an object that can be discarded as soon as it is perceived as inadequate. At a social level it may become an organising principle and one can conjectures what it will mean for the way the state treats pensioners …

The characteristic of the new psychic economy is that it does not contain the death drive but aspires to it. When your appetite is only for realised satisfaction, sustaining life does not in any way constitute a limiting factor.

The subject's responsibility

The subject becomes less responsible, insofar as its subjective determination does not depend upon a personal journey, or a single choice but on participating in a collective hysteria. As a consequence the subject considers it legitimate to think that his or her destiny is the consequence of exterior and collective factors. In the same logic, the subject feels that the collective owes him or her whatever is missing in his or her life, or that he or she should be compensated for anything that is damaged in his or her life because he or she was conceived by the collective. Clinically this leads to cases where the analysand expects the analyst "to repair" their misfortune. This claim is not the classical hysterical claim in that, to the subject, it appears completely legitimate, unequivocal, and does not lead to any questioning about its meaning. It is not a figure of speech addressed to others, it is the characteristic of her discourse, its truth. There is no response to this for the analyst, the patient expects to be fixed, to be given a *pharmacon* … Transference arises in a paranoid form, from a paranoid claim and any attempt at showing the patient that the analyst understands her claim can only increases the paranoid dimension.

Language

Violence appears when words have lost their efficiency, when the one who talks is not recognised. In the NEP the subject is often not recognised because the subject has not been properly set. So, violence can happen for anything, it becomes a trivial mode of social relationships.

Patriarchy, matriarchy, sexual orientations

Freud remarks that the passage from matriarchy to patriarchy constituted a progress for humanity. It was a form of spiritual progress that humanity moved from evidence to belief. Matriarchy resolved the question of causality: the mother is the cause of the child. This leads to a regime in which the mother, present in reality, is invested with the supreme power, that of procreation, which does not involve any mystery but derives from her own power, her own authority. Invested with this power, the mother becomes the incarnation of the phallus. The function of the father is accessory, not in any way necessary. Mother and child are sufficient to ensure the continuity of generations. In this regime, the world is a simple place where words, signifiers, refer directly to the thing, have no other signified than the thing itself. What is before is the cause of comes after, it is a world organised by continuity, by metonymy. The call upon the father as metaphor introduced a break in this happy simplicity. The father, like the mother, is present in reality but his power is not conferred to him by himself. He owes his power to being the metaphor of an elusive, invisible instance in the realm of the Real. The phallic instance has moved from reality where it was incarnated in the mother in matriarchy, to the Real with the father being not the incarnation but the representative of this instance in patriarchy. This introduces an almost traumatic aspect, as the objects we will derive satisfaction from are always substitutes, semblances. Something has been lost and desire will be correlated against this loss. In patriarchy the father becomes a causal agent. He becomes the cause of the generational chain but he is a "spiritual" cause not a natural cause as the mother was. In the new psychic economy it seems that there is a movement back towards matriarchy, illustrated by the increasing number of single parent families. This goes together with the rejection of the impossible that the paternal function introduced. The system of language always implies a part of Real, that that cannot be said. This is an impossible. But is this impossible, a characteristic of language, always sexual? Is it possible that changes could lead to a system in which this impossible would not concern sex? It could be considered that these changes could even lead to another type of sexual relationship.

At present by moving away from the patriarchy something of the matriarchy is coming back. Matriarchy contains the promise of an always-possible conjunction between the mother and the child, even at the cost of a foreclosure of sex. This position seems to be replicated between partners in the new economy, with a social promotion of perfect agreement, collusion, capture of each other, in such a way that the two partners don't have to speak, speech can be switched off, they only need to exchange signs. Classically, all relationships with a partner or an object are bound by the common experience of a fundamental loss that defines human desire—a loss that unites and dis-unites, separates, and makes closer the partners or the subject and the object in a symbolic pact. Matriarchy offers a world of sweetness, gentleness, benevolence; a regime in which signifiers in language refer to a substantivised ideal object which can therefore be possessed and consumed. The child has nothing to ask from anybody else but his or her mother. In relationships this means that the subject will expect his or her partner to have and to provide the substantivised ideal object, extinguishing all need for questions or for a quest. The establishment of sexuality has a traumatic, a cruel dimension. In the new economy this establishment loses its traumatic dimension and there is no need to defend oneself against it. This could make the homosexual solutions less attractive for the psyche, leading maybe to forms of bisexuality.

Social psychosis

One of the effects of this new economy is to push towards a social psychosis. When you see people in the street walking while listening to music in their earphones, being on a conversation or playing video games on their mobile, it feels as if people were attempting mechanically to produce a constant hallucinatory noise. The new subject appears unable to bear the silence of the Other and seems constrained to enter a world incessantly noisy where voices are overwhelming. People are trapped in a kind of masturbatory enjoyment of autistic quality provided by an artificial hallucinatory system. In the domain of the written word the equivalent is to be found in articles which are clearly inconsistent, presenting no coherence in their arguments or structure. They give the feeling that anything can be said in any order. From papers to internet blogs, the reader notes that the content of the article is perfectly incoherent, like some delusions just before they reveal their paranoid dimension. The subject seems to change the place from which he or she is speaking. His belonging to a certain "community" is transient and the listener/reader does not deal with the same subject all through the article. One does not only zap through images and channels but also through subjects. The interlocutor seems never firmly set on what they are thinking. This new freedom from ideology has unexpected consequences, as in order to communicate, the subject is constrained to refer to a system Other. In the absence of a subjective position, of an assumed ideal, it is information that takes the place of ideology. In this system, the subject faced with the discourse addressed to him or her has no retreat, he is wrapped, caught in a net, as the information can be entirely manipulated to make him or her feel or decide in a certain way—unsurprising therefore that politicians can now do without economists, wise advisers, religious leaders but not without good PR.

If the system is psychotic the subject is not. The subject is a non-psychotic participant in a psychotic system, lured by the promises of the new economy: it is possible to have multiple lives, experience different forms of enjoyment, explore every possible situation including different gender identities and choice of sexual objects. It is not polygamy it is polysubjectivity. A new subjectivity brings into the field of reality a new man that I would gladly call "liberal man". But will this new man be ballasted with an unconscious? If yes, it may not be by the Freudian unconscious, an unconscious that speaks, makes itself heard, interferes with the subject's affairs ... There is today in our clinical practice a "liberal man" a new subject "without gravity" whose sufferings seem different from what they were in previous generations. I do not regret the "good old" neurosis articulated around the love of the father but the problem is that the civilisation's discontent is managed in a way that is an accomplishment of the fantasy of the neurotic: to imagine that perversion would be the cure of neurosis.

The past and the future

The new psychic economy represents an attempt at avoiding the dead-end towards which the laws to which we were subject were driving us. It is a liberation attempt from the constraints inherent to the type of subjective organisation until then prevalent. But one of the consequences was that the subjects have been cast off, but far from floating freely they revolve around the object, the object of enjoyment, which gives direction to their lives.

Economic liberalism encouraged and allowed an unbridled hedonism that introduced a cultural mutation. The new psychic economy is not centred by the lost object and its representatives but by an accessible object and the accomplishment of enjoyment to its end. The new ideology is anonymous, no one is responsible for it and there is no need for authors. The Real has become so improbable that people have difficulties distinguishing reality from virtuality, as it is the Real that marks off the fields of reality. Identity does not have a language, ancestors, ideals as reference points but derives from a community of enjoyment of an accessible object. The individual does not exist as subject but as consumer, leading to a community organised by individualism and competition of one against all. From *Homo Faber*, the creature that makes things, we are moving to the *Fabricated Man*. Will this new man and its new psychic economy completely replace the speaking being, the one always obliged to pay the price of his or her desire? Will the human subjected to the laws of language survive or will they be drowned in the search for immediate enjoyment? Is it possible that a part of the new man, who aspires to becoming a subject, will persevere and eventually find a way to have a voice? Maybe there is a way to avoid both returning to old fashion Freudian neuroses or a flight forward to generalised perversion. We will see.

References

Freud, S. (1939a). *Moses and Monotheism: Three Essays. S. E., XXIII* (1937–1939). London Hogarth.
Lacan, J. (1991). *Le Séminaire Livre VIII, 1960–1961*. Paris: Seuil.
Melman, C. (2002). *L'Homme sans gravité*. Paris: Denoël.
Melman, C. (2009). *La Nouvelle Economie Psychique*. Paris: Eres.

INDEX